Greenhill Books

T. E. Lawrence in War and Peace

T. E. Lawrence in War and Peace

*An Anthology of the Military Writings of
Lawrence of Arabia*

Edited and Presented by Malcolm Brown

Foreword by Michael Clarke

Greenhill Books, London
Stackpole Books, Pennsylvania

Greenhill Books

T. E. Lawrence in War and Peace
An Anthology of the Military Writings of Lawrence of Arabia

First published 2005 by Greenhill Books/Lionel Leventhal Ltd, Park House,
1 Russell Gardens, London NW11 9NN
and
Stackpole Books, 5067 Ritter Road, Mechanicsburg, PA 17055, USA

ISBN 1-85367-653-5

Typeset by Servis Filmsetting Ltd, Manchester

I want to rub off my British habits and go off with Feisul for a bit.
Amusing job, and all new country
Captain T. E. Lawrence to Major Kinihan Cornwallis,
27 December 1916

One Afghan on a donkey was more effective than four Russians in a
tank
Attributed to a Russian general, Soviet–Afghan War, 1979–89

War upon rebellion was messy and slow, like eating soup with a knife
T. E. Lawrence, Seven Pillars of Wisdom

Contents

Part One
In Time of War

Part Two
In Time of Peace

Illustrations

IWM *refers to the Imperial War Museum*

Maps

Adapted from the 1935 edition of Seven Pillars of Wisdom

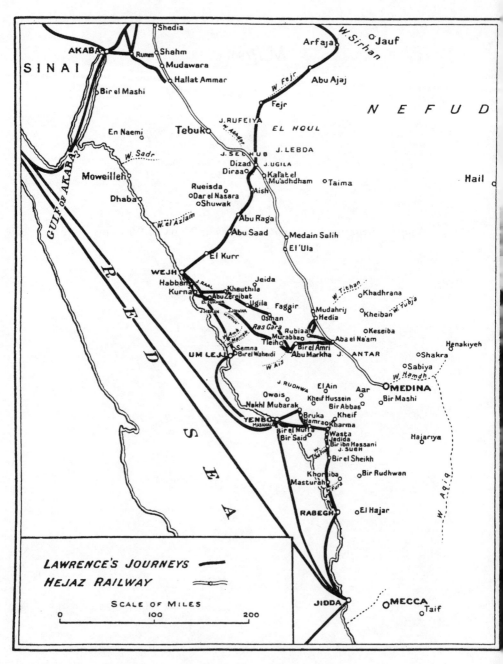

1 The Hejaz: from Mecca to Akaba

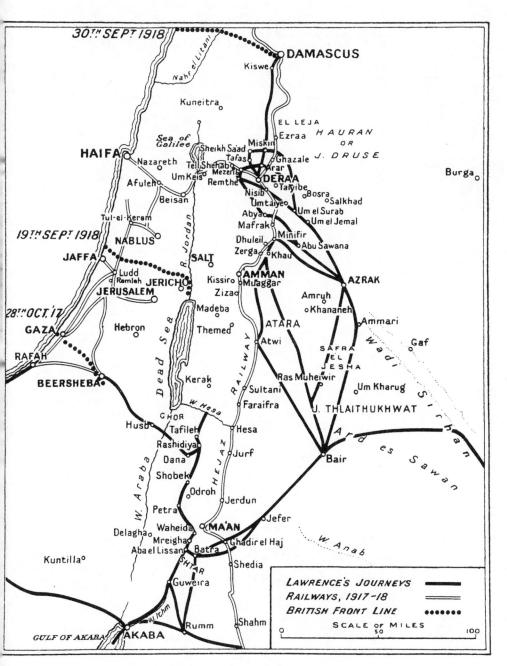

2 Syria and Palestine: from Akaba to Damascus

Foreword

Good writing never goes out of fashion, even if the writers themselves are subject to the whims and revisions of history. T. E. Lawrence was always a controversial warrior, brilliant military tactician, acute political analyst, philosopher, egotist – complex and tortured by turns, he was throughout his life a literate and self-aware writer of wonderful prose. He is somewhat back in fashion at the moment, as western policy-makers and military leaders try to rediscover some of the understanding he developed in the art of insurgent warfare in the particular cultural circumstances of the Arabian peninsula. *Seven Pillars of Wisdom* has become an oft-consulted work among military officers presently struggling with the attempt to create order in Iraq following the US-led invasion of March 2003. His famous political reflection that first appeared in *The Changing East* is quoted all too frequently: 'We have to be prepared to see them doing things by methods quite unlike our own, and less well: but on principle, it is better that they half-do it than that we do it perfectly for them.' But this comes hard to a political establishment schooled in management and homogeneity, and sensitive to the world looking over its shoulder at every turn. And what he wrote in this context should in any case be understood partly in terms of his more scurrilous, later approach to establishment thinking, exemplified in *The Mint*.

The truth is that, like all great writers, Lawrence is quoted more often than he is understood. And he cannot be fully understood through *Seven Pillars* alone. Much of the writings collected here subsequently found their way into that work in more mature and considered form. These writings, however, covering both the evolving tactics of the war and his often bitter reflections on the peace, present Lawrence at his most immediate. They are an essential pillar of *his* wisdom nurtured during those years, and his intellectual contributions to both war and peace can only be properly grasped in light of them.

In working through the mechanics of creating an insurgency against Turkish forces in the Arabian war of 1916–18, Lawrence came to understand the principles of effective counter-insurgency. He learnt from brutal experience that insurgencies worked not by confronting the enemy at its centre, but by stretching it out like elastic. Insurgencies, he appreciated, would seldom by themselves defeat an enemy, but they could deny victory to an enemy almost indefinitely, while more conventional forces, be they military or political, would work to defeat it. If he was reflecting Sun Tsu in discovering this, he was nevertheless some way ahead of Mao Tse-tung, Ho Chi Minh or Che Guevara in doing so. He had no formal military education, thought little of the military writers he had come across, was schooled only in the campaigns of the ancients, and in 1917, after some near disasters, 'was compelled suddenly to action, to find an immediate equation between my book-reading and our present movements'. His military accomplishment arose from his instinctive tactical appreciation of his situation.

Lawrence appreciated just as instinctively how politically astute an insurgency must be to succeed. The same applies to counter-insurgency. It takes time and patience to establish the political legitimacy of counter-insurgency forces in a foreign country. Such forces can be beaten far more effectively by their own lack of understanding of the societies they would protect than by any amount of violence on the part of the insurgents. Understanding is all. It is not a euphemism for a necessarily soft approach to policing. Counter-insurgency may require tough measures, but, if they are not consistent with the legitimate understanding of the population as to their motive, even 'soft policing' will be counter-productive. Above anyone, Lawrence would have appreciated that such understanding could be better achieved through literature than manuals. Indeed, his own youthful attempts to create manuals actually became literature in their own right.

Nevertheless, if the insight and brilliance contained in these despatches and articles are effectively timeless, this quality is only evident when these writings are placed in their own historical context, as this volume does. Lawrence lived in the era of imperialism and saw the task of building political legitimacy through that particular lens. He understood the growing power of nationalism around the world that was to prove a major political driver of the twentieth century, and he entertained the notion that colonial and then dominion status for emerging nation states could provide a framework to accommodate the diverse forces of nationalism without Britain relinquishing its own influence in the world. Indeed, like the United States today, he assumed that the sheer magnetism of the Great Power was a political force that could be manipulated for good. If he thought the British Empire was a construction that could, and should, endure, he was nevertheless certain it could not do so only by force in the years to come. He also seemed to understand that Britain's own political classes still had a lot to learn in this respect.

This may seem like a very modern approach to imperialism, but Lawrence was certainly not immune from the desensitising and numbing effects of the cruelty characteristic of all insurgent warfare against imperial power – in this case Ottoman power. In 'The Destruction of the Fourth Army' (pp. 167–74), he writes quite candidly of the atrocities they witnessed in Tafas, a village occupied by a Turkish column. After routing the Turks, he continues: 'We ordered "no prisoners" and the men obeyed, except that the reserve company took two hundred and fifty men . . . alive,' including, as it happened, many Germans. Later, however, one of Lawrence's wounded men was found bayoneted, and the response was immediate, almost offhand: 'Then we turned our Hotchkiss [machine gun] on the prisoners and made an end of them, they saying nothing.' To those who later criticised, he observed calmly that 'they had not entered Turaa or Tafas'.

Perhaps we should not be surprised that such a man was an enigma to almost all those around him. Lawrence's enduring appeal for biographers, film-makers, playwrights and historians is largely based on the glamour and tumult of his life after 1916. While he is easy to quote, he is, admittedly, a difficult man to understand. But if the man still somehow remains mysterious to us, his writings certainly do not. The scope, incisiveness, and sheer human depth of his accounts guarantee that, as long as we have the texts, what we do not know about the man is eclipsed by what, thankfully, we do know about the issues he addressed. It is an observation commonly made in the literary world about the great writers, from Homer to Shakespeare. In the more bounded and restrained intellectual world of political and military analysis I venture to offer the same observation of T. E. Lawrence. In a tradition of politico-military writing that too seldom allows itself the free expression to capture at its best both insight and inspiration, Lawrence is a glorious and liberating exception.

PROFESSOR MICHAEL CLARKE
Director
International Policy Institute
King's College London
June 2005

Preface

Shortly after the sudden, tragic death of T. E. Lawrence in May 1935, his account of the desert war of 1916–18, *Seven Pillars of Wisdom*, which had hitherto appeared only in a limited subscribers' edition in 1926, was published to immediate public acclaim. This started a surge of interest which one book alone could not satisfy. Two years later a substantial volume of reminiscences, compiled and edited by his brother, A. W. Lawrence, appeared under the self-explanatory title of *T. E. Lawrence by His Friends*. This was followed in 1938 by a selection of his letters, almost nine hundred pages long, compiled with scrupulous and careful scholarship by David Garnett. All these works came from the (at that time) relatively new publishing house of Jonathan Cape, which Lawrence had helped to stabilise a decade or so earlier when he provided an Introduction to a two-volume reprint of one of his favourite and most influential works, Charles Doughty's *Arabia Deserta*, which made it an instant best-seller. Other publishers, however, were now eager to share in the pickings. Thus the year 1939 saw two additions to the canon. One was *Oriental Assembly*, an anthology of his minor writings with a Middle Eastern connection, which appeared under the imprint of Williams & Norgate (see introduction to 'The Changing East', p. 248). The other, a compilation of his wartime reports, was published by the Golden Cockerel Press, of Waltham St Lawrence, Berkshire, under the eye-catching title of *Secret Despatches from Arabia*. In both cases A. W. Lawrence acted as editor.

Since the documents contained in this second volume were Crown Copyright and thus formally embargoed under the then pertaining fifty-year rule, a special dispensation to print was obtained, this being acknowledged by the statement 'Published by permission of the Foreign Office' on the title page. The book was published in a limited edition of one thousand copies.

In 1990, two years after the publication of my own collection of Lawrence's letters (published in Britain as *The Letters of T. E. Lawrence*, and in the United States as *T. E. Lawrence: The Selected Letters*), I was approached by Bellew Publications, London, with an invitation to introduce and edit a volume of Lawrence's wartime despatches. Curiously, the originator of the idea who had brought the project to Bellew seemed unaware that such a collection already existed, if only in an edition so rare as to be virtually unavailable. However, I saw at once that here was an initiative worth supporting, in that it was clear that many people interested in Lawrence would welcome the publication of the text of the Golden Cockerel compilation in a new format and at an affordable price. At a time when that finely produced volume, if it came up on the book market, which it did but rarely, was likely to cost a would-be purchaser £500 (or as much as £950 in its deluxe pigskin-bound format), it seemed a gesture worth making. There was another factor that rendered such a reprint attractive. The despatches alone, at the modest length of some sixty thousand words, would scarcely fill a modern standard hardback, thus allowing space for the inclusion of a number of Lawrence's other writings on subjects related to the desert war. With the blessing of the original editor, A. W. Lawrence, the project went ahead. The result, published in 1991, was a palatable, handsomely produced volume, entitled *Secret Despatches from Arabia and Other Writings by T. E. Lawrence*, which retailed at the then standard price of £14.95.

The book was well received and now graces, or so I understand, not a few shelves in not a few countries around the world. In my own case, never having dreamed of acquiring anything published under the august banner of the Golden Cockerel Press – a prince among such small independent presses in its heyday – this meant that I could have a copy of Lawrence's secret despatches myself.

Sadly, at a time when certain publishing houses prospered while others went to the wall, the Bellew imprint was one of those that joined the latter category, despite having originated a remarkably wide range of attractive and well-conceived titles (though it is good to be able to state that its founding publisher, the lively and irrepressible Ib Bellew, has successfully relocated to the United States). It might be thought that in such circumstances any unsold copies would be released to the market at a favourable price in order to raise the maximum amount of capital. This, however, was not the case. The outcome was that all outstanding copies of all the company's titles were destroyed.

Fortunately, I did not realise what had happened to the 1991 volume until well after Greenhill Books, some eighteen months ago, approached me with a view to producing a new book about T. E. Lawrence. My immediate reaction was to suggest a remake of that work. Greenhill responded warmly, though I insisted that permission to proceed should be sought from the original publishers. It was then that the story of Bellew Publishing's unhappy demise, and of the sad fate of the 1991 volume, came to light. The original book was not only out of print, it was also, in a sense, legally deceased.

This, in effect, cleared the ground. It would have been feeble, however, simply to recreate a book which had ceased to exist. In short, the circumstances provided a positive challenge: to make a new book for a new time and with a new purpose, taking into account that between the early 1990s and the present the world had undergone a remarkable transformation.

The 1991 edition was commissioned and compiled in 1990, just one year after the fall of the Berlin Wall, an event which was hailed as marking the end of a 'cold war' which for decades had seemed in imminent danger of becoming a hot one. Yet the focus was still on superpowers, despite the fact that in the long-standing duel between the USA and the USSR clearly the game was up. A distinguished America-based academic even proclaimed the end of history. Democracy 1: Communism 0: we could relax. It was as though the ghosts of two World Wars had finally been despatched to the shades. We could all look forward to what Winston Churchill – in a memorable phrase coined in the dark days of 1940 – had called 'broad sunlit uplands'. Paradise regained.

Yet even as the book was being completed the world's political climate was changing. The invasion of Kuwait by Saddam Hussein's Iraq in August 1990 provoked a serious crisis in the Middle East, which led to the swift international response which was instantly labelled the Gulf War – the gulf in question being the Persian Gulf, an area of significant controversy over decades, if not centuries. The war was successful in that it liberated Kuwait; it was also legal in that the attack on Iraq and her armed forces was carried out with the authorisation of the United Nations. The boil seemed lanced, but Saddam Hussein remained in power, and even the most optimistic of Middle Eastern watchers sensed there would be more trouble to come from that far from empty quarter. Yet for the moment it was still possible to believe that, in spite of such regional difficulties, the end of the cold war had produced a safer world overall. There was, after all, only one superpower and therefore no prospect of a clash of giants; the concept of 'mutually assured destruction', which had helped notably to keep the peace for almost forty years, could, for the time being at least, be safely put on the shelf marked 'history'.

Then on 11 September 2001 two aircraft flew into the World Trade Center in New York while a third caught a wing of the Pentagon in Washington DC and a fourth, almost certainly intended for the Capitol, crashed in a field in Pennsylvania. The grim formula '9/11' – the date, American-style, of the New York attack – entered the world's vocabulary overnight and stuck. In a trice we were in a different, less predictable territory. Suddenly those broad sunlit uplands were shadowed by frightening smoke clouds. The casualty count was appalling, if substantially smaller than the deaths resulting from the atom-bomb air raids on Hiroshima and Nagasaki in 1945, but when future historians look back on this troubled period (that is, if the world survives to do so), both sets of events will surely find themselves in the same category.

Overnight we had to switch our assumptions. The enemy was no longer the Kremlin, which at least had a geographical identity with a location and a calling address, but Al-Qaeda – a name we could barely pronounce, let alone spell – which had neither. In short order there were Western attacks

first on Afghanistan, Al-Qaeda's reputed homeland, and then, more contro-
versially, on Iraq. To some the latter attack was a legitimate assault on
another source of international terrorism; to others it seemed like a deliberate attempt by the USA to complete 'unfinished business': President Bush
Mark II taking over where his father, President Bush I, had left off. There
was an even more massive onslaught than had occurred in 1991: the key
slogan of the moment was 'shock and awe'. Yet what seemed in a matter of
weeks to look like 'mission accomplished' rapidly turned into a dangerous
period of insurgency. There was what could almost be defined as a new Arab
Revolt. Lawrence had once described his Arab Revolt as a 'side-show of a
side-show': see his essay 'The Evolution of a Revolt', published in this
volume (pp. 260–73). What was happening in Iraq beginning in 2003 was
no side-show of a side-show. It was the biggest show in town.

Before long a familiar name that had for decades been caught up in the
glamour of one of the most popular movies Hollywood ever made (while pro
and ante biographers spilled angry ink in endless arguments as to whether
or not the person in question should be outed as a homosexual or condemned as a fraud) was brought out from the closet and made a subject of
serious consideration and academic study. That name, of course, was T. E.
Lawrence. This was a man who, it now seemed, might have some wisdom
to offer as the West found itself in both a military and a psychological
quandary in the Middle East.

Significantly, *The Times* (the newspaper to which Lawrence first turned in
late 1918 when launching his political campaign on behalf of the Arab cause)
published articles on the subject. The *New York Times* also ran with the
story. Other newspapers echoed the cry. Military experts on both sides of the
Atlantic blew the dust off Lawrence's books on their shelves and began to
scan their pages. Lawrence was back.

I hope readers will forgive me if I state that I made my own modest contribution to this process: a letter in *The Times* on 8 March 2003, in which I
quoted a comment by Lawrence in 1929 when responding to a question
raised by an American journalist asking how he had coped with the challenge of working with Arab forces during his desert campaign. He wrote:
'You handle Arabs, I think, as you handle Englishmen, or Laplanders or
Czechoslovaks, cautiously, at first, and kindly always.'

This rediscovery of Lawrence has governed the remaking of this book.

The present volume has much in common with its 1991 predecessor. The
'secret despatches' which were its prime justification are reproduced here in
full. Several of the 'other writings' it included have also been reprinted.
However, it also contains material of substance for which that volume had
no space or which was deemed inappropriate to its concept. More import-
antly, the whole cast of the new book is so different that it seemed to require
a new title.

The 1991 volume began with two introductory sections entitled 'The
History of *Secret Despatches from Arabia*', and 'The Lawrence of *Secret*

Despatches from Arabia', the intention of the latter piece being to discuss Lawrence's role in the desert war largely in relation to the way he wrote about it, at the time in his despatches and later in *Seven Pillars*. Both these items had, essentially, a literary purpose. The Introduction to the present volume, although it includes some elements from the earlier version, has a markedly different aim. It represents an attempt to write something substantial and worthwhile about a subject with which I have skirmished, rather than engaged directly, over the many years of my involvement with the matter of Lawrence of Arabia: his virtue and value as a man of action in the campaign which gave him his fame and also the name to which he has become indissolubly attached. It also discusses his post-war dealings with questions and problems still on the Middle Eastern agenda when that campaign was over. For Lawrence was not a man to walk away from his war and wash his hands of it. It was to stay with him in one way or another for the rest of his life.

So this volume bears a new and challenging title: *T. E. Lawrence in War and Peace*. It is in two sections. Part One shows us Lawrence caught up in the rigours and challenges of war. Part Two shows us Lawrence trying to cope with the consequences of war in the circumstances of peace. The essential author of this anthology is Lawrence himself, with myself playing the role chiefly of a guide but also, occasionally, that of a modest barrister pleading, or perhaps sometimes not pleading, his cause. The juror is the reader. It is he or she who must judge.

Whatever the verdict on this compilation, it is not, as was its 1991 forerunner, a nostalgic re-visitation of a now distant period of our history through the medium of old writings piously reprinted. It is a book, I hope, with something to say about the present time and about the challenges facing the world as we move deeper into a new century and towards ever greater perils.

A final, personal word: I interrupted the writing of the Introduction to this volume to attend the Symposium of the T. E. Lawrence Society held in Oxford in September 2004 at which the principal guest was Professor John E. Mack, MD, Harvard Professor of Psychiatry and author of a groundbreaking and deeply researched biography of Lawrence entitled *A Prince of Our Disorder*, which won a Pulitzer Prize in 1977. He firmly believed that there were lessons to be learned from Lawrence as to how the Western nations, especially his own, might conduct themselves in relation to the problems of the Middle East, and it is tragic in the extreme that his voice should have been silenced by his sudden death, in a traffic accident in London on the day after the Symposium ended. He gave me some of his recent writings on this subject during the Symposium and I have taken the liberty of quoting briefly from them in my Introduction. Had he lived I would certainly have passed that Introduction and this Preface to him for his comments, and I have no doubt that they would have emerged the richer and more worthy of notice from his scrutiny. My acquaintance with him was brief, but it was most rewarding, and it has left me with a vivid impression of a brilliant, far-sighted and deeply compassionate man whom I am glad and grateful to have known. I should like to dedicate this book to his memory.

MALCOLM BROWN
Imperial War Museum, London
May 2005

Note on the Spelling of Arabic Names

T. E. Lawrence followed no consistent pattern in the spelling of Arabic proper names. When *Revolt in the Desert*, the abridged version of *Seven Pillars of Wisdom*, was being prepared for publication in 1927, his publishers, Jonathan Cape, took up this subject with him. He replied:

> Arabic names won't go into English exactly, for their consonants are not the same as ours, and their vowels, like ours, vary from district to district. There are some 'scientific systems' of transliteration, helpful to people who know enough Arabic not to need helping, but a washout for the world. I spell my names anyhow, to show what rot the systems are.

Thus the reader will find such variations in the following pages as Feisal and Feisul, Auda and Audah, Jiddah and Jedda, Talfila and Tafileh. However, although Lawrence's orthography might be seen as characteristically eccentric, it can fairly be claimed that in no way does it affect the clarity of his writing.

Chronology

1888	*16 August*: T. E. Lawrence born at Tremadoc, North Wales
1896	Family settles in Oxford; at City of Oxford High School (until 1907)
1906–8	*Summer*: in France, studying castles
1907	*October*: commences study at Jesus College, Oxford
1909	*Summer*: in Syria, studying crusader castles
1909–10	*Winter*: works on thesis, *Crusader Castles*
1910	*Summer*: graduates with 1st Class Honours in Modern History; travels to the Middle East
	Winter: at Jebail, Lebanon, learning Arabic
1911	*February–March*: travels to Carchemish
	April–July: excavating at Carchemish under D. G. Hogarth and R. Campbell Thompson
	Summer: walks through northern Mesopotamia
1912	*January*: in Egypt excavating under Flinders Petrie
	Spring: excavating at Carchemish under C. L. Woolley (until Spring 1914)
1913	*Summer*: at home in Oxford, with Hamoudi and Dahoum
1914	*January–February*: Sinai survey with Woolley and Captain Newcombe
	Summer: at Oxford and London, completing *The Wilderness of Zin* (archaeological report on Sinai co-written with Woolley)
	October: Joins War Office (geographical division of military intelligence)
	26 October: commissioned as Second Lieutenant on the special list (i.e. without regimental attachment)
	16 December: in Egypt as Intelligence Officer (until October 1916)
1916	*20 March*: promoted Captain
	March–May: on special duty in Mesopotamia

5 June: Sherif Hussein of Mecca launches the Arab Revolt

16 October: arrives at Jidda as part of a British military mission

23 October: first meeting with Emir Feisal

7–11 November: in Khartoum

18–25 November: in Cairo; leaves to return to Arabia

18 December: attached as liaison officer to Arab forces (until October 1918)

1917

4 January: first raid at Jebel Dhifran

14 January: leaves Yenbo on HMS *Suva* for Um Lejj

18 January: commences overland journey to Wejh with Feisal's army, arriving 25 January

10 March: leaves Wejh for Wadi Ais (away until 16 April)

11 March: British take Baghdad

26 March: First Battle of Gaza, Palestine Front

17 April: Second Battle of Gaza

9 May: start of Akaba expedition under Sherif Nasir

June: Lawrence's northern journey

6 July: seizure of Akaba

10 July: arrives in Cairo; first meeting with General Sir Edmund Allenby

22 July: returns to Arabia

5 August: promoted Major

7–22 September: Haret Ammar raid

27 September–9 October: Bir esh-Shediyah raid

24 October–3 December: extended raid to Yarmuk, etc.

31 October: Third Battle of Gaza; Beersheba captured

20–1 November: capture and rape at Deraa

9 December: Allenby takes Jerusalem

11 December: takes part in Allenby's ceremonial entry into Jerusalem

28 December: starts to recruit bodyguard

1918

20 January: at Tafileh

24 January: Battle of Tafileh

5–11 February: winter journey to and from Guweira

21 February: at Beersheba; asks to be relieved, persuaded to remain

24–7 February: at Jerusalem; meeting with Lowell Thomas

12 March: promoted Lieutenant-Colonel; joint actions by Allenby's and Arab forces postponed because of pressing need for troops in France following launch of major German offensive

18–19 April: with Imperial Camel Corps to Tell Shahm station

25 June–1 July: at Jidda; abortive attempt to meet Sherif Hussein

31 July–4 August: with Imperial Camel Corps at Akaba, Wadi Rumm, etc.

4 September: leaves Abu el Lissan for Azrak prior to final stage of campaign

19 September: Allenby launches final offensive (Battle of Megiddo) against Turkish forces in Palestine with Feisal's Arabs acting as right wing in the desert

1 October: arrival at Damascus

4 October: leaves Damascus for Cairo

24 October: arrives in England and returns to Oxford

29 October: attends Eastern Committee of War Cabinet

30 October: Turkey signs armistice with the Allies

November–December: with Feisal in France and Britain

1919   *January–October*: in Paris for peace conference

May–June: journey by air to Egypt

August: Lowell Thomas's Middle Eastern entertainment opens in London

November: elected as Fellow at All Souls College, Oxford; at Oxford and London until 1921, working on *Seven Pillars of Wisdom*

1921   Appointed adviser to Winston Churchill at the Colonial Office

August–December: on missions to Aden, Jidda and Transjordan

1922   *July*: resigns from Colonial Office

August: joins Royal Air Force as John Hume Ross; sent to RAF training depot, Uxbridge

November: transferred to RAF School of Photography, Farnborough

27 December: discovered by the press

1923   *January*: discharged following disclosure of his identity

25 March: enlists in the Army as Private T. E. Shaw, Royal Tank Corps (serves until August 1925)

Summer: acquires cottage at Clouds Hill, near Bovington Camp, Dorset

1925   *18 August*: rejoins the RAF as Aircraftman T. E. Shaw; sent to RAF Cranwell, Lincolnshire

1926   Subscribers' edition of *Seven Pillars of Wisdom* completed

1927   *9 January*: arrives in India (stays until January 1929)

Revolt in the Desert (popular abridgement of *Seven Pillars*) published, later withdrawn

1928   *The Mint* completed; work begun on translation of *Odyssey*; formally adopts the surname Shaw by deed poll

December: ordered home by Air Ministry following press stories claiming his involvement in a rebellion in Afghanistan

1929   Posted to various air stations in England (until 1935)

	September: working with Sydney Smith on Schneider Trophy, subsequently on high-speed marine craft
1934	*November*: moves to his final RAF base, in Bridlington, Yorkshire
1935	*26 February*: Lawrence leaves RAF, with a view to retirement at Clouds Hill
	13 May: has accident on motorcycle near Clouds Hill
	19 May: dies in Bovington Military Hospital
	21 May: funeral at Moreton, Dorset

General Introduction

During his two years of war service in the desert, T. E. Lawrence wrote numerous reports about his activities. Many of these were printed in a confidential publication called the *Arab Bulletin*, produced by the Arab Bureau, an intelligence organisation created with Foreign Office support in mid-1916 to deal with the consequences of the launch of the Arab Revolt. Later he was to draw extensively on these reports in writing his war memoir *Seven Pillars of Wisdom*.

That work, a worldwide best-seller since its first general publication in 1935, constantly in print and translated into seventeen languages, is the book on which Lawrence's reputation largely depends, both as writer and as man of action. Part adventure story, part polemic, part apologia, and written with distinct pretensions to high style, it is a book which attracts, annoys or mystifies its readers in roughly equal proportions. People either like it or they don't. While countless readers have been drawn into its labyrinths and have yielded to its spell, other equally large, or larger, crowds have been repelled by it and have consciously turned away. Lawrence is not a man about whom many people stay neutral. A full lifetime on – this Introduction is being written for publication seventy years after his death – he still has the power to divide. People who admire him come together to share often deeply felt enthusiasms; those who do not, walk by uncomprehending on the other side.

What is known or believed about the writing of the book can also attract or repel. Versions begun, versions discarded. A manuscript lost, or not lost, at a railway station halfway between Oxford and London. A near-manic figure writing through the night in a borrowed flat in London, a stone's throw from Westminster Abbey and within earshot of the boom of Big Ben, thence to emerge in the small hours to walk the streets of the capital like a ghost out of Dickens. Surely we finished with writers slaving in garrets far back, in the days of the Romantics. Yet here we go again: 'I nearly went off my head in Barton Street,' he wrote to the poet Robert Graves in 1923, 'heaving at this beastly book of mine.' These could be the words of a

Chatterton, though without the poverty (he had enough funds to support himself) or that tragic youth's fatal resort to arsenic. Yet, as is now widely acknowledged, suicide was far from being a closed option for him in these troubled years. If his schemes went awry or his mood irredeemably crashed, it was a permanent fall-back.

It is the contrast with all that which gives a special value to the secret despatches from Arabia which form Part One of the present volume. These were not written by a neurotic depressive racked with guilt and wounded by failure, yet still trying consciously to fashion a masterpiece. They were written by a young man full of the freshness of the world to be, ranging with dash and purpose through one of the globe's greatest and most historic landscapes, engaged in a task which extended and invigorated him. The ages and the ancient civilisations were with him. William Blake wrote, 'Great things are done when men and mountains meet, / This is not done by jostling in the street.' For mountains read the great sweeps of the Arabian desert or the 'stupendous hills' of Wadi Rumm.

The problem with T. E. Lawrence is that he was several people in one: scholar, archaeologist, soldier, diplomat, writer, publisher, mechanic – the *Who's Who* definitions could run on and on. When in the late 1980s I undertook the editorship of a selection of his letters, my daunting task was to try to reflect all the facets of this remarkable man (in a volume of six hundred pages) over a period of almost four decades. The despatches reproduced in this book date from just two years, and present, in essence, one aspect of him only. From its pages emerges a Lawrence who is shrewd, ingenious, resilient, enthusiastic, and thoroughly competent and committed in the execution of his duties – though, as was inevitable in the circumstances of a wartime campaign, bad moments punctuated the better ones. It is good to see someone so often a prey to self-questioning so evidently on top of his job. A many-minded man, he is single-minded here; or very largely so, because though he had several targets on his horizon – military, political, literary, and personal – for most of the time they were sufficiently conjoined to make this the most positive and productive period of his life.

These are the years – from late 1916 to late 1918 – in which Lawrence fought with the Arabs in their revolt against Turkey. He found them in the Arabian peninsula having only moderate success against their better-armed and more organised enemy, and left them installed, if only temporarily, in Damascus, with the Turks in full retreat. Of course the Arabs were far from alone in this effort, and by 1918 had become the right wing, or, perhaps more appositely, the 'desert support group', of a great advance under the command of General Sir Edmund Allenby. Lawrence's natural place was with that right wing, which was largely a guerrilla force quite different in style from Allenby's professional uniformed army, though it also included a substantial body of uniformed Arab regulars, most of whom were deserters from the Turkish army, commanded by Lawrence's military superior (but also, after getting to know him, admiring friend) Colonel Pierce

Joyce.* Throughout his period as an officer on active service Lawrence had been involved in the kind of war to which he was ideally suited. He understood the people and the terrain and had a useful command of the language, and he had been attached to an Arab leader, Emir Feisal, in whom (for most of the time) he believed and whose instincts he trusted. He had also been given substantial freedom to make his own judgements and decisions. All this was meat and drink to an individualist with strong views on the conduct of warfare and no great love of conventional military discipline. In short, if ever the right man was in the right place at the right time, it was T. E. Lawrence.

Lawrence's basic role was twofold: to act as adviser and liaison officer with the Arab forces, and to report in detail and at length on all relevant aspects of the campaign. He also carried out some effective practical harassment of the enemy in the field. In brief, his weapons were the explosives he used to blow up Turkish trains, tracks and bridges, techniques of persuasion which made him virtually a prime mover in terms of strategy and tactics, and, to use his own phrase from *Seven Pillars of Wisdom*, 'a fluent pen'.

Moreover, he was aware that those who had placed him there trusted him and believed in what he was doing. The despatches printed in this book brim with the confidence of a man who clearly appreciates that his work is respected and that his job is not under threat. More, Lawrence knew that in writing them he was not wasting his time. They were destined not for some ever-deepening in-tray at the base, but for immediate and serious appreciation, and very probably, as in the case of the reports collected here, immediate printing and circulation in a wide range of high places. The high places to which the *Arab Bulletin* was distributed, according to its first issue, make an impressive list; they included the War Office, the Admiralty, Army HQ India, Khartoum, Cyprus, Aden, as well as the British High Commissioner (who also had three copies for the Foreign Office) and the Commander-in-Chief of the Egyptian Expeditionary Force.

Although it is possible to argue that his two years in the desert both made him and broke him, it is undeniable that he had, to use the well-known phrase, a 'good war'. Not only did he emerge from it – despite his own doubts on the matter – a proven man of action, he also came out of it with the raw material of a major book. As he was to write in Chapter 99 of *Seven Pillars of Wisdom*, he found in his involvement in the Arab Revolt 'a theme ready and epic to a direct eye and hand . . . offering me an outlet in literature'. Or, as he would put it elsewhere: 'The story I have to tell is one of the finest given a man for writing.'

The wartime despatches printed in this book can, therefore, be interpreted

---

* Joyce's first reaction on seeing Lawrence was an intense desire to tell him to get his hair cut and have his buttons polished; he later came to acknowledge, when seeing Lawrence in Arab robes in conclave with Arab chiefs, that he was in the presence of a very unusual and gifted personality.

in more ways than one. They are not only intelligence reports from the field; they are also early attempts at giving literary expression to his war experience. They are forays along the road which was to lead, after many twists and turns, to *Seven Pillars of Wisdom*. As a glance at almost any page of this book will show, these despatches are not terse factual annotations to be worked up into decent prose at a later date. They are extremely well crafted, at times excitingly so. They marshal the information they are meant to convey with clarity and pace. They have the unmistakable hallmark of a writer of quality in that they make the reader want to keep on reading.

Here due tribute must be paid to the editor who set the style of the publication in which these reports first appeared and from which they are here reprinted. Good correspondents are always the better for good editors, and with the temporary naval officer whose personality dominates the *Arab Bulletin* Lawrence could not have had a more fruitful relationship. This was his mentor and friend from Oxford days, D. G. Hogarth, Keeper of the Ashmolean Museum and Fellow of Magdalen College, Oxford – the college which, at Hogarth's instigation, had given Lawrence a postgraduate scholarship after he had achieved his First Class Honours degree in History at Jesus College in 1910 – and briefly his chief during his archaeological stint in Carchemish, Syria, from 1910 to 1914. Colleagues in peace, they were now colleagues in war, for at this time Hogarth held the rank of Lieutenant-Commander (later Commander), RNVR,* with his sphere of activity centred on Middle Eastern intelligence. There could have been no one better qualified to oversee the reports of those officers who were involved in the Arab Revolt. As already indicated, that upheaval had produced a specialist unit in Cairo under the name of the Arab Bureau, of which Hogarth became a leading member. The *Arab Bulletin* was the Arab Bureau's voice. The idea of such a publication was T. E. Lawrence's, and indeed the latter's name appears as editor in the first and ninth issues, but the most influential mind behind it was Hogarth's, and he can be seen as the chief guarantor of its excellence. If Lawrence, or any of the other officers who wrote for the Bulletin, had turned in dull and turgid stuff, Hogarth would not have been pleased. He would have made clear his views just as he would have done to a student arriving for a tutorial with an ill-conceived and ill-expressed essay.

'Army prose is bad,' Lawrence wrote to his Oxford friend Vyvyan Richards in 1918, 'and one has so much of it that one fears contamination.' He could have had no better inoculation against such hazards than the influence of D. G. Hogarth. For Hogarth's firm belief, expressly stated in relation to the *Arab Bulletin*, was that 'it was as easy to write it in decent English as in bad, and much more agreeable'. The result was that the *Bulletin* had 'from the first a literary tinge not always present in intelligence summaries'. This was not, however, an unmixed blessing. 'Coupled with good type and

* i.e. Royal Naval Volunteer Reserve, a description assigned to 'hostilities only' officers; the attribution 'RN' (= Royal Navy) applied exclusively to regular officers.

paper', it seems to have led to a revision of the list of recipients, and the taking of 'other precautions . . . to preclude the dangers of over-circulation'. These quotations are from the editorial which Hogarth wrote for the *Arab Bulletin* in August 1918 to celebrate its hundredth edition – an essay which describes the context of the main content of this book so well, and so readably, that it has been reprinted in full in this book (see Appendix A: 'The *Arab Bulletin*', pp. 285–8).

There were some very articulate officers among the *Bulletin*'s contributors – Sir Ronald Storrs, Stewart Newcombe, Herbert Garland, Hogarth himself, later the redoubtable traveller H. St J. B. Philby – but there is no question that Lawrence was, as it were, the star correspondent, and not just on account of his fine writing. His previous training as wandering scholar and archaeologist, and the work in which he had been engaged from 1914 in the area of Middle Eastern intelligence, had provided him with excellent qualifications.

The point is well made by Jeremy Wilson in his authorised biography:

No other reports from British officers in the Hejaz compare with Lawrence's, either for detailed observation or quality of writing. His talent for description had been refined by the discipline of making notes about architecture and archaeological finds, and he now had a remarkable ability to portray what he saw. Work on maps had taught him to record the shape of the landscape through which he travelled, and he kept a detailed log of travelling times and compass bearings throughout his journeys. Later these were used, together with his sketches of hill contours, as a basis for map revisions in Cairo. The route reports included valuable military information such as the location of wells and the suitability of terrain for wheeled vehicles. Although it was normal practice to write notes on 'personalities', his comments were particularly impressive, both for their physical descriptions and their shrewd evaluation of character.*

Of course, the darker aspects of Lawrence's war must not be forgotten in reading these brisk and often exhilarating despatches. We will not find what he called 'the agonies, the terrors, and the mistakes' of the campaign, nor the sense of guilt that haunted him throughout concerning the ultimate intentions of the Allies vis-à-vis the Arabs, nor the response of an essentially fastidious man to the squalors of war.

These are selected rather than collected despatches. Lawrence wrote numerous other reports which for one reason or another did not find their way into the *Arab Bulletin*. Even if they had, a complete reprint would not have

* Jeremy Wilson, *Lawrence of Arabia: The Authorised Biography* (Heinemann, London, 1989; Atheneum, New York, 1990), pp. 315–16.

provided a comprehensive account of Lawrence's achievements and exploits. There would have been large gaps. (This is particularly true of 1918, during which only five of his reports appeared in the *Bulletin*, while one other – 'Syrian Cross-Currents', pp. 162–6 – was printed as a supplementary document.) So this book does not, nor should it, stand alone.

The obvious companion volume to have at one's elbow when reading the despatches is *Seven Pillars of Wisdom*. But to save the reader the trouble – and *Seven Pillars* is no pushover even for the most adept of skim-readers – here is the plot of that *magnum opus* in a nutshell. It is in fact a nutshell of considerable interest in that it was written by a famous writer who was a friend of Lawrence's and an admirer of his work, whose own reputation has stayed steady for decades while Lawrence's has risen and dipped according to the dictates of taste and fashion. The writer in question is the novelist E. M. Forster, best known for such works as *A Room with a View*, *Howard's End* and *A Passage to India* (all of which, like Lawrence's own story, have been turned into successful films). *Abinger Harvest*, Forster's anthology of articles, essays, reviews and poems, published in 1936, includes a piece entitled simply 'T. E. Lawrence', written during the previous year after the appearance, following Lawrence's death, of the first generally available edition of *Seven Pillars*. In it Forster wrote of that work:

What is this long book about?

It describes the revolt in Arabia against the Turks, as it appeared to an Englishman who took part in it; he would not allow us to write 'the leading part'. It opens with his preliminary visit to Rabegh and understanding with Feisul; then comes the new idea: shifting north to Wejh and harrying thence the Medina railway. The idea works, and he leaves Feisul for a time and moves against Akaba with Auda, another great figure of the revolt. A second success: Akaba falls. The war then ceases to be in the Hejaz and becomes Syrian. Henceforward he co-operates with the British Army under his hero Allenby, and his main work is in Trans-Jordania; it leads to the cutting of the three railways around Deraa. Deraa isolated, the way lies clear to the third success, the capture of Damascus; the united armies enter Damascus, the revolt has triumphed.*

Of course, in reducing *Seven Pillars* to such basic elements, Forster was not so much doing the would-be reader a kind favour as setting a literary trap. He continued: 'That is what the book is about, and it could only be reviewed authoritatively by a staff officer who knows the East. That is what the book is about, and *Moby Dick* was about catching a whale.' By adding this double codicil to his summary, Forster was not only implying, correctly, that *Seven Pillars* is a far cry from the average military memoir; he was

---

* E. M. Forster, *Abinger Harvest* (Edward Arnold, London, 1936), p. 140.

also – as he well knew – bringing into the equation one of those titanic works (of which *War and Peace* and *The Brothers Karamazov* were others) which Lawrence greatly admired and which he had consciously tried to emulate in writing *Seven Pillars*. Moreover, he was acknowledging the right of *Seven Pillars* to be discussed in such a context.

Seven Pillars, however, is not the subject of this Introduction, but its engaging, fledgling predecessor, *Secret Despatches*, to which Forster's two-hundred-word summary can serve equally well as a thumbnail guide. If written more to impress than to inform, Forster's is nevertheless a useful synopsis which has the added virtue of being a literary curiosity from the hand of one of the last century's most admired writers.

In recent years I have written several books on war subjects, drawing heavily on personal accounts. Such accounts fall into two obvious categories: contemporary material, i.e. letters and diaries, and material produced later, i.e. memoirs or recorded reminiscence. I have a bias in favour of the first category. There is a special quality, I believe, about evidence dating from the time of the event, as opposed to evidence written or spoken in hindsight. For me the letters or diaries of men, say, fighting the Battle of the Somme have a greater authenticity than the accounts of men remembering it in post-war tranquillity. Not knowing whether you will live to the following day can concentrate the mind wonderfully, whereas the veteran who has survived his St Crispin's day experience and come safe home has an altogether different perspective. There may be no overall view, but this is compensated for by a sense of immediacy.

Secret Despatches is clearly in this first category. Lawrence is filing his reports with no clear idea of the events to follow, though it is obvious he intends to do all he can to shape them. As we read on we see the campaign develop stage by stage. Perspectives change. Attitudes vary. Characters applauded one moment can be sternly criticised the next. Take, for example, the fluctuating fortunes of the veteran Howeitat chief, Auda Abu Tayi, undoubtedly one of the vintage figures of the Revolt. Auda is introduced in the *Arab Bulletin* of 24 July 1917 ('The Howeitat and Their Chiefs') almost with the kind of flourish one associates with the first appearance of a major character in a Victorian novel – or, perhaps more aptly, the arrival on the scene of a heroic figure in Malory or William Morris:

> He has married twenty-eight times, has been wounded thirteen times . . . He has only reported his 'kill' since 1900, and they now stand at seventy-five Arabs; Turks are not counted by Auda when they are dead . . . He sees life as a saga and all events in it are significant and all personages heroic. His mind is packed (and generally overflows) with stories of old raids and epic poems of fights.

The rich phrases roll on and on, more mediaeval than modern – certainly, no First World War citation for gallantry ever read like this. Yet in the issue of 8 October ('The Raid at Haret Ammar', pp. 147–50) Lawrence reports that Auda is 'making trouble by his greediness and his attempts to assume authority over all the Huweitat', and in the next *Bulletin* (21 October, 'The Raid near Bir esh-Shediyah', pp. 150–2) he is writing of another crop of 'difficulties caused by Audah Abu Tayi's pretensions'.

Auda, it should be added, was only briefly a broken reed. He is applauded in Lawrence's post-war articles in *The Times* and he is undoubtedly the most heroic Arab figure in *Seven Pillars*. Thus the reference in the despatches to his worrying quirks and instabilities underscore the contemporary nature of these writings; this was history in the making, quite a different matter from history having been made. When events are recorded as they unfold, not only the tense is different; there is a distinct difference in the tension.

For a prime example of this quality of urgent immediacy see 'The Destruction of the Fourth Army' (pp. 167–74), Lawrence's account of the hard and often brutal campaigning in September 1918 that culminated in the seizure of Damascus. It is a fast, raw, vivid piece, rushed out with the exaltations and horrors of those final weeks still fresh in his mind. He must have written it, if not in Damascus, then just after leaving it, presumably during his brief stay in Cairo before returning to England, since it appeared in the *Arab Bulletin* on 22 October. This is history caught on the run with the torrent of events still flowing. It would be invidious to quote from it to show its flavour. It requires reading from end to end and at speed.

There is another appealing aspect to *Secret Despatches*. In *Seven Pillars* one is often aware of the effort behind the carefully crafted chapters. Lawrence is trying very hard to write well and he is also trying, as stated, to get into the big league – to be up there with Tolstoy, or Dostoevsky, or Melville; in a word, to prove himself a mature artist in the matter of the making of books. By contrast, *Secret Despatches* is poured out breezily, with (as one can tell from the original manuscripts held in the National Archives) hardly any corrections or rewriting. The impression created is that this is a born writer whose hand is racing across the page untroubled by doubts and hesitations, and who is revelling in the fact that his day job is throwing up more good things to write about than he could possibly have imagined.

I have deliberately referred to him as a young man at this stage of his career. It is worth noting, however, that had he served on the Western Front, he would have been a comparatively elderly subaltern; born in 1888, he was twenty-eight when he went to the desert, thirty when he reached Damascus. But in the milieu in which he found himself on arriving in Cairo in 1914 he was certainly a relative junior, and, it might be claimed, rejoiced in the fact. His colleagues were almost all older men: Hogarth had been born in 1862; Brigadier General Clayton, his Military Intelligence superior in Cairo to whom he frequently reported, had been born in 1875; Newcombe, later his fellow raider in the desert, had joined the Egyptian army in 1901; the Hon. Aubrey Herbert (born 1880) and George Lloyd (born 1879) were already

Members of Parliament; Captain Buxton, of the Imperial Camel Corps, with whom he campaigned for a time in 1918, was five years his senior. Among these men he was the brilliant, energetic youth, the maverick, almost the *enfant terrible* ('I was all claws and teeth, and had a devil,' he writes in Chapter 6 of *Seven Pillars*, when placing himself in the Cairo scene). Throughout the war he could, and frequently did, infuriate his superiors, but he also knew how to dazzle them. It was Hogarth who, as early as the autumn of 1917, could write of his reputation as being 'overpowering'. There is no hint of criticism in Hogarth's comment; rather it shows a genuine admiration for someone who has performed so well that he has outstripped and outshone his more mature colleagues.

However, in claiming *Secret Despatches* as a young man's book, I am not suggesting that when he wrote *Seven Pillars* he had disowned the youthful stance of his war years. Far from it. See, for example, his classic statement in its Introductory Chapter:

> We lived many lives in those whirling campaigns, never sparing ourselves: yet when we achieved and the new world dawned, the old men came out again and took our victory to re-make in the likeness of the former world they knew. Youth could win, but had not learned to keep: and was pitiably weak against age. We stammered that we had worked for a new heaven and a new earth, and they thanked us kindly and made their peace.

One is almost reminded of Wilfred Owen's searing poem 'The Parable of the Old Man and the Young', a twentieth-century version of the story of Abraham and Isaac, in which Abraham binds his son for sacrifice while an angel entreats his father in vain to spare him:

> Behold! Caught in a thicket by his horns,
> A Ram. Offer the Ram of Pride instead.
>
> But the old man would not so, but slew his son,
> And half the seed of Europe, one by one.

These are both major formulations of the eternal paradox of war, that the younger generation does the fighting and the dying while the older generations give the orders and keep the spoils.

In certain respects Lawrence and Owen (whose name reminds us that there was another and far greater campaign going on throughout Lawrence's two years in Arabia) were not unalike. Both were 'hostilities only' officers of high intelligence and unusual sensitivity. Both were products of a strong religious upbringing and both were men of high moral purpose and ambition. Both wanted to write their war experience into a form of which the world would take notice. Both were acutely aware of the pity of war. For the sake of history and literature it is well they were where they were. Owen is indispensable to the understanding of the Western Front. Lawrence is indispensable to the understanding of the Middle Eastern war, and – as it is part of the purpose of this book to suggest – to the understanding of the Middle East ever since. But they were both part of the same overall scene.

As someone who has attempted to study many aspects of the First World War, I feel that too often students of T. E. Lawrence fail to see him in his wider context. It is as though the Arab Revolt was a war on its own. People can become so used to seeing the Middle Eastern campaign as a thing of itself that it comes almost as a shock when Lawrence records that on meeting Emir Abdullah in his desert camp in Wadi Ais in March 1917, the latter was less interested in talking about the task in hand than in discussing other subjects such as the Battle of the Somme. But Lawrence did not compartmentalise the war himself; he was always aware of what he once described as 'the big war' going on elsewhere. After all, two younger brothers had died in France while he was still making maps and composing intelligence reports at General Headquarters in Egypt. When he went to the desert he was aware that he was fighting the allies of the enemy who had killed his brothers. Later, the major Allied setback in Europe in the spring of 1918 severely affected Allenby's, and therefore his, plans for the final push against the Turks. Troops were drawn away to France and new, longer-term plans had to be devised. Moreover, the initiatives in which he was involved were, particularly in the later stages, regularly referred to and discussed in London. They even reached the desk of the Chief of the Imperial General Staff, Sir William Robertson, who was responsible for the prosecution of hostilities in all theatres, including and especially that most famous and crucial of battle sectors, the Western Front. This was one war, not several.

A substantial amount of the foregoing appeared in the Introduction to the 1991 edition of *Secret Despatches*, a fact for which I make only a muted apology, for it says much of what needs to be said in this section of the new volume, and I see no advantage in rewriting now what I laboured hard to put into readable prose fourteen years ago. But from this point forward I am deliberately stepping into less charted territory, effectually aping the epigraph by Lawrence which I quoted at the beginning of that edition and have repeated again in this one, with its reference to an 'amusing job, and all new country'. Of course, one should be wary of the word 'amusing', clearly used by the original writer with a distinct, if not untypical, sense of irony, and by myself with a pale, apologetic imitation of his. In practice his job was far from amusing, nor should the term apply to any serious attempt to analyse it, for it is in this analysis that, for better or worse, this new edition has its focus, and therefore, if the case is made even half satisfactorily, its justification.

So, to pose a central, necessary question: when Captain T. E. Lawrence rubbed off his British habits and went 'off for a bit' with Feisul (or Feisal, according to choice), was he wasting his time, and therefore, by definition, ours? Or to put it another way: did he make a significant contribution to the 1914–18 war? Did he have anything to offer the 'side-show of a side-show' in which he was engaged – this relatively minor theatre of a world conflict – other than through lively, stylish essays which made good reading for his elders and betters sipping their gin and tonics in Cairo and Whitehall? And implicit in this is the more important general question, what did the Arab Revolt contribute to the successful outcome of the Middle Eastern war? To this last question, in the light of recent research on this subject, I offer the following brief, if admittedly austere, answer.

Undoubtedly, Allenby's conventional force was the prime mover in this formidable and, apart from certain setbacks, impressively executed enterprise. In terms of the numbers of men and the weight of weaponry involved, and of the impact on the manpower and morale of the retreating Ottoman army, there can be no other interpretation. Thus with the best will in the world, the Arab contribution can only be seen as supplementary, and, since some of the Arab tribes wanted to make sure they were on the winning side before they jumped (they would have been in deep trouble if they had got things wrong), as a somewhat uncertain element, militarily difficult to quantify.

This summarises what might be described as a standard viewpoint among contemporary British historians of the First World War, and not just those so focused on the war in Europe that the campaigns of the Middle East can seem all but irrelevant. There are, however, other interpretations. The following is the verdict of the distinguished Australian historian, Trevor Wilson, author of an authoritative history of Britain's contribution to the 1914–18 conflict published in 1986, *The Myriad Faces of War*. 'Plainly, it was not decisive,' he commented. 'Yet it had not been inconsiderable: in protecting Allenby's right flank, helping to mislead the enemy concerning the whereabouts of his initial thrust, and disrupting the Turks' communications.' Wilson also called to witness General Glubb, famous as the last commander of the Arab Legion, in whose opinion the Arab Revolt was an extraordinary example of what could be achieved by guerrilla tactics, in that tens of thousands of regular Turkish troops had been pinned down by an adversary barely capable of engaging a brigade of infantry in pitched battle. 'Such economy of force', Wilson commented, 'was rare on either side in this war.'*

A historian of an earlier generation whose comments are worth recording in this context is Cyril Falls, who served in France throughout the First World War, but also compiled the *Official History of the Egypt and Palestine Campaigns* published in 1930. In his classic one-volume history of the war

---

* Trevor Wilson, *The Myriad Faces of War* (Polity Press, Cambridge, in association with Basil Blackwell, Oxford, 1986), p. 622.

which appeared in 1960 (by which time, it might be noted, Lawrence's reputation was a matter of some dispute), Falls acknowledged that Allenby
had given substantial credit to the contribution of the irregular Arab forces
to the success of the campaign. Bracketing Allenby's approach with that of
his predecessor as Commander-in-Chief, General Sir Archibald Murray,
Falls stated:

> Murray had consistently supported the Arab Revolt; Allenby, whose
> vivid imagination belied his conventional image, saw still more in it and
> gave it even more potent aid. The link between him and the Arabs was
> a little body of British officers, most notable among whom was T. E.
> Lawrence, who had a spiritual affinity with the Bedouin and was a
> master of guerrilla tactics and strategy.*

Another strongly supportive view of the Arab achievement appears in the
book *Images of Lawrence*, by two American authorities, Stephen E.
Tabachnick and Christopher Matheson, published in 1988. The authors
cited the opinion of General Liman von Sanders, German Commander-in-
Chief of the Turkish armies in Palestine, who recognised that because of the
Arab Revolt, the British 'were fighting under conditions as though in their
own country, while the Turks in defence of their own country had to fight
amongst a population directly hostile'. Von Sanders, the authors claimed,
was not one to dismiss the Arab capture of Akaba in June 1917 as militarily unimportant, nor to regard as insignificant the Arab attacks on the Hejaz
Railway, especially in the later stages of the campaign when spare parts were
no longer available to effect repairs to engines and rolling stock. Claiming
Lawrence's 'flexibility' as crucial, they stated:

> Owing precisely to this flexibility of approach, Lawrence was able to
> take a poorly organized band of warring Bedouin tribes and turn them
> (and the civilian population of the Hejaz and Syria) into an unorthodox
> weapon that helped bring about the collapse of the Turks . . . The
> Turks' confidence was undermined, and they were transformed into
> worried and isolated garrisons in a hostile land . . . When the Arabs
> marched into Damascus on 1 October 1918 (just two years after he pre-
> dicted that he would) Lawrence's theory that an unconventional force
> could be valuable received its final proof.†

Tabachnick and Matheson, well known as serious students, indeed admirers, of Lawrence, might be expected to take a generally favourable view, but
such is certainly not the case with Robert B. Asprey, whose encyclopaedic

---

* Cyril Falls, *The First World War* (Longmans, London, 1960), p. 375.
† Stephen E. Tabachnick and Christopher Matheson, *Images of Lawrence* (Jonathan Cape,
London, 1988), pp. 119–20.

work *War in the Shadows: The Guerrilla in History*, published in the 1970s, surveyed the whole saga of irregular warfare, from the Scythian guerrillas who plagued Darius or Alexander and the doomed exploits of Spartacus to the crises of the late twentieth century, with the special agenda of warning his fellow Americans against the dangers of being drawn into another Vietnam. Nevertheless, he found space for a whole chapter on Lawrence, of which the following is a keynote paragraph:

> He did not insist on grafting his own and his country's standards on a body incapable of reception. Instead, and thanks to linguistic ability, imagination, perception, intellectual and moral honesty, and, not least, immense energy, he went to the tribes, found a leader, determined a viable goal, weighed capabilities, and hit on a type of war compatible to leadership, capabilities, and the political goal. The estimate of the situation that Lawrence brought forth from the sand-dunes in 1917 is a military equivalent of the British constitution – one of the most interesting unwritten documents of all time.*

So far so good. But it is important to add that there are contrary views, sometimes expressed by people generally deemed to be cast in the Lawrence mould. No one was more outspoken in this respect than the man dubbed by many as the T. E. Lawrence of the Second World War, Orde Wingate, brilliant as a guerrilla leader most notably in Burma and Palestine, and, as it happens, a remote kinsman of Lawrence (he was a distant cousin through his mother's side). In a scathing passage in an essay entitled 'Palestine in Imperial Strategy', written in 1939, he wrote of the Arab Revolt:

> The vanity of the principals plus a great amount of romantic dust has been allowed so far to obscure what did happen. A ragged horde of at most a few thousand and often only a few hundred Bedouin, paid in gold for approximately two days' fighting per month . . . caused the Turks a certain amount of embarrassment and anxiety . . . In return for the highly paid assistance of this small rabble of Hedjazi Bedouin, we have handed over to the 'Arabs' the whole of Saudi Arabia, and the Yemen, Iraq, Transjordan and Syria. A more absurd transaction has never been seen.†

Yet this view must be put in context. If Wingate despised Lawrence, Lawrence could be said to have had his own back on Wingate. I quote from the scholarly Introduction by Kathi Frances McGraw to a catalogue

---

* Robert B. Asprey, *War in the Shadows: The Guerrilla in History* (Doubleday, Garden City, NY, 1975), pp. 289–90.
† John Bierman and Colin Smith, *Fire in the Night: Wingate of Burma, Ethiopia and Zion* (Random House, New York, 1999; Macmillan, London, 2000), p. 131.

produced for a Lawrence exhibition held at Brown University, New Jersey, in 1998:

> During the Second World War, there were several generals who recognized and appreciated TE's particular military genius. British Field Marshall A. P. Wavell, one of the great Allied commanders, held TE in great esteem as did German Field Marshall Erwin Rommel. On this side of the Atlantic, American field commander General George S. Patton had studied the *Seven Pillars of Wisdom*. TE's legacy to that war is reflected most strikingly perhaps in the ascension of Orde Wingate. When Prime Minister Churchill was firing British generals left and right, he was looking for a commander of the caliber of TE – unconventional, effective, able to make do with small forces and inflict maximum damage to the enemy. He turned to Wingate, described by Churchill's private secretary John Martin as 'an interesting and striking person, not unlike my idea of T. E. Lawrence.' Wingate employed Lawrencian tactics effectively, leading the notorious [*sic*] Chindits in long-range penetrations against the Japanese. His exploits won him unofficial titles such as Lawrence of Judea (for his activities in Palestine), Lawrence of Ethiopia, and Lawrence of Burma. When the Royal Central Asian Society recognized Wingate's achievements, they awarded him the Lawrence of Arabia memorial medal.*

Another notable leader in a vastly different context who took deliberate notice of T. E. Lawrence was Mao Tse-tung, who gave mediocre performances in standard warfare, but proved invincible when adopting irregular techniques. Edgar Snow, Mao's American admirer and interpreter, even compared 'Mao's Reds' to Lawrence's Arabs. Other Chinese and Vietnamese generals took Lawrence seriously. Writes McGraw:

> It is instructive to note that Vo Nguyen Giap, another self-taught guerrilla general who successfully drove first the French and then the Americans out of Vietnam, was familiar with TE. During an interview by *Paris Match* in 1977, the questioner comments: 'You . . . General, were nicknamed "The Cause". You have become a legend in your own time,' to which Giap laughingly responds: 'I'm not Lawrence of Arabia.'

Significantly, it has been stated that Vo Nguyen Giap went to war with *Seven Pillars of Wisdom* in his hand. This raises a possible claim on T. E. Lawrence's behalf accepted even by those not inclined to accept the more extravagant elements in his reputation: that whatever his expertise in the

---

* Kathi Frances McGraw and Andrew Carvely, *T. E. Lawrence, A 20th Century Retrospective* (Andrew Carvely Corporation, Summerduck, VA, 1998).

matter of practising guerrilla warfare in the field, he was arguably the subject's finest exponent.

This was affirmed in an influential work entitled *The Art of Counter-Revolutionary War: The Strategy of Counter-Insurgency*, by John J. McCuen, lieutenant-colonel in the US Army, published in Britain in 1966. McCuen referred to Lawrence's *Seven Pillars* as 'brilliant', and in a section on the role of advisers states that the book should be required reading for anybody engaged in the matter of helping emergent nations in their insurgency. He described Lawrence as 'the epitome of successful advisers – teacher, counsellor, supporter, and friend to the leaders of the British-supported Arab revolt'.*

On this matter of Lawrence's role as exponent of and propagandist for irregular warfare, a voice worth hearing is that of the distinguished British expert on the matter of insurgency and counter-insurgency throughout the last two or three centuries, Professor Ian Beckett, a historian with a proven record on both sides of the Atlantic.

For him, the palm for expertise in guerrilla warfare in the 1914–18 war should be assigned to the outstanding German regular commander in German East Africa, Paul von Lettow-Vorbeck, who fought so brilliant a campaign against the Western Allies that he laid down his arms a fortnight or so after the conclusion of the war in Europe, having teased and outwitted his enemies to the last. In his (edited) book *The Roots of Counter-Insurgency: Armies and Guerrilla Warfare, 1900–1945*, published in 1988, Beckett gave Lettow-Vorbeck his due, then added: 'However, where Lawrence did make a significant contribution was in the sheer elegance of his written account of his experiences, *Seven Pillars of Wisdom* in particular being a classic exposition of guerrilla theory underlined by a real comprehension of its political implications for Arab nationalism.'†

More recently, Beckett has written on this vast subject at much greater length in his book entitled *Modern Insurgencies and Counter-Insurgencies: Guerrillas and Their Opponents since 1750*, published in 2002. In a notable passage in his Introduction he picks out three modern guerrilla leaders worth mentioning as 'displaying a thoroughly modern understanding of the political and socio-economic potential of insurgency, namely Nestor Makhno, Augusto Sandino and Thomas Edward Lawrence'. The first two names need not detain us: Makhno was a Ukrainian anarchist who fought against the Bolsheviks in the latter stage of the Russian Civil War of 1917–21; Sandino was a Nicaraguan radical who waged a campaign against the Nicaraguan National Guard and its American marine allies between 1927 and 1933. Beckett's passage on Lawrence, however, is worth quoting at some length:

---

* John J. McCuen, *The Art of Counter-Revolutionary War: The Strategy of Counter-Insurgency* (Faber & Faber, London, 1966), p. 67.
† Ian F. W. Beckett (ed.), *The Roots of Counter-Insurgency: Armies and Guerrilla Warfare, 1900–1945* (Blandford Press, London, 1988), p. 7.

The third individual and arguably one of the most influential theorists of the twentieth century in terms of revolutionary war was not a revolutionary at all, but T. E. Lawrence (1888–1935). Lawrence's precise role in the 'Arab Revolt' against the Turks during the First World War remains a matter of some controversy. There is little doubt that his military achievements were exaggerated, not only by his own hand but also by that of the British military writer Basil Liddell Hart, who saw Lawrence's theories and methods as ideally complementary to his own concept of the 'indirect approach'. In essence, the Arab Revolt was a sideshow in a subsidiary theatre of war, although it has been calculated that 3,000 Arabs tied down up to 50,000 Turkish troops. Nevertheless, the significance of the campaign derived from Lawrence's account of it, in which it might be added he generally underestimated the impact of the British Army's conventional operations in Palestine. Arguably, Lawrence appears to be an original theorist because he had no literary competitors among contemporary practitioners, but there have been few better descriptions of guerrilla conflict.*

Clearly Beckett is no facile admirer of Lawrence, yet he is certainly ready to give credit where credit is due, namely by asserting that even those not entirely persuaded by his performance might find value in his prose.

However, Beckett can perhaps be faulted in what he wrote next, in that he roots Lawrence's military theories in his post-war writings, in 'The Evolution of a Revolt', written in 1920, and in *Seven Pillars of Wisdom*. For Lawrence students, this is an assumption verging on heresy, in that it can be seen as bolstering the view advanced by some of his critics that he made everything up after the war, rationalising in grand theoretical terms what had happened by mere good fortune.

Such was certainly not the case. And this is where the secret despatches in this volume come into their own. For they give us not the Lawrence of the post-war period, when he was fighting his own corner and that of the Arabs, who, as he knew in his bones, were small battalions in the conflict between the Great Powers as to who would win the spoils, but the voice of the Lawrence of the war years, when there was a mass of real work to be done and everything to play for. And in those war years his voice is not an uncertain sound, but an eloquent and incisive one, focusing rapidly on the essential elements of the odd kind of war into which he suddenly found himself thrust in late 1916.

It has to be admitted that the most eloquent exposition of his views on the subject of guerrilla war is in the famous Chapter 33 of *Seven Pillars* (or Chapter 35 in the 1997 edition of the 1922 version which arguably offers us a better and more authentic text than that published in 1935). However, an

---

* Ian F. W. Beckett, *Modern Insurgencies and Counter-Insurgencies: Guerrillas and Their Opponents since 1750* (Routledge, London and New York, 2002), pp. 19–20.

equally outstanding, if not in overall terms more important, treatise on guerrilla warfare is to be found in Lawrence's 'Twenty-Seven Articles' (pp. 142–7), his list of dos and don'ts for British officers attached to the Arab armies published in the *Arab Bulletin* of 20 August 1917. It is a brilliant thesis which only a Lawrence could have written. There is the same confident, precocious talent at work here that bemused the examiners in his Oxford days. Indeed, there is a certain amount of sheer youthful cheek in the writing, as he pours out his pearls of wisdom like so many commandments (which is precisely what he calls them, if with a hint of apology). Moreover, it is clear that he meant his advice to be heeded by his elders and betters as well as his subordinates, and he knew that, being published in the *Bulletin*, his 'commandments' would be widely read. (One can almost imagine eyebrows rising in the Cairo corridors: 'Twenty-seven? The Deity only needed ten!') But this was not mere showing-off; there was also a political purpose behind the piece. It put on the table his clear belief that the Arabs were worth fighting with, and for; if they had not been up to the effort put into supporting their cause, he would not have bothered.

The reader might be wise to turn to 'Twenty-Seven Articles' and read it before proceeding, or at least access its salient points. This, in a sense, is his central credo, his Sermon on the Mount to those about to leave the comforts and familiar atmosphere of Allied Headquarters in Cairo and head for the entirely different culture of the desert.

The central point to be made about this document is, however, that it was written *at the time*. For an even earlier statement showing Lawrence's understanding of the kind of war in which he was involved, the reader might turn to a forceful paragraph at the end of 'Military Notes', a postscript headed '*Argument against landing foreigners at Rabugh*'. It reads:

> The Hejaz war is one of dervishes against regular troops – and we are on the side of the dervishes. Our textbooks do not apply to its conditions at all. It is the fight of a rocky, mountainous, ill-watered country (assisted by a wild horde of mountaineers) against a force which has been improved – so far as civilised warfare is concerned – so immensely by the Germans, as almost to have lost its efficiency for rough-and-tumble work.

The despatch to which the postscript was attached is datelined '*Jiddah, 3 November 1916*'. When he wrote it – itself part of an extraordinary outpouring of lucid and incisive writing produced at this time – Lawrence had been in Arabia for less than a month. Far from being a retrospective theorist, he was a military thinker from the moment he became a military activist, living his philosophy and expounding it at the same time.

Thus Lawrence as the polemicist of his war. What of Lawrence's writings on war in time of peace?

The second half of this book is devoted to this subject, and each item included has its own separate introduction. Essentially what this section comprises is a mixture of expository articles and letters to the press written as comments on events which had excited Lawrence's interest, or more often his anger. Sometimes the authorship is evident; at other times it is concealed – as in the three articles for *The Times* published in November 1918 (pp. 216–31). In the editorial introduction to the first article he appears as 'a correspondent who was in close touch with the Arabs throughout their campaign against the Turks'; variations on this theme head the second and third. But anonymity was the standard usage of the nation's most famous newspaper (see introduction to 'Three Articles from *The Times*', pp. 216–17), and in any case at this time his name was not known: so much so that the first peacetime document reproduced here, 'Reconstruction of Arabia' (pp. 211–15), obviously typed from a handwritten original, was assigned to 'T. E. LAURENCE, *Lieut.-Colonel*'. But this was dated 4 November 1918; it was only a month since he had begun his return journey from Damascus, and the war had still a full week to run before the armistice of 11 November brought hostilities to an end.

All the material in this section of the book has been printed elsewhere, notably in David Garnett's wide-ranging collection of 1938, *The Letters of T. E. Lawrence*, or in the valuable anthology of early post-war writings brought together by Stanley and Rodelle Weintraub under the title *Evolution of a Revolt*, which was published by the Pennsylvania State University Press in 1968. The fact that both these books are long out of print makes the case for these items being given a further lease of life.

The final item, however, is of an interesting and unusual provenance. Reprinted from the *Encyclopædia Britannica* of 1929, it is not normally cited as one of Lawrence's writings, being basically a compilation of his thoughts on guerrilla warfare put together by Captain Basil Liddell Hart. Necessarily it recycles material to be found elsewhere in this book, but it is compiled with such skill that it reads with the pace and coherence of an entirely new document and thus pays a compliment to both men involved. Having had the privilege of meeting and discussing Lawrence with Liddell Hart in his latter years, I am particularly pleased to include an example of his handiwork here.

The virtue of these items being reprinted here, of course, is that, together with the despatches, they make up a before-and-after composite, offering, as it were, a snapshot of Lawrence in the active stage of his career and in the campaigning stage that followed. Essentially he is an armchair warrior in this second phase, though anyone less likely to enjoy the comfort of an armchair is hard to imagine. Curiously, for a man who normally loathed his attempts at literature – he endlessly denigrated *Seven Pillars of Wisdom*, in spite of the unstinted approval of such literary friends as E. M. Forster and Siegfried Sassoon – these items exude few such doubts. Writing on practical matters, or for practical purposes, he did so with speed and confidence, as had been the case with his reports in the war. Agonies over style were irrelevant to his purposes, but he wrote with style nevertheless.

The events that produced the material republished in this book are now old history. Yet there is strong evidence that interest in Lawrence has re-emerged with new vigour in our own day. This has largely been attributed to the situation in Iraq following the coalition attack led by the United States and Great Britain in 2003. Yet even before that some military analysts were pointing to Lawrence as a key figure whose views should be re-examined and, in appropriate circumstances, emulated. One such was Dr George W. Gawrych, of the US Army Command and General Staff College at Fort Leavenworth, Kansas, who at a conference in May 2000 gave a presentation which he entitled 'T. E. Lawrence and the Art of War at the Dawn of the Twenty-First Century'.

In a powerful passage under the heading 'Intellect and Military Theory', he criticised the 'anti-intellectualism' which he described as 'rampant in the [American] armed forces'. In the context of the Vietnam War he quoted a noted expert on that conflict as describing the attitude of the US military towards the Communist Vietnamese as (in a deft distortion of the usual phrase) 'vincible ignorance': 'One does not know, one realises one does not know, and yet one feels no need to change the fact that one does not know.' In a section headed 'Coalition Warfare', he praised Lawrence for being 'well prepared to meet the challenge of working as a British liaison officer with Bedouin Arabs', continuing: 'True to his desire for both action and contemplation, Lawrence reflected seriously about his mission within a British–Arab coalition. His ideas set out in the "Twenty-Seven Articles" serve as excellent advice for working in any coalition.'

Gawrych went on to accuse the American commander of the Gulf War of 1990–1, General Norman Schwarzkopf, of falling short in this regard. He quoted Khaled bin Sultan, the commander of Arab forces in Operation Desert Storm, as saying of his American colleague that 'the people, the leading personalities of Arab politics, the families, the customs, attitudes, language, history, way of life – indeed all the complexities of our Arab world – were as foreign and unfamiliar to him as they are to the average American'. By contrast, Gawrych praised Lawrence for demonstrating that 'a proper attitude to one's ally is essential in order to avoid unnecessary friction and problems. In reflecting on his experiences with the Hejaz Arabs, Lawrence counselled patience, respect, tact and even a good dose of humility.'

It might be added as an aside that other powers confronting nations of a totally different culture were prone to a similar 'vincible ignorance'. One recent case that might be cited is the Soviet attempt in the 1980s to subjugate Afghanistan, a confrontation in which the mailed fist was found to be singularly ineffective against forces which used terrain, scatter and the tactics of insurgency to outwit a greatly superior conventional enemy. Hence the epigraph quoted at the head of this book attributed to an unnamed Russian general who claimed that one Afghan on a camel was more effective than four Russians in a tank. Smashed tanks on Afghan hillsides would remain one of the enduring images of that ugly, futile conflict.

Not all American commanders fell below the standard Gawrych and those of like mind advocated. He had special praise for the generalship practised by the future President Dwight D. Eisenhower in his role as supreme commander in Europe during the Second World War:

> Eisenhower demanded collegiality and courtesy from subordinates and staff; reached decisions by consensus; and devoted most of his time to coalition politics. To avoid unnecessary friction, American soldiers received a booklet instructing them on British customs and habits. Lawrence approached his assignment with a similar mindset, one that stressed flexibility, adaptability and collegiality.

In his concluding paragraph, Gawrych strongly recommended that Lawrence should be read. 'In the spectrum of twenty-first century conflict, from conventional to unconventional warfare and peacekeeping operations, Lawrence offers a military theory that effectively addresses the nature of guerrilla warfare, the middle part of that spectrum.'

Gawrych's praise is both eloquent and impressive. For those many students and even historians, especially in Britain, who dismiss Lawrence as a shady figure of dubious validity out of a minor campaign of a ninety-year-old war, this might prove a testimony worth noting.

Dr Gawrych's observations related to a Gulf war now more than a decade in the past. Since then a second conflict has erupted in that long-troubled part of the world, beginning with the coalition attack of early 2003, mounted by the United States and Britain effectively to complete the unfinished business of that earlier conflagration and rid the world of the regime of the Iraqi dictator, Saddam Hussein. The pretext for war was Saddam's alleged ownership of weapons of mass destruction capable of almost instant deployment, which, on the back of his defiance of a series of resolutions emanating from the United Nations, had made him a prime target. In relatively short order the regime collapsed. The falling statue of the Iraqi dictator in the heart of Baghdad became the symbol of the hour, and the American president proclaimed 'mission accomplished' to sustained applause on the deck of one of his huge aircraft carriers. Yet the peace, goodwill and democracy which were meant to flow from the ousting of one of the world's most notorious tyrannies singularly failed to appear. Instead, the country fell into a condition of virtual anarchy. Anger was turned not only on the would-be liberators but flared viciously between different sections of Iraqi society, the pot being stirred by terrorists (according to one interpretation) or freedom fighters (according to another) pouring in to pursue their own often fanatic purposes. There were atrocities on all sides. A notorious prison in Saddam's day, Abu Ghraib, won a different kind of notoriety thanks to serious, and widely publicised, violations of the rights of Iraqi prisoners. If there were American excesses, there were also British ones. The winning of hearts and minds – vital to any political success in a situation of insurgency – seemed all but a lost cause.

Suddenly Lawrence was back in the frame, being treated with the kind of respect that had been conspicuously rare in recent times among historians of the twentieth-century in Great Britain. On 1 March 2004 *The Times* quoted Professor Andrew Lambert of King's College, London, formerly of the Royal Military Academy, Sandhurst, as stating: 'Lawrence teaches us that you can succeed only by immersing yourself in the culture. He also tells us very important things about insurgency.' Professor Michael Clarke, Director of King's College's International Policy Institute, was quoted to similar effect: 'There is an enormous amount of counter-terrorism that is to do with understanding cultural background. One of the reasons Lawrence was so successful was because he had such a good insight into Arabian politics.' Even more impressively, Clarke was reported as having made the remarkable assertion that Lawrence was as important as Nelson in understanding combat. The newspaper also recorded a 50 per cent surge in sales of *Seven Pillars of Wisdom* since the first rumblings of conflict in Iraq in August of the previous year.

The Lawrence cause was taken up even more vigorously in the United States. In *Finest Hour*, the journal of the Churchill Society, Charles Anderson, in an article entitled '*Seven Pillars* Today', described Lawrence's epic as 'a must book for those wanting to understand Arab psychology, and, to almost as great an extent, military history as applied in a hostile environment in a guerrilla fashion', concluding with the admonition, 'President Bush and Mr Blair need to read this book.'

More significantly, the late Professor John E. Mack, a Lawrence expert and author of the 1977 Pulitzer Prize-winning biography *A Prince of Our Disorder*, weighed in with a powerful article in the *Boston Globe*, in which he referred to his researches in the Arab world while preparing his book. He wrote:

Above all, Lawrence was able to command the respect of the men with whom he fought. Arab tribesmen who had been with Lawrence during the revolt made clear to me that he understood their culture, psychology and particular needs. They were proud to follow him. In the present situation in Iraq these essential elements of effective leadership seem to be largely missing. Most striking is the almost reflexive tendency of senior American officials to find others to blame for whatever goes wrong.

Even more pointedly, Mack discussed Lawrence's loathing of too swift a resort to arms, quoting him as stating: 'Only as a last resort we should be compelled to the desperate course of blood and the maxims of "murder war" . . . To man rationale, wars of nationality were as much a cheat as religious wars.' Mack concluded: 'We have been plunged into a moral chaos that can only end when saner minds, "man rationale" in T. E. Lawrence's words, can once more assume authority in this country.'

Another striking tribute to Lawrence appeared under the name of a writer on military subjects for the *Washington Post*, Thomas E. Ricks, in November 2004. Hitherto Ricks had, as he put it, 'faltered' whenever he had attempted to read *Seven Pillars of Wisdom*, until the experience of being embedded with the US 1st Infantry Division in Iraq made him try again. 'As it happened,' he wrote, in his article entitled 'Lessons of Arabia', 'I had been carrying the book around in my knapsack . . . and when I took it out, it seemed like a different book. This time I whipped through its 656 pages.' He cautioned:

> Let me emphatically state here that I am not likening the cause of the Iraqi insurgents to that of Arab rebels against the Turks. I was reading this as a tactical manual of military operations against another military, not of terrorist attacks on civilians.
>
> In those terms, the tactics employed by Lawrence and his Arab tribesmen were strikingly similar to those used against US forces today in Iraq. American truck convoys constantly come under attack, sometimes by rocket-propelled grenades but most often by anonymous roadside bombs. Likewise, for most of his war, Lawrence wasn't interested in direct confrontation with the Turkish military. Rather, he strove to avoid the set-piece slugfests that Western militaries – and Western journalists – tend to think of as the essence of war, such as the recent battle of Fallujah. He relentlessly chipped away at the railroad that supplied Turkish forces deep in what is now Jordan and Saudi Arabia, dropping railway bridges and blowing up locomotives . . .
>
> When I read his description of why he thought his outgunned, outmanned, unsophisticated force could prevail, a chill ran down my spine. His rebellion, he wrote, faced 'a sophisticated alien enemy, disposed as an army of occupation in an area greater than could be dominated effectively from fortified posts.' Meanwhile, his side was supported by 'a friendly population, of which some two in the hundred were active, and the rest quietly sympathetic to the point of not betraying the movements of the minority'.

Ricks praised Lawrence for his capacity to wage war psychologically, quoting a passage describing the wait for reinforcements: 'We could do little but think – yet that . . . was the essential process.'

But even Lawrence, Ricks noted, for all his knowledge of Arab culture, could be stunned by the thoroughness of Arab looting. Of the fall of Mezerib, Lawrence wrote: 'Men, women and children fought like dogs over every object. Doors and windows, door-frames and window-frames, even stairs, were carried off . . . Tons were carried off. Yet more were strewn in wreckage on the ground.' Ricks commented: 'That paragraph could have been written about the fall of Baghdad nearly 20 months ago.'

Yet for Ricks, Lawrence's overall understanding of the imperatives of counter-insurgency remains consistently impressive. Quoting another dictum from *Seven Pillars*, 'War upon rebellion was messy and slow, like eating soup with a knife', he reported that an officer who had served in Iraq in 2003, Lieutenant-Colonel John Nagl, had woven that concept into a doctoral thesis for Lawrence's own university, Oxford, and that, according to Pentagon insiders, the army Chief of Staff had distributed copies of his book to all US army generals, though 'Whether they will learn from Lawrence's lessons', he commented, 'remains to be seen.'

The thesis in question predated the 2003 conflict, being published in 2002 under the title *Counterinsurgency Lessons from Malaya and Vietnam*, with 'Learning to Eat Soup with a Knife' as its subtitle. John Nagl was a former West Point graduate and Rhodes Scholar of St Antony's College, Oxford, who had served as commander of a tank platoon in Iraq in 1991, earning a Bronze Star for his efforts. Returning to Iraq in 2003 as an operations officer gave him, as a student of guerrilla warfare, the opportunity of a lifetime. In a powerful article dated 11 November 2004, *New York Times* writer Peter Maass compared him to a 'palaeontologist given the chance to go back in time and walk with the dinosaurs'. Maass, himself with a distinguished track record as a reporter from Iraq, quoted Nagl as saying to him personally:

I didn't realize how right Lawrence of Arabia was. My first experience of war was the Gulf War. We shot the tanks that didn't look like ours, we shot the enemy wearing a uniform that didn't look like ours, we destroyed the enemy in 100 hours. That's kind of what I thought war was. Even when I was writing that insurgency was messy, the full enormity of that did not sink in on me. I am [now] seeing appreciable progress, but I am starting to understand in the pit of my stomach how hard, how long, how slow counterinsurgency is. There is no prospect it's going to end anytime soon.

Another writer with high praise for Lawrence in the present climate is Joel Turnipseed, author of a memoir about the first Gulf War entitled *Baghdad Express*, who in a major article in the online magazine *Salon* wrote of *Seven Pillars*:

It preceded Hemingway's first war novel, *A Farewell to Arms*, and Remarque's *All Quiet on the Western Front*. Thus Lawrence was the creator of both the individual soldier tormented about the aims of his war, but also, in his dual role as soldier and spy, the entire stock of Graham Greene and John Le Carré's characters . . . When all the books are written on our latest Gulf War – the one at hand and the decade-plus ellipsis that will ultimately join the adventures of 1990–91 and 2003 – *Seven Pillars* will be remembered as the greatest Gulf War memoir.

If there is a codicil worth adding to the argument it is perhaps this. On the day that Saigon fell in 1975 at the end of the Vietnam War, the English poet James Fenton found a framed quotation on a wall in the looted American embassy: '"Better to let them do it imperfectly than do it perfectly yourself, for it is their country, their war, and your time is short." The words are from T. E. Lawrence.' Versions of this quotation have appeared on many walls in Iraq in the course of the insurgency that followed the military defeat of Iraq in 2003. The correct text should read:

> Do not try to do too much with your own hands. Better the Arabs do it tolerably than you do it perfectly. It is their war, and you are to help them, not to win it for them. Actually, also, under the very odd conditions of Arabia, your practical work will not be as good as, perhaps, you think it is.

This is no. 15 of Lawrence's 'Twenty-Seven Articles'.

How long this surge in T. E. Lawrence's reputation will last is anyone's guess. Everything depends on how the global war against terrorism progresses in the years to come. Yet what the foregoing shows, surely, is that the unorthodox young officer who was posted to Arabia in 1916 and served in a minor campaign of the First World War has had an afterlife as influence and military expositor way beyond his own or anyone else's imaginings. It should be emphasised that not all his efforts were positive or effective. In particular, the 1921–2 settlement of the Middle East, in which he collaborated with the forceful and ebullient Churchill, has come in for serious criticism, especially in relation to Iraq. Feisal's emergence as monarch in Baghdad with British blessing could make him seem a puppet king, the fate of his dynasty – ousted bloodily in 1958 – being adduced as evidence of a flaw in the basic concept. However, the idea of creating the state of Iraq – seen by many as an artificial construct yoking disparate entities – was not Churchill's or Lawrence's, but a solution initially proposed by the government of British India, well used to ruling a large area with religious and ethnic divisions. With regard to that other focus of continuing anxiety, the territory then known simply as Palestine, Lawrence was wise enough to see that what in 'The Changing East' (see pp. 248–59) he called the 'Jewish experiment' – the settling of Jews from elsewhere among the existing Arabic-speaking population ('a people of kindred origin, but far different social condition') – would succeed only if it was carried out sensitively. Much depended, as he put it, 'on the course of the Zionist effort'. But there was encouragement in this, not criticism. I see

no sign in him of the facile, instinctive anti-Semitism of so many of his con-
temporaries. If anything he was ardently *pro*-Semitic, his vision including the
Semites of the Diaspora as well as of the desert, all of them (as his deep
acquaintance with the Bible from childhood would have taught him) the
children of that patriarch of patriarchs, Abraham. Notably, he counted the
Zionist Chaim Weizmann as well as numerous leading Arabs among his
friends. But he could not have foreseen the consequences of the Holocaust,
of the Jewish guerrilla struggle against the British, of the Arab–Israeli wars,
of the long history of hope and disappointment which has turned the territory he fought over into one of the most troubled places of the modern
world.

Not many figures of the 1914–18 war have much to contribute to the
debates of the military thinkers of the twenty-first century. Famous for its
sacrificial set-piece battles – what Ricks tellingly called 'slugfests' – that
war set a style that produced many such encounters in later conflicts, up to
and including the Iraq–Iran War of the 1980s, while the Gulf War of 1990–1
narrowly avoided what even so perceptive an observer as Alistair Cooke
feared could easily have become a rerun of the Battle of the Somme.
But now warfare has taken on a different dimension, and in this new
dispensation – which is really as old as war itself – T. E. Lawrence has come
to be acknowledged as a voice worth hearing. The key word in his own
seminal work is 'wisdom'. To show that he has some words of wisdom to
offer us in the circumstances of the present age is the prime intention, and, I
hope, the justification of this book.

Part One

In Time of War

Introduction

Lawrence's war could not have begun less dramatically. While volunteers by the thousand, including three of his brothers, crowded the recruiting stations clamouring to fight for King and Country, Lawrence, together with his close colleague of pre-war years, Leonard Woolley, was quietly preparing for publication a long, arcane report on the archaeology of the region of Sinai, to be published by the Palestine Exploration Fund under the title *The Wilderness of Zin*. There *was* a patriotic twist to the situation, in that the research which gave rise to the report had been undertaken in early 1914 as scholarly cover for a military survey undertaken by an officer of the Royal Engineers on the orders of Lord Kitchener, who was concerned that Sinai (sensitively close to the British Empire's famous lifeline, the Suez Canal) might prove to be an area of contention if Turkey, whose territory it was, became a belligerent on the other side in the event of war. Woolley and Lawrence, at that time based in Syria where they were involved in a major archaeological dig at Carchemish on the River Euphrates, were obvious candidates (or, in Lawrence's words, suitable 'red herrings') for such a role.

As soon as the report was finished, Woolley was commissioned into the Royal Artillery, while Lawrence, initially as a civilian, joined the Geographical Section of the General Staff (Intelligence) of the War Office in London. Although, according to the colonel who appointed him, he arrived hatless, in grey flannels and looking about eighteen (he was in fact twenty-six), he was shortly commissioned as a second lieutenant on the 'special list' (i.e. without regimental attachment). Before 1914 was out he found himself back in the Middle East as part of an intelligence cadre of the wise and the good brought together in Cairo to devise ways of destabilising the Ottoman Turks, who had indeed, as Kitchener had anticipated, joined the war on the German and Austro-Hungarian side.

There he remained for most of two years, fighting a war from behind a desk (though, together with his distinguished colleague, the Hon. Aubrey Herbert, he did undertake a potentially high-risk mission to Mesopotamia in 1915 at the time of the siege of Kut), turbulent with ideas but also disturbed by the death in France of two of his brothers, one in May 1915 and one in September. This prompted him to the much quoted comment: 'They were both younger than I, and it doesn't seem right, somehow, that I should go on living peacefully in Cairo.'

The outbreak of the Arab Revolt in June 1916 gave him the opportunity he now sought, to move from a passive to an active role. In October 1916 he undertook his first mission to Arabia, and shortly the make-over began that would transform him from junior officer in untidy khaki with unpolished buttons and badly in need of a haircut to charismatic camel-rider in flowing robes criss-crossing the desert at the head of groups of fearsome campaigning tribesmen. He would serve in Arabia, with brief intermissions, for almost two years.

The pages that follow are, in effect, the cream of the prose product of those two years. He also found time for letters to his family or to friends, though usually with long gaps in between, but his prime duty was to report to Cairo, and this was a man who wrote to his highest capacity whatever the occasion – whether he was devising a military signal, a letter to the great or humble, or, as in this case, urgent reports from the field. His despatches from Arabia, therefore, from the first, demanded and received his best in terms of content and style. He was also (as is discussed at length in the General Introduction) drafting material in advance for the book he planned to produce after the war, assuming he survived, aware that he was being given almost daily, by the chance of war, the raw material for an epic. It would not normally be deemed necessary, for example, to include in a military report a vivid description of a desert sandstorm: this in no way could affect the outcome of the campaign. Yet one such appears here, in 'Raids on the Railway' (pp. 111–21); it would later slip seamlessly into his book *Seven Pillars of Wisdom*.

'Secret' is, of course, the key word in this section of the book: a term which it must be assumed was chosen by A. W. Lawrence when editing his brother's despatches for their first publication in 1939. At the time it must have given them an attractive hint of cloak and dagger, and it is good to give the title a prime place in this new publication in 2005.

I

Secret Despatches from Arabia

I. Letter from Sherif Feisal
8 November 1916

Al-Hamra, Hegga 28, 1334 (26.10.16)

My Lord and Master, Ali Bey,

After kissing your noble feet, I acknowledge receipt of your noble order, sent with Abd el-Aziz Yadi. Its intimations were understood, and especially what you have mentioned about your marching, because I want to know seriously. I beg you to be very careful, because it is quite evident that if the movement should not be in combination, then the result will not be good. Therefore, I beg that you should make all possible arrangements concerning your movements; otherwise you had better not start from Rabegh unless my lord, Abdullah, starts from Mecca, and he should start four or five days before you start. When he arrives at El-Hijrieh, you can march; and you must divide your forces into two; the smaller part of the two, say about 300 or 400 dromedary men, under the command of one of the family, should go to El-Milaf, where Ahmed ibn Mansur is, and there he will have all Sobh, Zebeid, Beni Yum, and Beni Mohammed with him, and will defend the place (El-Milaf), and Beni Salem will follow those in El-Sidada, as I told them. The second division, which is the general force, must march as soon as possible towards the Fari road and camp at Mijaz, and cut the communication of the line of the enemy at El-Ghayir to threaten Medina; and I myself am going north to cut the railway line and besiege Medina, by the will of God. I am awaiting your reply to Bir Said, and you must inform me:

1. About the number of your forces.
2. About the number of Abdullah's forces.
3. About the time of Abdullah's start, and with how many men.
4. About the day of your start.

I shall advance before you in order to attract the attention of the Turks, so that it will be easy for you to advance.

There is another idea which is that you may attract their (Turks') attention towards yourself, and may wait for two or three days, and then I will advance quickly to destroy the line. I am awaiting your reply and information. At any rate, one of the members of the family, either Zeid or

Sharaf, must be sent to El-Milaf. Were it not for the movement of Juheina, I would have gone there myself. God willing, my stay will be at Buat or El-Jafr. I am awaiting your immediate orders my lord.

Your slave, Feisal

II. Extracts from a Diary of a Journey
18 November 1916

21 October

At 6 p.m. started off from Aziz Bey El-Masri's tent at Rabugh. Sidi Ali, Sidi Zeid and Nuri saw me off. I had Sidi Ali's own camel, with its very splendid trappings. This secured me a vicarious consideration on the way. The Abadilla wasm is the 'secret sign' of the Port Sudan messengers.

Sheikh Obeid el-Rashid of the Hawazim Beni Salim Harb, and his son Abdullah came with me.

We marched through the palm-groves, and then out along the Tihama, the flat and featureless coastal desert of Arabia. The Sultani road runs along this for the first fifty miles.

At 7 p.m. we crossed a belt of blown sand and scrub, about 500 yards broad, but only about a foot deep. It could probably be circumvented, but it was too dark to see. After that between 7.30 and 8 p.m. crossed several similar but smaller sandy hollows, and at 9.20 p.m. a deeper one. At 9.30 we stopped and slept.

22 October

Got going again at 3 a.m. The same sort of country till 4 a.m. when we came to the foot of a very low stony ridge, which proved to be a narrow saddle of harrah, joining a small flat block of harrah near the sea to the main mass inland. I could not see how far off the sea was, but it is said to be only five or six thousand yards, and if so the place should be ranged for ship's fire. The neck crossed by the road is stony, and rather narrow, between low shoulders. It has been cumbered up by many tiny cairns, but it is not a difficult passage, except for low-built cars, for which some of the larger stones would have to be rolled aside. By 4.45 a.m. we were across the ridge and had descended into the Masturah, which is really the delta of Wadi Fura. Bir Masturah is at the north bank of the wadi bed, which is a gravel and sand area, well covered with scrub and thorn trees up to twenty feet in height. It seems to extend for some fifteen minutes west of the road, after which bare country extends towards the sea, and inland seems to run back for some two hours, and then contracts into the mouth of Wadi Fura, one hour up which is Khoreiba. Khoreiba may be a point of great importance, and should be examined. It is reported to contain wells, and a spring and running water, with palm-groves.

We reached Bir Masturah at 6.45 and stayed till 8 a.m. The well is stone-lined, and about twenty feet deep and nine feet in diameter. On one side is a chimney (with hand and foot holes) running down to the water, which might be plentiful, if the well were clean. As it is the bottom is half full of stones. Forty yards south of the well is a rubble shelter, perhaps visible from the sea, and some reed huts for three or four families.

We left Bir Masturah at 8 a.m. and marched till 11 a.m., and again from 12.30 p.m. till 4 p.m. when the Sultani road leaves the Tihama towards the NE. Till this point the going has been much as before, though it gets slowly worse for wheels, as the surface becomes softer. The ground is made up of chips of porphyry and basalt, set in sand, or sometimes of pure sand only, with a hard under-soil. Thorn trees are not plentiful after Bir Masturah. Tareif Beni Ayub, a very steep and bare range of hills, stretches away on the east of the Tihama. It seems to be about fifteen miles long, and rather narrow. North of it is a tangle of small rocky hills (covering much the same space) and then Jebel Subh, a great mass of rocks going up to beyond Bir ibn Hassani. North of Jebel Subh is Jebel Gheidh. Jebel Radhwa is in sight to the NW, and across the top of the Tihama, from near Ras el-Abyadh (Rueis) from SW to ENE runs a range of low hills (Jebel Hesna) as though to meet Jebel Subh. The Sultani road runs north up Wadi Hesna towards these hills; but we turned off NE at 4 p.m. by a short cut. Wadi Hesna was sand with much broom-like scrub, and it marked the beginning of an intermediate area, between the flat Tihama and the rocky hills of the interior. The underlying characteristics of this intermediate area were low basalt ridges, but nearly everywhere they are covered with sand, on which is a good deal of coarse grass and trees, and sheep and goats were grazing in the shallow valleys which drained SE.

At 5 p.m. we passed a stone that marked the north boundary of the Masruh dira, and the south end of the Beni Salim. At 5.30 we rejoined the main road, and followed it down slopes of loose and rather heavy sand to Bir el-Sheikh at 6 p.m. This is a Beni Salim village, with a short, broad street of brushwood huts and a few shops; also two stone-lined wells (said to be thirty feet deep) with plenty of good water. We left again at 9 p.m., and in the dark struck up more rough sandy slopes with some hard patches, trees, etc., till 12 p.m., when we slept.

23 October

Started again at 3 a.m., and followed down Wadi Maared between sharp hills. Many trees about. At dawn (5 a.m.) reached Bir ibn Hassani, at the junction of three great wadis. The confluence is about half-a-mile wide, of hard soil, and the village (where lives Ahmed el-Mansur, brother of Mohsin of Jiddah, and the Sherif's Emir-el-Harb) consists of about thirty stone houses. There are three wells. The Sultani road to Bir Abbas turns off to the NE up Wadi Milif or Mreiga, which drains off SW as Wadi Milif, towards Bir el-Sheikh and the sea.

Jebel Subh, just E of Bir ibn Hassani, is fretted into the most fantastic shapes along the sky-line.

As we came by night I cannot say if cars would pass Bir el-Sheikh. I think not, though the run down to Bir ibn Hassani and the surface of the valleys there are quite excellent. The mountains are apparently impassable except for Arabs or birds.

At 6 a.m. we left Bir ibn Hassani, turning NW up Wadi Bir ibn Hassani. The country changed instantly, as we had reached the third zone of the Hejaz littoral, that in which sand hills give place to bare rocks. The hills on each side of the wadi were as steep as possible, perhaps 2,000 feet high, of dull red granite or porphyry with pink patches, but with foot-hills, about one hundred feet high, of a dark green rock, that gave the lower slopes a cultivated tint. There were many trees (acacia to thirty feet, sunt, etc.), and enough tamarisk and soft shrubs to make the view from a little distance most delightful, almost parklike. The ground surface was of shingle and light soil, quite firm, with occasional rocky patches, and the valley was from 200 to 500 yards wide. We ascended it (a very gentle rise) till 8.15 a.m., when we reached a low watershed, across which were the ruins of two small rooms, and a wall of broken blocks from sky-line to sky-line. It may have been a former tribal boundary, or a fortified frontier. Across the watershed we were in the basin of Wadi Safra. The valley became more bare and stony, and the hills each side less variegated. After half-an-hour we passed a well on the east, next a little stone ziaret in the mouth of a side valley. An hour later the valley joined a larger one coming from the NE and running SW down a gorge into Wadi Safra, on the further side of which we could just see the palm-groves of Jedida. Our track crossed this larger wadi, and went up a small affluent for half-an-hour, across another divide, and down a broad wadi for three-quarters of an hour to Wadi Safra in the middle of Wasta. The going underfoot from Wadi Bir ibn Hassani to Wasta, was rough and hard.

Wasta used to be a town of about 1,000 houses, divided into four hamlets scattered about Wadi Safra, which is here broad. The houses are built on earth mounds or the foot-hills, to be out of the floods, and there are palm-groves all about them. The place had had about 4,000 people, but a flood has broken through the banks and destroyed much of the groves, so that to-day many of the houses are deserted. It will take years to repair the damage, as the soil is gone.

We stopped in Wasta till 2 p.m. The houses are mud built, with ceiling of quarter palm logs, palm ribs, and pressed earth all over. There is a small market, in which the best things were dates, very sweet and good, and still plentiful, in spite of the locusts, which were bad this year. There is a running stream in Wasta; where this is artificially confined, it is a swift channel a foot or two wide. Lower down it is released, and becomes a clear slow rivulet, about ten feet broad, and eighteen inches deep, between thick strips of soft green turf. The palm-trees have little canals, a foot or two deep, dug among them, and are watered in rotation; in consequence there is a lot of rank grass in all the groves, and flowering shrubs. The same is the case in every hollow in the wadi, for water can apparently be found almost anywhere about two feet deep. The spring (the right to so many minutes of whose water daily or weekly is sold with each plot of ground), is not very good water, being a little brackish, and warm. Some of the wells of private water in the groves are excellent. Wadi Safra floods every year, sometimes several times. The water may be eight feet deep, and occasionally runs for two or three days. This is not astonishing, for every drop of water that falls on these polished hills must run off them as off glass, and Wadi Safra is the channel of a great drainage area.

The land and the trees are all owned by Beni Salim Harb, and the whole tribe lives on the produce of the valley. This is mainly dates, though a little tobacco, and some melons, marrows and cucumbers are grown, and grapes and fruits have been tried with success. The surplus dates are exported *via* Reis and Boreika to the Sudan, etc., and there exchanged for cereals and luxuries. This export seems to reach about 1,000 to 1,500 tons in a normal year.

The householders of the valley are all Beni Salim, but the actual work of cultivation is done by slaves (Khadim), of which every well-to-do house has four or five. These slaves are negroid, and with their thick bodies and fat legs look curiously out of place among the birdlike Arabs. They come from Suakin and Port Sudan originally, when small, with Takruri pilgrims, passing as their children, and are sold on arrival in the Hejaz. When grown, the price of a male ranges from £60 to £30, according to season and trade conditions. Being of such value, they are treated fairly well. In the towns they do household work, and have easy lives. In the villages they have to work hard, but have the envied solace of being allowed to marry the female slaves, and bring up families. These families are, of course, the property of the master, but etiquette prescribes the granting of reasonable privileges to a father and mother. Their work becomes light, and they are usually not separated from their children until these are grown up. They are all Moslems, but have no legal status, and cannot appeal to tribal custom, or even to the Sherif's court. When they fail to satisfy their master they are beaten, but by public opinion cruelty is discouraged, and on the whole they seemed a very contented lot. They are generally allowed a little pocket money, with which they add to their stock of clothes. About 5 per cent of Feisal's army was composed of them, the younger lads being preferred for service. There are supposed to be about 10,000 of them in Wadi Safra, and perhaps half as many again in Wadi Yenbo, which is the other great cultivated area in the middle Hejaz. The villages in Wadi Safra from its mouth to its source are Bedr Honein (the largest, said to have about 6,000 people), Bruka, Alia, Fara, Jedida, Husseiniya, Dghubij, Wasta, Kharma, Hamra, Um Dheiyal, Hazma and Kheif (or Jedida as the Turks call it).

I left Wasta at 2 p.m., and rode up Wadi Safra past Kharma (ten minutes) to Hamra at 3 p.m. The wadi is from 100 to 300 yards broad, of fine shingle and sand, very smooth swept by the floods. The walls are of absolutely bare red and black rock, with edges and ridges sharp as knife blades reflecting the sun like metal. Thanks to the green of the grass and the gardens, the whole effect was very beautiful. At Hamra the place was swarming with Sidi Feisal's camel-convoys and soldiers. I found him in a little mud house built on a twenty-foot knoll of earth, busied with many visitors. Had a short and rather lively talk, and then excused myself. Zeki Bey received me warmly, and pitched me a tent in a grassy glade, where I had a bath and slept really well, after dining and arguing with Feisal (who was most unreasonable) for hours and hours.

24 October

Awoke late. Sidi Feisal came to see me at 6.30 a.m., and we had another hot discussion, which ended amicably. This lasted till nearly noon, when I went out and explored Hamra, and went up towards Kheif to the sentinels, who were not in any danger! Hamra itself is a small place of, perhaps, 150 houses (hidden in trees on twenty-foot earth mounds), a little stream, and very lux-uriant groves and grass plots. I talked to all of Feisal's men I could. They were dotted about all over the place, mostly Juheinah, and Beni Salim, Ahamda, Subh, Rahala, and Beni Amr. They seemed a very tough lot, and were mostly amusing; also, in the best of spirits imaginable for a defeated army.

Then saw Feisal again. This time everything went smoothly, and he seemed less nervy. His optimism, or his contempt of the possibility of a Turkish advance, was curiously fixed.

At 4 p.m. mounted; with a new escort of fourteen Sherifs, all Juheinah, and mostly relatives of Mohammed Ali el-Bedawi of Yenbo, whither I am to go, by the Haj road. To reach this we went down Wadi Safra for a few minutes, crossing its bank, and entered a side wadi which opens on Kharma. The going is excellent, at first through very thick brushwood, but from 5.30 to 5.45 the path turns more west, up a stiff and narrow pass, confined on both sides by dry walls of large unhewn stones. This work continues down the other side of the watershed, for about two miles. It had obviously been a graded road, which had been in places only a revetted bank, but elsewhere a causeway sometimes six to eight feet high, through the gorge. The surface may have been paved, but is to-day all in ruins, and breached by the stream. From the remains it may have been twenty feet wide, but I saw it in the dark only, and could not examine it. It might have been the work of almost anybody, down to Mohammed Ali.

At 6.30 p.m. reached the bottom of the pass (now a very steep and rough descent) and took a road that passes a little to the north of Bir Said, across a most intricate system of wadis and small hills with some larger wadis bearing S or SW and loose blocks of lava here and there. At 8.30 p.m. we reached Bir el-Moiya or Moiya el-Kalaat, a well just under the ruins of a small fort on a low hill. It was probably a guard house of the Pilgrim road, over the water.

25 October

Started again at 3 a.m., up and down the same labyrinth of wadis, till 5 a.m., when dawn broke finding us in the middle of a confused harrah with sandy floor. The rocks were bent and twisted and cracked, most oddly. At 5.45 a.m. had got clear of this harrah, which died away in a great sea of sand dunes, interspersed with rocky hills, all spattered with sand to their tops. Numerous wadis drained this area, trending rather rapidly downhill towards the sea, which was visible to the SSW.

We now held steadily west, with an occasional aimless tack towards the north. At 7.30 a.m. we were over the dunes and came out on a flat sandy plain, with a good deal of scrub and acacia on it at first, and with low hills, to the south, prolonged westward into a small coastal range. On the north were other low hills, spurs of the central mass to the north of them. (An easier road bending to the north, avoids the worst of the dunes.) From 7.30 to 8.45 a.m. we stopped, and then rode across an empty shingle plain till 10 a.m., when we entered a northern off-shoot of the small coastal range. Between it and the inland range was a rolling open space, falling from an indeterminate watershed a little north of our road into Wadi Yenbo, whose palm-groves were visible about six miles away on the NNW. Behind the groves was the huge bulk of Jebel Rudhwa, the most striking hill in the district.

The foot-hills we crossed were low, and enclosed a thorn-grown plain with a sandy floor. At 11 a.m. we came to the end of this, and rode over a small saddle on to the basin of Wadi Yenbo, which here was a very broad green belt of tamarisk and thorn, having on its eastern edge a conspicuous low hill with a domed lava head, called Jebel Araur el-Milh, which deflects the wadi from SSW to SW or even WSW. Above us the main channel trended up 30°N, for some distance. We stopped under an acacia tree in the wadi from 11.15 a.m. to 3 p.m. and then again at 3.15 to water the camels at a little water-hole of brackish water, about four feet below the surface in the main wadi, behind a wall of tamarisk. After that we went on for an hour and three-quarters and stopped for the night. The country is again Tihama, made up of ten-foot slowly-swelling ridges and shallow valleys between. Wadi Yenbo main bed, where we crossed it, is about a mile and a half wide, but there are several smaller wadis, apparently subsidiary mouths, further west, and the stream, after crossing the track seems to swing round far to the west. The land between the track and the sea has a lot of scrub growing on it, so that the actual outlet of the wadi was not visible. The Tihama here is all so flat, that most of it goes under water whenever Wadi Yenbo comes down in strong flood.

26 October

Started again at 2 a.m. and reached Yenbo at 5.30 a.m. across a featureless but hard shingle and wet sand flat. Yenbo stands on a low stone outcrop, a few feet above the plain. I went to the home of Abd el-Kadir el-Abdo, Feisal's agent for military business, and a very well-informed, efficient, and well-inclined official. He put me up for four days, during which I wandered back to Wadi Yenbo again to see the palm-groves.

On 1 November, got on board the 'Suva'

Yenbo, 29 October.

III. Extracts from a Report on Feisal's Operations
18 November 1916

In June, Feisal's first attack on Medina failed, partly because he was met by Kheiri Bey's troops; but more because his own men were short of arms and ammunition. The people of Awali, on whom he had relied to hold the water supply of Medina, went over to the Turks, out of fear, and were promptly butchered by them. The lost ground could not be recovered, and Feisal had to retire further and further till finally he came down to Yenbo and saw Colonel Wilson.

After this he was a little encouraged, and notified the Sherif that he could hold up the Turkish advance for fifteen or twenty days, till a diversion was made by another road, or till reinforcements came to him; and ever since he has been fighting by himself on the Sultani road. At first he drove in the Turkish outposts, and did them some damage, but then Fakhri himself came down to inspect, and increased the Turkish force at Bir Abbas to some 3,000 men. These pushed back Feisal into the hills. The Egyptian artillery had come up, and the Arabs had recovered confidence, but lost it again when they saw it was quite useless against the Turkish guns. No advantage was taken of its mobility, but it was used like field artillery against the Turkish pieces, of which one is said to have been a howitzer. The Egyptian shells never went near the Turks, but the latter by indirect fire nearly hit Feisal's tent, and terrified the Arabs beyond measure. Partly to prevent their utter demoralisation, but more, I think, because he was bored with his own obvious impotence, Feisal withdrew to Hamra, leaving only a covering force to act on the defensive in the hills. The Turks made no attempt to push forward after him.

The effect of the fighting was to emphasise the Arab's old [*silly*] regard for artillery. From Feisal down to the most naked of his men, they all swear 'If we had had two guns we should have taken Medina'; for they will not appreciate that the Turks are not as foolish as themselves in this matter. I don't think they have ever been near taking Medina, as Feisal's forces are only a mob of active and independent snipers. [*But we have got to reckon with this artillery mania of theirs, and give them the guns necessary as tokens to restore their spirits.*]

Feisal from Hamra proposes to retire to Bir Said for a few days, and then devote his personal attention to the Hejaz railway, the primary importance of which he is beginning to recognise. He will, however, not entertain the idea of cutting it by surprise, by small raiding parties, but wishes to take the Juheinah army, now at Tareif and Kheif Hussein (2,500–3,000 men), and make a grand assault on Buwat and Bir Nasif. He does not want to do this till Abdullah is approaching Medina on the eastern road, and till Ali or Zeid, or Sherif Shakir has reinforced Sherif Ahmed el-Mansur (Feisal's successor), on the Sultani road. His idea is to distribute the Arab forces – each of which is available for service only in its own tribal district – as widely as possible, partly so as to raise the maximum number of men, and partly to break up the present Turkish concentration of almost all their force at Bir Derwish, which, as a common point of the Ghayir (Fura), Gaha and Sultani roads, threatens Rabegh unpleasantly. [*The difficulty is the faulty intercommunication, inevitable till we supply field wireless sets.*]

It is, of course, hardly safe to prophesy, but I think that if the scheme works out, the Turks may have to retire from Bir Derwish to Medina, and to allot most of their present force to the duty of guarding their railway communications; and if the railway is cut, and kept cut, Medina may fall more quickly than is expected, as its civil population is reported to be already short of food, in spite of the date harvest being only just in. The locusts and the needs of the troops have caused a shortage. The railway is at present very insufficiently guarded.

If the plan fails, the next move is with the Turks. After what I have seen of the hills between Bir Abbas and Bir ibn Hassani, I do not see how, short of treachery on the part of the hill tribes, the Turks here can risk forcing their way through. The hills are not so high, and there is a good deal of water in the valleys, but the beds of these valleys are the only practicable roads, and they take the nature of chasms and gorges for miles, of an average width of perhaps 200 yards, but sometimes only twenty yards, full of turns and twists, without cover, and flanked on each side by pitiless hills of granite, basalt and porphyry; not bare slopes, but serrated and split and piled up in thousands of jagged heaps of fragments as hard as metal and nearly as sharp. Over these cliffs the Arabs run barefoot, and they know hundreds of ways from one hill-top to another. The average range possible is from 200 to 300 yards, and at point-blank ranges the Arabs shoot quite well. The hill belt is a very paradise for snipers, and a hundred or two of determined men (especially with light machine-guns, capable of being carried by and uphill), should be able to hold up each road.

To break the determination of the Arabs, the Turks have their artillery – and I do not see how that will help them much in the hills – their aeroplanes, which have not so far taken an active part in the fighting, but which appear to have reached Bir Derwish, and caused a panic by their mere rumour which may die off on acquaintance – and, best weapons of all perhaps, money and moral suasion. They are actually spending a good deal of money (some say £70,000 a month), and receive the most gratifying verbal assurances in exchange, except perhaps at Awali, when the outcome gave little encouragement to Arab participation on the Turkish side in future. They have a few

Juheinah with them, and some Billi near Wejh, but the only Arabs with the
main Turkish army appear to be three hundred Shammar, sent by Ibn
Rashid, and some Ageyl, mostly Medina townspeople. The latter do not do
much fighting.

The tribes taking Turkish money are mostly in touch also with the Sherif,
and from what I could see the Sherif's is by far the most profitable and
popular side at present. Not only does he spend more, but Feisal has made
arrangements for rewards for booty taken; thus he pays £1 per Turkish rifle,
and gives it back to the taker, and pays liberally for captured mules, or
camels, or Turks.

Other things being equal, the Arab side will always have a definite prefer-
ence, for sentimental reasons. To-day the Turks are feared and hated by the
Arabs (except by such tribes as have been corrupted by the influence of
Hussein Mabeirig), and the Sherif is generally regarded with great pride, and
almost veneration, as an Arab Sultan of immense wealth, and Feisal as his War
Lord. His cause has for the moment reconciled the inter-tribal feuds, and Feisal
had Billi, Juheinah, and Harb, blood enemies, fighting and living side by side
in his army. The Sherif is feeding not only his fighting men but their families,
and this is the fattest time the tribes have ever known; nothing else would have
maintained a nomad force for five months in the field. The fighting men in the
Hejaz include anyone strong enough to hold a gun, between the ages apparently of twelve and sixty. Most of the men I saw were young. They are a tough
looking crowd, all very dark-coloured, and some negroid: as thin as possible,
wearing only a loose shirt, short drawers, and a headcloth which serves for
every purpose. They go about bristling with cartridge-belts, and fire off their
rifles when they can. They are learning by practice to use the sights. As for
their physical condition, I doubt whether men were ever harder. Feisal rode
twelve days' journey in six with 800 of them, along the eastern road, and I
have had them running and walking with me in the sun through sand and over
rocks for hour after hour without turning a hair. Those I saw were in wild
spirits, as quick as hawks, keen and intelligent, shouting that the war may last
for ten years, and screeching 'Allah yinsur el Din' whenever they get to close
quarters with the Turks, as they generally do; for on account of their fear of
artillery all fighting has been taking place at night. These fights are rather
quaint contests of wits, for the crowning piece of abuse, after the foulest words
in their language have been sought out, is when the Turks in frenzy call the
Arabs 'English', and the Arabs call the Turks 'Germans'. The Arabs take a
number of prisoners, and some Syrians and others have deserted. The Turks
cut the throats of all their prisoners with knives, as though they were butcher-
ing sheep. [*This fact depresses the Egyptian artillerymen, and perhaps we
might arrange them preferential terms if they get captured by the Turks.*]

I wandered about amongst the Arab soldiers by myself a good deal, to hear
what they were saying. They usually took me for a Turk, and were profuse
in good-humoured suggestions for my disposal. The only other theme of
their talk was artillery, artillery, artillery, the power and terror of which they

have on the brain. The report of the coming of the five inch howitzer to Rabugh nearly restored the balance of their last retreat from Bir Abbas in their own minds. It is, perhaps, worth mentioning that the Beni Amr (who has been weakened by Hussein Mabeirig's action), asked Sidi Feisal, when he retreated, if he now intended to make peace with the Turks, and received an indignant reply. I think most of the tribes (whose casualties have been almost nil), would regret peace at present, though perhaps the townspeople, who do not favour the Sherif, would welcome it.

If the Turks increase their force, and pass to the offensive, there are several courses open to them. They might invade the Tihama through the hills by the Sultani road, if the tribes break down. Such a move might be very dangerous for them, for one could never feel quite sure that the tribes would not collect again (the Rahala, particularly concerned, seem to be Feisal's best fighters), and it would almost be worse to have such hills behind one, across one's communications, than in front, to carry by assault. The Turks only own the ground they stand on, and can never neglect their flanks, till they have the tribes on their side. Also by the Sultani road they are brought down into the Tihama, where water and food are both scarce, and long camel trains will be necessary. [*It might be worth while keeping sea-planes and armoured cars at Rabugh for Fakhri is an untried man under orders of Jemal P. who is a fool: he is acting without German advice on the spot against an enemy he despises which might at any time give us a gift such as should be a Turkish advance into the Tihama when we have organised a Rabugh force.*]

Another possible route towards Rabugh is by the central (Fura) road. Wadi Fura starts from near Ghayir, up to which the Turks have been smoothing the track from Bir Derwish. From Ghayir it runs down with half-a-dozen oases of palms and water to Bir Ridwan, and thence to Khoreiba, which is three hours inland of Masturah. It is the most direct route from Medina to Rabugh, and the best watered, but for some reason was not used by the Haj. I could get no details about its surface.

It must also be remembered that the rains begin in November, and may continue intermittently till January. In the rocky country no moisture soaks in; therefore wadis run in flood very quickly, and pools are formed everywhere. This works both ways, for while there is plenty of water for two months, you may find your road a chest-deep roaring torrent in three minutes. In the matter of water, what has impressed me in the Hejaz (apart from the Tihama which is always parched), is not its scarcity, but its comparative abundance, and this at actually the dryest season of a year whose preceding rains were very small.

Another possible Turkish course, and perhaps the wisest, in view of the danger to the railway, is to proceed with a gradual pacification of the Hejaz from north to south. The action of Basri Pasha in going to Wejh may be the first step in such a course, by confirming the Billi in their allegiance. The Sherif has forbidden the Billi his markets, and they are in the greatest straits for food. He is also in communication with most of the sheikhs, and is fanning discontent against Suleiman Rifada, to whom he has sent a twenty day ultimatum (expiring about 15 November), threatening him with the fate of Hussein Mabeirig. The Billi are very anti-foreign, and much annoyed with the German–Turk alliance. A party of them in the Shefa have held up and kept a Turkish caravan, and Saad Ghoneim has increased his reputation by chasing a Turkish camel-patrol into Wejh. At present it is a toss-up which way the Billi go, and if they decide against the Turks it will make the subjugation of the Hejaz longer and more difficult.

If Basri Pasha succeeds in retaining the Billi, his next step should be to detach the Juheinah from the Sherif. They are newer subjects than the Harb, and should fall away the more easily, since economically they depend entirely on Wadi Yenbo for their existence. Wadi Yenbo runs from Yenbo up towards Buwat on the Hejaz railway, and in its lower course contains twenty-four oases of running water and palm-gardens, with a population of perhaps 20,000, mostly slaves, who cultivate the land. The entire tribe of the Juheinah feeds on the produce of this valley, whose occupation, as it is surrounded by rather easy down-country, seems a feasible operation for a considerable Turkish force. The Sherif would then be confined to the Hamra–Mecca area, and could no longer threaten the railway.

The next step would be the occupation of Wadi Safra, similar to, but smaller than, Wadi Yenbo, which is to the Beni Salim what Wadi Yenbo is to the Juheinah. By occupying Wadi Safra the Turks would ensure the extermination or submission of the Beni Salim, and would be in a position to make direct use of the disaffection caused by Sheikh Hussein.

This process seems to me a possible one for the conquest of the Hejaz, if the Arabs by working against the railway can frighten the Turks from an immediate advance down the Sultani or Fura roads. At the same time I do not think it can be done by force, by the Turkish troops now available, or by fraud on their present expenditure. On the other hand the news we picked up of the Turkish intentions looks as though they did mean to push through to Mecca: in which case either Wadi Fura is practicable, or they are, in my opinion, under-estimating the country with which they have to deal. [*Looked at locally the bigness of the Revolt impresses me.*]

We have here a well-peopled province, extending from Um Lejj to Kunfida, more than a fortnight long in camel journeys, whose whole Nomad and semi-Nomad population have been suddenly changed from casual pilferers to deadly enemies of the Turks, fighting them, not perhaps in our manner, but effectively enough in their own way, in the name of the religion which so lately preached a Holy War against us. This has now been going on for five months, during which time they have created, out of nothing, a sort of constitution and scheme of government for the areas behind the firing line. [*They believe that in liberating the Hejaz they are vindicating the rights of all Arabs to a national political existence, and without envisaging one state or even a federation, they are definitely looking north towards Syria and Bagdad. They do not question the independence of the Imam or of ibn Saud. They wish to confirm them . . . but they want to add an autonomous Syria to the Arab estate.*

Above and beyond everything we have let loose a wave of anti-Turkish feeling, which embittered as it has been by some generations of subjection may die very hard. There is in the tribes in the firing line a nervous enthusiasm common I suppose to all national risings. A rebellion on such a scale as this does more to weaken a country than unsuccessful foreign wars, and I suspect that Turkey has been harmed here more than it will be harmed elsewhere till Constantinople is captured and the Sultan made the puppet of European advisers.]

The Yeni Turan movement is keenly discussed in the Hejaz, where its anti-Arab and anti-Islamic character is well understood. The peace conference will, I think, see a demand from the Sherif for the transfer of the Holy Relics from Constantinople to Mecca, as a sign that the Turks are unworthy longer to be the guardian of such things.

The Arab leaders have quite a number of intelligent level-headed men among them, who, if they do not do things as we would do them, are successful in their generation. Of course they lack experience – except of Turkish officialdom, which is a blind leader – and theory, for the study of practical economies has not been encouraged. However, I no longer question their capacity to form a government in the Hejaz, which is better, so far as the interests of the subjects are concerned, than the Turkish system which they have replaced. [*They are weak in material resources and always will be, for their world is agricultural and pastoral and can never be very rich or strong. If it were otherwise we would have had to weigh more deeply the advisability of creating in the Near East a new power with such exuberant national sentiment. As it is, their military weakness which for the moment incommodes us should henceforward ensure us advantages immeasurably greater than the money, arms and ammunition we are now called upon to spare.*]

Yenbo, 30 October.

IV. Sherif Hussein's Administration
26 November 1916

With the country in its present critical state of war, only the main outlines of the Sherif's administration have emerged. There is seen to be an opposition between town and country. The former continues under a simplification of the Ottoman system; the latter is becoming patriarchal, for the Sherif deals with the sheikhs direct as his officials, and does not hesitate to remove them and replace them by others of their family (as we are doing in Mesopotamia) when they prove unsatisfactory. Their authority and status as intermediaries between their tribesmen and the central power are being increased by the Sherif, instead of sapped, as by the Ottoman system. Within the tribe of course, their rule is a nominal autocracy, so hedged about by tribal opinion and custom as to be little more than general assent in practice.

In the towns the Sherif has nominal governors, but the real business may be in the hands of an agent who is his man, but who has to act gently, to avoid arousing the jealousy of the less competent but great local man, who would be easily driven into the arms of the Turks. Strong men found the Turkish government not uncongenial, for it allowed scope for partiality, and the Sherif seems by nature just.

The Turkish civil code has been abolished. In the towns the cadis administer the undiluted Sharia, and in the tribes matters are still to be settled by tribal law, with final reference to the Sherif or his Kaimmakam. The Sherif intends, when there is time, to extend the principles and scope of the Sharia to cover modern difficulties of trade and exchange!

The multiplicity of Turkish officials has been abolished. Most of the offices are working on a fraction of the old staff.

The Turkish system of internal taxation is in abeyance. The taxes used to be only occasionally collected, and then by flying columns of gendarmes, and the vexation was greater than the profit. Also at present the manhood of the Hejaz is under arms, and so exempt from dues. The ten per cent *ad valorem* customs rate on imports, and the five per cent on exports remain in force. In Jiddah the yield is said not to be very great, as the Sherif's imports are so generous, as to discourage private enterprise. At Yenbo the customs receipts average about £600 a month, and more than cover the salaries and public improvements now in hand.

The urban *octroi** *is* retained.

The police are usually the Sherif's own Bishawi retainers, and seem quiet and efficient; but the return to chthonic conditions has meant the restoration of tribal or family authority, and a great decrease in the exercise of the central government. Sherif Hussein is a student of Bedouin policy and customs, and with his usual wisdom has silently sanctioned their restoration wherever they have retained their vitality. The higher government, in Arab areas, has always been an excrescence, only troubling the people when it touches them.

Finance

The two ports, Jiddah and Yenbo, probably each make a small profit of receipts over administrative charges. Mecca and the army are the two great expenses of the Hejaz government, and the actual cost of each it is not possible yet to estimate. At Mecca, the Imaret expenses before the war were £1,000 a month. They have since largely increased. In addition there are expenses in the town, and just now large charitable doles to replace the diminished pilgrimage receipts.

On the army the expenditure is heavy. Dhelul riders (rikab) are paid £2 a

---

* A French expression meaning town dues or city toll.

month, and £4 or £5 for their camel and its food. Arabs get about £3 a month, and soldiers £2 a month. All men are fed, and generally, their families as well.

The forces actually mobilised are continually shifting. A family will have a gun, and its sons will serve in turn, perhaps week by week, and go home for a change as often as replaced. Married men drop off occasionally to see their wives, or a whole clan gets tired, and takes a rest. For these reasons the paid forces are more than those serving, and this is necessary, since by tribal habit wars are always very brief, and the retention in the field of such numbers as the Sherif has actually kept together is unprecedented. Policy further often involves the payment to sheikhs of the wages of their contingent, and many such payments are little more than disguised bribes to important individuals.

Sherif Feisal receives a lump sum of £30,000 a month from his father, and complete discretion. He keeps on foot about 8,000 men with this money (3,000 Sultani road and Hamra, 1,000 at Tareif, 800 near Bowat, 1,000 with Saad el-Ghoneim, 2,000 at Kheif Hussein) and with the surplus (perhaps £6,000) is working on the cupidity of the more distant tribes. Representatives of the Fakir, the Billi and Nuri Shaalan were with him when I was there, and with them all were being arranged the foundations of a complete understanding of common action, when the Sherif's forces were near enough to lend efficient support.

Sidi Ali has no fixed allowance, but receives from Mecca what he asks for. He says it is not less than £25,000 a month, and has been £35,000. He keeps about 3,000 men with him, and has a large, but rather nebulous contingent watching the Ghayir, Fura, and other central roads.

Sidi Abdullah, as the Sherif's most politic son, has probably what money he wants, though since Taif fell he cannot have spent very much. He has now, however, a force of Ateibah, Harb and Meteir mobilised for action on the eastern road.

On the whole, therefore, one may perhaps suggest for the Hejaz monthly expenses:

	£
Mecca	5,000
Jiddah, etc.	2,000
Emirate	3,000
Sidi Ali	30,000
Sidi Abdullah?	30,000
Sidi Feisal	30,000

It is not likely that Sherif Hussein makes any real economies in gold at present, and one can see everywhere that money, and money only, is going to give us the breathing space necessary to equip the Arab armies for the taking of Medina.

V. Military Notes
26 November 1916

Sherifial Forces

(a) Numbers
I think to-day the Sherif has probably in all about 15,000 to 20,000 men mobilised. These are divided up in local forces, from Um Lejj to Kunfida. The largest bodies of men are probably the 3,000 formerly with Feisal, and those with Sherif Ali at Rabugh. Sherif Abdullah may have as many with him.

(b) Composition
With the exception of the Bishawi retainers and the 'soldiers' at Rabugh, these forces are entirely tribal. About ten per cent are camel corps and the rest infantry, some of whom are desert tribes, and some hill tribes. I did not see much (or think much) of the desert tribes, but the hill men struck me as good material for guerrilla warfare. They are hard and fit, very active, independent, cheerful snipers. They will serve only under their tribal sheikhs, and only in their home district or near it. They have suspended their blood feuds for the period of the war, and will fight side by side with their old enemies, if they have a Sherif in supreme command; except in exceptional circumstances they would not, I think, obey the orders of a man belonging to any other tribe. The lack of discipline – or rather of control – allows them to go home and see their wives and families when they please, if they produce a substitute; the personnel of the army thus changes incessantly; this is inevitable in tribal warfare.

There is a sheikh usually to every hundred or so men. He is paid their wages, and is responsible for their being fed, and ready for action in their stated strength when called upon.

(c) Tactics
The tribal armies are aggregations of snipers only. Before this war they had slow old muskets, and they have not yet appreciated fully the uses of a magazine rifle. They would not use bayonets, but enjoy cutting with swords. No man quite trusts his neighbour, though each is usually quite wholehearted in his opposition to the Turks. This would not prevent him working off a family grudge by letting down his private enemy. In consequence, they are not to be relied on for attack in mass. They are extremely mobile, and will climb or run a great distance to be in a safe place for a shot – preferably at not more than 300 yards range, though they are beginning to use their sights empirically. They shoot well at short ranges, and do not expend much ammunition when in contact with the enemy, though there is any amount of joy-firing at home. Feisal gives them fifty cartridges each, keeps a tight hold of his reserves, and prevents waste as far as possible.

The Arabs have a living terror of the unknown. This includes at present aeroplanes and artillery. The sound of the discharge of a cannon sends every man within earshot to cover. They are not afraid of bullets, or of being killed – it is just the manner of death by artillery that they cannot stand. They think guns much more destructive than they really are, but their moral confidence is probably as easily restored, as it is easily shaken. A few guns – useful or useless – on their side would encourage them to endure the Turkish artillery, and once they get to know it, most of their terror will pass. At present they fight only at night, so that the Turkish guns shall be blind.

(d) Possibilities

I think one company of Turks, properly entrenched in open country, would defeat the Sherif's armies. The value of the tribes is defensive only, and their real sphere is guerrilla warfare. They are intelligent, and very lively, almost reckless, but too individualistic to endure commands, or fight in line, or help each other. It would, I think, be impossible to make an organised force out of them. Their initiative, great knowledge of the country, and mobility, make them formidable in the hills, and their penchant is all for taking booty. They would dynamite a railway, plunder a caravan, steal camels, better than anyone, while fed and paid by an Arab authority. It is customary to sneer at their love of pay, but it is noteworthy that in spite of bribes, the Hejaz tribes are not helping the Turks, and that the Sherif's supply columns are everywhere going without escort in perfect safety.

I do not think the tribal armies will break up unless:

(a) money runs short with the Sherif
(b) the Turks occupy their home waters and palm-groves.
(c) they attempt a pitched battle (when their defeat and casualties would appal them).
(d) the Sherif loses his prestige as an exclusively Arab sovereign.

Turkish Forces

(a) Numbers

The two armies are not dissimilar in numbers; though the Turkish force is concentrated, and the Arab force is excessively distributed.

A difference in character between the Turkish and Arab armies, is, that the more you distribute the former the weaker they become, and the more you distribute the latter the stronger they become. This point is now going to be made use of by the Sherifs.

(b) Composition

The Turkish forces contain about 600 Arab infantry, and about 500 Arab (Ageyl) camel-men; also 300 Shammar tribesmen from Nejd. The rest of their men are Turks, and all infantry, except for the camel corps, a handful of cavalry, and detachments of mule-riders.

Their composition renders them deficient in mobility, and the Shammar are the only light troops they possess capable of extended mounted raids; the latter will probably (being tribesmen) not remain very long.

(c) Tactics
The Turks have so far restrained themselves entirely to action in the plains, where they have the support of their artillery. They have not yet attempted to attack the hills.

(d) Plans
The Turks have plenty of food for the men; there has generally been a shortage of hay, not much barley, enough water. They can allot 130 camels per battalion for the Bir Abbas force, and at the same time maintain their troops at Bir Derwish.

It is not easy to see why they have not advanced. Their cause is steadily losing ground among the tribes, who are also gaining experience in the new mode of fighting. It may be that the cholera at Medina is serious . . . or they may be short of the necessarily very large reserve of food required for an advance to Mecca; or they may be afraid of our landing forces at Rabugh.

They also know that as long as Feisal's army is in being – and it should be in being as long as he preserves its present elasticity and avoids a decisive action – their communications with a column advancing on Mecca from Medina would be almost impossible to keep open, without very greatly increased forces or a block-house system.

It would, I think, be quite possible for a small self-contained force to retake Mecca; and, if the tribes still kept their present determination, impossible to retain it.

[*The Sherif's present forces are tribal volunteers. Their virtues are mobility and knowledge of the country, and therefore we can increase neither their numbers nor their baggage. Foreign artillery units, like the Egyptian, are a mistake. On the other hand these tribal forces must be strengthened by light machine-guns, manned by themselves. As many Lewis guns as are available at once, as a sniper's accessory, and some mountain guns as amulets to restore public confidence are immediately required. This tribal force will never finish the war (unless the Turks have not enough men to defend their railway) as it will never be capable of an offensive. We should utilise it as a screen behind which to build up for the Sherif a field force with good mobility, which shall be capable of meeting a Turkish force distracted by guerrilla tactics, and defeating it piecemeal. This force will have to be recruited from townspeople, slaves and villagers.*]

[*Argument against landing foreigners at Rabugh.*]
The Hejaz war is one of dervishes against regular troops – and we are on the side of the dervishes. Our textbooks do not apply to its conditions at all. It is the fight of a rocky, mountainous, ill-watered country (assisted by a wild

horde of mountaineers) against a force which has been improved – so far as civilised warfare is concerned – so immensely by the Germans, as almost to have lost its efficiency for rough-and-tumble work.

Jiddah, 3 November 1916.

VI. Personal Notes on the Sherifial Family
26 November 1916

One can see that to the nomads the Sherif and his three elder sons are heroes. Sherif Hussein (Sayidna as they call him), is outwardly so gentle and considerate as to seem almost weak, but this appearance hides a deep and crafty policy, wide ambitions and an un-Arabian foresight, strength of character and persistence. There was never any pan-Arab secret society in Mecca, because the Sherif has always been the Arab government. His influence was so strong in the tribes and country districts, as to be tantamount to administration; and in addition he played Arabs' advocate in the towns against the Turkish government.

Particularly have his tastes and sympathies been always tribal. The son of a Circassian mother, he is endowed with qualities foreign to both Turk and Arab, but he determined to secure the hearts of the nomads by making his sons Bedouins. The Turks had insisted that they be educated in Constantinople, and Sherif Hussein agreed most willingly. They have all had a first-class Turkish education, and profit by their knowledge of the world. However, when they came back from Constantinople as young Levantines, wearing strange clothes and with Turkish manners, Sherif Hussein at once made them change into Arab things, and rub up their Arabic. He gave them Arab companions, and a little later sent for them, to put them in command of some small bodies of Arab camel corps, patrolling the pilgrim roads against the Auf. The young Sherifs fell in with the plan, as they thought it might be amusing, but were rather dashed when they were forbidden to take with them special food, or bedding, or saddle cushions, and still more when they were not given permission to come to Mecca for the Feast, but had to spend all the season out in the desert with their men, guarding the roads day and night, meeting nomads only, and learning to know their country and their manners.

They are now all thorough Bedouins, and as well have from their education the knowledge and experience of Turkish officials, and from their descent that blend of native intelligence and vigour which so often comes from a cross of Circassian and Arab blood. This makes them a most formidable family group, at once admired and efficient. It has, however, left them curiously isolated in their world. None of them seems to have a confidant or adviser or minister, and it is doubtful whether any one of them is fully intimate with another or with their father, of whom they all stand in awe.

Sidi Ali. Short and slim, looking a little old already, though only thirty-seven. Slightly bent. Skin rather sallow, large deep brown eyes, nose thin and a little hooked, face somewhat worn and full of lines and hollows, mouth drooping. Beard spare and black. Has very delicate hands. His manners are perfectly simple, and he is obviously a very conscientious, careful, pleasant, gentleman, without force of character, nervous and rather tired. His physical weakness makes him subject to quick fits of shaking passion with more frequent moods of infirm obstinacy. Apparently not ambitious for himself, but swayed somewhat too easily by the wishes of others. Is bookish, and learned in law and religion. Shows his Arab blood more than his brothers.

Sidi Abdullah. Aged thirty-five, but looks younger. Short and thick built, apparently as strong as a horse, with merry dark brown eyes, a round smooth face, full but short lips, straight nose, brown beard. In manner affectedly open and very charming, not standing at all on ceremony, but jesting with the tribesmen like one of their own sheikhs. On serious occasions he judges his words carefully, and shows himself a keen dialectician. Is probably not so much the brains as the spur of his father. He is obviously working to establish the greatness of the family, and has large ideas, which no doubt include his own particular advancement. The clash between him and Feisal will be interesting. The Arabs consider him a most astute politician, and a far-seeing statesman: but he has possibly more of the former than of the latter in his composition.

Sidi Feisal. Is tall, graceful, vigorous, almost regal in appearance. Aged thirty-one. Very quick and restless in movement. Far more imposing personally than any of his brothers, knows it and trades on it. Is as clear-skinned as a pure Circassian, with dark hair, vivid black eyes set a little sloping in his face, strong nose, short chin. Looks like a European, and very like the monument of Richard I, at Fontevraud. He is hot-tempered, proud and impatient, sometimes unreasonable, and runs off easily at tangents. Possesses far more personal magnetism and life than his brothers, but less prudence. Obviously very clever, perhaps not over-scrupulous. Rather narrow-minded, and rash when he acts on impulse, but usually with enough strength to reflect, and then exact in judgement. Had he been brought up the wrong way might have become a barrack-yard officer. A popular idol, and ambitious; full of dreams and the capacity to realise them, with keen personal insight, and a very efficient man of business.

Sherif Zeid. Aged about twenty. Is quite overshadowed by the reputation of his half-brothers. His mother was Turkish and he takes after her. Is fond of riding about, and playing tricks. Has not so far been entrusted with any important commission, but is active. In manner a little loutish, but not a bad fellow. Humorous in outlook, and perhaps a little better balanced, because less intense, than his brothers. Shy.

Yenbo, 27 October 1916.

VII. Nationalism among the Tribesmen
26 November 1916

Tribal opinion in the Hejaz struck me as intensely national, and more sophisticated than the appearance of the tribesmen led one to expect. These ideas can hardly have been acquired from the educated in the town, for Jiddah and Mecca are not Arab in their composition, but are collections of Javanese, Sudanese, Hindus, Turks, and Bokhariots, without sympathy with Arab ideals, and at present suffering somewhat from the force of Arab sentiment, which is too lately released from Turkish compression to be quite under control.

Seeking the cause of this sudden growth of national feeling, I was informed that German propaganda was an important contributory factor. The Germans preached Jihad the first few months of the war, till they saw that the idea had fallen flat. They then skipped across at once to a base of nationalism, and tried to awaken in the provinces, the (in their opinion) dormant Ottoman sensibility. They taught that Germans were Germans, and British, British; and, therefore, it behoved the Ottomans to be Ottoman, and to assert their separate existence, in the name of the principle of nationality. The fate of the Armenians was the Turkish reading of that lesson . . . and the Hejaz rising was the Arab reaction to this and other influences. Instinct (the Arab believes himself superior to all other races), money, and the counsels and example of the family of Sherif Hussein found an unexpected ally in German propaganda and Neo-Turk and Yeni Turan dogma.

Whatever the cause, Arab feeling in the Hejaz runs from complete patriotism amongst the educated Sherifs down to racial fanaticism in the ignorant. One thing, of which the tribes are convinced, is that they have made an Arab government, and consequently that each of them is it. The towns are sighing for the contented obstructionist inactivity of the Ottoman government, or for the ordered quiet of our own rule; the tribes know they are independent, and mean to enjoy their independence. This will not entail anarchy, since the family tie and the system of tribal responsibility will be tightened, but it entails the practical disappearance or negation of central power in internal affairs. The Sherif may have his political sovereignty abroad, and shall have it – so far as the tribesmen can secure it; but their home affairs must be settled by their own tribal sheikhs. 'Is Damascus to rule the Hejaz, or can we rule Damascus?' said a Sherif, and it would be hard to say which would be the bigger problem. However, they will not allow it to be set for decision: for their idea of nationality is the independence of tribes and parishes, and their idea of national union is episodic, combined, resistance to an intruder. Constructive politics, an organised state, and an extensive empire, are not only beyond their capacity, but anathema to their instincts. They are fighting to get rid of empire, not to win it, and the only unity that is possible is one to which they are forced by foreign influence, or control. Unless we, or our allies, make an efficient Arab empire, there will never be more than a discordant mosaic of provincial administrations.

Any such assumption of foreign right to organise them is bitterly rejected by the Arabs. 'We are delighted to be your friends, most grateful for what you have given us, but do, please, remember that we are not British subjects. We should feel more at ease if you were not so disproportionate an ally.'

Feisal meant that the touchiness of Arab tribesmen at any suggestion from us in internal affairs was due, not to rational offence, but to consciousness of material and physical weakness. Their government will have something of a cripple's temper until it has found its feet.

In my supposed capacity of a Syrian I made some sympathetic reference to the executions by Jemal Pasha of the Arab leaders of Damascus. The Sherifs, and those who knew the real history, abhorred the act. The others said: 'But Jemal Pasha published papers showing that these men had sold their country to the French and English. If he had not put them to death, it would have been our duty as Arabs to have done his work.'

The feeling seemed to grow in intensity towards the north. The Harb were less keen than the Juheinah, and the Juheinah less chauvinistic than the Billi. The Billi, I believe, hold back from the Sherif, not because they like the Turk, but because they fear that the Sherif means the British.

Of religious fanaticism I found little trace. The Sherif has refused in round terms to give a religious twist to his rebellion. The tribes know that the Turks are Mohammedans, and think that the Germans are probably true friends of Islam. They know that we are Christians, and that we are their friends. In the circumstances their religion would not be of much use to them, and they have put it aside. 'Christian fights Christian, so why shouldn't Mohammedan do the same? What we want is a government that speaks Arabic, and will let us live in peace. Also, we hate those Turks.'

VIII. The Turkish Hejaz Forces and Their Reinforcement

26 November 1916

On 9 June 1916, there was in Medina part of a battalion of the 129th Regiment, a Mohafiz Alai, the Yemen Mofraza of the Stotzingen Mission, and some train troops, with the fortress gunners of the Medina forts.

When the news of the revolt arrived the Turkish government sent down the two battalions of the 130th Regiment which had been for six months at Tartus watching Ruad Island, and parts of Regiments 42 and 55 of the 14th Division intercepted at Aleppo on their way to the Caucasus. Some artillery and technical details were also sent, and such of the units as were below strength were re-made from the Yemen Mofraza, which has apparently been entirely broken up in the process.

This force was named the Hejaz Expeditionary Force, under the supreme command of Jemal Pasha. Fakhri Pasha commands in Medina, and Basri Pasha the El Ula section. Fakhri is a Turk of the pre-German school, with long administrative experience. He was the executive of the Adana massacre of 1909, and the recent affairs at Zeitun and Hajin. Basri was the Turkish Mohafiz of Medina, and a popular official.

The present composition and distribution of the force appears to be roughly as follows:

Medina
OC Abd el-Rahman Bey.

4/131st Regiment. A gendarmerie unit from Aleppo province, of about 600 Turks.

1/129th Regiment. A nominal battalion of regimental details and drafts. About 700 strong. Probably eighty per cent Turks.

Regiment Camel Corps. About 500 strong, patrolling to Bir Derwish. Turks.

79th Machine-gun Company. Four machine-guns; mule transport (pack). Personnel: probably partly Arab.

Fortress Artillery. Turks. Several masonry forts with old guns of position.

Three Companies of Engineers. Turks, taken respectively from the 47th, 48th and 49th Divisional Engineers.

Bir Derwish District
OC Ghalib Bey.

1, 2, 3/55th Regiment. Mostly Turks. Battalions perhaps 800 strong.

2, 3/42nd Regiment. Mostly Turks. Battalions perhaps 8–900 strong.

3/130th Regiment. Camel Transport Battalion, mostly Arabs.

Two Companies, Mule MI. Turks.

Regiment of Camel Corps. Patrolling to Bir Raha.

One Battery, Camel Mountain Artillery. 22nd Artillery Regiment.

Field-gun Batteries. ?

Aeroplane Section. Three aeroplanes, of which two are probably disabled. A fourth perhaps to come.

Bir Raha District
OC Amin Bey.

1, 2/130th Regiment. About 700 strong, each containing about thirty per cent Arabs.

Camel Corps. 300 Shammar Arabs.

Company Mule MI.

Three Mountain-guns.

Two Field-guns.

Wireless Section. Apparatus on three carts. From them wires are taken to pole twenty-five feet high, 100 yards away.

Lines of Communication Units

Railway
Mohafiz Alai. 800 strong.

Regiment Camel Corps. H. W. Bueir, with one company and two guns. Company at Abu el-Naam, and one at Bowat (two guns).

El Ula
One Battalion. Turks. Perhaps the missing 1/42nd.
   Ageyl Camel Corps. Arabs.

El Wejh
One Battalion Gendarmes. 800 strong. Turks.
   Ageyl Camel Corps. Arabs.

Total numbers perhaps:

	Dismounted	Mounted
Wejh	800	400
El Ula	800	300
Railway	900	600
Bir Raha	2,000	400
Bir Derwish	4,500	700
Medina	1,300	600
	10,300	3,000

Between Medina and Bir Derwish there were about 2,000 camels, and the two battalions at Bir Abbas were allowed 130 camels each for food, water, ammunition and baggage transport. Water was a very small item, as there were local supplies, and men were only given a water-bottle per day.

Possible Reinforcement

It is possible that Turkish and German opinions on the importance of the Hejaz operations are divergent. The Turks see their national reputation, enhanced by their preliminary successes over us, endangered by the Sherif's continuance. The Germans may think Maan easier to defend than Medina. It is, perhaps, risky to over-estimate the German influence in the Turkish war-council. The Turkish official is as difficult to guide or drive as anyone on earth, and his German advisers, no doubt, have many revolts and obstructions in their way.

Another governing factor must be the carrying capacity of the Hejaz railway. This is a vexed point, requiring exhaustive treatment and full materials, not yet available.

The Turkish army to-day consists of forty-two divisions, and the Medina force. The paper strength of a division is 12,000 rifles, and the actual strength in rifles of an untouched division seldom exceeds 9,000. An engaged division may be anything from 3,000 rifles upwards. Turkey's weakness of reserve prevents her making good her losses. The total strength of her armies in rifles to-day appears to be less than 350,000 and her depôts are nearly dry. She has been reduced to spreading reports that she has found her population larger than she expected, and that great reserves of man-power are, therefore, available when the moment comes. Unfortunately, much of the force of this new discovery was taken off by her coincident reduction of twelve divisions (which had in 1915 a strength of 114 battalions of 800 men each), to twelve regiments each of three battalions of 800–1,000 men.

The distribution of the Turkish army is now; eighteen divisions against the Russians in Armenia, five in Mesopotamia and Persia, six in Syria, three in southern Arabia, one at Smyrna, and nine in Europe. Those in Europe used to be concentrated in Thrace and formed a reserve army, till the needs of their allies forced the Turks to scatter one to Bulgaria, two to Galicia, two or three to the Dobruja: so that to-day they have only one in Constantinople, and three or two in the Dardanelles on which to draw for further military efforts.

If Turkey has a strategical reserve to-day, it would appear to be in the Syrian army, the only considerable body of troops not in actual contact with the enemy; and the Syrian army, being under Jemal Pasha is also the most likely to send reinforcements to the Hejaz. In consequence its situation is of direct importance in Hejaz operations.

The military district of the 4th (Syrian) army extends from the Taurus to Medina, and the divisions composing it are the 3rd, 23rd, 27th, 41st, 43rd and 44th. Syria has been split into divisional zones, and each commander made responsible for part of the coast.

In the northern sectors the troops are thickest. From Mersina to Aleppo, Syria is the line of communications for the Southern Army of the Caucasus, for Mesopotamia and Persia, as well as for Sinai and Arabia. The railway on which these fronts depend runs very close to the sea and accidents of terrain make it easy to attack. In consequence we have the 23rd Division (two regiments, perhaps 5,000 men in all and mainly Turks) guarding from Mersina to Adana, with its main strength at Tarsus, and the 44th Division (complete, of perhaps 9,000 men, ninety per cent Turks) takes over from it round the head of the Gulf of Alexandretta almost to Aleppo, with its headquarters at Erzin. Alexandretta itself, and Aleppo, and the main part of Syria, down to the Tripoli–Homs gap, are in the area of the 41st Division (perhaps 8,000 strong, seventy per cent Turks), whose main force is concentrated at Beilan. South of the 41st Division comes the 43rd with an independent regiment (the 67th) in Lebanon. Its duty is to cover Damascus, but we know so little of it that we suspect it is inchoate. It is probably mainly Turk, but the 67th Regiment is largely Arab, and so in the Hauran is a reserve of troops, some of them line battalions, some of them depôt-troops, sent there no doubt to overawe the Druses, but also to simplify the problem of feeding them. They must be 4,000 or 5,000 strong. In Haifa district was the 27th Division, (8,000 strong, including many Arabs), which has been in movement southward, apparently to relive the 3rd Division (6,000 strong, all Turks) in Sinai. The 27th Division used to be the Sinai garrison, and then gave way to the 3rd, which lost about fifty per cent of effectives at Katia, and is perhaps to be rested and repaired in the rich and quiet district about Nazareth.

The term 'strategic reserve', tentatively applied to the Turkish army in

Syria alone, is, therefore, seen to be rather illusory, since the Syrian garrison is playing an essential part either in defending the main L. of C. (three divisions) on controlling a restless population (one division, one regiment, and the composite force at Deraa), or opposing the British canal army (one division in line, and one in reserve).

The 27th and 3rd Divisions are indispensable – to the Turks – and can hardly afford to send large drafts to Medina – even though the weakness of the railway link with Damascus, while the Hejaz needs a daily train, may make it unwise to reinforce them heavily. The force in Lebanon is also necessary, and the Sherif's policy with the Hauran Druses and Arabs should hold the Deraa force in its place. The retention of Divisions 23, 41 and 44, about the Gulf of Alexandretta is dependent on the opinion entertained by the Turkish staff about the necessity for guarding this, the most vulnerable point on its line of communication from the Caucasus, Mesopotamia and Syria – a point where an Allied landing would wreck, at one stroke, all three campaigns.

IX. Sherif Feisal's Army
11 December 1916

At the end of November, Feisal decided to form a regular infantry force on the lines of that suggested for Sherif Ali by Aziz el-Masri. The battalions were to be composed, not so much of Nomads, as of their fellahs, poor men and slaves. They were to be formed into eight battalions each of 600 men, and by November 28th, several were already over 400 strong. Internal organisation consists of 20 men under one reis, and 5 reis (100 men) under each 'Sherif'. Ten 'Sherifs' to each battalion.

The battalions were contributed as follows:

1. Hudtheil (Mecca).
2. Ibn Shefia (Juheinah).
3. Rifaa (Juheinah).
4. Wuld Selim (Harb).
5. Bishawa (Asiris from Wadi Bishah).
6. Ashraf (Juheinah).
7. Wuld Mohammed (Harb).
8. Muretteb of Ageyl and others.

X. Diary of a Second Journey
26 December 1916

Left Yambo on Saturday, 2 December, about 4.30 p.m., with Abd el-Kerim, Sherif and Emir of the Juheinah, younger brother of Mohammed Ali el-Beidawi. He is the son of a negro woman, very dark, about twenty-six years old, obviously half-African, but energetic, active, and endowed with a humour which is as salacious as it is easy. He is a tremendous rider, doing camel journeys at three times the normal speed, and is strongly anti-Turk. With him there were three or four men, and we had a very rapid and merry journey. We rode straight over the plain till 7.30 p.m., when we stopped till 9 p.m., eating a little bread and drinking coffee, while Abd el-Kerim and his men played games on each other and exchanged japes. Everything was very free, very good-tempered, and not at all dignified.

After we re-started, an hour's journey brought us to the end of a low range of hills (rock and sand) which cuts off the plain in which Yambo stands from Wadi Yambo. The Bir Said road passes south of this range along the Tihamah; our present road turned up Wadi Agida, a narrow winding sandy valley between the hills. It had flooded lately, and the going was, therefore, good. I think even in normal times a car would get over it. At 11 p.m. we came to the watershed, next an old cistern called only the 'Sebil', on the left hand side of the road. We then galloped down to Nakhl Mubarrek, which we reached at 11.30 p.m.

When we got near, we saw through the palm-trees the flame and smoke of many fires, and the whole valley was full of shouting and rifle shots, and the roaring of camels. We rode past an end of the groves and turned up a narrow street, forced the door of the first empty house we came to, and led our camels inside to hide them while Abd el-Kerim went off quietly down the street towards the noise to find out what was happening. He came back in half-an-hour to say that Feisal had just arrived in the village from Sueig with his camel corps, and that I was to go to see him at once. So we led the camels out and mounted again, and rode down the narrow lane between houses and the wall of a sunk garden on the right, pressing through a solid crowd of Arabs and camels, mixed up in the wildest confusion, and all shouting like mad.

At the end of the lane we came out suddenly on to the bed of Wadi Yambo, as it ran between the palm-groves of Nakhl Mubarrek and Bruka on the one side, and the hills of Wadi Safra on the other. It was a broad open space, very damp, for it had just flooded, with a few tamarisk and thorn trees in it, but now filled from side to side with Feisal's army. There were hundreds of watch-fires burning, with Arabs round them making coffee, or eating, or just sleeping, as well as they could in the confusion of camels. I have never seen so many tied up, or couched here and there all over the camping ground, and more were ever coming up, and the old ones were leaping up to join them, and patrols were going out, and convoys being unloaded, and some dozens of Egyptian mules were bucking all over the middle of the picture.

We shouldered our way through all this din, and made our camels kneel down opposite Sherif Feisal, who was seated on a carpet in the wadi bed, reading reports and writing orders by the light of a lamp. The night was quite windless. With him was Sherif Sharraf, Kaimmakam of the Imaret and of Taif, his second in command, and Mulud ibn Mukhlus his Mosul ADC. He received me very cordially, and apologised for the accommodation, which was not improved a minute later, when the hay bales of a baggage camel behind Feisal's head became untied, and he, the lamp, Sharraf and myself were temporarily overwhelmed in an avalanche of hay. I sat down with him, and listened to the news and petitions and complaints and difficulties being brought in and settled before him. The position was, that the Turks, after clearing Zeid out of Wadi Safra, had come forward very fast to Wasta and Bir Said, and were threatening to advance rapidly on Yambo or Nakhl Mubarrek, either to destroy Feisal, or to cut of his sea bases. Feisal's spy system was breaking down, and most wild and contradictory reports were coming in from one side and from another, about the strength of the Turks, and their movements. In the absence of news, he had moved suddenly down here, to watch the Yambo roads, with about 2,000 camel-men, and 2,000 infantry, and had got in, an hour before I came.

We sat on the rug talking till 4.30 a.m. It got very cold and the damp of the wadi rose up through the carpet and soaked our cloaks, and a white mist collected slowly over the whole camp, which gradually became quiet as the men and the camels all went to sleep, and the fires burnt out. Immediately north of us, rising out of the mist and quiet clear in the moonlight, was the eastern end of Jebel Rudhwa, which looks even more steep and rugged close by than it does from the sea. At about 4.30 Feisal decided that we should go to sleep, so we ate half-a-dozen dates, and stretched out on the very wet carpet on which we had been sitting. The Bishah men came up and spread their cloaks over him as soon as he had dropped asleep.

At 5.30 we got up (it was too cold to do anything else) and lit a fire of palm-ribs to warm ourselves. Messengers were still coming in from all sides, and the camp was not far off panic. Feisal decided to move then, partly to avoid the strong probability of being washed out next rain, and partly to occupy his men's minds. So everybody began to mount at once, and drew off to right and left, leaving a path for Feisal to ride up. He came along on a horse with Sherif Sharraf a pace behind him, and then his standard bearer (a splendid wild Arab with many luxuriant plats of hair) on a camel, and behind him all the mob of Sherifs and sheikhs and household slaves – and myself – pell-mell. There was about 800 in the bodyguard that morning.

He rode about up and down, looking for a camping ground, and finally stopped on the further bank of a little side-wadi (the road to Yambo), that runs down into Wadi Yambo from the west, just north of Nakhl Mubarrek village. On the south bank of this wadi (in whose bed I made a landing ground), was a raised slope, backed by some little rocky knolls, and beneath them Feisal pitched his camp. There were about ten tents with headquarters, and the Egyptians had theirs, too, so that the place soon looked business-like.

We stayed here two days, most of which I spent in Feisal's tent, and so I got a certain experience of his manner of command. The circumstances were very difficult, and the morale of his men was obviously suffering heavily under the scare reports brought in, and the defection of the northern Harb. Feisal was fighting all these two days to keep up their spirits. He is accessible to any man who stands outside his tent till he is noticed, and never cuts short a petitioner. He hears every case, and if he does not settle it himself, calls one of his staff to settle it for him. His patience was extreme, and his self-control rather wonderful. When Zeid's men came in to try and explain away the really shameful story of their surprise and retreat, he rallied them gently, and jested at them, chaffing them for having done this or that, for having inflicted such losses or suffered so much. He has got a very rich tenor voice, and uses it carefully in making speeches to his men, which he does in the broadest of Bedouin dialects. I heard him speak to the Rifai sheikhs, when he sent them forward to picket the plain this side of Bir el-Fagir. He told them quite quietly that the Turks were coming on, and that it was their duty to hold them up, and give God a victory, adding that he hoped they would not go to sleep. The older men particularly were enthusiastic, and after saying that God would give him the victory, and then two victories, decided that his life would be prolonged, to enable him to accumulate an unprecedented number of victories.

Generally speaking, I thought the spirits of the infantry rather good, and those of the Juheinah less firm; neither party was anything like so cheerful as the Harb and Juheinah had been in Hamra a month before.

In the afternoon I walked round Nakhl Mubarrek and Bruka, which are pleasant little mud villages, with very narrow streets, built on high earth mounds encircling their palm-gardens. Nakhl lies to the north, and Bruka 150 yards south of it across a thorny valley. I think each has about 300 to 600 houses, but it was very difficult to judge. The earth mounds round the villages were fifty feet high in places, and formed from the stuff dug out of the gardens, which are divided up into narrow plots by fences of palm-leaves, or by mud walls, and are watered from two or three narrow streams of sweet water running through them. The palms, very regularly planted and well cared for, are the main crop, but between the trunks are grown barley, radishes, marrows, cucumbers and henna. The villages in the upper part of Wadi Yambo have grapes.

The views from the little knolls behind our camp were very fine. Rudhwa bore N 20°E, or the SE end of it did, and it seemed to be about fifteen miles away. The whole time I was there, one part of it or another was wrapped in rain clouds, and it formed the most striking part of every outlook. Wadi Yambo itself is a broad tree-covered plain, relieved by odd-coloured and odd-shaped rocks sticking out of its bed at intervals. It seemed to be about two miles wide, and runs up 40°E of N to the fork, where the Bugaa branch leaves the main stream. Bugaa is half-Harb and half-Juheinah. Mjeil, Madsus, Ain Ali and Shaatha are wholly Harb; the rest of the valley seems to be Juheinah. Bir Said is Harb, and Hafira is Juheinah. All the villages in the main bed of Wadi Yambo are on its northern side. The water flows in little stone-lined channels underground from springs to villages.

Beyond the fork of the valley it was obvious that the country rose rapidly and got very hilly. The district behind Buwat is very high. Buwat itself stands on the watershed of Wadi Yambo and Wadi Hamdh, and is about twelve miles west of the station of Buwat.

Between Bruka and Bir Said is a long hollow valley, with an imperceptible watershed somewhere in the middle of it, at Bir el-Fagir, a well surrounded by thick groves of acacia and tamarisk. On the left of this plain or valley is the great massif of hills bounding the western edge of Wadi Safra, and on the right is Gebel Fijeij. Towards Bir Said are dunes of some height.

Wadi Yambo itself runs first north and then west of Fijeij, to Milha and the sea near Masahali. It has no more sweet water in it, from Nakhl Mubarrek to the *themail* at Masahali. Its right bank is made up of the low range of hills out of which Wadi Agida flows.

After the landing ground was finished I decided to come back at once to Yambo, to instruct the aeroplanes on the ground they would have to reconnoitre. So at 9.15 p.m. on 4 December, I left Feisal's tent, on his own camel, on which I had also come. He paid £30 for it and it is a magnificent animal. Because of a scare of Turkish patrols we left the Agida road, and marched across the heads of its tributaries from the north by a very good and easy hard-surfaced road, into Wadi Messarid, which led us down into the maritime plain at El-Zuweidr, an area that was, apparently, once cultivated. Bedr ibn Shefia rode with me, and we stopped nowhere. Reached Yambo 3.30 a.m., very tired after three sleepless nights, and constant alarms and excursions during the days.

XI. Genesis of the Hejaz Revolt
26 December 1916

Sidi Feisal's account of the genesis of the Arab rising, as communicated in conversation to Captain T. E. Lawrence in December 1916, was briefly as follows:

It was first imagined by his brother Abdullah, who reckoned that the Hejaz was capable of withstanding Turkey, with the aid of the Syrian and Mesopotamian armies, and our diplomatic help; but the scheme was put off on Feisal's representing that Turkey was too strong for them. When the Great War broke out, Sherif Husein decided that this was his opportunity, and sent Feisal to Damascus to prepare the ground for a rising in Syria. The latter found the time inopportune, and reported to his father that further delay was necessary. Abdullah told his father that Feisal was afraid, and the revolt was ordered for June. The Sherif had been holding the Bedouin in for some months, and telling them not to move till ordered.

XII. The Arab Advance on Wejh
6 February 1917

When the deadlock in the Medina–Hamra area declared itself in October 1916, the new idea of an attack on the Turkish rear at El-Ala, by way of

Wejh, was brought forward. The situation in the south was that the Turks held Medina too strongly for direct attack by the Arab forces, and that Feisal held the Kheif-Milif hills too strongly for direct attack by the Turkish forces. In the rear, almost blockaded in Rabugh, lay Sidi Ali profitlessly with his army.

Feisal decided to carry out the northern expedition to Wejh, and to do it himself. He, therefore, brought up Sidi Zeid to Wadi Safra, and transferred to him the whole of his Harb forces and his Southern Juheinah. He then withdrew to Wadi Yambo to organise a force of Northern Juheinah for the march on Wejh.

While he was in Wadi Yambo in early December the unexpected happened. The Arabs under Sidi Zeid became slack and left a by-road near Khalis unguarded. A Turkish mounted infantry patrol pushed up along it into Wadi Safra near Kheif. The front line of Arabs, hearing news of this enemy six miles in their rear, broke with a rush to rescue their families and property in the threatened villages. Zeid's main body followed suit. Zeid himself fled at top pace to Yambo; and the astonished Turks occupied Hamra and Bir Said unopposed.

This situation made Feisal's march north impossible. He moved into Nakhl Mubarak with his forces and the still-trembling remnant of Zeid's army, and after a few excited days fought a long range action against a strong Turkish reconnaissance. In this he found his troops lacking in many respects: his centre and right wing held and repulsed the enemy; the left wing (Juheinah) retired suddenly behind his centre, without hostile pressure. He suspected treachery and ordered a general retreat on Yambo, the next water supply. The defaulting left wing refused to retire, put up an independent stubborn resistance against the Turks for another twenty-four hours, and then rejoined Feisal at Yambo. It explained that the retirement during the action was to find an opportunity for brewing a cup of coffee undisturbed.

The army of Sidi Ali at Rabugh was stirred into life by these events and began a sudden advance of its own towards Bir ibn Hassani, in spite of Feisal's appeals that it should wait till he was in a position to support it by a thrust from Yambo. Ali persisted in his movement, and Feisal eventually collected what men he could and hurried out to Nakhl Mubarak again. He was preparing a stroke against Kheif and Hamra to synchronise with Ali's arrival at Bir ibn Hassani when he got the news that Ali's forces had fallen back sixty miles on hearing a (false) report of the defection of the Subh. He, therefore, retired again, in a very bad temper, to Nakhl Mubarak.

The move on Wejh now appeared not merely the convincing means of securing a seige of Medina, but an urgent necessity if a Turkish advance on Mecca was to be prevented. Colonel Wilson came up to Yambo and pressed the point on Sherif Feisal, who agreed entirely, but pointed out that the Rabugh force had proved hollow, and that the Turks in Hamra were open to strike at Rabugh or Yambo as they pleased. Now that Zeid was discredited, and Ali shown a broken reed, he could not risk leaving the area himself. In the circumstances Colonel Wilson gave Feisal his personal assurance that the Rabugh garrison (with British naval help) would be capable of resisting any Turkish attack until Feisal had occupied Wejh. There was no means of giving force to this assurance, but it seemed a reasonable and necessary risk to take, since without it Feisal would not have moved north. Colonel Wilson strengthened his position a few days later, by sending Feisal direct orders from the Sherif of Mecca to proceed to Wejh at once.

The other Arab factor in our hands was Sherif Abdullah with an untarnished reputation and a force in being north-east of Medina, an area of very secondary military importance. It was pointed out to Feisal how effective Abdullah might be made if he was moved to Wadi Ais, a natural fortress about 100 kilometres above Medina on the railway line. He would there be astride the Medina lines of communication, and no Turkish advance towards Mecca, Yambo, or even Rabugh would be possible till he had been dislodged, and to dislodge him troops would have to be withdrawn from Ghayir and Hamra since the coincident Sinai push of the EEF made reinforcements from the north improbable. Feisal saw the point, and sent off Raja ibn Khuluwi at once to Abdullah with the scheme.

In view, however, of the situation at Rabugh, it seemed to Colonel Wilson that Feisal's move on Wejh should be undertaken as soon as possible. Preparations were, therefore, made for the start, before a reply had arrived from Abdullah. Feisal was very nervous during this period. The operation involved a flank march of about 200 miles parallel to the Turkish communications, by an inferior fighting force, leaving its base (Yambo) entirely undefended, and evacuating its only possible defensive position (Wadi Yambo) in the face of an enemy force of nearly divisional strength in Wadi Safra, not thirty miles away across easy country. The manoeuvre was only made possible at all by the absolute command of the sea and the ungrudging co-operation in transport of ammunition and supplies afforded Feisal by the SNO Red Sea Patrol. The situation at Yambo appeared likely to be so insecure that all possible rifles and ammunition were embarked from the town store-houses before we left.

Sherif Abdullah fortunately fell in with the Wadi Ais scheme, and said he would arrive there on 11 January. Feisal, therefore, fixed 20 January as a provisional date for his attack on Wejh. Actually, Abdullah was not able to reach Wadi Ais till 17 January, and Feisal did not reach Wejh till 25 January.

The occupation of Wejh is of importance, since it means a prolongation of the Arab front along the Hejaz railway by rather more than 200 miles, the accession to the Sherif's cause of the Billi, and later of the Beni Atiyah and Huweitat. Its direct military value is that it is the only possible base for operations against El-Ala, which is the vital point of railway communication between Syria and Medina, and a base for the future.

Sherif Abdullah's occupation of Wadi Ais rendered possible Feisal's move north to Wejh, and Abdullah's occupation was indirectly secured by the operations at Arish and Rafah.

XIII. The Sherifial Northern Army
6 February 1917

Feisal moved away from Owais (sixteen miles north of Yambo), towards Wejh, with the following force:

Juheinah Tribal Volunteers

Contingent	Mounted	Infantry	Officer Commanding
Ashraf	270	296	Sherif Mohammed Ali Abu Sharrain
Gufa	690	854	Sherif Abd el-Kerim
Erwa	244	298	Sherif Jabar el-Aiaishi, Jerabih ibn Rubaia, Maazi
Zueida	260	80	Ali Seyyid, Mifleh el-Hansha and Thali el-Urfi
Beni Ibrahim	916	800	Mohammed ibn Jebbara, Abd el-Rahman, Abu Rageiba
Rifaa	261	836	Audah ibn Zuweid
Sinan	150	100	
	2,791	3,264	

Harb Tribesmen

	Mounted	Infantry	
Wuld Mohammed	176	212	Salih el-Jiddah

Other Units

	Mounted	Infantry	
Ibn Shefia's battalion	95	400	Mohammed ibn Shefia
Ageyl and Ateibah bodyguard	800	400	Abdullah ibn Dakhil, Sherif Ahmed ibn Hadhaa
Mule Mounted Infantry	100		Mulud ibn Mukhlus
Mountain-battery	4 2.95 quick-firing guns		Rasim
Machine-guns	10 (= 2½ companies)		Abdullah

Near Wejh Feisal was joined by:

Juheinah Tribesmen

	Mounted	Infantry	
Marawin	800	500	Saad el-Ghaneim Mohammed el-Ghaneim
Hameida Samarra Foweida	400	308	Murzuk el-Tihaimi

HMS *Hardinge* transported to Wejh:

150 Bisha police	Sheikh Aamr
450 Juheinah infantry, mainly belong to Ibn Shefia's unit	Salih ibn Shefia

This makes in the whole northern army, 5,162 mounted men, and 5,084 infantry (total 10,246 men), with four quick-firing guns and ten machine-guns.

The forces left in the Yambo area by Feisal comprised the following:

Anezah

Wuld Suleiman	550	Sent to Wadi Ais

Juheinah

Beni Kelb	250	Bowat

Harb (Beni Salim) | | Wadi Safrah

		Officer Commanding
Subh	1,200	Abd el-Mayin ibn Aasai, Suleiman el-Teiah, Nassar ibn Wahis
Sumeidat	300	Assaf (Paramount of all Beni Salim)
Mahamid	600	Hetaihet
Hawazim	1,300	Selman; Jebr ibn Hemeid; Mastur ibn Aiyj
Dawahir	300	Ibn Balud
Seraha	400	Suleiman; Afnan
Beni Amr	500	Nasir ibn Derwish
Sakharna	800	Abu Bekr ibn Motlog; Naji ibn Rubia
Fedhallah	200	Feisal ibn Ahmed
Rehalah	900	Raba; Atiet Allah; Mohammed ibn Nafia
Dhikara	300	Mabruk
Radadah	600	Barakat
Hejela	550	Sheteiwi

In Yambo

500 Hudheil and a few Bishah.
In all, about 9,250 men.

Of the above force, since the Turkish occupation of Wadi Safrah, only about sixty per cent could be counted on as effective, and some large contingents were cut off from communications with Yambo. They were handed over to Sherif Sharaf, with orders to do what he could to get them together again. A few of the Hawazim and Sheikh Khallaf had surrendered to the Turks, but the remainder (about ninety-six per cent) withdrew into their hills with their rifles, and stood on the defensive waiting orders; or, if they were on the Turkish L. of C., carried out raids on camel convoys and local posts.

XIV. Feisal's Order of March
6 February 1917

(i) Yambo to Um Lej

From Owais, Feisal moved to Akhdar (water), and thence to Nubt (water), and so to Um Lej. He took five days over the journey, which is one of only eighty miles, and experienced great difficulty for lack of water. I was not able, owing to difficulties of the local situation at Yambo, to travel this stretch with the army, and can give no details of the route.

The troops were given six days rations, and ordered to carry two gallons of water per man. The order of march was that the force was divided into nine sections, each under a Sherif or sheikh of importance, and instructed to march separately to Um Lej, and concentrate there. Actually there proved to be no water at Um Lej, and so Feisal camped at Bir el-Waheidi, five miles north-east of the town. He reached there on 14 January, and in the next four days was gradually joined by his other contingents, who settled down at all available water holes in the district.

(ii) Um Lej to Wejh

The more serious part of the march was that from Um Lej to Wejh. The best road for camels is up the coast, to Wadi Dhulm, and then to Abu Zereibat for water. The drawback to the road is that the sixty miles between Semna and Abu Zereibat have no permanent water. For this reason an interior road, from Semna to Khuf, Towala and Abu Zereibat is usually chosen, as well-water exists at each station. Between Yambo and Wejh there is no single spring of running water, and the wells depend intimately on the rainfall, which for the last three years has been almost nil. In consequence, little water is anywhere obtainable, and the supply of forage presents serious difficulties. There is almost no grazing (and in any case a worked camel cannot subsist by grazing alone), and the price of dried hay has reached unprecedented prices. A particular local measure of hay, calculated to be sufficient for a riding camel for one day, now costs six shillings and eight pence. Feisal only pays £6 a month camel-hire, and in consequence, all the animals are under-fed, and quite a number died along our march, simply from physical weakness. The Arabs care for them so far as possible, and there is little sickness among them; but their carrying capacity is impaired, and their number is also limited. For the transport of his army of 4,000 camel corps, and 4,000 infantry (the army is organised on a basis of rikab and redif to each camel), mountain-guns, machine-guns, and mule mounted infantry, Feisal had 380 baggage camels, in all. He carried eight days food, thirty-six hours water, 500 rounds of 2.95 ammunition and a small reserve of SAA, over the 100,000 rounds of the machine-gun companies, on these 380 camels.

It will be understood from the above, that the material needs of an Arab army (even when of the size and complexity of Feisal's), are much below that of a Turkish or European force. Feisal's mountain-battery, in the hands of its Egyptian personnel, required 360 camels for its proper transport. Since the Egyptians have been replaced by Arabs, the battery has moved with thirty-two camels for two-day marches, and on this expedition of fourteen days found less than eighty sufficient. The same quantity of ammunition was carried in both cases. At Bir el-Waheidi Feisal heard that casual rain-pools had formed at two places on the coast road, and decided to take that road to Abu Zereibat with his own guard and three other sections of the army. He ordered the rest to march by Khuff and Towala. The local Arabs (Musa Juheinah) on whom we had to rely for local information and as guides proved most unreliable. They were never able to say what the yield of any well really would be, or where and how far off the wells were. The numbers of Feisal's armies are much in excess of anything which tribal warfare has conceived, and the Juheinah – being uneducated – have no unit of time smaller than the day, or of distance longer than the span and shorter than the stage (from six to sixteen hours march, according to your wish and camel), and cannot realise a number larger than the digits. Inter-communication between units of the Arab forces is often hindered by there being no person in a force who can read and write. In the circumstances a great deal of delay, confusion, and actual danger for lack of water and food occurred on our march, which would have been obviated had time allowed of previous reconnaissance of the route. The animals were without food for two and a half days, and the army marched the last fifty miles on half a gallon of water per man and no food. This did not seem in any way to affect the spirits of the men, who trotted gaily into the Wejh singing songs and executing sham charges; nor did it affect in any way their speed or energy. Feisal said, however, that another thirty-six hours of the same conditions would have begun to tell on them.

XV. Nejd News
6 February 1917

The following information about central Arabian matters, past and present, is based on notes of a conversation with Sherif Feisal.

'About five years ago Ibn Saud began to move the people of Western Nejd against the Meccans. He sent Seyyids and preachers among the former, and taught that the people of Mecca were *kufar* and quite intolerable in such

Holy Places. He won over to his side (by various arguments) some of the Buqum and Sebai, and threatened Taif. This stirred up the Sherif of Mecca, who took effective counter-measures. In consequence Saad ibn Saud was sent down to arrange terms of peace. By mediation all Wadi Dawasir (to the point where it becomes Wadi Ranyah) was recognised to be Ibn Saud's, and Wadis Kharmah and Bishah and Ranyah were confirmed to the Sherif. Ibn Saud was recognised as overlord of all the Kahtan, and the Sherif as overlord of the Ateibah. The trouble about the Ateibah is that they are a Hejaz stock, recently moved into Nejd. Geographically they should be Ibn Saud's, but by origin and custom they are Sherifian. Two years ago Ibn Saud again got active, and sent agents among the Ateibah and other tribes. So Sherif Abdullah went out over the whole dira, further than ever before to the east, and received again the allegiance of the Ateibah.'

Feisal regards Ibn Saud as very powerful, but at home only; for his forces are not organised, and he cannot move abroad in great strength. I noticed, as before, among the Hejaz Arabs and their leaders strong distrust and dislike of Wahabi principles and sectaries.

Feisal is informed that 300 Turks with two mountain-guns, have been put under Ibn Rashid's orders in Hail. They are unpopular, and local disturbances in Hail recently ended in the deaths of two of them.

Persistent rumours are current amongst the Ageyl of a quarrel between Sheikh Jabir and Ibn Saud, in which Jabir was killed. The rumours originated apparently in Jebel Shammar.

The Senha section of the Qahtan are wild. A cord is knotted about the necks of young lads, and not removed till they have killed a man in battle.

XVI. With the Northern Army
15 February 1917

Route Notes

On 2 January 1917, I left Yambo and rode across the plain to the mouth of Wadi Agida in five hours. From the mouth of Wadi Agida to the watershed into the Wadi Yambo basin was one hour, and thence to Nakhl Mubarak was one hour; all done at four miles an hour walk. The lowest third of the ascent of Wadi Agida was over sand: soft, slow going. The upper parts were harder and better: the divide was low and easy, and it gave at once to the eastward, on to a broad open valley, coming from the left with only very low hills on each side (Jebel Agida?), down which the road curved gently into Nakhl Mubarak. The 'Sebil' stands about 400 yards east of the watershed.

The road down to Nakhl looked very beautiful to-day. The rains have brought up a thin growth of grass in all the hollows and flat places. The blades, of a very tender green, shoot up between all the stones, so that looked at from a little height and distance there is a lively mist of pale green here and there over the surface of the slate-blue and brown-red rocks. In places the growth was quite strong, and the camels of the army are grazing on it.

In Nakhl Mubarak I found Feisal encamped in tents: he himself was in his private tent, getting ready to go out to his reception. I stayed with him that day, while rumours came in that the Turkish force had evacuated Wadi Safra. One reported that from Bir Sheriufi to Bir Derwish was one great camp, and that its units were proceeding to Medina; another had seen a great force of camel-men and infantry ride east past Kheif yesterday. We decided to send out a feeler towards Hamra, to get news.

On 3 January, I took thirty-five Mahamid and rode over a dull tamarisk- and thorn-grown plain past Bir Faqir (not seen) to Bir Wasit, which is the old Abu Khalaat of my first trip. We waited there till sunset, and then went to Bir Mura, left our camels with ten of the men, and the rest of us climbed up the hills north of the Haj road up to Jebel Dhifran, which was painful, for the hills are all of knife-like strata which are turned on edge, and often run in straight lines from crest to valley. It gives you abundance of broken surface but no sound grips, as the strata are so minutely cracked that almost any segment will come away from its socket in your hand.

The top of Dhifran was cold and misty. At dawn we disposed ourselves in crevices of the rocks, and at last saw three bell tents beneath us to the right, behind a spur at the head of the pass, 300 yards away. We could not get round to them to get a low view, so put a few bullets through their top. This turned out a crowd of Turks from all directions. They leaped into trenches and rifle pits each side of the road, and potting them was very difficult. I think they suffered some loss, but I could not be sure. They fired in every direction except towards us, and the row in the narrow valley was so awful that I expected to see the Hamra force turn out. As the Turks were already ten to our one this might have made our getting away difficult, so we crawled back and rushed down into a valley, almost on top of two very scared Turks, who may have been outposts or may have been at their private morning duty. They were the most ragged men I have every seen, bar a British tramp, and surrendered at once. We took them with us, and bolted off down the valley for another 500 yards. From there we put a few shots into the Turks, which seemed to check them, and so got off gently to Bir Murra by 6.30 a.m. The prisoners could speak only Turkish, so we mounted them and raced up to Nakhl to find an interpreter. They said it was the 5th Coy of the 2/55th Regiment which was posted on Dhifran, the rest of the battalion and two companies of the first battalion being at Hamra village. The other companies of the 1/55th were guarding the Derb el-Khayaa from Hamra to Bir Ibn Hassani; 3/55th in Bir Derwish; OC 55th Regiment, Tewfik Bey.

At Nakhl Mubarak I found letters from Captain Warren saying that Zeid was still in Yambo, and that the 'Dufferin' would wait in Sherm Yambo till I came. As Feisal was just starting for Owais, I changed my camel and rode down with him and the army to the head of Wadi Messarid by 3 p.m. The order of march was rather splendid and barbaric. Feisal in front, in white;

Sharaf on his right in red headcloth and henna dyed tunic and cloak; myself on his left in white and red; behind us three banners of purple silk, with gold spikes; behind them three drummers playing a march, and behind them again, a wild bouncing mass of 1,200 camels of the bodyguard, all packed as closely as they could move, the men in every variety of coloured clothes, and the camels nearly as brilliant in their trappings, and the whole crowd singing at the tops of their voices a war song in honour of Feisal and his family. It looked like a river of camels, for we filled up the wadi to the tops of its banks, and poured along in a quarter of a mile long stream.

At the mouth of Wadi Messarid I said good-bye to Feisal and raced down the open plain to Yambo by 6 p.m. I was riding Feisal's own splendid camel, and so managed to do the twenty-two miles fairly easily. To my great relief I found the 'Dufferin' had already left for Rabugh with Zeid, and so I was saved a further ten miles' march to Sherm Yambo.

Arab Forces

The troops in Nakhl Mubarak were mostly camel corps. There were very many – according to Feisal's figures, over 6,000 – but their camps were spread over miles of the Wadi and its tributaries, and I could not manage to see all of them. Those I did see were quiet, and I thought in fair spirits. Some of them have now served six months or more, and these have lost their enthusiasm but gained experience in exchange. They still preserve their tribal instinct for independence of order, but they are curbing their habit of wasting ammunition, have achieved a sort of routine in matters of camping and marching, and when the Sherif approaches near they fall into line and make the low bow and sweep of the arm to the lips which is the official salute. They do not oil their guns – they say because they then clog with sand, and they have no oil handy – but the guns are most of them in fair order, and some of the men know how to shoot. They are becoming separate but coherent units under their sheikhs, and attendance is more regular than it was, as their distance from home increases. Further, they are becoming tempered to the idea of leaving their own diras, and Feisal hopes to take nearly all to Wejh with him. As a mass they are not formidable, since they have no corporate spirit or discipline, or mutual confidence. Man by man they are good: I would suggest that the smaller the unit that is acting, the better will be its performance. A thousand of them in a mob would be ineffective against one fourth their number of trained troops: but three or four of them, in their own valleys and hills, would account for a dozen Turkish soldiers. When they sit still they get nervous, and anxious to return home. Feisal himself goes rather to pieces in the same conditions. When, however, they have plenty to do, and are riding about in small parties tapping the Turks here and there, retiring always when the Turks advance, to appear in another direction immediately after, then they are in their element, and must cause the enemy not only anxiety, but bewilderment. The mule mounted infantry company is very promising. They have got Mulud, an ex-cavalry officer, training them, and already make a creditable appearance. The machine-gun sections were disappointing. They say that the Egyptian volunteers are improving these and the artillery details.

Camp Life

The camp routine at HQ, is much as follows. At 5 a.m. the Army 'Imam' gets on to the best hill-top and calls to prayer. He has an astonishing voice, and wakes up every man and animal in the camp. Immediately after him Feisal's private Imam calls gently and musically by his tent. A few minutes later a cup of sweet coffee turns up, for each of us (Feisal has five slaves), and at 6 a.m. or a little later we go to breakfast with Feisal in his tent, where he has two modern, but not bad carpets, and a delightful old Baluch prayer rug. Breakfast in favourable moments may include Mecca cakes and cooked dhurra besides dates: after breakfast two little glasses of sweet tea are produced for each of us. From after breakfast till 8 a.m. Feisal works with his secretary, or discusses things privately in his tent with important people. At 8 a.m. he gives audience in his diwan tent, which is furnished with two bad *kilims*. The routine is for him to sit at the end of it, on one side, and callers or petitioners sit in front of the tent in a half circle, until he calls them up to him. All questions are settled very summarily, and nothing is left over till later. At 11.30 a.m. he rises, and walks back to his living tent, where a little later we collect for lunch. Lunch again, on fortunate days, consists of several dishes: stewed thorn-buds, beans or lentils, with bread, and afterwards rice or honey cakes. They eat with fingers or spoons, as pleases them. After lunch comes short delay of talk, while coffee and sweet tea turn up. Then till 2 p.m. Feisal writes, or dictates letters, or sleeps. From 2 p.m. till 4.30 p.m. he again sits in the reception tent and disposes of the afternoon cases. From 4.30 to sunset (5 p.m.) he often walks about, or sits outside and talks to a few chiefs. From 5 till 6 p.m. he gives private audience in his living tent to necessary people, and discusses the night's reconnaissance and duties, for most field work is done in the dark. About 6 p.m. comes the evening meal, like lunch, but with large fragments of sheep crowning the rice heap. After it comes intermittent glasses of sugared tea till bed time, which may not be till late hours. He sees all sorts of people at this time; his servants bring them in one by one, according to their business. If there is not much doing, he sends out for some local sheikh, and discusses with him the country round about, roads, tribal histories, etc., or simply tells us stories of what he saw in Syria, Turkish secret history, or family affairs.

Feisal's Table Talk

Talking one day about the Yemen, as they call anything south of Mecca and Jiddah, Feisal remarked on the great docility and reasonableness of the

Southern tribes, compared with the Harb, Juheinah and Ateibah of the North. He said that no Arabs of his acquaintance were so easily to hold and to rule. To imprison an officer, his sheikh had only to knot a thin string about his neck and state his sentence, and the man would henceforward follow him about with protestations of innocence and appeals to be set at liberty. Another good custom is that of naming boy or girl children after a favoured guest. They then belong literally to their name-father, who can dispose their actions as he pleases, to the exclusion of parental authority; they even incur their part-responsibility of the blood feuds of the name-parent. He was down south between Taif and Birk and inland up to Ebhah for months, and says that now whole tribes of boys are called Feisal, and that, over them and indirectly over their fathers, he has wide personal influence. Particularly he spent four months fortifying Muhail for the Turks and made great friends of Suleiman ibn Ali and his family. He says that, given ten days leave, he would undertake to raise every fighting man in Asir against Muhieddin. Ebhah he says is not formidable to an attacking force with a battery of field-guns. The present bar on action is that Nasir is not weighty enough to counterpoise the Idrisi. The tribes all believe that Idrisi would egg on his friendly sheikhs to attack them in the rear, if they moved openly against the Turks. The presence of Feisal or Abdullah would allay these fears.

Feisal says that Abdullah, though quick when he does move, is rather luxurious in taste and inclined to be lazy.

Stotzingen told Feisal in Damascus that, from the Yemen, arms and ammunition were to be shipped across to Abyssinia, and an anti-foreign war begun in that country. He himself was going afterwards to German East Africa.

Frobenius (calling himself Abd el-Kerim Pasha) turned up in Jiddah one morning by sea from Wejh soon after war had begun. Feisal was in Jiddah, and headed him off from Mecca. British naval activity dissuaded him from going on further south. Feisal, therefore, got him a boat, and gave him a letter of recommendation, and sent him back north again. When he got to Rabugh, however, Hussein Mubeirik took suspicion of him and locked him up in the fort. Frobenius had some difficulty in getting out, and made great complaints of his treatment when he got back to Syria.

In March 1916, Jemal Pasha took Feisal to a cinema in Damascus. The star film showed the Pyramids, with the Union Jack on top, and beneath them, Australians beating the Egyptian men and raping the women, and, in the foreground, an Egyptian girl in an attitude of supplication. The second scene showed a desert, with camel-convoys and a Turkish infantry battalion marching on for ever and ever. The third scene returned to the Pyramids with a sudden appearance of the Ottoman Army in review order, the killing of the Australians and the surrender of General Maxwell, the joy of Egypt, the tearing down of the British flag from the Pyramids, and its replacement by the Turkish flag. Feisal said to Jemal: 'Why go on troubling my father and myself for recruits for your army if this film is true?' Jemal said: 'Well, you know it encourages the people. We do not expect or try to conquer Egypt yet. Out policy is to hold the British forces there with the least cost to ourselves; and Germany has promised us that the last act of the war shall be the conquest of Egypt by Germany and its restoration to the Ottoman Empire. On these terms I agreed to join her in arms.'

Oppenheim came to see Feisal in Constantinople in early 1915. He said he wanted to make rebellions. Feisal asked of what and why? Oppenheim said there were to be rebellions of Moslems against Christians. Feisal said the idea was sound. Where did he propose to start them? Oppenheim said, 'everywhere' – in India, Egypt, the Sudan, Java, Abyssinia, North Africa. Feisal said they might consider India first. There was the technical difficulty of lack of arms. Oppenheim said that would be put right by a German–Turk expedition into Persia. He asked if the Sherif would be prepared to co-operate with the Indian Moslem societies. Feisal said his father would want to know whether, afterwards, the Indian Moslems would be independent and supreme, or would Hindus rule them, or India fall to another European power? Oppenheim said he had no idea: that it was previous to think so far ahead. Feisal said he was afraid his father would want to know all the same. Oppenheim said, 'Very well, how about Egypt? We can arrange to give your family office there, when it is conquered.' Feisal quoted the Koran to the disparagement of Egyptians, and said that he had lately been in Egypt, and had been offered the crown by the Nationalist party. (This took place in Piraeus.) Egyptians were weather-cocks, with no political principle except dissatisfaction, and intent only on pleasure and money getting. Any Egyptian who talked of raising a rebellion in Egypt was trying to touch you for something on account. Oppenheim said, 'Well then, the Sudan?' Feisal said, 'Yes, you are right. There is in the Sudan material to cause a real rebellion: but do you know the Sudan?' Oppenheim said, 'Why?' Feisal said, 'They are ignorant negroes, armed with broad-bladed spears, bows and shields. He, who would try to stir them up against the English and their rifles and machine-guns, is no good Moslem. The men, however, are sound material. Give me arms, money and the command of the Red Sea for about six weeks, and I shall be Governor-General of the Sudan.' Oppenheim has hardly spoken to him since.

In January 1915, Yasim, Ali Riza, Abd el-Ghani, and others approached the Sherif of Mecca and suggested a military rebellion in Syria. The Sherif sent Feisal up to report. He found Divisions 25, 35 and 36 ready to revolt, but public opinion less ready, and a general opinion in military circles that Germany would win the war quite rapidly. He went to Constantinople, and waited till the Dardanelles was in full blast. He then came back to Damascus, judging it a possible moment; but he found the well disposed divisions broken up, and his supporters scattered. So he suggested to his father that they delay till England had been properly approached, and Turkey had suffered crippling losses, or until an Allied landing had been effected at Alexandretta.

XVII. Syria: The Raw Material
12 March 1917

Geographically, Syria is much parcelled out. The first and greatest longitudinal division is made by the mountains, which run like a rugged spine north and south close to the sea, and shut off the peoples of the coast from those of the interior. Those of the coast speak a different Arabic, differently intoned; they live in different houses, eat different food, and gain their living differently. They speak of the 'interior' unwillingly, as a wild land full of blood and terror.

The interior is divided again longitudinally. The peasants in the valleys of the Jordan, Litani and Orontes are the most stable, most prosperous yeomen of the country; and beyond them is the strange shifting population of the border lands, wavering eastward or westward with the season, living by their wits only, wasted by droughts and locusts, by Bedouin raids, and if these fail them, by their own incurable blood-feuds.

Each of these main north and south strip-divisions is crossed and walled off into compartments mutually at odds: and it is necessary, if political composition of Syria is to be gauged, to enumerate some of the heads of these.

The boundary between Arab and Turkish speech follows, not inaptly, the coach-road from Alexandretta to Ezaz, and thence the Baghdad railway to Jerablus. On the west it begins among Ansariya, disciples of a strange cult of a principle of fertility, sheer pagan, anti-foreign, distrustful of Mohammedanism, but drawn for the moment to Christianity by the attraction of common persecution; the sect is very vital in itself, and as clannish in feeling and politics as a sect can be. One Nosairi will not betray another, and they will hardly not betray Mohammedan and Christian. Their villages are sown in patches down the main hills from Missis to Tartus and the Tripoli gap, and their sheikhs are Aissa and old Maaruf. They speak Arabic only, and they have lived there since, at least, the beginning of Greek history. They stand aside from politics, and leave the Turkish government alone in hope of reciprocity.

Mixed among the Ansariya are colonies of Syrian Christians, and south of the Orontes are (or were) solid blocks of Armenians, who spoke Turkish, but would not consort with Turks. Inland, south of Harim, are settlements of Druses (who are Arabs) and Circassians. These have their hand against every man. North-east of them are Kurds, speaking Kurdish and Arabic, settlers of some generations back, who are marrying Arabs and adopting their politics. They hate native Christians most, and next to them Turks and Europeans. Just beyond the Kurds are some Yezidis, Arabic-speaking, but always trying in their worship to placate a spirit of evil, and with a warped admiration for crude bronze birds. Christians, Mohammedans and Jews unite to spit upon the Yezid. After the Yezidis lies Aleppo, a town of a quarter of a million of people, and an epitome of all races and religions. Eastward of Aleppo for sixty miles you pass through settled Arabs, whose colour and

manner becomes more and more tribal as you approach the fringe of cultivation, where the semi-nomad ends and the Bedawi begins.

If you take another section across Syria, a degree more to the south, you
begin with some colonies of Mohammedan Circassians near the sea. They
speak Arabic now and are an ingenious but quarrelsome race, much opposed
by their Arab neighbours. Inland of them are districts reserved for Ismailiya.
These speak Arabic, and worship among themselves a king Mohammed,
who, in the flesh, is the Agha Khan. They believe him to be a great and wonderful sovereign, honouring the English with his protection. They hate Arabs
and orthodox Muslimin, and look for the crumbling of the Turk. Meanwhile,
they are loathed and trampled on by their neighbours, and are driven to
conceal their beastly opinions under a veneer of orthodoxy. Everyone knows
how thin that is, and they maintain among themselves signs and pass-words
by which they know one another. Miserably poor in appearance, they pay the
Agha a princely tribute every year. Beyond the Ismailiya is a strange sight, villages of Christian tribal Arabs, some of semi-nomad habits, under their own
sheikhs. Very sturdy Christians they are, most unlike their snivelling brethren
in the hills. They live as do the Sunnis round them, dress like them, speak like
them, and are on the best of terms with them. East of these Christians are
semi-nomad Muslim peasants, and east of them again some villages of
Ismailiya outcasts, on the extreme edge of cultivation, whither they have
retired in search of comparative peace. Beyond them only Bedouins.

Take another section through Syria, a degree lower down, between Tripoli
and Beyrout. To begin with, near the coast, are Lebanon Christians,
Maronites and Greeks for the most part. It is hard to disentangle the politics
of the two churches. Superficially, one should be French and the other
Russian, but a part of the Maronites now have been in the United States, and
have developed there an Anglo-Saxon vein which is not the less vigorous for
being spurious. The Greek church prides itself on being old Syrian, autoch-
thonous, of an intense local patriotism that (with part) would rather fling it
into the arms of the Turk than endure irretrievable annexation by a Roman
power. The adherents of the two churches are at one in unmeasured slander
of Mohammedans and their religion. They salve a consciousness of inbred
inferiority by this verbal scorn. Behind and among the Christians live families of Mohammedan Sunnis, Arabic-speaking, identical in race and habit
with the Christians, marked off from them by a less mincing dialect, and a
distaste for emigration and its result. On the higher slopes of the hills are
serried settlements of Metawala, Shia Mohammedans who came from Persia
centuries ago. They are dirty, ignorant, surly, and fanatical. They will not eat
or drink with an infidel (the Sunni as bad as the Christian), follow their own
priests and notables, speak Arabic but disown in every way the people, not
their co-sectarians, who live about them. Across the hills are villages of
Christians, yeomen, living at peace with their Sunni neighbours, as though
they had never heard the grumbles of their fellows in the Lebanon. East of
them are semi-nomad Arab peasantry.

Take a section a degree lower down, near Acre. There are first, Sunni Arabs, then Druses, then Metawala to the Jordan valley, near which are many bitterly-suspicious Algerian colonies, mixed in with villages of aboriginal Palestinian Jews. The latter are an interesting race. They speak Arabic and good Hebrew; have developed a standard and style of living suitable to the country, and yet much better than the manner of the Arabs. They cultivate the land, and hide their lights rather under bushels, since their example would be a great one for the foreign (German inspired) colonies of agricultural Jews, who introduce strange manners of cultivation and crops, and European houses (erected out of pious subscriptions), to a country like Palestine, at once too small and too poor to repay efforts on such a scale. The Jewish colonies of North Palestine pay their way perhaps, but give no proportionate return on their capital expenditure. They are, however, honest in their attempts at colonisation, and deserve honour, in comparison with the larger settlements of sentimental remittance-men in South Palestine. Locally, they are more than tolerated; one does not find round Galilee the deep-seated antipathy to Jewish colonists and aims that is such an unlovely feature of the Jerusalem area. Across the eastern plain (Arabs), you come to the Leja, a labyrinth of crack-led lava, where all the loose and broken men of Syria have foregathered for unnumbered generations. Their descendants live there in rich lawless villages, secure from the government and Bedouins, and working out their own internecine feuds at leisure. South of them is the Hauran, peopled by Arabs and Druses. The latter are Arabic-speaking, a heterodox Mohammedan sect, who revere a mad and dead Sultan of Egypt, and hate Maronites with a hatred which, when encouraged by the Ottoman government and the Sunni fanatics of Damascus, finds expression in great periodic killings. None the less, the Druses are despised by the Mohammedan Arabs, and dislike them in return. They hate the Bedouins, obey their own chiefs, and preserve in their Hauran fastnesses a parade of the chivalrous semi-feudalism in which they lived in the Lebanon, in the days of the great emirs.

A section a degree lower would begin with German Zionist Jews, speaking a bastard Hebrew and German Yiddish, more intractable than the Jews of the Roman era, unable to endure near them anyone not of their race, some of them agriculturists, most of them shopkeepers, the most foreign, most uncharitable part of its whole population. Behind these Jews is their enemy, the Palestine peasant, more stupid than the peasant of North Syria, materialist and bankrupt. East of him lies the Jordan valley, inhabited by a charred race of serfs, and beyond it, group upon group of self-respecting tribal or village Christians, who are after their co-religionists of the Orontes valley, the least timid examples of their faith in the country. Among them, and east of them, are semi-nomad and nomad Arabs of the religion of the desert, living on the fear and bounty of their Christian neighbours. Down this debatable land the Ottoman government has planted a long line of Circassian immigrants. They hold their ground only by the sword and the favour of the Turks, to whom they are consequently devoted.

These odd races and religions do not complete the tale of the races of Syria. There are still the six great towns, Jerusalem, Beyrout, Damascus, Hama, Homs, and Aleppo to be reckoned apart from the country folk in any accounting of Syria.

Jerusalem is a dirty town which all Semitic religions have made holy. Christians and Mohammedans come there on pilgrimage; Jews look to it for the political future of their race. In it the united forces of the past are so strong that the city fails to have a present: its people, with the rarest exceptions, are characterless as hotel servants, living on the crowd of visitors passing through. Questions of Arabs and their nationality are as far from them as bimetallism from the life of Texas, though familiarity with the differences among Christians in their moment of most fervent expression has led the Mohammedans of Jerusalem to despise (and dislike) foreigners generally.

Beyrout is altogether new. It would be all bastard French in feeling, as in language, but for its Greek harbour and its American college. Public opinion in it is that of the Christian merchants, all fat men, who live by exchange, for Beyrout itself produces nothing. After the merchants its strongest component is the class of returned emigrants, living on their invested savings, in the town of Syria which, to them, most resembles the Washington Avenue where they 'made good'. Beyrout is the door of Syria, with a Levantine screen through which shop-soiled foreign influences flow into Syria. It is as representative of Syria as Soho of the Home Countries, and yet in Beyrout, from its geographical position, from its schools, from the freedom engendered by intercourse with many foreigners, there was a nucleus of people, Mohammedans, talking and writing and thinking like the doctrinaire cyclopaedists who paved the way for revolution in France, and whose words permeated to parts of the interior where action is in favour. For their sake (many of them are martyrs now, in Arab eyes) and, for the power of its wealth, and for its exceeding loud and ready voice, Beyrout is to be reckoned with.

Damascus, Homs, Hamah, and Aleppo are the four ancient cities in which Syria takes pride. They are stretched like a chain along the fertile valleys of the interior, between the desert and the hills; because of their setting they turn their backs upon the sea and look eastward. They are Arab and know themselves such.

Damascus is the old inevitable head of Syria. It is the seat of lay government and the religious centre, three days only from the Holy City by its railway. Its sheikhs are leaders of opinion, and more 'Meccan' than others elsewhere. Its people are fresh and turbulent, always willing to strike, as extreme in their words and acts as in their pleasures. Damascus will move before any part of Syria. The Turks made it their military centre, just as naturally as the Arab opposition, or Oppenheim and Sheikh Shawish established themselves there. Damascus is a lode-star to which Arabs are naturally drawn, and a city which will not easily be convinced that it is subject to any alien race.

Hamah and Homs are towns which dislike one another. Everyone in them manufactures things – in Homs, generally cotton and wool, in Hamah, silk and brocade. Their industries were prosperous and increasing; their merchants were quick to take advantage of new outlets, or to meet new tastes. North Africa, the Balkans, Syria, Arabia, Mesopotamia used their stuffs. They demonstrated the productive ability of Syria, unguided by foreigners, as Beyrout demonstrated its understanding of commerce. Yet, while the prosperity of Beyrout has made it Levantine, the prosperity of Homs and Hamah has reinforced their localism, made them more entirely native, and more jealously native than any other Syrian towns. It almost seems as though familiarity with plant and power had shown the people there that the manners of their fathers were the best.

Aleppo is the largest city in Syria, but not of it, nor of Turkey, nor of Mesopotamia. Rather it is a point where all the races, creeds and tongues of the Ottomon Empire meet and know one another in a spirit of compromise. The clash of varied characteristics, which makes its streets a kaleidoscope, has imbued in the Aleppine a kind of thoughtfulness, which corrects in him what is wanton in the Damascene. Aleppo has shared in each of the civilisations which turn about it, and the result seems to be a lack of zest in all that its people do. Even so, they surpass the rest of Syria in most things. They fight and trade more, are more fanatical and vicious, and make most beautiful things, but all with a dearth of conviction that renders their great strength barren. It is typical of Aleppo that here, where yet Mohammedan feeling runs high, there is more fellowship between Christian and Mohammedan, Armenian, Arab, Kurd, Turk and Jew, than in, perhaps, any other great city of the Ottoman Empire, and more friendliness, though less licence, is accorded to Europeans on the part of the average Mohammedan. Aleppo would stand aside from political action altogether but for the influence of the great unmixed Arab quarters which lie on its outskirts like overgrown, half-Nomad villages. These are, after the Maidan of Damascus, the most national of any parts of towns, and the intensity of their Arab feeling tinges the rest of the citizens with a colour of nationalism, which is by so much less vivid than the unanimous opinion of Damascus.

In the creeds and races above described, and in others not enumerated, lie the raw materials of Syria for a statesman. It will be noted that the distinctions are political or religious; morally the peoples somewhat resemble one another, with a steady gradation from neurotic sensibility, on the coast, to reserve, inland. They are quick-minded, admirers (but not seekers) of truth, self-satisfied, not incapable (as are the Egyptians) of abstract ideas, but unpractical, and so lazy mentally as to be superficial. Their wish is to be left alone to busy themselves with others' affairs. From childhood they are lawless, obeying their fathers only as long as they fear to be beaten, and their government later for the same reason: yet there are few races with greater respect than the upland Syrian for customary law. All of them want something new, for with their superficiality and their lawlessness is combined a passion for politics, the science of which it is fatally easy for the Syrian to gain a smattering, and too difficult to gain a mastery. They are all discontented with the government they have, but few of them honestly combine their ideas of what they want. Some (mostly Mohammedans) cry for an Arab kingdom, some (mostly Christians) for a foreign protection of an altruistic thelemic order, conferring privileges without obligation. Others cry for autonomy for Syria.

Autonomy is a comprehensible word, Syria is not, for the words Syria and Syrian are foreign terms. Unless he has learnt English or French, the inhabitant of these parts has no word to describe all his country. *Syria* in Turkish (the word exists not in Arabic) is the province of Damascus. *Sham* in Arabic is the town of Damascus. An Aleppine always calls himself an Aleppine, a Beyrouti a Beyrouti, and so down to the smallest villages.

This verbal poverty indicates a political condition. There is no national feeling. Between town and town, village and village, family and family, creed and creed, exist intimate jealousies, sedulously fostered by the Turks to render a spontaneous union impossible. The largest indigenous political entity in settled Syria is only the village under its sheikh, and in patriarchal Syria the tribe under its chief. These leaders are chosen, not formally, but by opinion from the entitled families, and they rule by custom and consent. All the constitution above them is the artificial bureaucracy of the Turk, maintained by force, impossible if it were to be carried out according to its paper scheme, but in practice either fairly good or very bad, according to the less or greater frailty of the human instruments through which it works.

Time seems to have proclaimed that autonomous union is beyond the powers of such a people. In history, Syria is always the corridor between sea and desert, joining Africa to Asia, and Arabia to Europe. It has been a prizering for the great peoples lying about it, alternately the vassal of Asia Minor, Egypt, Greece, Rome, Arabia or Mesopotamia, and when given a momentary independence by the weakness of its neighbours, it has at once resolved itself fiercely into northern and southern, eastern and western discordant 'kingdoms', with the areas and populations at best of Yorkshire, at worst of Rutland; for if Syria is by nature a vassal country, it is also by habit a country of agitations and rebellions.

The proposals to make Syria an Arab or foreign-protected country are, of course, far from the hearts of the 'autonomy' party, but the conviction of their internal divisions, and the evident signs that Syria's neighbours are not going to be of the weak sort that enable it to snatch a momentary independence, have reconciled these parts to having such proposals constantly on their lips.

By accident and time the Arabic language has gradually permeated the country, until it is now almost the only one in use; but this does not mean that Syria – any more than Egypt – is an Arabian country. On the sea coast there is little, if any, Arabic feeling or tradition: on the desert edge there is much. Indeed, racially, there is perhaps something to be said for the suggestion – thrown in the teeth of geography and economics – of putting the littoral under one government, and the interior under another.

*

Whatever the limits of future politics, it can hardly be contested that, like a European government, an Arab government in Syria, to-day or to-morrow, would be an imposed one, as the former Arab governments were. The significant thing is to know what local basis, if any, such a government would have; and one finds that it would be buttressed on two fronts, both contained in the word 'Arab', which seems to strike a chord in some of the most unlikely minds. The Mohammedans, whose mother tongue in Arabic, look upon themselves, for that reason, as a chosen people. The patriotism which should have attached itself to soil or race has been warped to fit a language. The heritage of the Koran and the classical poets holds the Arabic-speaking peoples together. The second buttress of an Arab polity is the dim distortion of the old glories and conquests of the Arabian Khalifate, which has persisted in the popular memory through centuries of Turkish misgovernment. The accident that these ideas savour rather of Arabian Nights than of sober history retains the Arabs in the conviction that their past was greater than the present of the Ottoman Turks.

To sum up – a review of the present components of Syria proves it as vividly coloured a racial and religious mosaic to-day as it has notoriously been in the past. Any wide attempt at autonomy would end in a patched and parcelled thing, an imposition on a people whose instincts for ever and ever have been for parochial home-rule. It is equally clear that the seething discontent which Syrians cherish with the present Turkish administration is common enough to render possible a fleeting general movement towards a new factor, if it appeared to offer a chance realisation of the ideals of centripetal nationalism preached by the Beyrout and Damascus cyclopaedists of the last two generations. Also, that only by the intrusion of a new factor, founded on some outward power or non-Syrian basis, can the dissident tendencies of the sects and peoples of Syria be reined in sufficiently to prevent destructive anarchy. The more loose, informal, inchoate this new government, the less will be the inevitable disillusionment following on its institution; for the true ideal of Syria, apart from the minute but vociferous Christian element, is not an efficient administration, but the minimum of central power to ensure peace, and permit the unchecked development that will find, in Moslem Syria, any really prepared groundwork or large body of adherents is a Sunni one, speaking Arabic, and pretending to revive the Abbassides or Ayubides.

XVIII. Geographical Notes and the Capture of Eshref
12 March 1917

Wadi Hamdh

The lower valley of Wadi Hamdh is a ten-mile wide depression. 'At 3 p.m.', writes Captain Lawrence, 'we entered the wadi itself. It proved to be an immense bed of sandy hillocks a few feet high, cut up with shallow channels, which bore no signs of any general *seil*, though evidently local showers fill one or other of them frequently. Channels and hillocks are alike overgrown with the thickest growth of *ethil* and *tarfa* imaginable. It was difficult for us to force our camels through in places. The bed was in all about a mile wide, running from 100°E to 300°W, and we cut across it obliquely till 3.30 p.m., when we passed a water-pool about eighty yards long, fifteen yards wide, and two feet deep in a clay bottom, and 200 yards further reached the bare flint ridge of the Billi bank of the wadi, which extends as an empty plain to the abrupt foot of Jebel Raal, four or five miles away. The pool of water is within a few yards of the well of Abu Zereibat, and one or other of them affords water all the year round.'

Wadi el-Ais

Feisal said to Captain Lawrence that the road up Wadi Yambo to the railway at Bowat station was very difficult for loaded camels. There is a road by Bowat village to Wadi Ais, and another from Kheif Hussein in Wadi Yambo to Bir Fueis, by Ras el-Magrah, between Jebel Radhwah and Jebel Tareif, and thence over a harrah to el-Ain, near Murabba in Wadi Ais. Murabba lies a long day's journey from the railway, and is said to be the last oasis in Wadi Ais. The water springs and plantations endure for a day's camel journey west of Murabba, and Wadi Ais itself for another day after that, up to a high pass between Jebel Tubi and Jebel Mertaba, a day from Wadi Girs and Um Lej. These passes (with Wadi Hamdh) are the only roads into Wadi Ais, which is bounded on both sides by difficult hills and harrahs. There are many springs and wells of water, but the groves are poorer than those of Wadi Yambo.

Wadi Aqiq

Feisal told Captain Lawrence that Wadi Aqiq, which rises between Lith and Taif, and flows through Taif, becomes Wadi Shaiba near the Harrat el-Muteir, and eventually flows between Ohod and Medina, as Wadi Aqiq, into the Wadi Hamdh. As the crowfly distance from beyond Taif to Medina is about 300 miles, this wadi, hitherto unexplored, must be one of the most important channels in Arabia. The Darb esh-Sharqi, from Mecca to Medina, is known to cross it at Birkah, about 80 miles NNE of Mecca: but, though this road may hit its course again more than once, the reports (e.g. Burtons's) show that it does not follow the valley continuously. A wadi of the same name reappears just south-west of Medina, in accounts of pilgrim marches between Medina and Bir Abbas, and possibly this is the lower end of the original Aqiq immediately before it loses itself in Wadi Hamdh.

The Capture of Eshref Bey

Eshref was met quite by accident about 2 p.m. in easy country at a spot called Gambila, about six hours from Kheibar, and was galloped down at once, before he could get off more than sixty or seventy rounds with his machine-gun. The Arabs lost four killed and four wounded, and captured the whole of his party. He had with him letters to Ibn Rashid, Ibn Saud, and the Yemen; £20,000 in gold; presents of carpets and clothes, a machine-gun with five spare barrels and 50,000 rounds, a box of Mauser pistols, etc.

Abdullah subsequently marched across the railway between Jedaha and Stabl Antar, without seeing any enemy patrols, and he left, between the metals, a letter to Fakhri with an account of the capture of Eshref. His force includes Muteir, Ateibah, Buqum, and Anezah, and he has got in a few Hutein mercenaries. The force left at Henakiyah is about 300 strong. The desert seems in a very lively state, and nothing gets through unplundered. Nejd caravans are making for Mecca rather than Medina, to avoid the danger zone.

Abdullah sent to Feisal Eshref's gaudy Medina-made dagger as a trophy (given subsequently by Feisal to Colonel Wilson), and there was great rejoicing in Feisal's army all night. The HQ poet (also chaplain, and as Muedhdhin, waker-up-in-general to the force) produced a creditable ode in sixteen minutes. The ode summed up the situation in favour of Abdullah, but said that Feisal's opportunities were coming.

XIX. Raids on the Railway
13 May 1917

I. Abu Markha to Abu el-Naam

From 15 March to 26 March I stayed in Sidi Abdullah's camp. On Monday, 26 March, we started off at 7.50 a.m. for the railway at Abu el-Naam. With me were Sherif Fauzan (Hurith, Emir of el-Modhiq), Sherif Suleima (Abdilla), Sidi Raho (Algerian officer in French service), and Mohammed el-Gadhi (Juheinah). We were joined shortly by Mufaddil, a Selqa Anazeh Sheikh. Total force, about thirty men. We went away down Wadi Ais till 8.50 a.m., when we turned slightly to the left, after rounding the mouth of Wadi Tleih coming from the north-west. At 9.20 a.m. we crossed to the right bank of the wadi, under a rock wall, and at 9.30 a.m. reached a corner and bore more to the right. This is El-Marraha. At 10 a.m. we turned a little to the left, and came out of the narrows on to a broad plain, formed by the confluence of the wadis from right to left. Just in front of us was Bir el-Amri, about twenty feet deep; water slightly brackish, but abundant. The hills on the right, beyond the bend of the wadi, are high. At 10.40 a.m. we halted under a great *sidr* tree, and spent the mid-day there. Wadi Ais proved almost luxuriant with its thorn trees and grass. There was a cool east wind, and the valley was full of white butterflies and the scents of flowers.

We mounted again at 3.40 p.m., and at 3.50 p.m. reached an old wall, which deflects the stream of the wadi to its left bank, and guards an earth terrace, about five feet high, on its south side, against floods. The wall is constructed of chosen unhewn blocks, about a foot square each, and tolerably coursed. It is about a mile and a half long, and fairly solid. Its present greatest height is about four feet, but it must go down some considerable depth below the wadi bed, to withstand the floods. In the terrace, about 400 yards wide, partitioned off by the wall, are remains of fields, house-foundations, and a large sunk water-basin, of correct masonry. At 4.10 p.m. we left Wadi Ais, which turned off northwards on our left towards Murabba. We went up a narrow valley into Jebel Serd. At 4.45 p.m. a valley came in on the right; at 5.5 p.m. we reached an easy watershed and crossed the heads of a valley flowing north to Wadi Ais. At 5.15 p.m. we crossed a second watershed, also easy, and went down a small valley into W. Serum at 5.25 p.m. We camped here for the night, watering from Ghadir Seriam (Moeit Hefna), ten minutes away in the foothills east of us.

Tuesday, 27 March

Started at 5.35 a.m. and crossed El-Mauggad to the north end of J. Serd, and went up and down its first spur by a very steep, sharp path (there is a much better road for guns, ten minutes south of our road, over J. Serd). This took us down into a deep wadi, which we crossed, and thence over a second wadi (Seil el-Howeiti) and a low divide, giving on a side valley, up which we wound to another steep saddle at 7.3 a.m., and a nasty descent into a long rough narrow valley leading down into Wadi Turaa, which enters Hamdh opposite the mouth of W. Tubja. We reached this W. Turaa at 7.45 a.m., and camped at 8.25 a.m. near Bir Fueir. W. Turaa is a plain, bearing north-west, full of trees, and grass, with a sandy surface, much cut up with *seils*. One of these had filled in the well this year, but water-pools exist in plenty in the hills, so that the many tents in the valley have no lack of water. Wadi Turaa is the best way down to Wadi Yambo, and Ras el-Fura (Kheif Husein) is about two days camel from here. The flat-topped straight-sided hills on the north bank of the valley are J. Um Rutba. The valley is Urwa dira.

We started again at 4.20 p.m. and at 5.5 p.m. turned 60° up a valley. At 5.20 p.m. about 120° and at 5.30 p.m. 60° again, up the upper course of W. Turaa, a broad smooth road, for half-an-hour till we lost the way, and wandered about the foot-hills, like Virgil's crippled snake, till 6.40 p.m., just across the watershed of W. Turaa and W. Meseiz. Our guides were at fault in bringing us (to be near some tents) too far north from our first entry into the Turaa plain. The quickest and best road is straight across to Ain Turaa, and up the east branch of the wadi direct to the watershed.

Wednesday, 28 March

Rode at 5.5 a.m. past north end of J. Tareif and down W. Meseiz, which is a steep, loose ramp of shingle and stones, scored deeply by water, unfit for wheeled traffic, into the great plain of el-Jurf, across which W. Meseiz cuts its way east to join W. Gussed, flowing north from J. Agrad. At 6.15 a.m. we were well into el-Jurf, and going due east, with J. Antar, a castellated rock with a split head perched on a cone, most conspicuous about ten miles off to the south. J. Jeddah, a group of needles, lay about six miles off down W. Gussed down beyond Aba el-Hellu. We rode 90° till 7 a.m. and then 140° till 7.40 a.m., and camped under a tree in Wadi Gussed. It is very fertile in a wild way – indeed all the Jurf is. We were camped nearly at the south end of a tongue of hills, which walls off el-Jurf from the Hamdh valley. To the south el-Jurf opens into el-Magrah, up which the railway climbs to a watershed near J. Bueir, and one comes down to join the Hamdh at Abu el-Naam; and our own Wadi Guad, rising a little further west, in the foot-hills of Azard (where is water in *themail*), runs down north to join the Hamdh near Jedahah, after giving the water hole of Abu el-Hella on its passage through the hills. J. Tareif, prolonged by Azrad, forms a blank wall of hill to Bowat. There is no way up it for camels into the valleys beyond, except a difficult pass just south of our camp.

In the afternoon we went up the Dhula of Abu el-Naam, just behind the camp, and examined the railway and the station at 6,000 yards. It has two large basalt and cement two-storeyed buildings, a circular water-tower, and a small house to the west; and about the houses were many bell tents and shelter tents. The perimeter was heavily entrenched, but there were no guns visible, and we only saw about 300 men. A trolley went off north with only one man on it, to the bridge over W. Hamdh, which Dakhilallah had attacked. It was a large bridge, of about twenty arches of white stone, and next to it were some shelters, and on the top of a coal-black mound just north of the bridge, some dozen white tents, with Turkish officers lounging in chairs beside them. At 2 p.m. a train (locomotive reversed), came in from the south. It had four water cisterns (improvised iron tanks on trucks), and four box-wagons, and after watering, went off north. The station of Istabl Antar was clearly visible on the Ras el-Magrah, but Jedhah was behind hills. Returned to camp at sunset, after sending snipers to Istabl and Jedhah to stop night patrolling. The Turks had been very active lately by night, but we succeeded in confining them to stations by the simple means of firing shots in the air near the stations at night. They expected an attack, and therefore concentrated the men in the GHQ and stood to arms in the trenches all night.

Thursday, 29 March
Up at 5.20 a.m. Very cold, with a restless dawn wind blowing down el-Jurf, singing in the great trees round our camp. We spent most of the day admiring Abu el-Naam from the hill-top. The garrison paraded, and we counted them as 390 infantry, and twenty-five goats. No camels or horses, except the two or three near the well, which we captured subsequently. A train came in from the north, and one from the south. That from the south went on and contained baggage and women. The northern trains stayed all day and the night in the

station. At midday we heard from Sherif Shakir, who was coming up with the main body (we were only the reconnaissance), that he would arrive at sunset, and we wandered out across el-Jurf to the last foot-hills of Dhula Abu el-Naam, till we found what seemed to be a good gun-position, about 2,000 yards west of the station. There were no Turkish outposts to be found, except that on the bridge. Behind the station is a steep hill, J. Unseih, about 400 yards distant, and we decided to put 400 men into it, to take the Turks in the rear.

The hills about us were typical of the eastern Hejaz hills. They were of glistening, sunburnt stone, very metallic in ring when struck, and splitting red or green or brown as the case may be. The upper part of the hill is a cap, of an outcrop of base rock, and the lower screes are hard at the foot, where they are packed with a thin soil, but loose and sliding on the slopes. From them sprout occasional thorn bushes, and frequent grasses. The commonest grass sends up a dozen blades from one root, and grows hand- to knee-high, of yellow-green colours. At the head are empty ears, between many feathered arrows of silvery down. With these and a shorter grass, ankle deep, bearing a bottle-brush head of pearl-grey, the hillsides are furred white, and dance gaily in the wind. One cannot call it verdure, but it is excellent pasture, and in the valleys are great tufts of coarse grass, waist-high, bright green in colour till it fades to a burnt yellow, and growing thickly in all water-lined sand or shingle. Between these tufts are thorn trees from eight to forty feet in height, and less frequently *sidr* trees, giving thick shade, and dry sugary fruit. Add some brown tamarisk, broom, a great variety of coarse grass and flowers, and everything that has thorns, and you exhaust the usual vegetation of the Hejaz. Only on steep hillsides is there a little plant, *hemeid*, with fleshy green heart-shaped leaves and a spike of white or red blossom. Its leaves are pleasantly acid, and allay thirst.

Shakir arrived at 5 p.m., but brought only 300 men, two machine-guns, one mountain-gun, and one mountain howitzer. The lack of infantry made the scheme of taking the station in rear impossible, since it would have left the guns without support; so we changed ideas, and decided on an artillery action only. We sent down a dynamite party to the north of the station, to cut rails and telegraph at dawn. I started at 8 p.m. with a company of Ateibah and a machine-gun, to lay a mine and cut the wire between Abu el-Naam and Istabl Antar. Mohammed el-Gadhi guided us very well, and we reached the line at 11.15 p.m., in a place where there was cover for the machine-gun in a group of bushes and a sandy valley bed about four feet deep, 500 yards west of the rails. I laid a mine, and cut the wire, and at 1 a.m. started back for the main body with a few Ageyl, but did not get in till 5 a.m., through various accidents, and was not able to go forward to the artillery position till 6.30 a.m. I found the guns just ready, and we shelled the station till 10 a.m., when Shakir found that the Ateibah infantry had no water, and we retired to W. Gussed without molestation. *Girbis* are mostly unobtainable in the eastern Hejaz, which makes it difficult for an Arab force of more than a dozen men to remain in action for half a day.

The results of the bombardment were to throw the upper storeys of the large stone buildings into the ground-floors, which were reported to contain stores and water-cisterns. We could not demolish the ground-floors. The water-tank (metal) was pierced and knocked out of shape, and three shells exploded in the pumping room and brought down much of the wall. We demolished the well-house, over the well, burned the tents and the wood-pile and obtained a hit on the first wagon of the train in the station. This set it on fire, and the flames spread to the remaining six wagons, which must have contained inflammable stores, since they burned furiously. The locomotive was behind the northern building, and got steam up, and went off (reversed) towards Medina. When it passed over the mine it exploded it, under the front bogies (i.e. too late). It was, however, derailed, and I hoped to see the machine-gun come into action against it, but it turned out that the gunners had left their position to join us in our attack on the station, and so the seven men on the engine were able to 'jack' it on the line again in about half-an-hour (only the front wheels were derailed) and it went off towards Istabl Antar, at foot-pace, clanking horribly.

The north end of the station now surrendered, and about 200 of the garrison of the north end rushed in driblets for the hills (J. Unseila) and took cover there. I examined the prisoners (twenty-four in number, Syrians, of 130th Regt), and also the brake-van of the train. The box-body had been lined with matchboard, at an interval of about four inches, and packed near the floor with cement (loopholed) and above with shingle, but it was burning hotly, and the Turks were too close for me to obtain accurate details.

We fired altogether fifty rounds (shrapnel) from 2,200 and 900 yards and about ten belts of machine-gun ammunition. Deserters reported about thirty dead (I saw nine only) and forty-two wounded. We captured the pedigree mare of Ali Nasir (the Egyptian 'Bab-Arab' in Medina) and a couple of camels from the well-house, and destroyed many rails. Our casualties were one man wounded. Had there been enough Arab infantry to occupy J. Unseila, which commanded the trenches at 400 yards (plunging fire), I think we could have taken the entire garrison. The Ateibah were not asked to do very much, and I do not think would have done it if asked. The Juheinah and the gunners behaved very well, and I think that the attack – as an experiment – justified itself. It had the effect, in the next three days, of persuading the Turks to evacuate every outpost and blockhouse on the line, and concentrate the garrison in the various railway stations. This action facilitated the work of the dynamite parties.

Friday, 30 March
We marched back to el-Jurf, and camped in the middle of it from 12.30 p.m. till 3 p.m. We then rode up the Wadi Meseiz (gradually turning west and south) till the watershed at 5.15 p.m., and at 5.30 p.m. had crossed the divide into W. Turaa, and rode down it till 6.30 p.m., when we camped at Ain Turaa, just where the eastern Wadi Turaa enters the great plain of Bir Fueis.

The march (like all Shakir's marches) was very fast. The water of the W. Ain is very good, and fairly plentiful.

Saturday, 31 March

Left el-Ain at 5.45 a.m.; rode across the plain, up the side of the wadi and over an easy pass (to the right) into Seil el-Howeita. From this we took the easy southern road into el-Muaggad, and stopped from 8.30 a.m. till 3.45 p.m. in Wadi Serum. We then marched to Bir el-Amri at 5.45 p.m. and camped there.

Sunday, 1 April

Rode from Birl el-Amri to camp at Abu Markha from 6 a.m. to 8.30 a.m.
   Abu Markha to Abu el-Naam: 14 hours, 20 minutes.
   Abu el-Naam to Abu Markha: 13 hours, 15 minutes.

II. Abu Markha to Madahrij

After returning from Abu el-Naam with Sherif Shakir, I stopped a short while with Sidi Abdullah, and on Monday, 2 April, marched at 2.20 a.m. for the railway to the north of Hadiyah. I took with me Dakhilallah el-Gadhi with 40 Juheinah, and had as well Sultan el-Abbud (Ateibah), Sherif Abdullah, and Sherif Agab (two sons of Hamza el-Feir), and Mohammed el-Gadhi. A machine-gun with six men and seven infantrymen (Syrians) came along also, as my hope was to derail a train with a Garland mine, and then attack it from a previously prepared machine-gun position. Sherif Shakir rode the first half-hour with us.

We marched down Wadi Ais by the same road as that to Abu el-Naam to the village site at 6.20 p.m. Instead of leaving Wadi Ais at this point, we turned north with the valley, and camped at 7 p.m. opposite Magreh el-Semn, under hills on the left bank of the wadi.

Tuesday, 3 April

Marched at 5.20 a.m. up the wadi at 50° till 5.35 a.m., and then swung round towards 20° in a curve till 6 a.m., aiming direct at J. Shemail, a great mass, which deflects the valley westward. At 5.40 a.m. we were opposite the mouth of W. Serum, and at 5.55 a.m. passed Bir Bedair on our left. At 6 a.m. we were opposite the point of J. Shemail, and the wadi, which had been clear and broad and shingly, narrowed down. At 6.30 a.m. Wadi Gharid came in on the left (it is the quickest way to Abu Markha, but steep), and at 6.40 a.m. we were opposite Bir Bedia, in the mouth of Seil Bedia on the left of our road. Seil Bedia rises near Seil Osman. The wadi now widened out and became full of large trees, and more green than any wadi I had seen in the Hejaz. It has come down in flood twice this year, and affords splendid pasturage. We were now going about 40° and at 7.15 a.m. reached Bir el-Murabba, in a broad part of Wadi Ais, where it became a small and very beautiful plain. We then turned 60° and marched down the wadi till 7.45 a.m., when we halted opposite the mouth of Seil el-Howeiti (from J. Serd). At 1.15 p.m. we marched again, and at 1.45 p.m. reached Ribiaan, the last well in Wadi Ais. The well is lined with a rough stone steyning, and is about ten feet in diameter and fifteen feet deep; water very slightly brackish. Wadi Ais at this point leaves the hills, and enters a great open plain, studded with low mounds. This plain is the common bed (or united beds) of, amongst others, Wadi Ais, Wadi Hamdh, W. Tubja, W. Turar, and W. Jizal (Gizal or Qizal, since the ق is pronounced ج by the Juheimah and eastern Billi). In the north the plain is bounded by J. Gussa, on the Billi bank of the Hamdh. On the west, to Wadi Ais, by J. Jasim (Kasim, Qasim or Gasim to taste; it is a ق), and south of Wadi Ais by J. Um Reitba, continued in J. Tareif and J. Ajrad. On the east it is bounded by J. Nahar, the east bank of W. Jizal, and then by el-Mreikat, J. Jindal, and J. Unseih. On the south it runs down into el-Jurf and el-Magrah, and J. Antar is clearly visible from the mouth of Wadi Ais, forming the southern boundary of the plain, miles away towards Medina.

We left the direct road a little, when we mounted at 2.10 p.m. and marched a little way north-east. At 2.40 p.m. we left Wadi Ais and crossed a low bank into el-Fershah, a parallel wadi, in which were many tents of Harb and Anazeh, come by permission into the Juheinah *dira* for pasture. We camped near them (they refused us hospitality) at 3.20 p.m.

Wednesday, 4 April
Rode at 5.30 a.m. and at 6.15 a.m. crossed the level bed of Wadi Turaa, and Wadi Hamdh at 6.45 a.m. The Hamdh was as full of *aslam* wood as at Abu Zereibat and had the same hummocky bed, with sandy blisters over it – but it was only about 200 yards wide, and shallow. We halted at 8 a.m. in W. Tubja, which was a sort of wilderness garden, with a profusion of grass and shrubs in which the camels rejoiced. The weather was very hot, with a burning sun that made the sandy ground impossible for me to walk on bare-foot. The Arabs have soles like asbestos, and made little complaint, except of the warmth of the air. There had been thunder all yesterday, and half-a-dozen showers of rain last night and today. J. Serd and J. Kasim were wrapped in shafts and sheets of a dark blue and yellow vapour that seemed motionless and solid. We marched across W. Tubja again at 1.20 p.m. About 1.40 p.m. we noticed that part of the yellow cloud from J. Serd was approaching us, against the wind, raising scores of dust-devils before its feet. It also produced two dust-spouts, tight and symmetrical – stationary columns like chimneys – one to the right and one to the left of its advance.

When it got nearer, the wind, which had been scorching us from the north-east, changed suddenly, and became bitterly cold and damp, from the south-west. It increased greatly in violence, and at the same time the sunlight disappeared and the air became thick and ochre-yellow. About three minutes later the advancing brown wall (I think it was about 1,500 feet high) struck us, and proved to be a blanket of dust, and large grains of sand, twisting and turning most violently with itself, and at the same time advancing east at about forty miles an hour. The internal whirling winds had the most bizarre effect. They tore our cloaks from us, turned our camels sometimes right round, and sometimes drew them together in a vortex, and large bushes, tufts of grass, and small trees were torn up clean by the roots, in a dense cloud of the soil about them, and were driven against us, or dashed over our heads, with sometimes dangerous force. We were never blinded – it was always possible to see seven or eight feet each side – but it was risky to look out, since one never knew if one would meet a flying tree, or a rush of pebbles, or a column of dust.

This *habub* lasted for eighteen minutes, and then ceased nearly as suddenly as it had come, and while we and our clothes and camels were all smothered in dust and yellow from head to foot, down burst torrents of rain, and muddied us to the skin. The wind swung round to the north, and the rain drove before it through our cloaks, and chilled us through and through. At 3 p.m. we had crossed the plain and entered the bare valley of W. Dhaiji, which cuts through J. Jindal at its southern end, from the railway to the Hamdh. It is fairly broad at first, sandy, with precipitous rock walls. We rode up it till 4 p.m. and left our camels in a side valley, and climbed a hill to see the line. The hill was of naked rock, and with the wet and the numbing cold the Ateibah servant of Sultan el-Abbud lost his nerve, pitched over a cliff, and smashed his skull to pieces. It was our only casualty on the trip.

When we got to the hill-top it was too thick weather to see the railway, so I returned to the camels, and shivered by them for an hour or two. We were stumbled upon by a mounted man, with whom we exchanged ineffectual shots, and were annoyed by this, as surprise was essential, and we could hear the bugles of Madahrij sounding recall and supper in the station, which was also an irritation. However, at 9 p.m. the explosives came up, with the rest of the party, and I started out with Sultan, Dakhilallah and Mohammed el-Gadhi for the line.

We had some delay in finding a machine-gun position, for the railway runs everywhere near the eastern hills of the valley, and the valley is about 3,000 yards broad. However, eventually, we found a place opposite kilometre 1121, and I laid a mine (trigger central, with rail-cutting charges 15 yards north and south of it respectively) with some difficulty owing to the rain, at 12 p.m. It took till 1.45 a.m. to cover up the traces of the digging, and we left the whole bank, and the sandy plain each side, as covered with huge footmarks as though a school of elephants had danced on it, and made tracks that a blind man could have felt. I wiped out most of those on the embankment itself, however, by walking up and down in shoes over it. Such prints are indistinguishable from the daily footmarks of the patrol inspecting the line.

We got back to the new position at 2.30 a.m. (still raining and blowing and very cold) and sat about on stones till dawn, when the camels and machine-gun came up. Dakhilallah, who had been guide and leader all night, now sent out patrols and sentries and outposts in all directions, and went on a hill-top himself with glasses to watch the line. The sun fortunately came out, so we were able to get dry and warm, and by midday were again gasping in the heat. A cotton shirt is a handy garment, but not adaptable to such sudden changes of temperature.

Thursday, 5 April
At 6 a.m. a trolly with four men and a sergeant as a passenger came from Hadiyah (Haraimil) to Madahrij, passing over the mine without stopping. A working party of sixty men came out of Madahrij, and began to replace five telegraph poles blown down near the station the day before by the *habub*. At 7.30 a.m. a patrol of eleven men marched south along the line, two inspecting each rail minutely, one walking along the bank in charge, and then at fifty yards interval right and left of the line, looking for tracks. At kilometre 1121 they found abundance of the latter, and concentrated on the permanent way, and wandered up and down it, and scratched the ballast, and thought for a prolonged period. They then went on to near J. Sueij (Sueij Sueik, or Sueiq, to taste), and exchanged greetings with the Hadiyah patrol. At 8.30 a.m. a train of nine trucks, packed with women, children and household effects came up from Hadiyah, and ran over the mine without exploding it, rather to our relief, since they were not quite the prize we had been hoping for.

The Juheinah were greatly excited when the train came along, and all rushed up to Dakhilallah's lookout, where we were, to see it. Our stone *zariba* had been made for five only, so that the hill-top became suddenly and visibly populous. This was too much for the nerves of Madahrij, which called in its working party, and opened a brisk rifle fire on us, at about 5,000 yards. Hadiyah (or rather its outpost on a hill-top) was encouraged by this to take a share. As they were about 1,200 yards off, they retained their fire, but played selections on the bugle from 8.30 a.m till 4 p.m.

This disclosure of ourselves put us in rather an unfortunate position. The Juheinah and myself were on camels, and therefore pretty safe, but the machine-gun was a sledge-maxim (German) and very heavy. It was on a mule, and the mules could only walk. Our position was between Madahrij (200 men) and Hadiyah (1,100 men), with Hadiyah in Wadi Tubja, behind our backs. I was afraid of their trying to cut us off in the rear, and after consulting Dakhilallah we rode past Madahrij to the head of W. Um Reikham, which runs into Tubja just north of J. Jindal, and sent the mules with an escort of fifteen Juheinah back to Wadi Ais. Had the Turks attacked us, the few Juheinah with me would not have been enough to cover the retreat of the gun: and the gunners were Meccan tailors, inexpert at handling it.

Dakhilallah, Sultan Mohammed and myself then rode back to the head of Wadi Dhaije, and camped at 9.40 a.m. under some good shady trees, from which we could see the line. This appeared to annoy the Turks, who shot and trumpeted at us incessantly, till about 4.30 p.m. No trains passed during this time – I fancy our presence held up the traffic, for a lone engine came down from the north to Madahrij, and there was also heavy smoke from Hadiyah station.

At 4.30 p.m. the Turkish noise stopped, and we got on our camels at 5 p.m. and rode out slowly across the plain towards the line. Madahrij revived in a paroxysm of rifle fire (4,000 yards, no damage) and all the trumpets of Hadiyah began again. Dakhilallah was most pleased. We went straight to kilometre 1121, and made the camels kneel beside the line, while Dakhilallah (whose strong piety has a vein of humour) called the *idhan*, and led the sunset prayer between the rails. As soon as it got dark the Turks became quiet, and I dug up the mine (a most unpleasant proceeding: laying a Garland mine is shaky work, but scrabbling along a line for 100 yards in the ballast looking for a trigger that is connected with two powerful charges must be a quite uninsurable occupation), and I found it had sunk a sixteenth of an inch, probably owing to the damp ground. We replaced it, and then fired a number of charges along the rails between us and Madahrij with great effect. We also cut up a good deal of telegraph wire and a number of poles, and at 7.30 p.m. rode off down W. Dhaije again. At 9 p.m. we reached the Tubja-Hamdh plain, and galloped across it furiously, passing Wadi Hamdh, W. Turaa, W. Abu Marra, and reaching El-Fershah and the machine-gun camp at 12.15 a.m.

Friday, 6 April

Started at 6 a.m., reached Rubiaan at 7 a.m., and left it at 7.15 a.m. Wadi Ais had been down in flood since we left, and the surface was all shining with white slime and pools of soft grey water. The camels slipped over this most amusingly, and most of the party went down. Dakhilallah therefore drew us up a mouth of Seil Howeiti, and across its delta, and over a little pass into the eastern bay of the plain of Murebba in Wadi Ais. We crossed this, passed Seil Badia, and halted at 9.15 a.m. in the mouth of W. Gharid. We mounted again at 2.45 p.m. and rode slowly (everything was stiff and tired) to the bend of Wadi Ais by the ruins at 4.45 p.m., where we camped for the night. Our two messengers who had been left in Dhaije came in late, and reported that the mine (which we had heard explode very vigorously at 7.30 a.m. this morning) had gone off north and south of a locomotive with rails and about 300 soldiers, arriving from Hadiyah to repair our damage. The quantity of Turks frightened our men away, so I cannot say if any inconvenience was caused the train; but the break in the line was not repaired for five days, which looks as though something had delayed the enemy.

Saturday, 7 April

We started at 1 a.m. and slept the rest of the night in Marraha from 2.30 a.m. till 6 a.m. Then rode and reached Abu Markha at 8 a.m.

The results of this trip were to show me the rare value of Dakhilallah and his son. Their humour makes railway-breaking a pleasure to them; their authority keeps the Juheinah in better order than ever I have seen; and old Dakhilallah has grown grey in successful *ghazzus*, and is as careful and astute as any raider could be.

It also showed that Garland mines, properly laid, are impossible for the Turks to detect. Eleven men searched for my mine for twenty minutes. Also that the Turkish garrisons suffer badly from nerves; and that a machine-gun party to deal with stranded locomotives may require great mobility in retreat or advance, and should be, if possible, mounted on the same kind of animal as the tribal escort.

XX. Notes on Hejaz Affairs
13 May 1917

Antecedents of the Hejaz Revolt

Talaat, in 1913, showed great anxiety about the situation in the Hejaz. Its subjugation and the imposition of military service there had been a favourite project. Mahmud Shevket and the Turkish Ministry generally looked upon the situation as disquieting, on account of the great hold Husein Pasha was getting on the people. This was the real reason of Wahib's appointment, and his withdrawal was a personal triumph for Feisal, who secured from Talaat a promise that Wahib would be tried by court-martial for infringing the privileges of the Hejaz.

Sherif Abdullah was regarded as the probable cause of trouble in the Hejaz, and to keep him out of it he was offered first the Wakf Ministry and then the Vilayet of Yemen. He saw the idea, and refused the appointments. Abdullah has a low opinion of Talaat's judgement, and regards him as brutal and ignorant.

The previous plan of Sherif Abdullah to secure the independence of Hejaz (as a preliminary to the formation of an Arab State) was to lay sudden hands on the pilgrims at Mecca during the great feast. He calculated that the foreign governments concerned (England, France, Italy, and Holland) would bring pressure on the Porte to secure their release. When the Porte's efforts had failed, these governments would have had to approach the Sherif direct, and would have found him anxious to do all in his power to meet their wishes, in exchange for a promise of immunity from Turkey in the future. This action had been fixed (provisionally) for 1915, but was quashed by the war.

Hejaz Tribes

Abdullah gave the eastern Ateibah (he has little control over them, and they would probably not have come to Hejaz to fight for him, had he asked them) orders to help Ibn Saud against Ibn Rashid. It was partly on account of this

that Ibn Rashid declared war on the Sherif. Abdullah doesn't really care at
all if they help Ibn Saud or not; but the order was an assumption of control
over all the Ateibah (which Abdullah pretends to) in a form to which Ibn
Saud could hardly object with grace.

The Turks gave decorations to Aida, Towala, and Fagir (Fuqara) Sheikhs.
The recipients decided to show their new orders to Sidi Abdullah, but, as
they were crossing the line near Toweria, they ran into a Turkish patrol, and
the camel carrying their personal baggage was killed and had to be abandoned. The Turks have thus received back their insignia.

The Ateibah believe that Christians wear hats so that the projecting brims
may intervene between their eyes and the uncongenial sight of God.

Dakhilallah el-Gadhi, who has had good means of judging, regards the
Billi as less than half the strength of the Juheinah, and a little less than the
tribes under Ferhan el-Aida. Ferhan (who is with Abdullah) is the Motlog
Allayda, Doughty's old host. Dakhilallah says that Billi and Huweitat are
much fiercer fighters than Wuld Ali or Ateibah. Indeed, I notice a contempt
for the Ateibah among the Juheinah, and think that there is a good deal of
justification for the feeling.

XXI. Wejh to Wadi Ais and Back
23 May 1917

I. Wejh to Wadi Ais viâ the Darb el-Gara

I left Wejh at 9 p.m. on 10 March, with four Ageyl and four Rifaa Juheinah,
for Sidi Abdullah's camp. We went out along the Khauthla road as far as J.
Jidra (el-Nebadein; but the northern hill of the two), at 12.30 a.m. We then
bore off right from the Khauthla road, across a sanded area of rough stones.
This lasted only till 12.50 a.m., when we entered a wadi, crossed it, and
passed over others and their tributaries till 1.15 a.m., when we stopped in
Seil Arja, which runs down to Munaibura. The going for the last hour was
rough.

11 March
Started at 6 a.m. up a tributary of Seil Arja, and continued in it till 6.30 a.m.,
when we reached the head of the valley and entered a plain, about a mile
wide. At 6.45 a.m. the road forked and we went right downhill, at 140°, into
Seil Mismah, at 7.10 a.m. Mismah runs into Arja and Munaibura. We
crossed it and rode up a side-valley (rough in parts) to a watershed at 7.40
a.m., and a steep descent of a few minutes into a great sand and gravel plain.
Across this we went at 110° till 8.15 a.m., when we crossed Wadi el-Murra,
which runs into the Sebakha at Kurna; J. Murra was about three miles away
to the north. At 10.10 a.m. we reached Wadi Abu Ajaj, running from 20° to
200°; it is not one bed, but a whole system of seils, all shallow and bushy,
with soft sandy water-courses winding about them. About three miles away

on the right lay J. Ajwi, overlooking Mersa Zaam. Ajwi is a very unmistakable square-sided flat-topped coral reef. We stopped at 10.45 a.m. in Wadi
Abu Ajaj and started again at 12.45 p.m. At 1.30 p.m. I was abreast of J.
Tibgila, about five miles off, and at 1.50 p.m. and 2.5 p.m. crossed the
branches of Wadi Ghorban, which passes just south of Tibgila. The going
across the plain was at first soft, and later rather more solid, but with very
soft sandy valleys, which would be bad for cars. The guide now took us too
far east, and the path entered the lower spurs of J. Raal, so that we did not
enter the Hamdh valley till 4 p.m. We bore across this to the *ghadir* at Abu
Zereibat, which we reached at 6 p.m. It was little, if any, smaller than it had
been in January last.

12 March
Started at 3.45 a.m. and proceeded to lose the road in the dark. At 4.30 a.m.
we entered low rough hills, J. Agumma, till 5.20 a.m., when we turned to
the right up Seil Aguna at 135°. At 5.30 a.m. reached the watershed, which
was easy, and rode down a short valley on luxuriant colocynth into el-Khubt,
at 6.10 a.m. Colocynth makes the best timber when crushed and dried. Its
juice is rubbed on the feet to produce a purgative effect, which is said to be
quite distinct, even when the drug is applied in this very diluted manner.
Horses which will eat its stalks and leaves can go without water for a considerable time.

El-Khubt is a great plain, draining at its extremity into Wadi Hamdh near
Abu Zereibat. A road goes up it to Um Lejj. We crossed it diagonally, aiming
for el-Sukhur (wrongly called J. Arban on the map). At 7.15 a.m. we reached
the east bank of el-Khubt, and turned right, up a side-valley, for ten minutes,
on to the plain (Magrah) of el-Darraj, a scrub-covered area leading right up
to the feet of el-Sukhur. We halted at 7.40 a.m. in the middle of a rain shower,
which lasted intermittently from 6 till 8.30 a.m. In el-Darraj were some half-
dozen tents of Waish Billi, with sheep, goats, horses and camels. There has
been no rain to speak of in the Bluwiya this year, and plenty in the Juheiniya,
and, therefore, many of the Billi have come over the border peaceably to
pasture. These tents were watering from Heiran.

We left el-Darraj halt at 10 a.m. and moved across to the feet of the
Sukhur. We wound up a valley till we were between them and the isolated
Sakhara south-west of them, and then scrambled for fifteen minutes up rock
shelves and along faults over a knife ridge and down a stony bed, past a huge
boulder all hammered over with tribal marks, into the basin of Wadi Heiran.
The Sukhur are huge striated masses of a reddish-coloured volcanic rock,
grey on the surface; the Sakhara is like a brown water-melon standing on
end: on its south and east faces it is absolutely smooth, and dome-headed,
polished till it shines, with fine cracks running up and across it, like seams.
The height above the plain must be about 700 feet.

At 11.5 a.m. we were over this pass and in a narrow valley, between
granite outcrops. This led into another valley, and so to another, till we

entered Wadi Herian (40° to 200°, its course) at noon. The well lay some way on our right, down the valley. We crossed the valley, rode up a tributary, and then till 12.45 p.m. went up and down over granite shards piled up in tiny 50-foot mounds all round us in wild confusion. There was no road and we kept no direction, but wandered where we could. Wadis ran in and out everywhere.

At 12.45 p.m. we descended sharply into Seil Dhrufi, a wooded valley 100 yards wide, along which we went at 120°. At 1.30 p.m. we got to the head of our branch of the valley, and ascended a narrow and difficult hill-path, with broken steps of rock, difficult for camels, round a shoulder of Jebel Dhrufi (it is a range) to a saddle from which a steep but short descent led into and across a valley sweeping down from north-east towards the sea. The ground again became a confusion of small mounds and valleys till a new watershed was reached at 1.40 p.m. This was easy and led us to a big valley running south; we bent on the left at right angles close by the rock-wall down which we had come. We turned up this gorge, which grew very narrow, and the path soon left the bed and began to climb the side of the hill to the north. The ascent was very steep, unfit for laden camels, owing to the rough surface and the narrowness of the path, between very sharp slopes above and below. At 2.20 p.m. we reached the watershed and descended a sandy valley into W. Hanbal, a large well-wooded tributary of W. Heiran. We stopped for twenty minutes to gather for the camels the luxuriant grass in a little sandy bay of the hills and then crossed the wadi and marched up a tributary of its east bank, W. Kitan. This is a stony valley with a good hard surface (no rocks), about 300 yards wide from hill to hill, and well wooded with thorn trees. We marched up till 4.15 p.m. and then halted; the valley had drawn in a little in the last half-hour. The hills on the south were small; but to the north is a very large hill, J. Jidwa, about six miles long and perhaps three miles distant, flanking the valley with a steep and high hog's back, running nearly north and south.

13 March

Started at 3.30 a.m. and reached the head of W. Kitan in a few minutes and went over a narrow pass between rock masses (steep but not difficult; too narrow for wheels) into Seil Jidha, which runs into W. Amk. It has sharp hills each side. At 4.30 a.m. we diverged to the right up a gorge running south. This was from eight to ten feet wide between its cliffs, but the bed of the torrent was all encumbered with fallen stones and trees, so that the passage was difficult. At 4.50 a.m. we reached its head and found a gentle valley running away south. At 4.50 a.m., when the wadi turned west about a mile above Bir Reimi, which is the only *themail* in the wadi bed. The water smelt one foul smell, and tasted equally unpleasantly but quite differently. We had high hills on the east and smaller hills to the west. We started again at 8.30 a.m., leaving Wadi Reimi by a side-wadi to the south, which ascended to a gentle watershed, from which we had a fine view down the broad and green

Wadi Amk, which passes through Khuff to the sea. This branch of it runs 150° and is bounded by considerable hills. At 9.10 a.m. the valley turned more to the east, and at 9.20 a.m. received a large feeder (on the main stream) from the north, and bore off 180°. We cut across the confluence, at 70°, making for the centre of a great hill in front of us. At 9.30 a.m. we found a side-valley and at 9.40 a.m. went over a patch of soft white sand in its bed. At 10.15 a.m. we entered Wadi Dhuhub el-Amk, coming from the north to join W. Amk. We went up a side valley from it, with high hills on the right about a quarter of a mile off, and then climbed a sandy valley between piles of the curiously warped grey granite, looking like cold toffee, that one finds frequently in the Hejaz. This valley led us to the foot of one of these great stone piles, up which runs a natural ramp and staircase, badly broken, twisting and difficult for camels, but short. This brought us at 10.30 a.m. back into W. Dhuhub again, above its northern bend. We followed the valley till 11.38 a.m. (its head). It runs about 120°, and has low hills on the right, and high hills on the left of the road, and is full of quite large trees; there are water-pools in the gorges about it. There were a number of Merawin tents here and there, with plentiful sheep and goats. At 11.15 a.m. the valley narrowed and began (from being excellent smooth shingle) to get stony. At 11.25 a.m. it became a mere ravine, on the north bank of which an execrable track led us up to the watershed between W. Dhuhub el-Amk and W. Marrakh. The view from the crest was beautiful, but the descent dangerous. We reached the foot at 11.45 a.m., and found ourselves in an absolutely straight valley, running steeply downhill at 130° towards a depression ahead, between two regular walls of moderate hills. At 12.25 p.m. a large side-valley entered on the right, showing, through its break in the hills, a parallel range a couple of miles away and broken ground behind. There was a corresponding (but small) break on the left. The hill walls then opened out in a double sweep like an amphitheatre of grey stone with veins of dark red brown granite running over them in up-and-down lines, looking like cockscombs, or a rustic scenic railway; and in front came down a steep black wall of harrah, with a low hill of brown granite in the middle of the line. We halted at 1.10 p.m. under the trees, shortly after passing a pile-circle of uncut stones about forty feet in diameter, with a central cairn, and some small square piles round about it, outside the circle. These were the first stone remains I had noted (bar simple cairns) on the way from Wejh, but from now onwards to the mouth of Wadi Ais they were to grow increasingly frequent. In parts of the harrah and its valleys are distinct remains of old villages and rough terrace constructions for cultivation. The Juheinah ascribe all these to the Beni Hillal, and never put up even a cairn of more than three or four stones themselves. Their only stone constructions are little square box-houses of the type they call 'nawamis' in parts of Sinai. These little places are made to shelter the young lambs and kids, and are put up, as needed, by the shepherd boys.

We have now got into a much more fertile area than the Tihamah or the hills near Wejh. My camel-men got milk to-day in the Merawi tents – the first milk they had tasted for two years – and this plain of fine quartz gravel and coarse sand is all studded over with a stubbly grass, in tufts sixteen inches high, of a slate green colour, white at the tips. The heat is very great, but there is a faint cool wind, which, however, has little effect on the plague of flies.

I have with me a Syrian, a Moroccan, a Merawi, four Rifaa, and three men from Aneizah, Rass, and Zilfi respectively. The last describes himself as an eyewitness of Shakespear's death. He says he was with Ibn Saud's artillery, looking through his field glasses and very conspicuous, since he was wearing full British uniform and a sun-helmet over all. He was therefore easily picked out, and was shot at long range. His helmet was taken into Medina, and publicly exhibited as proof to all Moslems that Ibn Saud was a traitor to Islam, and had permitted Christians into his country. There were great demonstrations in Medina, and the hat is still displayed in the Serai, with an inscription pointing its moral.

We started again at 2.35 p.m. (120°) across Wadi Marrakh, which runs out to westward to the Makassar just south of Harrat Gelib, and at 3 p.m. entered Harrat Gara. It fills a wadi, running north, and falls down in steps or waves to Wadi Marukh, where it is cut short. We had mounted its first terrace by 3.25 p.m., and found a small sand and grass plain in the lava of the second step. We then turned east, up Wadi Gara, which is one of the main sources of the lava flow. The lava was in a great rope, down the centre of the valley, whose water had cut for itself a deep bed in the granite each side. At 4 p.m. a stream of lava came in from the south, and we crossed it, and the edge of the main stream, and other side streams, very slowly and painfully till 4.50 p.m. The north bank of the wadi was a straight line of hills. At 4.50 p.m. we passed a first crater, of fine sifted black ash and earth, just south of the road, and at 5.10 p.m. halted at the tent of Sheikh Fahad el-Hamshah, who produced bowl after bowl of milk, till 10 p.m, and then rice and a dismembered sheep. Camels and men all very tired, for the going over the harrah is vile. Harrah looks like scrambled eggs that have gone very wrong, and affords the worst going imaginable for man or beast.

14 *March*

Started at 5.40 a.m., and at 6.25 turned 120° with the valley, and then sharply to the left up the slope between a group of cones of black ash from a huge crater to the south. At 7.10 a.m. reached the watershed (Ras Gara) and went down the eastern slope of the valley, passing the remains of what was perhaps a fort, of rough uncut stones, rectangular, about 40 feet wide and 100 feet long. Walls about three feet thick, and now not more than four feet high. Descent was very bad; at 8 a.m. left the main valley and stopped at 8.20 a.m. at the end of the harrah, up a side-valley, in the tents of Sheikh Mualeh, a relative of Fahad. We halted till 9.35 a.m., and then marched 120° till 10 a.m. when we reached the head of the valley, across remains of old settlement and fields. At 10.10 a.m. we had crossed a small spur into a tiny valley between hills, which led us at once to a kind of chimney, up which the camels had to climb till 10.25 a.m. It was dangerous riding up, and most of us walked. From the top there was an easy run down Wadi Shweita till 11.20 a.m., when it ran into Wadi Murramiya, one of the most important tributaries from the Juheiniya into Wadi Hamdh. The wadi is filled all across the middle with bristling harrah, but a clear path exists each side. We marched along the west edge till 11.50 a.m., when we struck round a bay of lava, and camped under a tree in a grassy dell. In the hollows and sandy places of the harrah you find wonderful vegetation, which affords the best grazing in the country. Flowers grow freely, and the grass is really green and juicy. The green looks the more wonderful in comparison with the blue-black naked crusts and twists of jagged rock all around. Harrah seems to be either loose piles of fist- or head-sized stones, rubbed together and rounded, possible for camels; or solid, almost crystallised, fronds of rock, which are impossible to cross.

We mounted again at 2.15 p.m. and crossed the remaining harrah in a few minutes to a flat plain, containing stone circles and cairns. At 2.40 p.m. this came to its end, and we turned 125° up an easy pass. At 3 p.m. reached the watershed (broad and flat) and entered Wadi Cheft, which is half-a-mile wide, straight, overgrown with brushwood and lined with hills. At its lower end (3.45 p.m.) was a field about a quarter of a mile square, ploughed two years ago. This was the first field I had seen in the Juheiniya, though many others are reported. The field ended in a harrah which we crossed – the worst road yet experienced on the march. We have had many bad roads, but this is awful. The path zig-zagged across the harrah, which is very deep and piled up and broken. At 4.30 p.m. we reached the southern side (it was going north) and climbed a low watershed into a smooth valley, which turned down towards W. Murramiya, at 4.40 p.m. We climbed a feeder for a few minutes, and then rode down into W. Murramiya. Its central harrah was easy to cross, and took five minutes only, and we then climbed up its further bank – it is here a plain about two miles wide, covered with large trees (W. Ghadirat Murramiya) till near the eastern hill border. Along this we marched, by a beautiful road, till dark. We could see the lava a mile and a half to our right, and behind it a break in the hills and high ranges in the distance. At 6 p.m. it got dark and a hill rose up in the centre of the valley. About 6.30 p.m. we crossed an imperceptible watershed, and rode down W. Tleib, till we stopped at 7 p.m.

15 March
Rode at 5.30 a.m. down the valley, which became more and more green as it got lower. The hills each side were low at first, but then J. Elif on the right, and later J. Keshra on the left, raised the level. At 8 a.m. we passed a conical hill in the valley, below Keshra, and at 8.30 a.m. went over a low watershed into a parallel valley; at 9.20 a.m. this opened into W. Ais at Abu Markha, where the valley is about a mile wide, more thickly wooded than most Hejaz

valleys, and with a great 30-foot deep water hole to an underground stream in its side. Wadi Ais is here sharply limited by hills on its south side, but is open on its north, with all the Tleib system of valleys running down into it. I found Sidi Abdullah at Abu Markha, just dismounting from his camel, after his march here from Bir el-Amri.

Time taken from Wejh to Wadi Ais: 47 hours.

Road was a by-road, impossible for any but pack-animals and not for regular or extended use by them.

Average speed of camels about three miles per hour.

II. Abu Markha to Wejh

When Sidi Abdullah had made arrangements for a nightly cutting of the railway, I decided that I might return to Wejh. I started therefore at 6 a.m., with three Ageyl, and Mohammed el-Gadhi, with about a dozen of his followers. Sherif Shakir put us on our way for the first half-hour.

At 7 a.m. we reached the low watershed into W. Tleib, which we had crossed on the journey down to Wadi Ais. We marched across Wadi Tleib, and up a steep side-valley to the north of Jebel Keshra. At 8.55 a.m. we reached the head of this, and went down an easy slope into W. Saura, turning a little right out of our road to some tents at 9.20 a.m., where we halted. They fed us very hospitably, and at 12.50 p.m. we rode across Wadi Saura, which comes from the east, and up a northern branch of it to the common origin of W. Osman and Wadi Bedia, on the eastern slope of J. Riam, at 2.5 p.m. On the western slope of Riam is the common source of W. Tleib and W. Murramiya. We rode down W. Osman (which is fit for gunwheels, except for about 150 yards at its head, where rock cutting would be necessary), twisting and turning with it, till 5 p.m., when, at a right-angled turn, we saw on our left Magrah el-Ithrara, whose western half drains into Murramiya. We halted at 6.15 p.m. in the mouth of W. Geraia.

Rode at 5.5 a.m. and at once Wadi Osman widened out. We rode across it to the tents of Dakhilallah at 5.55 a.m. We had to stop there till 1.35 p.m. while they prepared saffron-rice and a lamb. We then rode up a side-valley, and down into Osman again at 2.15 p.m. We followed it down (it was not so zigzag in its course as it had been yesterday) till 4 p.m., when we turned abruptly to the right, and found ourselves in Wadi Hamdh, which here flows in a narrow rock-walled valley, about 200 yards wide. The valley is bare at the edges, of hard damp sand. In the middle it is packed with aslam wood, the ground being leprous, and of a white salty colour, with soft bulging patches where bushes grow or grew. The water-beds are cut in a clean light clayey soil from one to eight feet deep, and in the central one was a *ghadir* (brought by W. Osman) about two feet deep, 250 feet long, and twelve feet broad. The water was sweet and good. Half-a-mile above the *ghadir*, Wadi Hamdh ran into Jebel Muraishida, and turned abruptly north to get round it.

Faqeir is said to be about seven miles up. From Ghadir Osman we rode at

6.30 p.m. along Hamdh, and at 7.15 p.m. were opposite the break where the road from Wadi Osman to Aqila ('Ugla) reaches the Hamdh. Our course now 280°. At 7.30 p.m. we turned 300°, and at 8.20 p.m. diverged from the bed of Hamdh to the left, to sleep. Wadi Hamdh is clearly distinguished from any other Hejaz wadi (except W. Yambo) that I have seen, by the damp chill that strikes up from its valley. This is of course most obvious at night, when the mist rises, and everything glistens with damp; but even in daytime Wadi Hamdh feels raw and cold and unnatural.

Started at 5.20 a.m. along Wadi Hamdh. At 6.15 a.m. Wadi Murramiya came in on the left; it forms by far the best road from Hamdh to Ais, and from Wejh to Sidi Abdullah's camp offers the quickest and smoothest road. We rode down it, into the brushwood of W. Hamdh, where we found large pools of rainwater, some fresh, others gone very green and stale. We then crossed the valley, left Wadi Dura on our right (the confluence of Dura and Murramiya makes the plain of Aqila, whose brackish well is the only permanent supply in the district till Faqeir is reached) and rode past Bir Aqila (on the left, in the Hamdh valley) over a low watershed, to the landing ground at Um Jarad at 7.20 a.m. From this point Major Ross's map is available. It is admirable. I rode till W. Methar at 10.15 a.m., camped till 3 p.m., and then rode slowly (one of us fell off his camel when racing and broke his arm and had to be left behind) till 6.20 p.m., when we halted, with a narrow gorge to the south in which are rock-pools of water.

Started at 5 a.m. Halted at 6 a.m. in Wadi Melha, north of the road, which contains good water-pools. Rode again, 6.45 a.m. till 10.10 a.m., when we halted till 2.20 p.m. We then marched to Bir ibn Rifada in Khauthla, at 4.50 p.m. There are at least five wells in and near W. Khauthla, and about them are small plants of *dôm*-palm, one or two grown-up *dôm*-palms, and, at Bir ibn Rifada, the drying remains of the palm and vegetable garden that Suleiman began to make. The well-water had a purgative effect on our camels. We rode again at 5.30 p.m. and camped between the Raals at 7.30 p.m.

Started again at 1.36 a.m. and rode till 8.45 a.m. in the south edge of Murra. From 8 a.m., when men and camels were all tired, it seemed fit to the boy, Mohammed el-Gadhi, to run races. So he took most of his clothes off, got off his camel and challenged any of us mounted to race him to a clump of trees on the slope ahead, for a pound English. All the party started off at once; the distance turned out about three-quarters of a mile, uphill, over heavy sand, which I expect was more than Mohammed had bargained for; though he won by inches, he was absolutely done and collapsed bleeding from his mouth and nose. Some of our camels were very fast, and when racing in a mob, as we were, they do their best. We put him on his camel, at 11 a.m.; when we started off to march to Wejh at 5 p.m., he was quite fit, and again playing all the little jests that had enlivened the march from Abu Markha. If you come up quietly behind a camel, poke a stick up its rump, and screech, it plunges off at a gallop, very disconcerting to its rider. It is also good fun to cannon another galloping camel into a tree; either the tree goes down (Hejaz trees are very unstable things) or the rider is scratched, or best of all, is swept off his saddle and left hanging on a thorny branch. This counts a bull, and is very popular with the rest of the party.

The Bedu are odd people. Travelling with them is unsatisfactory for an Englishman unless he has patience deep and wide as the sea. They are absolute slaves of their appetites, with no stamina of mind, drunkards for coffee, milk or water, gluttons for stewed meat, shameless beggars for tobacco. A cigarette goes round four men in the tent before it is finished; it would be intolerable manners to smoke it all. They dream for weeks before and after their rare sexual exercises, and spend their days titillating themselves and their friends with bawdy tales. Had the circumstances of their life given them greater resources or opportunity, the Beduins would be mere sensualists. It is the poverty of Arabia which makes them simple, continent and enduring. If they suspect you want to drive them, either they are mulish or they go away: if you know them, and have the time and give the trouble to present things their way, then they in turn will do your pleasure. Whether the results you gain are worth the effort you put forth, no man knoweth. I think Europeans could not or would not spend the time and thought and tact their sheikhs and emirs expend each day, on such meagre objects. Their processes are clear, their minds moving as one's own moves, with nothing incomprehensible or radically different, and they will follow us, if we can endure with them, and play their game. The pity is, we break down with exasperation, and throw them over.

XXII. In Sherif Abdullah's Camp
23 May 1917

Captain T. E. Lawrence, whose report on his journeys to and from Sherif Abdullah's camp, as well as on the two chief raids in which he took part, have appeared separately, sent also an account of his stay in the camp itself. From this we take the following notes:

Abdullah had a force of about 3,000 men, mostly Ateibah. These Capt. Lawrence thought very inferior as fighting men to the Harb and Juheinah, being unadulterated Bedouins. Their Sheikhs are ignorant men, lacking in influence and character, and they appear to be without interest in the campaign. They also knew nothing of the country they are in. Abdullah himself was leading rather an irresponsible hedonistic existence. His tastes appear to be pronouncedly literary. He takes great interest in the war in Europe and follows the operations on the Somme and the general course of European politics most closely (through Arabic newspapers which he spends most of the day in reading). [*Stayed Abdullah's camp 15 March to 25 March. 1st boils: 2nd dysentery: 3rd 10 days malaria.*] 'I was surprised to find', says Capt. Lawrence, 'that he knew the family relationships of the Royal Houses of Europe and the names and characters of their ministers.' He believes that he could make himself supreme in Yemen. If he succeeded, 'It would transform the Sherif's state from a loose hegemony of Bedouin tribes into a populous, wealthy and vigorous kingdom of villagers and townspeople.' Capt. Lawrence adds, with justice, that all past movements of importance in Arabia have been the work of the settled peoples, not of the tribes.

Sheikhs Shakir and Dakhilallah el-Gadhi were the two outstanding personalities in the camp. Both are men of action, and the first has an authority hardly inferior to that of the king or his sons. The Ateibah worship him. Dakhilallah is hereditary lawman of the Juheinah and possesses some science, speaking Turkish well. In fact, he was with the Turks up to December last and came down with them to Nakhl Mubarak. He seems to be a man of energy, resolution and persistence.

In regard to railway raids, Capt. Lawrence gives a rough list of those carried out during his stay from 24 March to 6 April.

'March	24	Bueir	Sixty rails dynamited and telegraph cut
	25	Abu el-Naam	Twenty-five rails dynamited, water-tower, two station buildings seriously damaged by shell fire, seven box-wagons and wood store and tents destroyed by fire, telegraph cut, engine and bogie damaged
	27	Istabl Antar	Fifteen rails dynamited and telegraph cut
	29	Jedahah	Ten rails dynamited, telegraph cut, five Turks killed
	31	Bueir	Five rails dynamited, telegraph cut
April	3	Hadiyah	Eleven rails dynamited, telegraph cut
	5	Mudahrij	200 rails blown up, four-arched bridge destroyed, telegraph cut
	6		Locomotive mined and put out of action temporarily
	6	Bueir	Twenty-two rails cut, culvert blown up, telegraph cut

'The Turks lost about thirty-six killed, and we took some seventy prisoners and deserters during the operations.

'From 7 April a regular service of dynamiters was begun, from Ain Turaa, working against the Mudahrij-Abu el-Naam section, and from Bueir against the Istabl Antar-Bowat section. Dynamiters have been ordered to blow up not more than five rails per night and do something every night. The result of the first three nights' work was satisfactory, but no later details have reached me.'

In conclusion, Capt. Lawrence pays a tribute to Abdullah's sincerity and earnestness, while he thinks him not a military commander or a man of action in any way. He is too fond of pleasure and, in a sense, evidently too civilised for his present wild work. Capt. Lawrence, however, got him to do a good deal – to pay up the Ateibah (whose allowances were in arrears), to take an interest in his guns and machine-guns, to send out his dynamite parties, and to begin to prepare for a general move towards the railway. The report ends with an optimistic forecast.

'As regards the situation at Medina, I think the great bulk of the troops and practically all stores have been evacuated northward in small parties by rail. The programme for a route-march of the main body to el-Ula has (wisely, I think, for the Turks) been abandoned, and the fall of Medina is now merely a question of when the Arabs like to put an end to the affair. The Turks have little food, but so small a garrison that the question has less importance. No food is going in from the north, so that sooner or later starvation will ensue. Till it does, the Arabs will probably not enter the town, since the emirs are all anxious to avoid warlike action against the place itself for religious reasons.'

XXIII. The Howeitat and Their Cheifs
24 July 1917

The Howeitat used to be all under Ibn Rashid – a family which still exists in the Akaba in the Hisma, but is grown poor and weak. They were then for a little presided over by Ibn Jazi; and from this period dates their sub-division into discordant sections with independent foreign policies.

The Abu Tayi sub-section is the joint work of Auda, the fighting man, and Mohammed el-Dheilan, the thinker. It fell out with Ibn Jazi over the latter's treatment of a Sherari guest of Auda's, and in the fifteen-year-old feud Annad, Auda's full-grown son was killed. This feud is the greatest of the Sherif's difficulties in the operations lately at Maan and has driven Hamed el-Arar, the 'ibn Jazi' of to-day, into the arms of the Turks, while Saheiman Abu Tiyur and the rest of the sub-tribe are at Wejh with Sidi Feisal. Auda has offered them peace and friendship at the request of Feisal; and it was perhaps the hardest thing the old man has ever had to do. The death of Annad killed all his hopes and ambitions for the Abu Tayi in the desert, and has made his life a bitter failure; but it is a fixed principle of the Sherif that his followers have no blood-feuds, and no Arab enemies, save the Shammar, who are enemies of the Arab. His success in burying the innumerable hatchets of the Hejaz, is the most pregnant indication of his future government. In all Arab minds the Sherif now stands above tribes, the tribal sheikhs and tribal jealousies. His is the dignity of the peacemaker, and the prestige of independent, superposed authority. He does not take sides or declare in their disputes: he mediates, and ensues a settlement.

The head man of the Abu Tayi is, of course, the inimitable Auda. He must be nearly fifty now (he admits forty) and his black beard is tinged with white, but he is still tall and straight, loosely built, spare and powerful, and as active as a much younger man. His lined and haggard face is pure Bedouin: broad low forehead, high sharp hooked nose, brown-green eyes, slanting outward, large mouth (now unfortunately toothless, for his false teeth were Turkish, and his patriotism made him sacrifice them with a hammer, the day he swore allegiance to Feisal in Wejh), pointed beard and moustache, with the lower jaw shaven clean in the Howeitat style. The Howeitat pride themselves on being altogether Bedu, and Auda is the essence of the Abu Tayi. His hospitality is sweeping (inconvenient, except to very hungry souls), his generosity has reduced him to poverty, and devoured the profits of a hundred successful raids. He has married twenty-eight times, has been wounded thirteen times, and in his battles has seen all his tribesmen hurt, and most of his relations killed. He has only reported his 'kill' since 1900, and they now stand at seventy-five Arabs; Turks are not counted by Auda when they are dead. Under his handling the Toweihah have become the finest fighting force in western Arabia. He raids as often as he can each year ('but a year passes so quickly, Sidi') and has seen Aleppo, Basra, Taif, Wejh and Wadi Dawasir in his armed expeditions.

In his way, Auda is as hard-headed as he is hot-headed. His patience is extreme, and he receives (and ignores) advice, criticism, or abuse with a smile as constant as it is very charming. Nothing on earth would make him change his mind or obey an order or follow a course he disapproved. He sees life as a saga and all events in it are significant and all personages heroic. His mind is packed (and generally overflows) with stories of old raids and epic poems of fights. When he cannot secure a listener he sings to himself in his tremendous voice, which is also deep and musical. In the echoing valleys of Arnousa, our guide in night marches was this wonderful voice of Auda's conversing far in the van, and being rolled back to us from the broken faces of the cliffs. He speaks of himself in the third person, and he is so sure of his fame that he delights to roar out stories against himself. At times he seems seized with a demon of mischief and in large gatherings shouts appalling stories of the private matters of his host or guests: with all this he is modest, simple as a child, direct, honest, kind-hearted, affectionate, and warmly loved even by those to whom he is most trying – his friends.

He is rather like Caesar's tribe, in his faculty for keeping round him a free territory, and then a great ring of enemies. Nuri Shaalan pretends only to love Auda – but in reality he and the Sukhur, and all friendly chiefs also, go about in terror lest they should offend in some way against Auda's pleasure. He loses no opportunity of adding to his enemies and relishes the new situation most because it is an ideal excuse to take on the Turkish government. 'To the Mutessarif of Kerak from Auda abu Tayi . . . greeting. Take notice to quit Arab territory before the end of Ramadan. We want it for ourselves. Should you not go, I declare you outlawed and God will decide between us.' Such was Auda's cartel to the government the day we struck.

After Auda, Mohammed el-Dheilan is the chief figure in the tribe. He is taller than Auda, and massively built, a square-headed intelligent, thoughtful man of perhaps thirty-five, with a sour humour and a kind heart carefully concealed beneath it. In his youth he was notoriously wild, but reformed himself the night he was condemned to be hanged by Nevris Bey,

Sami Pasha's Staff Officer, and has repaid many of the injuries he once wrought. He acted as business manager of the Abu Tayi and their spokesman with the government. His tastes are rather luscious, and his ploughed land at Tafileh and his little house at Maan introduced him to luxuries which took root among the tribe: hence the mineral waters and parasols of a Howeitat *Ghazzu*. Mohammed is greedy, richer than Auda, more calculating, deeper – but a fine fighting man too, and one who knows how to appeal to everything in his hearers' natures, and to bend them to his will by words.

Zaal ibn Motlog is Auda's nephew. He is about twenty-five, with *petite* features, carefully curled moustache, polished teeth, trimmed and pointed beard, like a French professional man. He, too, is greedy (of all Arabs I have met the Howeitat were the most open, most constant, most shameless beggars, wearying one day and night with their mean importunities and preposterous demands), sharp as a needle, of no great mental strength, but trained for years by Auda as chief scout to the tribe, and therefore a most capable and dashing commander of a raid.

Auda ibn Zaal is the fourth great man of Abu Tayi. He is silent and more unusual in type than Auda, Mohammed, or Zaal, but the Howeitat flock to his side when there is a raid, and say that in action for concentrated force he is second only to Auda, with something of the skill of Mohammed superadded. Personally I have seen all four chiefs under fire, and saw in them all a headlong unreasoning dash and courage that accounted easily for the scarred and mutilated figures of their tribesmen.

The fighting strength of the Abu Tayi is 535 camel-men and twenty-five horsemen.

XXIV. The Sherif's Religious Views
12 August 1917

On 28 July 1917, the Sherif of Mecca explained at some length to Colonel Wilson before me his dogmatic position. He began by sketching the original tenets of the Wahabi sect – its Puritanism, its literalism and its asceticism. After the Egyptian conquest of Nejd the sect fell away very quickly in numbers and enthusiasm, till of late years it was practically confined to Aridh. The Nomads, Wushm and Qasim had all weakened so much as to be practically Sunni.

About four years ago there was a sudden revival. The Sherif is doubtful as to whether this can be ascribed to Ibn Saud or not. At any rate, funds were obtained from somewhere, and Wahabite missionaries went up to Qasim, amongst the Ateiba, Meteir and Sbei, and into Mecca and Taif. The first tenet of the new preachers was that the orthodox Sunnis and Shias (especially the Shias), were infidels. The Emir of Mecca was as convicted a Kafir as the Turks. The constructive side of the new creed was curious; they preached an exaggerated fatalism: 'God does everything'; they forbade medicine to the sick, discouraged trade, building and forethought. A favourite saying was, 'If a man fall into a well, leave it to God to pull him out.'

The missionaries were at first successful in great part, and the Sherif took alarm at the prospect. He sent Sidi Abdullah rapidly into Nejd, and by a show of force recovered the Atieba, and most of the Meteir, and bound them again to the Emirate of Mecca. He also seems to have taken steps to counter-preach the new dogmas in Qasim itself, and in a short time the second Wahabite movement appeared to have spent itself. It was, however, only dormant, and in the last year or so missionaries have again been issuing from Aridh, and agitating the neighbourhood.

Ibn Saud has increased the unrest by his military policy. He has called out his levies two and three times in the year, discriminating between town and town; from one he will demand a contribution of men; and from another a composition in money. This has particularly annoyed Aneyza, Boreyda and Russ, rich and comfortable towns, fond of silk and tobacco, and not too fond of prayer. Their disaffection is wide, and the Sherif regards it as an embarrassment, since his ambitions extend to the limits of the Ateiba and Meteir only, and he has no desire to be involved in any question of the suzerainty of the Qasim towns. At present there is a sharp cleavage between Aridh and Qasim, which any external encouragement, or unwise internal act, might inflame into an open breach.

We then asked the Sherif about the position of the Shias. Towards the Wahabis, he said, they were extremely hostile. Other than that, he could not see in them any particular policy. They loved his family, since Shias have a greater respect for the person of the Prophet than have the Sunnis. Some such as the Zeidis and Jaafaris were, in his opinion, more reasonable in their attitude than the Shafeis who oppose them. The Hanefite objection to the Shias was political and not doctrinal.

He, in common with all orthodox Islam, was not prepared to deny the Khalifate of Abu Bekr, and regarded the Shias who condemned Abu Bekr, Omar and Othman, as mistaken. The Shias in India are largely heretical in their views, as are many of the Persian sects.

(The Sherif is ostensibly a Shafei. In this conversation he took up a middle position between moderate Shia and Sunni; it is generally believed that his real beliefs are Zeidi. Sidi Abdullah is nearly openly a Shia of the Jaaferi wing; Sidi Ali is a Sunni, and a fairly definite one; Sidi Feisal is not a formalist, and tends to an undefined undogmatic position, more Shia perhaps than Sunni, but vague. They are all nervous of betraying their real attitude, even to their friends, and maintain a noncommital Shafei profession in public.)

I then mentioned to the Sherif that the Northern Arabs commonly called him Emir el-Muminin, and asked him if this title was correct and if it met with his approval. After a short reflection he said 'No' and made his refusal more definite later. He said that people ascribed to him ambitions which he did not possess; he had even heard talk of his reviving the Khalifate. He explained his position with regard to the Khalifate. It was the simple Shia one (already impressed on me by Feisal and Abdullah), namely, that the

Khalifate expired with Abu Bekr, and that any resurrection of the idea
to-day was not only grammatically absurd but blasphemous. He will have
absolutely no truck with such a notion. (Sidi Abdullah is weaker than his
father in this respect. If he saw profit from the Sunni side in the assumption, he might do it, and cut the loss of the Shia element; yet, as matters
stand, if the decision lies with him it is improbable that it will ever be
adopted.) The idea of a Moslem Khalifate was, said the Sherif, suggested
to Abdul Hamid by the British, and exploited by him as a stick to beat us
with. Its exponents to-day were Obeidullah, Abd el-Aziz Shawish, Shekib
Arslan, and Assad Shucair, four blackguards without an ounce of Islam or
honesty between them, and its nominal holder, the Sultan of the Turks, was
a pitiable laughing-stock; the invention had been fatal to Islam; it tried to
twist a religion into a political theory and was responsible for unrest in
Turkey, Arabia, Egypt, North Africa, Java, India and China. It had plunged
Turkey into the present war, and caused the Arab revolt, and with this
example before his eyes, and in view of his own policy of friendship with
Great Britain, he could neither acknowledge another's Khalifate, assume
one himself, or admit the existence of the theory.

The title Emir el-Muminin was one that a sincere Moslem might adopt. It
made no pretence to any succession to the prophet, but was objectionable
politically, on account of the word 'emir'. It was no use being emir, without
the power or pretence of giving orders, not to a sect, or a country or two,
but to the Moslem world. The main divisions of Shia and Sunni would unite
under this title, but the smaller sects, and especially the alien congregations
in India and Africa, would resent the implication of authority, as, no doubt,
would the Great Powers.

His policy for Islam was to provide in Mecca and Medina for the honourable upkeep of the Holy Places, to facilitate the pilgrimage, and to issue
Fetwas and Sheria decisions as required. The Moslem world must have a
head, but it would be a less tempestuous body of thought if the head was the
Sherif and Emir of Mecca, basing his right on the concrete possession of the
Holy Places, and on an authentic descent, not on a supposed implicit apos-
tolic authority, inherited from an unbroken succession of Khalifas. His
motives in rebelling against the Turks were two. The first is a political object;
the liberation of the Arab world from Turkish domination; this he will effect
without question of creed; Christian, Druse, Shia and Sunni meet on a
common base of nationality, and must co-operate with him on level terms if
the aim is to be achieved. His second motive was a religious one, purely
Islamic in character; it is to provide for the Mohammedan world an independent sovereign, ruling in the Holy Places, of the Sherifian family, whose
claims to the spiritual leadership of Islam will be so transcendent as to be
generally admitted, but whose weakness in material resources (money, ships,
and guns) will at once make him acceptable to the Christian Powers, and
purge Islam of the lunatic idea that it is a polity, bound temporally to a single
infallible head. His ideal is a spiritual city, not a theocracy. To attain this aim

he must have temporalities enough, free of foreign control, to establish his claim to political competence, and must be delivered from the hierarchical theories which have plunged Turkey, the Senussi and Ali Dinar into suicidal jehads. His temporalities he will hold as king of the Arab countries, and his spiritualities as Emir of Mecca.

My personal opinion is that the title of Emir el-Muminin would not be repugnant to him, if it came not as his assumption but as the homage of his followers. It is generally used by the tribes to-day from Kaf to Kunfida, and will apparently be acceptable to the sheikhs of urban Syria. His present objection, that it involves the power of command in Islam, does not hold good, since it is as fair to interpret it only in a doctrinal sense.

As for the Khalifate, the sincere disgust he expressed of Abdul Hamid's bogus claims, and his only half-veiled acknowledgement of Shia tenets himself, made me certain that this opposition to the idea is a matter of principle. Further, I do not think that all the temptations of the world would persuade Sherif Hussein to run counter to his principles. His transparent honesty and strength of conviction (while they may prevent him distinguishing between his prejudices and his principles) will at all costs ensure his shaping his conduct exactly in accordance with his promised word. It would be easy to influence him in coming to a decision, but once his mind is made up it would be a thankless task to try and make him change it.

He appears to hope that, by ignoring the political disintegration of Islam, he may be able to concentrate attention on its dogmatic differences and do something to reduce the friction between sects. His appeal would be to moderate Sunni and moderate Shia to meet together under his presidency, and try to restrain the extremists in their camps.

XXV. The Occupation of Akaba
12 August 1917

By Monday, 18 June, we had enrolled 535 Toweiha (of whom twenty-five were horsemen), about 150 Rualla (under Benaiah ibn Dughmi, Durzi's brother) and Sherarat (under Geraitan el-Azmi), and thirty-five Kawachiba, under Dhami. Of these we chose nearly 200, and left them as guards for the tribal tents in Wadi Sirhan. With the rest we marched out of Kaf in the afternoon, and on 20 June entered Bair, after an easy but waterless march over the Suwan. At Bair we found one well filled in, two seriously damaged, and a fourth unhurt: the Turks had come there a little time before with Hamd el-Arar, and tried to blow them in with gelignite. They used an electric exploder clumsily, and we removed many tamped charges from the sides of the still open wells.

Circumstances forced us to stay in Bair till Thursday, 28 June. The time was spent in negotiations with Ibn Jazi and the smaller sub-sections of the Howeitat on the Akaba road. We also carried out demolitions against the railway at Atwi, Sultani, Minifir, and elsewhere. The Ageyl dynamitards were inefficient, and our supply of dynamite small, so that the demolitions were of a pin-prick character, meant only to distract the Turks, and advertise our coming to the Arabs. The staffs of two stations were killed, to the same intent.

From Bair we marched to El-Jefer, where we stayed till 1 July. The Turks had been more successful in their efforts against the wells here, and we had some difficulty in digging one out. The water proved sufficient for about 300 men and camels, when it was obtained. The station buildings of Maan and Hamra are visible from El-Jefer, about twenty-four miles off, but the Turks did not realise that we had arrived in force, owing to the operations near Amman, undertaken at this time by a flying column of 100 men, under Shiekh Zaal. This led them to believe us still in Wadi Sirhan, and on the 30th they sent a force of 400 cavalry with four machine-guns, and Nawaf ibn Shaalan as guide, from Deraa to go to Kaf and find us. The Turks seem unable to discriminate the true from the false, out of the flood of news unquestionably brought them by the local Arabs.

From El-Jefer a flying column rode to Fuweilah, about seventeen miles south-west of Maan, and in concert with the Dhumaniya Howeitat (Shiekh Gasim) attacked the gendarme post on the motor road to Akaba. In the fighting some mounted gendarmes got into a group of undefended Howeitat tents, and stabbed to death an old man, six women and seven children, the only occupants. Our Arabs in consequence wiped out the post, but not before some had escaped to Maan.

This news reached Maan at dawn on the 1st and a battalion of the 178th Regiment which had arrived at Maan from Zunguldak on the day before, was immediately ordered out to Fuweilah to relieve the post. The same afternoon we descended on the line at kilometre 479, near Ghadir el Haj, and carried out extensive demolitions till nearly sunset, when we marched westward, intending to sleep at Batra. On the way, however, we were met by messengers from our Fuweilah column, reporting the coming of new troops from Maan, and we swung northwards, marching a great part of the night, till we were able at dawn to occupy the crests of the low rolling grass-covered hills that flank each side of the Akaba road near Ain Aba el-Lissan. The Turks had reached Fuweilah, to find only vultures in possession, and moved to Aba el-Lissan, fourteen miles from Maan, for the night. The spring has been built round, and piped, and is much smaller than it used to be before the war, but is still sufficient for perhaps 2,000 men and animals. The battalion camped next the water, and kept together in the bottom of the valley, so that we were able to take the higher ground (at from 400 to 600 yards range) without difficulty.

We sat here throughout 2 July, sniping the Turks steadily all day, and inflicted some loss. The Turks replied with shrapnel from a mountain-gun, firing twenty rounds, which were all they had. The shells grazed our hill-tops, and burst far away over the valleys behind. When sunset came, Auda Abu Tayi collected the fifty horsemen now with us, in a hollow valley about 200 yards from the Turks, but under cover, and suddenly charged at a wild gallop into the brown of them, shooting furiously from the saddle as he came. The unexpectedness of the move seemed to strike panic into the Turks (about 550 strong), and after a burst of rifle fire, they scattered in all directions. This was our signal, and all the rest of our force (perhaps 350 men, for some were watching the road on the east) dashed down the hillsides into the hollow, as fast as the camels would go. The Turks were all infantry, and the Arabs all mounted, and the mix-up round the spring in the dusk, with 1,000 men shooting like mad, was considerable. As the Turks scattered, their position at once became hopeless, and in five minutes it was merely a massacre. In all I counted 300 enemy dead in the main position, and a few fugitives may have been killed further away, though the majority of our men went straight for the Turkish camp to plunder it, before the last shots were fired. The prisoners came to 160 (three officers) mostly taken by Sherif Nasir and myself, since the Arabs in the Maan area are very bitter against the Turks, and are set on killing all they can. They have some reason for this attitude, in the slaughter of the women and children mentioned above, and in the previous execution of Sheikh Abd el-Rahman, a Belgawiya from Kerak. He was popular, and anti-Turk, but the government caught him and harnessing him between four wild mules tore him to death. This was the culmination of a series of executions by torture in Kerak, and the memory of them has embittered local opinion.

The Arab losses in the fight came to two killed (a Rualla and a Sherarat) and several wounded, including Sheikh Benaiah ibn Dughmi. Considering the amount of firing, the confusion, the close quarters at which we were, and the Turkish casualties, the Arabs must be held to have got off very luckily. Several horses were hit in the cavalry charge and Auda himself (in front, of course) had a narrow escape, since two bullets smashed his field glasses, one pierced his revolver holster, three struck his sheathed sword, and his horse was killed under him. He was wildly pleased with the whole affair.

Unfortunately, many of our prisoners were wounded and we had very few spare camels with us. Those who could hold on were mounted behind Arabs on the spare camels; but we had to abandon the worst cases at Aba el-Lissan, and of those we took with us about fifty died of heat, hunger and thirst on the road down to Akaba. The heat in the Hesma and Wadi Itm was terrible, and the water between Fuweilah and Akaba only sufficient for perhaps 200 men and animals. For the matter of food, Nasir and I had taken two months' supply with us from Wejh, and were now two months out; the Bedu had their own food with them in their saddle bags, but Arab rations are ill-adapted, in quality and quantity, for Turkish soldiers. We did what we could for the prisoners, but everybody went short.

From Aba el-Lissan we marched to Guweira (22 miles) after sending out a column which destroyed Mreiga, the nearest gendarme post to Maan, on the Akaba road. At Guweira we received the surrender of the garrison (of about 120 men), their intermediary being Hussein ibn Jad, who joined us here on 4 July. The motor road is finished to the foot of Nagb el-Star, from Maan, but not metalled anywhere. As the soil is fairly hard loam, I think it should suffice for the passage of a series of light cars. The Nagb is very steep, with bad hairpin corners, and will require improvement. The Hesma is of fine red sand, soft along the track, but harder in the bed of the water-course which runs down from the foot of the Bagb to Guweira. From Guweira we marched down Wadi Itm to Kethira (18 miles) where we overran a Turkish post of about seventy infantry and mounted men, taking most of them prisoners, and thence we went on to near Khadra, at the old stone dam in Wadi Itm (15 miles), where we came into contact with the garrison (300 men) of Akaba. They had retired from the village itself (about six miles away) to be out of view of the sea, and on the line of retreat towards Maan. The news of our fight at Fuweilah had reached Akaba quickly, and all the Amran, Darausha, Heiwat and sub-tribes of the Howeitat near Akaba had risen, and collected round the Khadra post, which had held them at bay from their trenches with small casualties for two days. When Nasir and the banner turned up the Arab excitement became intense, and preparations were made for an immediate assault. This did not fall in with our ideas, since (*pour encourager les autres*) we wanted the news to get about that the Arabs accepted prisoners. All the Turks we met were most happy to surrender, holding up their arms and crying 'Muslim, Muslim' as soon as they saw us. They expressed themselves willing and anxious to go on fighting foreigners and Christians till they dropped, but with no intention of adding a Moslem enemy to the powers already against them. To save the Khadra garrison from massacre Sherif Nasir had to labour from afternoon till dawn, but he eventually carried his point (by our going ourselves between the Arab and the Turkish lines, to break their field of fire), and with the prisoners (now about 600 in number) we marched into Akaba on the morning of 6 July. The astonishment of a German NCO (well-boring at Khadra) when the Sherif's force appeared was comic. He knew neither Arabic nor Turkish, and had not been aware of the Arab revolt.

The situation at Akaba was now rather serious, economically. We had no food, 600 prisoners and many visitors in prospect. Meat was plentiful, since we had been killing riding camels as required, and there were unripe dates in the palm-groves. These saved the day, but involved a good deal of discomfort after the eating, and the force in Akaba was very unhappy till the arrival of HMS *Dufferin* on the 13th with food from Suez. Before she arrived, Arab forces were sent northward to occupy the hills up to Wadi Musa (Petra), some sixty miles from Akaba, and southward to join up with the Beni Atiyeh, and reconnoitre the country with a view to an eventual offensive against the railway south of Maan.

XXVI. The Sherif and His Neighbours
20 August 1917

In Bulletin No. 58 we referred to an interview which Colonel Wilson had with the Sherif on the subject of the latter's relations with Ibn Saud and the Idrisi. We have now received from him a detailed account of this interview, written by Captain Lawrence, who was present. The Sherif, after explaining the misunderstanding caused by Ibn Dakhil, said that his relations with Ibn Saud for many years had been friendly, and he had no intention of giving offence in the manner suggested by Sidi Abdullah.

On the contrary, he had invited Abd el-Rahman, Ibn Saud's father, to come to Mecca for the Haj, and to reconcile with Ibn Saud such fugitives of the emir's family as had taken refuge with him in Mecca. He hopes to hear in a few days that Abd el-Rahman is coming.

The Sherif also said that Sidi Abdullah was on the best of terms with Ibn Saud, and insisted that he went to Shaara in 1914–15 to assist Ibn Saud against Ibn Rashid. He also said that Abdullah's presence there had prevented Ibn Rashid from following up the victory at Jerab. This is also Sidi Abdullah's present view of his action on that occasion, and it is worth noting, from Captain Shakespear's reports before the battle (Arab Bulletin, 1916, p. 336), that Abdullah and Ibn Saud were in direct relation at that time.

Colonel Wilson suggested to the Sherif that it might be desirable to send letters officially to Idrisi and Ibn Saud, informing them that his assumption of the royal title was not intended in any way to suggest interference with their internal affairs, and proposing common action against the Turks. He suggested that if Said Mustafa and Turki could come to Mecca as representatives of Idrisi and Ibn Saud, the relations of the three rulers could be put on a satisfactory basis.

The Sherif said he did not agree with him. He thought it unwise to raise the question of the inter-relations of the Emirates of Arabia while the Turks were still in possession of the Hejaz. His future policy towards the other emirs would be guided, when the time came, by the wishes of the British government. For the present he intends to make no demand, suggestion, or protest to them, in any event. He did not believe they could harm him, even if they wanted to, and as for their co-operation with him against the Turks, they all had cause enough against the Turks, and treaties with the British government, and if that did not move them, he was not going to try.

Later he said that Idrisi's promise of neutrality to Muhieddin in Asir had enabled the Turks to operate against the Beni Shihir, who had however repulsed them and inflicted a loss of twenty-five killed on them. He said that Ibn Saud's conduct towards Ibn Rashid was a disappointment, especially his recent retirement from northern Qasim. He had asked Salih ibn Athil for the reason for the latter move, and Salih had replied that he was not in a position to explain it.

He mentioned that Ibn Saud had permitted the Turkish military envoys, with specie for the Yemen force, to pass through his country, on payment of £10,000, and expressed some disgust at the meanness which would break a treaty obligation for so small a bribe. He also said that the ruling family of Koweit was negroid, and that Mohammerah, as Persian, was hardly in a position to enter an Arab confederation.

The Sherif mentioned later that the Ajman who had turned on Ibn Saud and killed his brother were now serving Sidi Zeid and Sidi Abdullah. He had no intention of making capital out of them; but he hoped, through Abd el-Rahman, to persuade Ibn Saud to make peace with them.

When asked what his ideas were with regard to Ibn Rashid, he promptly said that Ibn Rashid was a young fool with no will or policy of his own. The visit of Ibn Ajil to Abdullah, the defeat of Rashaid Ibn Leila by Zeid, and the interview between Ibn Rimmal and Sherif Nasir were then quoted as possible indications of an early submission of the Shammar to his authority, and he was asked what his attitude towards proposals of peace would be. He replied that when the time came, he would consult with Colonel Wilson and act in accordance with the wishes of His Majesty's government.

It was evident throughout the interview that the Sherif has no intention at all of adjusting the relations of the Hejaz government with the emirs of Arabia until after the fall of Medina. He said quite frankly that they were not going to do him good or harm at present, and felt that his position would then by sufficiently improved to give him the advantage in negotiation. He insisted at the same time upon his good personal relations with the various rulers, and seemed to anticipate no difficulty in arriving eventually at an agreement with them, agreeable to the wishes of the British government.

XXVII. Twenty-Seven Articles
20 August 1917

The following notes have been expressed in commandment form for greater clarity and to save words. They are, however, only my personal conclusions, arrived at gradually while I worked in the Hejaz and now put on paper as stalking horses for beginners in the Arab armies. They are meant to apply only to Bedu; townspeople or Syrians require totally different treatment. They are of course not suitable to any other person's need, or applicable unchanged in any particular situation. Handling Hejaz Arabs is an art, not a science, with exceptions and no obvious rules. At the same time we have a great chance there; the Sherif trusts us, and has given us the position (towards his government) which the Germans wanted to win in Turkey. If we are tactful, we can at once retain his goodwill and carry out our job, but to succeed we have got to put into it all the interest and skill we possess.

   1. Go easy just for the first few weeks. A bad start is difficult to atone for, and the Arabs form their judgements on externals that we ignore. When

you have reached the inner circle in a tribe, you can do as you please with yourself and them.

2. Lean all you can about your Ashraf and Bedu. Get to know their families, clans and tribes, friends and enemies, wells, hills and roads. Do all this by listening and by indirect inquiry. Do not ask questions. Get to speak their dialect of Arabic, not yours. Until you can understand their allusions, avoid getting deep into conversation, or you will drop bricks. Be a little stiff at first.

3. In matters of business deal only with the commander of the army, column, or party in which you serve. Never give orders to anyone at all, and reserve your directions or advice for the CO, however great the temptation (for efficiency's sake) of dealing direct with his underlings. Your place is advisory, and your advice is due to the commander alone. Let him see that this is your conception of your duty, and that his is to be the sole executive of your joint plans.

4. Win and keep the confidence of your leader. Strengthen his prestige at your expense before others when you can. Never refuse or quash schemes he may put forward; but ensure that they are put forward in the first instance privately to you. Always approve them, and after praise modify them insensibly, causing the suggestions to come from him, until they are in accord with your own opinion. When you attain this point, hold him to it, keep a tight grip of his ideas, and push him forward as firmly as possibly, but secretly, so that no one but himself (and he not too clearly) is aware of your pressure.

5. Remain in touch with your leader as constantly and unobtrusively as you can. Live with him, that at meal times and at audiences you may be naturally with him in his tent. Formal visits to give advice are not so good as the constant dropping of ideas in casual talk. When stranger sheikhs come in for the first time to swear allegiance and offer service, clear out of the tent. If their first impression is of foreigners in the confidence of the Sherif, it will do the Arab cause much harm.

6. Be shy of too close relations with the subordinates of the expedition. Continual intercourse with them will make it impossible for you to avoid going behind or beyond the instructions that the Arab CO has given them on your advice, and in so disclosing the weakness of his position you altogether destroy your own.

7. Treat the sub-chiefs of your force quite easily and lightly. In this way you hold yourself above their level. Treat the leader, if a Sherif, with respect. He will return your manner and you and he will then be alike, and above the rest. Precedence is a serious matter among the Arabs, and you must attain it.

8. Your ideal position is when you are present and not noticed. Do not be too intimate, too prominent, or too earnest. Avoid being identified too long or too often with any tribal sheikh, even if CO of the expedition. To do your work you must be above jealousies, and you lose prestige if

you are associated with a tribe or clan, and its inevitable feuds. Sherifs are above all blood-feuds and local rivalries, and form the only principle of unity among the Arabs. Let your name therefore be coupled always with a Sherif's, and share his attitude towards the tribes. When the moment comes for action put yourself publicly under his orders. The Bedu will then follow suit.

9. Magnify and develop the growing conception of the Sherifs as the natural aristocracy of the Arabs. Inter-tribal jealousies make it impossible for any sheikh to attain a commanding position, and the only hope of union in Nomad Arabia is that the Ashraf be universally acknowledged as the ruling class. Sherifs are half-townsmen, half-Nomad, in manner and life, and have the instinct of command. Mere merit and money would be insufficient to obtain such recognition; but the Arab reverence for pedigree and the Prophet gives hope for the ultimate success of the Ashraf.

10. Call your Sherif 'Sidi' in public and in private. Call other people by their ordinary names, without title. In intimate conversation call a Sheikh 'Abu Annad', 'Akhu Alia' or some similar by-name.

11. The foreigner and Christian is not a popular person in Arabia. However friendly and informal the treatment of yourself may be, remember always that your foundations are very sandy ones. Wave a Sherif in front of you like a banner and hide your own mind and person. If you succeed, you will have hundreds of miles of country and thousands of men under your orders, and for this it is worth bartering the outward show.

12. Cling tight to your sense of humour. You will need it every day. A dry irony is the most useful type, and repartee of a personal and not too broad character will double your influence with the chiefs. Reproof, if wrapped up in some smiling form, will carry further and last longer than the most violent speech. The power of mimicry or parody is valuable, but use it sparingly, for wit is more dignified than humour. Do not cause a laugh at a Sherif except amongst Sherifs.

13. Never lay hands on an Arab; you degrade yourself. You may think the resultant obvious increase of outward respect a gain to you; but what you have really done is to build a wall between you and their inner selves. It is difficult to keep quiet when everything is being done wrong, but the less you lose your temper the greater your advantage. Also then you will not go mad yourself.

14. While very difficult to drive, the Bedu are easy to lead, if you have the patience to bear with them. The less apparent your interferences the more your influence. They are willing to follow your advice and do what you wish, but they do not mean you or anyone else to be aware of that. It is only after the end of all annoyances that you find at bottom their real fund of goodwill.

15. Do not try to do too much with your own hands. Better the Arabs do it tolerably than that you do it perfectly. It is their war, and you are to help

them, not to win it for them. Actually, also, under the very odd conditions of Arabia, your practical work will not be as good as, perhaps, you think it is.

16. If you can, without being too lavish, forestall presents to yourself. A well-placed gift is often more effective in winning over a suspicious sheikh. Never receive a present without giving a liberal return, but you may delay this return (while letting its ultimate certainty be known) if you require a particular service from the giver. Do not let them ask you for things, since their greed will then make them look upon you only as a cow to milk.

17. Wear an Arab headcloth when with a tribe. Bedu have a malignant prejudice against the hat, and believe that our persistence in wearing it (due probably to British obstinacy of dictation) is founded on some immoral or irreligious principle. A thick headcloth forms a good protection against the sun, and if you wear a hat your best Arab friends will be ashamed of you in public.

18. Disguise is not advisable. Except in special areas, let it be clearly known that you are a British officer and a Christian. At the same time, if you can wear Arab kit when with the tribes, you will acquire their trust and intimacy to a degree impossible in uniform. It is, however, dangerous and difficult. They make no special allowances for you when you dress like them. Breaches of etiquette not charged against a foreigner are not condoned to you in Arab clothes. You will be like an actor in a foreign theatre, playing a part day and night for months, without rest, and for an anxious stake. Complete success, which is when the Arabs forget your strangeness and speak naturally before you, counting you as one of themselves, is perhaps only attainable in character: while half-success (all that most of us will strive for; the other costs too much) is easier to win in British things, and you yourself will last longer, physically and mentally, in the comfort that they mean. Also then the Turks will not hang you, when you are caught.

19. If you wear Arab things, wear the best. Clothes are significant among the tribes, and you must wear the appropriate, and appear at ease in them. Dress like a Sherif, if they agree to it.

20. If your wear Arab things at all, go the whole way. Leave your English friends and customs on the coast, and fall back on Arab habits entirely. It is possible, starting thus level with them, for the European to beat the Arabs at their own game, for we have stronger motives for our action, and put more heart into it than they. If you can surpass them, you have taken an immense stride toward complete success, but the strain of living and thinking in a foreign and half-understood language, the savage food, strange clothes, and stranger ways, with the complete loss of privacy and quiet, and the impossibility of ever relaxing your watchful imitation of the others for months on end, provide such an added stress to the ordinary difficulties of dealing with the Bedu, the climate,

and the Turks, that this road should not be chosen without serious thought.

21. Religious discussions will be frequent. Say what you like about your own side, and avoid criticism of theirs, unless you know that the point is external, when you may score heavily by proving it so. With the Bedu, Islam is so all-pervading an element that there is little religiosity, little fervour, and no regard for externals. Do not think from their conduct that they are careless. Their conviction of the truth of their faith, and its share in every act and thought and principle of their daily life is so intimate and intense as to be unconscious, unless roused by opposition. Their religion is as much a part of nature to them as is sleep or food.

22. Do not try to trade on what you know of fighting. The Hejaz confounds ordinary tactics. Learn the Bedu principles of war as thoroughly and as quickly as you can, for till you know them your advice will be no good to the Sherif. Unnumbered generations of tribal raids have taught them more about some parts of the business than we will ever know. In familiar conditions they fight well, but strange events cause panic. Keep your unit small. Their raiding parties are usually from one hundred to two hundred men, and if you take a crowd they only get confused. Also their sheikhs, while admirable company commanders, are too 'set' to learn to handle the equivalents of battalions or regiments. Don't attempt unusual things, unless they appeal to the sporting instinct Bedu have so strongly, or unless success is obvious. If the objective is a good one (booty) they will attack like fiends, they are splendid scouts, their mobility gives you the advantage that will win this local war, they make proper use of their knowledge of the country (don't take tribesmen to places they do not know), and the gazelle-hunters, who form a proportion of the better men, are great shots at visible targets. A sheikh from one tribe cannot give orders to men from another; a Sherif is necessary to command a mixed tribal force. If there is plunder in prospect, and the odds are at all equal, you will win. Do not waste Bedu attacking trenches (they will not stand casualties) or in trying to defend a position, for they cannot sit still without slacking. The more unorthodox and Arab your proceedings, the more likely you are to have the Turks cold, for they lack initiative and expect you to. Don't play for safety.

23. The open reason that Bedu give you for action or inaction may be true, but always there will be better reasons left for you to divine. You must find these inner reasons (they will be denied, but are none the less in operation) before shaping your arguments for one course or other. Allusion is more effective than logical exposition: they dislike concise expression. Their minds work just as ours do, but on different premises. There is nothing unreasonable, incomprehensible, or inscrutable in the Arab. Experience of them, and knowledge of their prejudices will enable you to foresee their attitude and possible course of action in nearly every case.

24. Do not mix Bedu and Syrians, or trained men and tribesmen. You will get work out of neither, for they hate each other. I have never seen a successful combined operation, but many failures. In particular, ex-officers of the Turkish army, however Arab in feelings and blood and language, are hopeless with Bedu. They are narrow-minded in tactics, unable to adjust themselves to irregular warfare, clumsy in Arab etiquette, swollen-headed to the extent of being incapable of politeness to a tribesman for more than a few minutes, impatient, and, usually, helpless without their troops on the road and in action. Your orders (if you were unwise enough to give any) would be more readily obeyed by Beduins than those of any Mohammedan Syrian officer. Arab townsmen and Arab tribesmen regard each other mutually as poor relations, and poor relations are much more objectionable than poor strangers.

25. In spite of ordinary Arab example, avoid too free talk about women. It is as difficult a subject as religion, and their standards are so unlike our own that a remark, harmless in English, may appear as unrestrained to them, as some of their statements would look to us, if translated literally.

26. Be as careful of your servants as of yourself. If you want a sophisticated one you will probably have to take an Egyptian, or a Sudani, and unless you are very lucky he will undo on trek much of the good you so laboriously effect. Arabs will cook rice and make coffee for you, and leave you if required to do unmanly work like cleaning boots or washing. They are only really possible if you are in Arab kit. A slave brought up in the Hejaz is the best servant, but there are rules against British subjects owning them, so they have to be lent to you. In any case, take with you an Ageyli or two when you go up-country. They are the most efficient couriers in Arabia, and understand camels.

27. The beginning and ending of the secret of handling Arabs is unremitting study of them. Keep always on your guard; never say an unnecessary thing: watch yourself and your companions all the time: hear all that passes, search out what is going on beneath the surface, read their characters, discover their tastes and their weaknesses, and keep everything you find out to yourself. Bury yourself in Arab circles, have no interests and no ideas except the work in hand, so that your brain is saturated with one thing only, and you realise your part deeply enough to avoid the little slips that would counteract the painful work of weeks. Your success will be proportioned to the amount of mental effort you devote to it.

XXVIII. The Raid at Haret Ammar
8 October 1917

I left Akaba on 7 September, with the two British gun instructors, and two sheikhs of the Ageilat Beni Atiyah, from Mudowarrah. My hope was to raise 300 men in Gueira and take Mudowarrah station.

We rode gently to Gueira, where were a large camp, little water, and great tribal heartburnings. The three sub-tribes I was relying on were not yet paid, and Audah abu Tayi was making trouble by his greediness and his attempt to assume authority over all the Huweitat. It was impossible to get either men or camels, so I moved to Rum, five hours SSE of Gueira. There are good springs, difficult of access, at Rum, some pasturage, and the most beautiful sandstone cliff scenery.

At Rum the Dhumaniyah came in on 12 September, mutinous. The situation became unpleasant, so I rode to Akaba, saw Feisal, and returned on the 13th with the promise of twenty baggage camels, and Sherif Abdullah ibn Hamza el-Feir, who tried to smooth over the local friction.

On 15 September the camels arrived, and on the 16th we started for Mudowarrah with a force of 116 Bedouins, made up of Toweiha, Zuweida, Darausha, Dhumaniyah, Togatga and Zelebani Huweitat, and Ageilat Beni Atiyah. Sheikh Zaal was the only capable leader, and Audah's pretensions had made the other sub-tribes determined not to accept his authority. This threw upon me a great deal of detailed work, for which I had no qualifications, and throughout the expedition I had more preoccupation with questions of supply and transport, tribal pay, disputes, division of spoil, feuds, march order, and the like, than with the explosive work which should more properly have been mine. The Sherif with me, Nasir el-Harith, went blind the first day out and was useless.

We reached Mudowarrah well on 17 September, in the afternoon, after thirteen hours march and went down at dusk to the station about three miles further east. We got within 300 yards of it, but could find no position for a Stokes gun. The station is large and the garrison seemed to be between 200 and 300 men, and I was doubtful whether it would be wise to take it on with the rather mixed force I had; so in the end I went back to the well and on the 18th moved southward into sandy country. It is hoped to make Mudowarrah the object of further operations.

In the afternoon of 18 September, I laid an electric mine, in about five hours work, over a culvert at kilo. 587, on the outside of a curve towards some low hills, 300 yards away, where Stokes and Lewis guns could be placed to rake the lengths of either north- or south-bound trains. The position was too high for the best machine-gun work, but the presence of a British machine-gunner made safety play advisable.

We slept near the mine, but were seen by a Turkish watching post near kilo. 590 in the afternoon, and at 9 a.m. on the 19th about forty men were sent from Haret Ammar (= Kalaat el-Ahmar on map Maan 1:500,000) to attack us from the south, where the hills were broken and difficult to keep clear. We detached thirty men to check them, and waited till noon, when a force of about 100 men moved out from Mudowarrah and came slowly down the line, to outflank us on the north. At 1 p.m. a train of two engines and ten box-wagons came up slowly from the south, shooting hard at us from loopholes and positions on the carriage roofs. As it passed I exploded the mine under the second engine, hoping the first would then go through the culvert: the Lewis guns cleared the roof meanwhile. The mine derailed the front engine, smashing its cab and tender, destroyed the second engine altogether, and blew in the culvert. The first wagon upended into the hole and the succeeding ones were shaken up. The shock affected the Turks, and the Arabs promptly charged up to within twenty yards, and fired at the wagons, which were not armoured. The Turks got out on the far side, and took refuge in the hollow of the bank (about eleven feet high) and fired between the wheels at us. Two Stokes bombs at once fell among them there, and turned them out towards some rough country 200 yards NE of the line. On their way there the Lewis gun killed all but about twenty of them, and the survivors threw away their rifles and fled towards Mudowarrah. The action took ten minutes.

The Arabs now plundered the train, while I fired a box of guncotton on the front engine and damaged it more extensively. I fear, however, that it is still capable of repair. The conditions were not helpful to good work, for there were many prisoners and women hanging on to me, I had to keep the peace among the plunderers, and the Turks from the south opened fire on us at long range just as the train surrendered, our covering force on that side having come in to share the booty. The baggage in the train was very large and the Arabs went mad over it. In any case a Bedouin force no longer exists when plunder has been obtained, since each man only cares to get off home with it. I was therefore left with the two British NCOs and Zaal and Howeimil of the Arabs, to ensure the safety of the guns and machine-guns. It was impossible to complete the destruction of the first engine or burn the trucks. We destroyed twenty rounds of Stokes shells and some SAA whose detonation kept back the Turks for a time. The north and south Turkish forces were both coming up fast, and our road back was commanded by hills which they were already occupying. I abandoned my own baggage and got away the men and guns to a safe position in the rear. Zaal was there able to collect thirteen men, and at 3 p.m. we counter-attacked the hills and regained our camping ground. We then managed to clear off most of the kit, though some of it, in the most exposed positions, had to be left. Sergeant Yells came up with a Lewis, and we retired ridge by ridge from 4.30 p.m. with no losses except four camels.

The Turkish killed amounted to about seventy men, with about thirty wounded (of whom many died later). We took ninety prisoners, of whom five were Egyptian soldiers captured by the Turks near Hadiyah, ten were women, and nine were Medina men, deported by the Turks. An Austrian Second Lieut. who (with about thirteen Sergeant Instructors) was on the train, was killed: only sixty-eight of the prisoners were brought into Akaba.

From 5 p.m. we rode hard northward, and on to Mudowarrah well, at 8 p.m. We watered that night, without interruption from the Turks, which was good fortune, for the station is only three miles away and the Arab camels were so loaded with booty as to be useless for a fight. We left the same evening, and got to Rum on the night of 20 September.

The promptness of the Turkish attack, the smallness of my force, and the amount of spoil made our retreat inevitable. I had hoped to hold up the line for a considerable time, and still hope that, with proper arrangements, it may be possible. The country about Mudowarrah (whose station well is, I feel sure, the key of the Maan–Tebuk railway) is so bare of grazing, that the maintenance of a large blockading force is not feasible; but the water difficulties for the Turks make a heavy attack by them, if Mudowarrah is once lost, improbable.

The Arab casualties were one killed and four wounded.

The mine was a sandbag of fifty pounds of blasting gelatine kneaded into one lump. It was set between the ends of two steel sleepers, in contact with each and with the base of the rail. Four inches of sand and ballast was laid over it. The spot chosen was over the south haunch of a three-metre arched culvert, and the contact wires were buried down the embankment, across a hollow, and up a low rocky ridge beyond. A naval waterproof detonator was used, as army detonators were not available. The burying of the contact wire took nearly four hours, since stiff single wires were supplied. A very light twin cable would be more use. It proved extremely difficult (on the score of weight) to carry off the wires after use.

The length of cable available was 200 yards, but for reasons of observation I had to stand at 100 yards only. The shock of the explosion was very severe, and parts of cylinders, wheels, pistons and boiler plating fell all over the place to a radius of 300 yards from the locomotive. The whole side of the engine was blown off and half the culvert brought down. People in the trucks complained of shock. Had I fired the mine under the front engine I think both would have been wrecked. One was a Hejaz locomotive and one a DHP (Damascus–Aleppo Railway).

XXIX. The Raid near Bir esh-Shediyah
21 October 1917

I left Akaba on 27 September, to test an automatic mine on the Hejaz railway. In view of the possibility of wider operations in October, I took with me Lieutenant Pisani, of the French section at Akaba, and three educated Syrians (Faiz and Bedri el-Moayyad, and Lutfi el-Asali), in order to train them in anti-railway tactics.

We marched to Rum on 29 September, where we stopped three days. Lieut. Pisani had fever, and I spent the time in showing him and the others the preliminary work of mining and arranging with Sherif Hashim, a Shenabra, who is OC, Rum, details of the Bedouin force required. Feisal's orders to him were to go where, when, and as I wanted. In an endeavour to get over the difficulties caused by Audah Abu Tayi's pretensions, I appointed Sheikh Salem Alayan (Dumaniyah) to be OC Bedouins, and asked for only Dumaniyah and Darausha tribesmen, about forty in all. This number would have been enough to deal with a wrecked train, and easy to handle in the

Fasoa district (for which I was bound), where the wells are small. However the enormous haul of booty in the train blown up early in September near Mudowarrah had completely turned the heads of the Huweitat, and hundreds clamoured and insisted on taking part in my new expedition. We had a great deal of difficulty, and in the end I accepted nearly 100 Darausha, and fifty Dumaniyah, including every sheikh in the two sub-tribes. All others were refused.

A feature of the Huweitat is that every fourth or fifth man is a sheikh. In consequence the head sheikh has no authority whatever, and as in the previous raid, I had to be OC of the whole expedition. This is not a job which should be undertaken by foreigners, since we have not so intimate a knowledge of Arab families, as to be able to divide common plunder equitably. On this occasion, however, the Bedouins behaved exceedingly well, and everything was done exactly as I wished; but during the six days' trip I had to adjudicate in twelve cases of assault with weapons, four camel-thefts, one marriage-settlement, fourteen feuds, two evil eyes, and a bewitchment. These affairs take up all one's spare time.

We marched up Wadi Hafri (which drains into el-Gaa, NE of Rum, a central basin into which W. Hisma and W. Rabugh also pour) to its head near Batra, where we watered with some difficulty owing to scarcity of supply, and the numerous Arab families at the well. The area between Batra and the railway is full of Arab tents. From Batra we marched on 3 October to near kilo. 475, where I meant to mine; but we found Turkish guard posts (of fifteen to twenty-five men) too close to the suitable spots. At nightfall, therefore, we went away to the south, till midnight, when we found a good place, and buried an automatic mine at kilo. 500.4. The nearest Turkish post was 2,500 m. away on the south. On the north there was no post for nearly 4,000 yards. The mine-laying took the five of us two hours, and then we retired 1,500 yards from the line and camped. On the 4th no train passed. On the 5th a water-train came down from Maan at 10 a.m., and went over the mine without firing it. I waited till midday and then, in two hours, laid an electric mine over the automatic. The Turks patrolled the line twice daily, but one may usually reckon on their all sleeping at noon. We then disposed the Arabs to attack the train when it should come, and waited till the morning of 6 October for one to arrive.

The line here crosses a valley on a bank twenty feet high, and 500 yards long. The bank is pierced by three small bridges, at intervals of about 200 yards. We laid our mines over the southernmost of these, took the cables along the track to the midmost (the firing position), and put two Lewis guns in the northernmost, from which point they were in a position to rake the embankment. From this northern bridge ran up westward a two-foot deep torrent bed, spotted with broom bushes. In these the men and guns hid till wanted.

On the 6th a train (twelve wagons) came down from Maan at 8 a.m. It arrived only 200 yards in advance of the Turkish patrol (of nine men), but this gave us time to get into position. From the open bed of the valley in front of the line, where I was sitting to give the signal for firing, it was curious to see the train running along the top of the bank with the machine-gunners and exploders dancing war-dances beneath the bridges. The Arabs behind me were beautifully hidden, and kept perfectly still.

The explosion shattered the fire-box of the locomotive (No. 153, Hejaz), burst many of the tubes, threw the l.c. cylinder into the air, cleaned out the cab, warped the frame, bent the two near driving wheels and broke their axles. I consider it past repair. Its tender, and the front wagon were also destroyed, with one arch of the bridge. The couplings broke, and the last four wagons drifted backwards downhill out of fire. I was too late to stop them with a stone. A Kaimmakam, General Staff, appeared at one window, and fired at us with a Mauser pistol, but a Bedouin blazed into him at twenty yards, and he fell back out of sight and I hope damaged. (We have heard since he got back safe to Maan: he was one, Nazmi Bey.) The eight remaining wagons were captured in six minutes. They contained about seventy tons of foodstuffs, 'urgently required at Medain Salih for Ibn Rashid', according to way-bills captured with the lot. We carried off about a third of this, and destroyed another third or more. The Turkish killed amount to about fifteen. Some civilians were released, and four officers taken prisoner.

The plundering occupied all the energies of our Bedouins, and Turkish counter-attacks came up unopposed from N and S. I rolled up the electric cables first of all, and as they are very heavy and I was single-handed, it took nearly three-quarters of an hour to do this. Then two chiefs of the Darausha came to look for me. I went up to the top of the bank, hoping to fire the train, but found about forty Turks coming up fast and only 400 yards off. As the nearest Bedouins were 1,000 yards away and they were all on foot, driving their laden camels at top speed westward, I felt that it would be foolish to delay longer alone on the spot, and so rode off with the two Arabs who had come back for me. We all reached Rum safely on the 7th, and Akaba on the 8th, where I found telegrams asking me to go to Suez and on to GHQ, EEF.

The raid was intended as an experiment only, and was most successful. The automatic mine failed, but I proved able to keep 150 Bedouins in a camp 1,500 yards from the line for three days without giving the Turks warning of our presence, in spite of the regular patrols passing up and down the line. This means that the rank and file of the Arabs, as well as the sheikhs, did as I ordered. The complete destruction of a captured train, and annihilation of relief parties, will be easy, as soon as I have the Indian MG section to support me in the actual action. The Lewis gunners on this occasion were two of my Arab servants, trained by me in one day at Rum. They killed twelve of the enemy's casualties, but of course went off to get booty immediately afterwards.

M. Pisani, Faiz el-Moayyad, and Lufti el-Asali, are now, I think, competent to lay mines by themselves. I was very well satisfied with all three of them.

XXX. Geographical Notes
21 October 1917

Wadi Sirhan

Major Lawrence has supplied some new information about this important wadi, which affords the main channel of communication between the Hauran, Jauf and North-Central Arabia. Kaf (pronounced Djaf), at its head, is grouped popularly with Wishwasha, Nebkh, Ithra and Jerjer, as el-Geraia or Geraiat el-Milh, on the ground of common possession of vast saltworks which seem to have escaped mention by European travellers. Major Lawrence found the wadi alive with snakes, of which some half-dozen varieties, ranging from nine to three feet in length are poisonous. His party lost three men from snake-bites. It is particularly dangerous to water after dark, as the wells and pools are then full of snakes swimming about. In the daytime they are to be found in every bush. There and in the country to the south many ostriches were seen, but none was caught. Major Lawrence and three others breakfasted off one of their eggs, boiled over a fire of gelignite sticks (!): it was about a month old. They obtained a good deal of oryx meat and saw several of these heavy-headed antelopes, very suggestive of oxen. The Huweitat had a fine baby oryx in their tents. After the war it ought to be arranged that this interesting species be represented by live specimens in London.

Maps of North-West Arabia

Major Lawrence, as a result of his journeys in north-western Arabia, reports that all existing maps leave much to be desired. The Arab Bureau Maan sheet (1:500,000) he found to be not bad as a sketch of the general lie of country; but the railway, he feels sure, is shown too far to the east, a mistake which leads to the underestimating of all distances from it in an inland direction. The Royal Geographical Society's 1:2,000,000 sheet he condemns for all the Wadi Sirhan and Jauf region, especially in its placing and spelling of localities. Miss Bell's traverse from Kaf to Seba Byar, the most important of the Wuld Ali watering places, he found to be good but too slight. Between Maan and Akaba he condemns all our maps, British, German and Turkish alike; e.g., an important watershed between the Hisma (he doubts the general application of this name to all the large plateau area usually so-called, and thinks it is to be used only of a single wadi) and Wadi Ithm, some eight miles southwest of Guweira, is nowhere properly marked. It is certainly very desirable to run a route-survey up Wadi Ithm, and to get the position of the railway fixed at several points between Maan and Medina. Major Lawrence's own route-sketches are not yet to hand.

XXXI. A Raid
16 December 1917

I left Akaba on 24 October, with Capt. G. Lloyd, Lieut. Wood, RE, and the Indian Machine-Gun Company. The Indians took two Vickers, and I took two Lewis guns with me.

We marched to Rum (25 October) and thence across El-Gaa and up W. Hafir to near Batra. We crossed the railway just south of Bir el-Shedia and reached el-Jefer on 28 October. Capt. Lloyd returned to Akaba from there. Sherif Ali ibn Husein overtook us, and the party marched to Bair, picked up Sheikh Mifleh el-Zebn and fifteen Sukhur and reached Amri on 2 November. On 5 November we camped at Kseir el-Hallabat, and on the 7th failed to rush the bridge at Tell el-Shehab, and returned to Kseir. Thence the Indian MG Company with Lieut. Wood, returned to Azrak. I went with sixty Arabs to Minefir, blew up a train at Kil. 172 on 11 November and reached Azrak on the 12th.

My intention had been to reach Jisr el-Hemmi on 3 November, but this proved impossible, since rain had made the Jaulaan plain too slippery for our camels, and the Turks had put hundreds of woodcutters in the Irbid hills. This closed both the north and south roads, and left Tell el-Shehab (Bridge 14) the only approachable bridge in the Yarmuk valley. My first plan was to rush it by camel marches of fifty miles a day. This idea also failed, since by their best efforts the Indian Machine Gun Company were only able to do thirty to thirty-five miles a day, and even this pace cut up their camels very quickly, owing to their inexperience. They all did their best, and gave me no trouble at all, but were simply unable to march fast.

I decided, therefore, to raise an Arab force, and descend on the bridge in strength. The Abu Tayi refused to come, only fifteen Sukhur would take it on, and I had to rely mainly on thirty Serahin recruits at Azrak. They were untried men and proved little use at the pinch. For the last stage to the bridge, as hard riding was involved, I picked out six of the Indians, with their officer, and we got actually to the bridge at midnight on 7 November. It is a position of some strength, but could, I think, be rushed by twenty decent men. The Indians with me were too few to attempt it, and the Serahin, as soon as the Turks opened fire, dumped their dynamite into the valley and bolted. In the circumstances I called everyone off as quickly as possible and went back to Kseir el-Hallabat. The Indians with us were very tired with the ride, which was a fairly fast one, of ninety miles in twenty-two hours. The Bedu and the Sherif wanted to do something more before returning to Azrak, and had the Indians been fitter, we could have put in a useful raid; but they were tired and had only half a day's ration left, since all extra stuff has been placed at Azrak.

The situation was explained to the Sherif, who said it would be enough to mine a train, without making a machine gun attack upon it. The Bedu agreed, and we went off together. The party was composed of Sherif Ali with

ten servants, myself with one, twenty Sikhur and thirty Serahin. None of us
had any food at all. We went to Minifir, to Kil. 172, where I mined the line
in June last. As the Bedu had lost my dynamite at the bridge I was only able
to put 30 lb into the mine, which I laid on the crown of a four metre culvert
(about eighteen feet high) and took the wires as far up the hillside toward
cover as they would reach. Owing to the shortage of cable this was only sixty
yards, and we had to leave the ends buried, for fear of patrols. A train came
down before dawn on the 10th, too fast for me to get to the exploder from
my watching place. In the morning of the 10th a train of refugees came up
at four miles an hour from the south. The exploder failed to work, and the
whole train crawled past me as I lay on the flat next the wires. For some
reason no one shot at me, and after it had passed I took the exploder away
and overhauled it, while a Turkish patrol came up and searched the ground
very carefully. That night we slept on the head of the wires, and no train
appeared, till 10 a.m. on 11 November. Then a troop train of twelve coaches
and two locomotives came down from the north at twenty miles an hour. I
touched off under the engine and the explosion was tremendous. Something
must have happened to the boiler for I was knocked backwards and boiler
plates flew about in all directions. One fragment smashed the exploder,
which I therefore left in place, with the wires. The first engine fell into the
valley on the east side of the line; the second upended into the space where
the culvert had been, and toppled over on to the tender of the first. The frame
buckled, and I doubt whether it can be repaired. Its tender went down the
embankment west, and the first two coaches telescoped into the culvert site.
The next three or four were derailed. Meanwhile I made quite creditable time
across the open, uphill towards the Arabs, who had a fair position, and were
shooting fast over me into the coaches, which were crowded with soldiers.
The Turkish losses were obviously quite heavy. Unfortunately many of the
Serahin had no rifles, and could only throw unavailing stones. The Turks
took cover behind the bank, and opened a fairly hot fire at us. They were
about 200 strong by now. Sherif Ali brought down a party of twenty-two to
meet me, but lost seven killed and more wounded and had some narrow
escapes himself before getting back.

The train may have contained someone of importance, for there were a
flagged saloon-car, an Imam, and a motor car in it. I suspect someone wanted
to go *via* Amman to Jerusalem. We riddled the saloon. The Turks, seeing us
so few, put in an attack later which cost them about twenty casualties, and
then began to work up the slopes to right and left of us. So we went off, and
reached Azrak next day.

This mine showed that sixty yards of cable is too little for firing heavy
charges under locomotives. I had first to survive the rain of boiler plates, and
then to run up a steep hill for 400 yards under fire. By good chance it was
impossible to carry off the wire, so the performance cannot be repeated till
more comes from Akaba.

The march also showed the staying qualities of the Bedouins. They rode ninety miles without food or rest on the 8th, ate a small meal on the morning of the 9th and sat out hungry two nights and three days of bitterly cold wind and rain (we had not the satisfaction of being steadily wet, but were wetted and dried five times) till the evening of the 11th when we killed them a riding camel; after which they rode into Azrak cheerfully.

XXXII. Abdullah and the Akhwan
24 December 1917

The following are notes of the talk of Sherif Feisal during a conversation which I had with him on 4 December:

It is not fair to condemn my brother, Abdullah, without reserve. He is taking no part in the war against the Turks, because his whole heart, his head, and all his resources are engaged in the problems of Nejd. He is king of the Ateibah and of part of the Meteir and Heteym, and is daily increasing his hold on the outliers of Qasim and Jebel Shammar. The responsibility for order in Western Nejd has always lain upon Abdullah. When my father came to the throne he found all the border tribes in a turmoil, and Abdullah led expedition after expedition against them (while I crushed the Idrisi, by the help of the Turks) until his name was feared from Taif to Shaharah, and all the chiefs of the Ateibah came to him for orders and directions. In those days we were beset by our religious enemies, the Wahabis and the Idrisis, and were fighting for our lives. After that there was peace until we had revolted against the Turks and marched to Wejh. Then again began troubles in Nejd. Abdullah garrisoned Henakiyah, and Ibn Saud took alarm. Once more he has sent out all his missionaries.

The name 'Akhwan', which you use is not properly applied to the converts. It began as the title of the brotherhood of preachers. Now it is used loosely of the disciples also. The Akhwan take over all the Senefiyeh tenets, especially the saying that Mohammed was a man with a message, who is dead. They add stricter rules of consanguinity, veil their women even in the house, are fatalists to a forbidden degree, and hold as first principle the law of Jihad, at the call of the Imam and the Ulema. I fear always that to-morrow, when the stress comes, they will reject the authority of the Koran (in the interpretation of which they differ greatly from us), as they reject the Prophet to-day. Their Imam is Ibn Saud, but the title is not significant; yet they regard him as the head of their *tarika* and submit themselves wholly to his orders. He pays the salaries of all the preachers, many hundreds of them; but the moving spirit of the whole is one of the Ulema of Riyadh. They appeal only to Bedu, and sow discord between them and the *hadhar*. Riyadh (or the *aalim* village near it) is the centre of the new doctrine. Eight out of ten Nejd Bedu follow the Akhwan, and the Taif branch is rapidly winning over the tribes of northern Yemen. The Zobeir men are influencing the Shamiyah Arabs; one fourth of the Shammar have allied themselves to it, and only the energy of Nuri has kept it out of the Anazeh. The converts stir each other up to a pitch of extreme fanaticism, but their subjection to the college at Riyadh is absolute, and the college is the creation of Ibn Saud, who pays and feeds the preachers. He insists on peace at present, and is friendly to you. He suffers Ibn Rashid to exist till he has converted the other Shammar. When his time comes he will direct the force of the Bedu in turn against the settled peoples of Arabia: taking piece-meal, first Qasim, then Hail, then the Hejaz, then Iraq and Syria, he will impose everywhere the new doctrine, and sway the peninsula.

Abdullah is making head against all this. The first step in his ambition is to win the Shammar, and in this he is making steady progress. He has lost the Heteym, who have gone over to the new faith; but his hold upon the Ateibah is very strong, and he is daily confirming it. Without the Ateibah Ibn Saud can never take the Hejaz. These measures are defensive, and so far as his means go, Abdullah is extending them. He is also carrying the war into Ibn Saud's camp, in Qasim, the weak point of the Akhwan scheme. Aneizah, Bureidah and Rass are comfortable towns. Their young men have enlisted in our, and the Turkish government's, *ageyl*, and there learnt tolerance and the use of tobacco. They return after three or four years to their homes, and tell the people of the Hejaz government, where the savagery of the *sheria* code, literal with Ibn Saud, is softened by the humanity of the ruler to accord with the spirit of the time. In consequence the eyes of Qasim turn longingly towards us, and if the Qusman could, they would rebel against the Imam and his Akhwan. Ibn Saud usually keeps forces in their towns, to prevent this movement gaining force, and so Abdullah has to work secretly. He does not really want Qasim, but he wants to make Ibn Saud afraid.

If we can unite the settle peoples of Arabia under my father's flag, we can strangle the new faith in the desert, until it becomes again a dogmatic abstraction, as the Wahabi faith was between Mohammed Ali and Emir Abd el-Aziz. If we fail, all our efforts and victories over the Turks will be wasted. Great Britain will not profit by the Arab revival, if the tomb at Medina and the Haram at Mecca are destroyed, and the pilgrimage is prevented. Abdullah is fighting all our battles, and if he has no leisure to campaign against the railway meanwhile, he should not be judged too harshly.

XXXIII. Akhwan Converts
27 January 1918

Among the recent converts to the Akhwan sect are Feisal, Watban and Lafi, of the Dueish section of the Ateibah. Parts of the Doshan got religion some months ago. Feisal became converted shortly after he had left Sidi Abdullah's camp. He has already sold off his camels, and assumed the white 'imama'. It is thought that he will settle in Dukhna, the Akhwan village shared by the Ateibah and Harb, but Suman and Dahana are other Dueish Akhwan colonies, and he might prefer either of these. Of the Hejna Atban, Sheikhs Nijr and Turki have gone over to the new Wahabi movement, with Bijad abu

Khusheim. Ghalib and Ali el-Himerzi, Naif el-Jithami and Naif el-Rueis are also converts, while Mohammed ibn Hindi is suspected. Ibn Shleiwi has refused to have anything to do with it.

The converted Muteir are mostly living at Artawiya, which seems likely to become one of the headquarters of the militant Akhwan. Ibn Skeiyan, Mohammed el-Hawamil, Dheihan el-Lafi, Azeir el-Sfeini (of the Hawamil), Ibn Sbeiyil of Athla, Mohammed el-Mizeini (of el-Gereiyat) and Mohammed ibn Mijal of Nifi are prominant Muteiri converts.

Of the Harb, Nahis and Feisal el-Dhueibi, Dhaar el-Saada, Zeid el-Hilali and Thellab ibn Ali are adherents. Some of the Furm sub-chiefs are rumoured to have joined.

All the above have been converted since 1914.

XXXIV. First Reports from Tafila
11 February 1918

Tafila had surrendered on the 15th after a little fighting, and the number of Turks captured there was 150.

Major Lawrence, writing from there on the 22nd, reported that the inhabitants were divided into two hostile factions, who were very afraid of each other, and there was shooting in the streets every night. Flour and barley were very dear and difficult to find, and there was a serious lack of mules and camels. The Sherifian officers, however, were arranging to police the town and organise supplies. The situation was complicated by the presence of a colony of Moors, who had been besieged by the Arabs, and a party of seventeen [*1,700!*] destitute but, apparently, well fed Armenians.

A force of local Arabs, under Sherif Abdullah el-Faiz and Hamud es-Sufi, of the Terabin (adds Major Lawrence) had gone to Mezraa, on the Dead Sea, to block any leakage of supplies westwards from Kerak; while Sherif Mastur was going northward to Seil el-Hesa, about half-way between Kerak and Tafila. Letters have been sent to the Kerak Arabs, whose attitude was doubtful. Rifaifan, the head of the Mujaliyah, was believed to be pro-Turkish, but Husein el-Tura, the other leading sheikh, was secretly pro-Sherifian.

News has since been received of the occupation of Mezraa by the Arabs, who captured sixty prisoners, including two officers, and burnt a launch and six sailing boats.

On 26 January a large force of Turks from Kerak attacked the Arabs at Seil el-Hesa, where severe fighting took place. This resulted in a brilliant victory for the Arabs, who killed 500 of the enemy and captured 250, including Hamid Bey, the OC 48th Division. Only about fifty Turks escaped in the direction of Kerak, and all officers were killed or captured. The booty consisted of two powerful Austrian mountain-guns, nine automatic rifles, twenty-three machine-guns (including fifteen German Maxim machine-guns) and 800 rifles. About 200 mules and horses were also taken and distributed among the Bedouin.

XXXV. The Battle of Seil el-Hasa
18 February 1918

A Turkish temporary regiment, commanded by Hamid Fakhri Bey, acting GOC 48th Division, and composed of 3/151, 1/152, a *murettab* battalion of 150, with a company of gendarmes, a detachment of 100 cavalry, two Austrian quick-firing mountain-guns, and twenty-three machine-guns, was railed to Kalaat el-Hasa station on 19 January, and left Kerak on 23 January to retake Tafila. The troops had been hurriedly collected from the Hauran and Amman commands, and came forward from Kerak short of supplies, and leaving no food and few men there.

On 24 January, they came in contact in the afternoon with our patrols in Seil el-Hasa, and by night had driven them back into Tafila. The Sherifian officers had laid out a defensive position on the south bank of the great valley in which Tafila stands, and Sherif Zeid left for this about midnight, taking with him the sixty regulars and 400 irregulars (Ageyl, Bisha, Muteir) who had come with him from Akaba. The Sherifian baggage marched away at the same time towards Buseira, and everybody thought that we were running away. I think we were.

Tafila of course panicked, and as Diab el-Auran (the busy-bodied sheikh) had given us ominous reports of the disaffection and treachery of the villagers, I went down from my house before dawn into the crowded street, to listen to what was being said. There was much free criticism of the Sherif, distinctly disrespectful, but no disloyalty. Everyone was screaming with terror, goods were being bundled out of the houses into the streets, which were packed with women and men. Mounted Arabs were galloping up and down, firing wildly into the air, and the flashes of the Turkish rifles were outlining the further cliffs of the Tafila gorge. Just at dawn the enemy bullets began to fall in the olive gardens, and I went out to Sherif Zeid and persuaded him to send Abdullah Effendi (the machine-gunner and the junior of our two officers) with two *fusils mitrailleurs* to support the peasants who were still holding the northern crest. His arrival stimulated them to a counter-attack in which they drove the Turkish cavalry back over the near ridge, across a small plain to the first of the low ridges falling into Wadi el-Hasa. He took this ridge also, and was there held up, as the Turkish main body was posted just behind it. The fighting became very hot, with huge bursts of Turkish machine-gun fire and a good deal of shelling.

Zeid hesitated to send forward reinforcements, so I went up to Abdullah's position (about seven miles north of Tafila) to report. On my way I met him returning, having had five men killed and one gun put out of action, and having finished his ammunition. We sent back urgent messages to Zeid to send forward a mountain-gun, any available machine-guns, and what men he could collect, to a reserve position, which was the southern end of the little plain between the Hasa valley and the Tafila valley. This plain is triangular, about two miles each way. The opening lay to the north, and was a low pass, through which the Kerka road ran, and up which the Turks were coming. The sides of the triangle were low ridges, and Abdullah's charge had taken all the western ridge.

After Abdullah had gone I went up to the front, and found things rather difficult. It was being held by thirty Ibn Jazi Howeitat, mounted, and about thirty villagers. The Turks were working through the pass, and along the eastern boundary ridge of the plain, and concentrating the fire of about fifteen machine-guns on the face and flank of the rather obvious little mound we were holding. They were meanwhile correcting the fusing of their shrapnel, which had been grazing the hill-top and bursting over the plain, and were beginning to sprinkle the sides and top of the hill quite freely. Our people were short of ammunition, and the loss of the position was obviously only a matter of minutes. A Turkish aeroplane came up and did not improve our chances.

The Motalga horsemen were given all the cartridges we could collect, and the footmen ran back over the plain. I was among them, since I had come straight up the cliffs from Tafila, and my animals had not caught me up. The mounted men held out for fifteen minutes more, and then galloped back to us unhurt. We collected in the reserve position, a ridge about sixty feet high, commanding an excellent view of the plain. It was now noon, we had lost about fifteen men and had about eighty left, but a few minutes later about 120 Ageyl came up, and my men with a Hotchkiss automatic, and Lutfi el-Aseli with two. We then held our own easily till 3 p.m. when Sherifs Zeid and Mastur came up with Rasim and Abdullah, one Egyptian army 2.95 mountain-gun, two Vickers, two large Hotchkiss, and five *fusils mitrailleurs*, with twenty mule MI, thirty Motalga horse, and about 200 villagers. The Turks were trying to shell and machine-gun our ridge, but found difficulty in ranging. They had occupied our old front line, and we had its range (3,100 yards) exactly, as I had paced it on my way back (this mountain country is very difficult to judge by eye). We mounted all our materials on our ridge, and Rasim took all the mounted men (now about eighty) to the right, to work up beyond the eastern boundary ridge. He was able to get forward unseen, till he had turned the Turkish flank at 2,000 yards. He there made a dismounted attack of ten men and five *fusils mitrailleurs*, keeping his horse in reserve. Meanwhile the Turks had just five Maxims and four automatics on the western ridge of the pass, and opened on our centre. We replied with Vickers and Hotchkiss, and put twenty-two rounds of shrapnel over the face of the mound. A reinforcement of 100 men from Aima now reached us (they had refused Sherifian service the day before over a question of wages, but sunk old scores in the crisis), and we sent them, with three Hotchkiss automatics, to our left flank. They crept down behind the western ridge of the plain till within 200 yards of the Turkish Maxims, without being seen, as we opened across the plain a frontal attack of eighteen men, two Vickers, and two large Hotchkiss. The ridge was a flint one, and the Turks could not entrench on it, as we had found in the morning; the ricochets were horrible. They lost many men, and our left flank were finally able by a sudden burst of fire to wipe out the Turkish machine-gunners and rush the guns. The mounted men then charged the retreating Turks from our right flank, while we sent forward the infantry and the banners in the centre. They occupied the Turkish line at sunset, and chased the enemy back past their guns into the bed of Wadi Hasa; where their cavalry in reserve put up a check that was not passed till dark. Our people mostly gave up the pursuit at this point (we had no food since the day before, and the cold was pitiful) but the Bedouins of Kerak took it up and harried the flying mob all night.

Our losses were about twenty-five killed and forty wounded. The Ibn Jazi Howeitat, under Hamad el-Arar, did splendidly, and the villagers were very steady and good.

The figures of the Turkish losses were given in the last Bulletin. Four more machine-guns have since been brought in, raising the number captured to twenty-seven.

XXXVI. Report on Khurma
9 July 1918

Ibn Saud began to collect *dhikat* (a semi-religious tax) from some sections of the Sbei this year, thus reviving his custom of four or five years ago. Shortly afterwards messengers from the Sherif, demanding the same tax, were imprisoned by Sherif Khalid ibn Elwi in Wadi Khurma.

Khalid (a lean fanatical silent man, said to be more capable than his elder brother Naif) was made Emir of Khurma by the Sherif years ago. He was converted to the Nejdean Religion four years ago, and was last year confined in the Sherif's prison at Mecca. On his release on Abdullah's intervention, he paid a secret visit to Ibn Saud, an old friend of his father's.

The imprisonment of the Sherifian messengers was an act of war, and Khalid at once collected his followers. Only the converts joined him, and they were a mixed lot of Beni Thor Sbei; Jithima, Khararis (whose sheikh, Naif, is in prison in Mecca), Shlawa and Hamarza Ateibah; and many Kahtan. The Kahtan were those formerly in the east, who fled from Ibn Saud over the Ajman affair, and have since been living in the upper reaches of Wadi Dawasir. They are not in any way under Khalid, and have only joined temporarily, for the Religion's sake.

Khalid began by expelling the other Shei, and all the villagers and freedmen, from Wadi Khurma, into the main valley Truba, of which it is a tributary. Wadi Truba (Tharba or Tarabat) runs south-west into a cultivated plain in Jebel Areysh, of the Goz aba el-Air (Joz Belair) district. Khalid proposed to install converted peasants in the palm-gardens in their place.

His brother, Naif, then waylaid and killed four Ageyl, two Ateibah, and four women, Sunnis from Mecca on their way to Khurma for the summer. They refused to be converted, but nevertheless Khalid protested against their slaughter.

The Sherif now sent against them a very ragged force, comprising Hamarja, Biyasha, Sbei, Mowalid, Hedhlan (Hudheil) and other Meccan sweepings, with two brass saluting guns and two automatic rifles, under the incompetent Sherif Ali, brother of Shakir ibn Zeid. They were surprised by night on Bir Goreish by an inferior force of Kahtan, and fled without resistance, losing fourteen killed, and their artillery.

Khalid then repented of his action, and went off to Ibn Saud with fifty-four riders and his trophies, to beg for help. On his way he crossed an Ateibah raiding party, under Fajir ibn Shelawih, on its way to Dawasir. The two parties fought, and Ibn Shelawih took thirteen camels, four horses and the artillery, killing four of the converted, and losing only one himself. Khalid fled towards Riadh.

The Kahtan are not likely to remain long in Wadi Khurma, and Naif ibn Elwi cannot hope, with only the Beni Thor, to keep the other Sbei indefinitely out of their properties. If Khalid fails in his mission in Aridh, the complete collapse of his movement may be expected.

The Sherif hopes to enrol a new force in Mecca to retake Khurma, but is trying to conscript the town Bedouins at half wages, and in consequence has made no progress. Should he make further attacks upon Khurma, with the materials at his disposal, he may reasonably be expected to suffer further reverses. If, however, he acquires wisdom enough to accept the temporary loss of the district, and if Ibn Saud maintains his present correct attitude, then no extension – or prolongation – of the rising need be feared.

XXXVII. Syrian Cross-Currents
1 February 1918

It used to be interesting before the war to ask a Syrian in French who were the leading spirits of Beyrout or Damascus, and a day or two later to ask him the same question in Arabic. You got two entirely different lists, alike only in that all were Moslem, since there are no Christians, in or out of Syria, whose 'nationalism' is more than a pretty name for a European control loose enough to give their co-religionists excessive place in the administration. For this reason Christians have no share in the political life of the country, and their voices and opinions are absolutely to be ignored.

The Moslems were divided rather sharply into the intelligentsia and the Arabs. The first were those who had thrown off Arab things, and bared themselves to the semi-Levantine semi-European fashions of the renegade Moslem – the Moslem who has lost his traditional faith, and with it all belief in all faiths. They spoke foreign languages as often as they could, wore European clothes, were often wealthy, used to entertain and be entertained by foreigners, and impressed themselves more deeply upon foreign visitors than their numbers or home influence warranted. Their political ideals were culled from books. They had no programme of revolt, but many ideas for the settlement after one. Such and such were the rights of Syria, such her boundaries, such her future law and constitution. They formed committees in Cairo, Paris, London, New York, Beyrout, Berlin, and Berne, to influence European powers to deliver them from the Turks, and lend them the sinews to go on spinning real dreams. Their habits made Syria uncongenial, and most of them lived in foreign countries.

There existed a bridge between these occidentalists and the classes that speak Arabic first and foremost. They were the translators, who were in touch with the foreign-veneered logocrats. They edited newspapers, and produced Arabic paraphrases of western political theories. When war broke out they remained in Syria, believing themselves secure. They had preached the completed revolution daily in their press, but their hearts were shining – innocent of all intention of revolutionary processes. Their tragic astonishment when Jemal Pasha arrested them and hanged them as leaders of rebellion betrayed their harmlessness. They saw the real conspirators, men who day and night preached armed action against the Turks, walking freely in Damascus, and crowding to see them executed. Some took up the dress of martyrs, and died silently. Some in their bitterness told the Turks the names all Arabs knew, trying to involve the guilty with themselves in punishment: but mostly Jemal only laughed.

Thus by January 1915, Syria was deprived of her Christian pseudo-nationalists, who were either silent with terror, or the Turks' best friends, of her Levantine-Moslems, who were reaping new delights abroad, in finding themselves taken seriously by foreign chancellors, and of her Arab-revival idealists, who were hanged and buried. For three years she has been a closed country, ignorant of the programmes made for her future in allied capitals, subject to the military autocracy of a particularly ruthless and unbridled dictator, and so forced to a more secret internal and intensive culture of such nationalist ideals as had real root in herself. Until the northern thrusts of the Sherifian army, to Akaba, and then to the Hauran, there was no outer door by which contact could be obtained with this re-born Syria of 1918, and only by casual indications could the force and direction of the new movements be guessed. Now that we can feel the full vigour we realise how jejune the former political groups have become, and how little they can claim to represent the feelings of Syria to-day. The Azm and Mutram factions go on blindfoldedly, balancing this party with that party, and offsetting this programme with that programme in memoranda and solemn interviews with European statesmen, while in the disputed country the Sherifians set their teeth and work, and the Turco-Germans bring down Abbas Hilmi into Asia.

This restoration of Abbas Hilmi may be called a renaissance of Oppenheim, and points to Germany's having at last gained a hand in Turkish internal politics. The Turks tried to use Abbas Hilmi in the early days of the war, found him double-edged, and threw him aside. Now in their extremity they are forced again to admit him, knowing that it hurts them if he succeeds. Abbas Hilmi will not serve the Turks to suppress the Arabs, but only to elevate himself – by the Arabs – to the level of the Turks. He may do this with Germany's approval. Oppenheim with his very rich Semitic nature was always pro-Arab rather than pro-Turk. He fought the ultra-Turk party in Germany till the first year of war, and was beaten. Prussia allied herself with Enver to raise a Jehad, and her Arab friends joined Arab parties. The day of the Sherif's revolt justified Von Oppenheim, too late to help Germany, but soon enough to give him another opportunity. Turkey to-day is [too] feeble to serve Germany's ends in the world. The Kaiser must have friends in Islam other than Enver and Carasso, and friends in Syria and Mesopotamia other than Jemal and Sheikh Shawish. Oppenheim has set out to find her allies on the Alexandretta–Basra lines of penetration, in readiness for the after-war.

His first pre-occupation must be the Sherif. Abbas Hilmi is beloved in Mecca, but the Sherif based his revolt on principles which are above private friendships (even in the Near East where the personal element is nearly all in all) and till the issue of the war is plain, Oppenheim will not overtake our influence there. When the Sherif drew sword he told us what he wanted, and we raised no vital objection to his claim. Since then we have helped him manfully, and his kingdom has grown from nothing to 100,000 square miles (such miles, perhaps, but the Arabs like Arabia!). He has involved himself and all his friends in the risk of gallows if they fail, or if we fail, and has pledged his honour to the Arabs in the magnificent ambition of adding Syria and Mesopotamia to his dominion. If the war lasts long enough he wins, at least enough to fire Arab minds for many years with the picture of Arabia Irridenta. The dice of the great game between us and the rest, for Arab suffrage after the war, will be cogged against the alien owners of any such province: but the asset in our hands, our control of the sea, has been so seared into the minds of the Sherif and his family, by the work of the Red Sea Patrol during this war, that its importance will probably outweigh to them any sins of commission or omission, that we may accumulate.

Oppenheim's second effort may well be to try and divide the Arab house against itself. The phrase 'Arab movement' was invented in Cairo as a common denomination for all the vague discontents against Turkey which before 1916 existed in the Arab provinces. In non-constitutional country these naturally took on a revolutionary character, and it was convenient to pretend to find a common ground in all of them. They were most of them very local, and very jealous, but had to be considered, in the hope that one or other of them might bear fruit. The day the Sherif declared himself, ended this phase of the question. We had found one Arab who believed in himself and his people, and fortunately it was the noblest family of them all. Since then there has been for us no question of any 'Arab movement'. We have supported the Sherifian movement, and have tried to help him gather into his own society such Arab side and sub-currents as his progress has encountered. Our exclusiveness has been justified, since to date no second Arab has had the courage to range himself independently against the Turk.

Needless to say the Arab parties are not all ready to welcome an imposed head. The renegade Moslems, the Christians, and all other sects (there are few parties whose real platform is not sectarian) are dissatisfied. Their arguments are specious, and not only persuade themselves, but give manoeuvre ground for Oppenheim (and indeed for all other powers who feel alarmed at our too great influence with the Sherif) to oppose us on the highest motives. 'The Sherif', they say, 'is Meccan and obscurantist. We are infidel and enlightened. Deliver us from him.' The Sherif, they imply, will be fanatical in religious questions, and crabbed constitutionally. The sacred words Progress and Nationality are to be ranged against him.

Unfortunately these charges are brought against the Sherif by parties ignorant of Arabia. The Sherif heads no religious revival, claims no hierarchical position. His revolt has divided the house of Islam, drawn the teeth of the Khalifate for a generation. His growth is the one factor in our hands which can aid us to stem the new fanatical revival in central Arabia. His rise has killed the idea of Jehad, the very real bogey which has so often paralysed our action in the East. In Moslem theology he heads the old and slightly effete professional orthodoxy. Legally he is rather lax. Even in the holy cities he dilutes the Sheria; in the provinces he abandons it altogether, for customary law. For a first offence in Wahabi Nejd the right hand is cut off, for the second the tongue torn out, for the third the offender banished to a desert without food or water. In Mecca the worst penalty is imprisonment. For his northern provinces, whose complex populations and commerce make a simple code impossible, he has designated his more plastic son, Feisul, as administrator. His promised programme for Syria may not be sufficient to enlist him the support of Syrians in Europe and America, but the Syrians of Syria are enlisting by thousands in the ranks of his armies. Arabs in Egypt and elsewhere have spoken and written against him. Feisul will not hear of a press propaganda of his ideas: but no free Arab has yet fired a shot against him or his forces, and every advance of his armies is done, not merely by the consent, but by the actual brains and hands of the local people, in the strenuous field of rebellion. There is no 'Hedjaz force' in Syria. Feisul accepts any volunteer for his service, allowing him to preach what he pleases, and pray as he pleases, so long as he will fight against the Turks. He says always that neither England nor France nor Turkey will give over to the Arabs one foot of unconquered ground, but that each new village occupied, each new tribe enrolled by Arab effort, is one more step forward towards the Arab State. For him questions of its boundaries, the composition of its upper house, and the colour of its policemen's boots, can wait till Turk is conquered. One may surmise, however, that his administration will differ rather in the spirit, than in the form, from the system which the Turks have gradually built up for their subject-provinces.

The Syrians abroad are as anxious as the Syrians in Syria to obtain deliverance from the Turk, but desire more elaborate reforms when he is removed, and particularly desire a leading voice in the decision of what these reforms are to be. They have a pathetic belief in the idiot altruism of Britain and France. Themselves hardly capable of courage or unselfishness, they accredit us with little else. For their sake (or rather for their words' sake) we are to pull down the new (and to us rather comfortable) Moslem Power we have so carefully set up, to launch armed expeditions into Syria, expel the Turks, and police the country at their direction, while they exhaust upon it the portfolio of constitutions the Abbé Sieyès must have bequeathed to them. In return we are to have their gratitude, afterwards. The only difference between the Sherif's conquest of Syria and theirs (and they call it such a little difference) is that the Sherif achieves it by the hands of the Syrians themselves, and they wish it achieved by our own blood. They would so much rather the Judean hills were stained with London Territorials, dead for their freedom, to save them from the need of taking dangerous rides . . . but from our point of view it may be argued that in these times of crisis our interests may lead us to support those who adventure their lives in arms on our side (even if they do not please all who call themselves our friends) rather than to rebuff the armed supporters in favour of wordy persons who claim to represent – behind our line – a higher form of culture. A spontaneous rebellion in Syria is an impossibility: the local people will take no action till the front tide of battle has rolled past them. If it is the Sherifian tide, they are enlisted by him, and serve at a later date to advance the allied cause another step. If it is our front line, they will get on with the ploughing of the fields, feeling no gratitude, and no obligation towards us. We have only given them the opportunity of unpunished politics, in the future. When the Sherif comes, neutrality is impossible, and their decision, as between Arab and Turk, inevitable. Our coming enables them to postpone for a season the necessity of rebellion, the gravest step that sedentary man can take. Not until the prosperity of foreign control has given them renewed leisure for politics, will the need for self-government revive. Oppenheim, and the financial interests that back the Mediterranean–Mesopotamian railway schemes would like to raise an Arab movement against the Sherif, since the Sherif is irrecoverably ours. If they succeeded in limiting the pro-British spheres to the Wahabis of Nejd, the Emir of Mecca, and the Bedouin of the Hedjaz, they would have a plausible case for tying the town and village communities of Syria and Mesopotamia to the Continental Powers for protection against these our friends, and could do it all the more freely, since the Arabic areas south of the Akaba–Basra line are not essential to anyone except ourselves. Their material interests are limited to the settled peoples, and if they can prevent our making ourselves 'founders' kin' to the Arab federated states that are inevitable among them, they will have gained a part of their ends. The moral element, the support of the head of Islam passed from them when the advance from Akaba closed the history of the Hejaz revolt. The success or failure of the Sherifian invasion of Syria – a new operation and a new movement – is going to affect the other phase of European rivalry in the Levant, by determining whose candidate is going to gain control of the trade routes and commercial centres of Western Asia.

XXXVIII. The Destruction of the Fourth Army
22 October 1918

With the two thousand camels, given us in July by General Allenby, we calculated that we could afford to send up to Azrak, for operations about Deraa, an expedition of four hundred and fifty camel corps of the Arab regular army, four Arab Vickers, twenty Arab Hotchkiss, a French battery of four mountain QF 65 guns, two British aeroplanes, three British armoured cars with necessary tenders, a demolition company of Egyptian Camel Corps and a section of camel-Ghurkas. Besides these, Sherif Nasir and myself had our private bodyguards of Arab camel-men. This made our total force one thousand strong, and its prospects were so sure that we made no provision (and had no means) for getting it back again. The supply problem, especially in petrol and ammunition, was a very great one, and we lived from hand to mouth, without, however, ever being in serious need.

The force left Ab el-Lissan in detachments early in September, and concentrated, without accident, to time at Azrak on the twelfth of the month. The distance from Akaba to Azrak was two hundred and ninety miles, and we used the wells of Jefer, Bair and Ammari on the way. At Azrak we had meant to collect the Rualla and descend in force on the Hauran, with direct assault on Deraa, which was only held by five hundred rifles – but this plan was spoiled by the unfortunate outburst of the king of Hejaz against Jaafar Pasha and the senior officers of the Northern Army, since the crisis he provoked upset the whole local temper, and delayed me in Ab el-Lissan till 4 September. As a result, the Rualla never came together, and we had to modify our schemes. In the end, we decided to carry out a flying attack on the northern, western and southern railways at Deraa, with our regular troops, the Rualla horse under Khalid and Trad Shaalan, and such Hauran peasants as should be brave enough to declare for us.

As we sat at Azrak we put in a strong bluff towards Amman. Money was sent to Mithgal with very secret instructions to collect barley dumps for us and the British, in our combined surprise attack against Amman and Salt on the 18th. The Beni Sakhr were to mass at Ziza to help us. The rumour of this, and the rumour of our simultaneous intention on Deraa, confirmed by other factors supplied them from Palestine, kept the Turks' eyes fixed on the Jordan and east of it, where their lines were very long, expensive in men, and, despite their best efforts, inevitably vulnerable to a force of our mobility and range.

On the 13th we left Azrak and marched over the long Gian el-Khunna into the basalt screes of Jebel Druse. The Egyptian and Ghurka units were sent westward to cut the Amman line by Mafrak, but, owing to a misunderstanding with their guides, never got so far. However, our Bristol Fighter the same day, brought down a German two-seater in flames near Umm el-Jimal: so all was well. We got to Umtaiye, thirteen miles south-east of Deraa, on the 15th. This (and its neighbour Um el-Surab) were our forward base, as about them were many cisterns of water of last year's rain. We were at once joined by the male population of the nearest villages, and by Sheikh Talal el-Hareidhin of Tafas, the finest fighter of the Hauran, who had come to me in Azrak in 1917. He had agreed to be our guide, and marched with us till he died near Deraa, helping us day and night, our sponsor and backer in every village. But for his energy, courage and honesty, things would have gone hard with us many times.

It was still necessary for us to cut the railway between Deraa and Amman, not only to give colour to our supposed attack on the Fourth Army, but to prevent the reinforcement of Deraa from the south. It was our plan to put ourselves between Deraa and Palestine, to force the enemy to reinforce the former from the latter. Had we merely moved troops from Amman to Deraa we should be doing Palestine no good, and should probably have been rounded up and caught ourselves. The only unit now in hand to do this cutting – since the army must go forward at once – were the armoured cars, which are not ideal for the purpose, as you are almost as shut in to them as the enemy are shut out. However, we went down in all the cars we had to the railway and took a post of open-mouthed Turks too suddenly for them to realise that we were hostile. The post commanded a very pleasant four-arched bridge (kilo. 149) about twenty-five metres long and six metres high, with a flattering white marble inscription to Abd el-Hamid. We wrecked all this with one hundred and fifty pounds of guncotton, and did what we could to the station.

On the way back we had a mishap to one of the cars, and a vile road, so did not catch our army till after dawn on the 17th, going down to the line near Tell Arar, five miles north of Deraa. We suppressed a little post and some Kurdish cavalry, and put our demolition party on the line. The French blew up part of the bridge, and the Egyptians, working up the line towards Ghazale, did six hundred pairs of rails before dark on our new 'tulip' system.* Meanwhile we climbed to the top of Tell Arar, which commanded a complete view of Deraa, about four miles off, and we realised that there were nine enemy machines on the aerodrome. Our Bristol had been badly shot about, so they had no competition to fear, and for a time they did what they liked to us with bombs and machine-gunning. We had luck, and used

---

* After long experiment we found this the cheapest and most destructive demolition for a line with steel sleepers. Dig a hole midway between the tracks under a mid-rail sleeper, and work out the ballast from the hollow section of the sleeper. Put in two slabs of guncotton, return the ballast to the hole, and light. If the charge is properly laid, and not in contact with the sleeper, a 12-inch fuse is enough. The gas expansion arches the sleeper eighteen inches above the rail, draws the metals six inches towards one another, humps them three inches above the horizontal, and twists the web from the bottom inwards. It drives a trough a foot deep across the formation. This three-dimension distortion of the rails is impossible to straighten, and they have to be cut or scrapped. A gang of four men can lay twenty 'tulips' in an hour on easy ballast, and for each two slabs (and single fuse) you ruin a sleeper, a yard of bank and two rails. The effect of a long stretch of line planted with these 'tulips' is most beautiful, since no two look just alike.

our mountain-guns and Hotchkiss for what they were worth, but were getting much the worst of it, till our only surviving machine, a BE 12 from Azrak turned up and sailed into the middle of the show. We watched with very mixed feelings, for the Turkish two-seaters, and their four scouts were all of them much more than its equal in the air: however, by good hap or skill the BE came through them and led the whole circus of them away westward, and after to Ghazale, in pursuit, while we took advantage of our respite to organise and send off a mixed column to Mezerib, to cut the Palestine line. Just after this was done, the BE came back again with its attendant swarm, and telling us that it had finished its petrol, landed near us and turned over on to its back in the rough, while a Halberstadt came down and scored a direct hit on it with a bomb. Our pilot was unhurt, and with his Lewis gun and tracer bullets was soon most usefully running about just outside Deraa in a Ford, cutting the railway to prevent any kind of sortie of rolling stock.

We reached the lake at Mezerib about one p.m., and by two, had taken and looted the French station. The main station on the Palestine line proved too difficult, and we waited till three for the Camel Corps and guns to arrive, and then attacked it formally, and carried it by assault a few minutes later. As our only demolition parties were on the Damascus line, still demolishing, we could not do anything very extensive, but cleared the station, burnt a lot of rolling stock and two lorries, broke the points, and planted a fair assortment of 'tulips' down the line. The interruption of their main telegraph between Palestine and Syria, here and at Tell Arar, bothered the Turks a good deal. We spent the night at Mezerib, and were joined by hundreds and hundreds of the Hauran peasants: during the night some of us marched to within three hundred yards of Tell el-Shehab, intending to attack, but found that a German colonel with guns and reinforcements had just arrived. It was a consolation to know that on the critical 18th of the month we had moved the reserve regiment at Afuleh up to meet us, and we also pleased ourselves with blowing up the line west of Shehab, and, further west, at Zeizun.

Next morning we did some leisurely work on Mezerib station, and then moved past Remthe till mid-afternoon, when we were in position west of Nasib station. After considerable resistance and artillery work, we were able to carry the post on the big bridge north of the station, and to blow up the bridge. This was my seventy-ninth bridge. It had three seven-metre arches, was about twenty-five feet high, and had piers five feet thick – quite one of the finest we have destroyed.

We slept at Nasib and next morning marched gaily away to Umtaiye, speeded by a field-gun which came to Nasib by train, and shelled our tail vigorously. At Umtaiye we rejoined the armoured cars, which had returned direct from Arar after covering the demolitions: and as we had that morning seen as enemy aeroplane land near the railway west of Umtaiye, we at once took two cars down to look at it. We found three two-seaters there, but for a deep gully could not rush their aerodrome. Two got up and troubled us, but we were able to put one thousand five hundred bullets into the third, and finished it. On our way back the other two machines returned from Deraa with bombs, and swooped at us four times; however, they placed them badly, and we escaped nearly unhurt. Armoured car work is fighting *de luxe*, but they give a sitting shot to a well-handled plane. All the rest of the day at Umtaiye we were much bothered by enemy aircraft.

That night (the 19th) an armoured car, with the Egyptian and Ghurka units, went down to the railway about kilo. 154 and blew up some culverts and many rails. The object was to hinder the repair parties which (with escort of guns, machine-guns, and infantry) were hard at work on our destroyed bridge of the 16th at kilo. 149. We were also able to engage the repair train (by armoured car and Ford) at eighty yards range, and persuade it back to Mafrak at top speed. Next day I went on to Azrak, thence by air to Ramleh, and returned on the 22nd to Um el-Surab, with three Bristol Fighters. Before these finished breakfast they had been up twice, bagged a Turkish two-seater, and driven down three scouts. After this the Turks troubled our air no more; and after breakfast I went again to Azrak, and returned to Um el-Surab in the evening with Feisal and Nuri Shaalan, to meet the Handley-Page. It turned the scale in our favour through all the Hauran.

Next day the regulars went down to bridge kilo. 149, as its repair was nearly finished, and after a sharp fight drove off its guards, including very persistent German machine-gunners, destroyed more of the line, and burned the timber framing which the Turks had erected in seven days' work. The armoured cars and French guns did specially well today, and the Rualla horse under Nuri Shaalan personally. Nuri is quiet, and retiring, but a man of few words and great deeds, intelligent, well-informed, decisive, full of quiet humour, and the best Arab sheikh I have ever met. His tribe are like wax in his hands, and he knows what should be done and does it. The British forces had now (24 September) advanced to such a point that the Turkish Fourth Army, whom we had arrogated to ourselves as our birds, were ordered back to cover Deraa and Damascus. As a result of their haste and our holding of the railway, they abandoned the idea of falling back from Amman by rail, and proceeded towards us by road with all their guns and transport. We sent our cavalry at them, and forced them to leave the guns and carts between Mafrak and Nasib. They also lost a lot of men, and what had been a formal column of route became a confused mass of fugitives, who never had time to reform again. It seemed to us, however, that we might now venture to put ourselves between Deraa and Damascus (at some such point as Sheikh Saad) so as to force the immediate evacuation of the former: we might then hope to be able to do business, not only with this mob of the Fourth Army as it emerged from Deraa, but with such remnants of the Palestine Army as escaped by Semakh and Irbid. Accordingly, the camelry, guns, and machine-guns, marched northward on the 25th, till, on the afternoon of the 26th, they were able to descend on the railway and cross it between Ghazale and Ezra.

This move took the Turks (by now panic-stricken) completely by surprise.

The railway had been opened for traffic (after our damage of the 17th) on the previous day, but we now cut it again – and it remained cut till the close of operations, and penned into Deraa six complete trains, which are now ours – took Ghazale with its two hundred men and two guns, took Ezra, held only by the Algerian, Abd el-Kader, a pro-Turk religious fanatic, and a good deal of stores. We then passed on and slept near Sheikh Miskin. The Turks received fantastic reports of our strength, and ordered the immediate evacuation of Deraa by road, while the Germans burnt their five remaining aeroplanes. This gave us a total of eleven enemy machines accounted for by our force since 13 September.

At dawn on the 27th we reached Sheikh Saad, in time to take prisoner two Austro-Turk machine-gun companies on their way to Kuneitra to oppose the British advancing by that road. We then stood on the hill at Sheikh Saad, and watched the country-side. When we saw a small enemy column we went out and took it: when we saw a large column, we lay low. Our excuse must be physical exhaustion – also we were only nine hundred strong.

Aeroplanes now dropped us a message that there were two columns of Turks advancing on us. One from Deraa was six thousand strong, and one from Mezerib, two thousand strong. We determined that the second was about our size, and marched the regulars out to meet it just north of Tafas, while sending our Hauran horse out to hang on to the skirts of the large column, and some unmounted peasants to secure the Tel el-Shehab bridge, which the Turks were mining. We were too late (since on the way we had a profitable affair with an infantry battalion) to prevent the Mezerib column getting into Tafas. They strengthened themselves there, and as at Turaa, the last village they had entered, allowed themselves to rape all the women they could catch. We attacked them with all arms as they marched out later, and bent the head of their column back towards Tell Arar. When Sherif Bey, the Turkish commander of the lancer rearguard in the village, saw this he ordered that the inhabitants be killed. These included some twenty small children (killed with lances and rifles), and about forty women. I noticed particularly one pregnant woman, who had been forced down on a saw-bayonet. Unfortunately, Talal, the sheikh of Tafas, who, as mentioned, had been a tower of strength to us from the beginning, and who was one of the coolest and boldest horsemen I have ever met, was in front with Auda abu Tayi and myself when we saw these sights. He gave a horrible cry, wrapped his headcloth about his face, put spurs to his horse, and, rocking in the saddle, galloped at full speed into the midst of the retiring column, and fell, himself and his mare, riddled with machine-gun bullets, among their lance points.

With Auda's help we were able to cut the enemy column into three. The third section, with German machine-gunners resisted magnificently, and got off, not cheaply, with Jemal Pasha in his car in their midst. The second and leading portions after a bitter struggle, we wiped out completely. We ordered 'no prisoners' and the men obeyed, except that the reserve company took two hundred and fifty men (including many German ASC) alive. Later, however, they found one of our men with a fractured thigh who had been afterwards pinned to the ground by two mortal thrusts with German bayonets. Then we turned our Hotchkiss on the prisoners and made an end of them, they saying nothing. The common delusion that the Turk is a clean and merciful fighter led some of the British troops to criticise Arab methods a little later – but they had not entered Turaa or Tafas, or watched the Turks swing their wounded by the hands and feet into a burning railway truck, as had been the lot of the Arab army at Jerdun. As for the villagers, they and their ancestors have been for five hundred years ground down by the tyranny of these Turks.

Our Rualla horse were then sent on straight to Deraa, with orders to scatter any Turkish formations met with on the road, and to occupy the place. They had two or three fights on their way down, and took Deraa station at a whirlwind gallop, riding over all the trenches, and blotting out the enemy elements that still tried to hold the place. Next morning they brought us three hundred mule mounted infantry prisoners, and about two hundred infantrymen and two guns. The Turks and Germans had unfortunately burnt their stores before we took it.

The regular troops spent that night – a very uneasy night it was – at Sheikh Saad. We did not yet know that we had won, since there was always a risk of our being washed away by a great wave of the enemy in retreat. I went out to see our Haurani horse, near Sheikh Miskin, where they were tenaciously clinging on to the great Turkish column from Deraa, giving much more than they were getting. At midnight I was back in Sheikh Saad, and found Nasir and Nuri just off for Deraa: we had a race, in which my camel corps beat the headquarters horses and joined Trad Shaalan in Deraa village at dawn. We had some little work to do then in making the necessary local arrangements.

Afterwards I rode out westwards till I met the outposts of the Fourth Division (British) and guided them into Deraa. They only stayed there one night and early on the 29th they left for Damascus, after assigning to us the duty of right-flank guard. Accordingly, we marched up the Hejaz line, which suited us very well, for first our three hundred Rualla and Abu Tayi horse, and then our nine hundred Rualla camels, caught up with our Hauran cavalry harassing the Turkish Deraa column near Mesmiye.

The aeroplanes had reported this column as six thousand strong. At Sheikh Miskin on the second day it looked about five thousand strong. At Mesmiye it was said to be three thousand strong, and at Kiswe, where our horse headed them into General Gregory's Brigade, there were about two thousand of them. The whole of this gradual attrition was the work of the irregulars, since the Arab Regular Army, not being skilled camel-men, marched little faster than the British cavalry, and never came into action after Deraa. The Kiswe fight was a satisfactory affair. The Turks came along the valley of the Hejaz line, in a long, straggling column, halting every few miles to bring their guns into action against the Arabs. Nasir knew that the leading brigade of the Fourth Division was nearing Khan Denun, so he galloped forward with his slaves, and Nuri Shaalan and his slaves, about thirty in all, headed the Turkish column off between Jebel Mania and the trees of Khiata, and threw himself into the trees to delay them till the British were ready. The British had not seen or heard of this enemy column, and were in order of march, but as soon as they had learned what was forward they got their cavalry to north, west, and south of them, and opened on them with their Horse Artillery. It was just sunset when the affair began, but before it was too dark to see, the Turks were a scattered mob, running up the steep slopes of Mania and over it, in their ignorance that the Wuld Ali and Abu Tayi were waiting for them there in force. This ended the history of the Fourth Army. Old Auda, tired of slaughter, took the last six hundred prisoners. In all we had killed nearly five thousand of them, captured about eight thousand (as we took them we stripped them, and sent them to the nearest village, where they will be put to work on the land till further notice) and counted spoils of about one hundred and fifty machine-guns and from twenty-five to thirty guns.

Our horse rode on that evening (30 September) into Damascus, where the burning ammunition dumps turned night into day. Away back at Kiswe the glare was painful, and the roar and reverberation of the explosions kept us all awake. In Damascus, Shukri el-Ayubi and the town council had proclaimed the King of the Arabs and hoisted the Arab flag as soon as Mustafa Kemal and Jemal had gone. The Turk and German morale was so low that they had marched out beneath the Arab flag without protest: and so good was the civil control that little or no looting took place.

Nasir, old Nuri, Major Stirling and myself, entered the morning of 1 October, receiving a tremendous but impromptu greeting from the Moslems of the town.

I think I should put on record a word of what happened after we got in. I found at the town hall Mohammed Said and Abd el-Kadir, the Algerians, who had just assumed possession of the provisional civil government, since there was no one in Damascus who could fight their Moorish bodyguard. They are both insane, and as well pro-Turkish and religious fanatics of the most unpleasant sort. In consequence I sent for them, and before the belediyeh and the shiyukh el-harrat, announced that, as Feisal's representative, I declared Shukri el-Ayubi Arab military governor (Ali Riza, the intended governor, was missing), and the provisional civil administration of the Algerians dissolved. They took it rather hard, and had to be sent home. That evening Abd el-Kadir called together his friends and some leading Druses, and made them an impassioned speech, denouncing the Sherif as a British puppet, and calling on them to strike a blow for the Faith in Damascus. By morning this had degenerated into pure looting, and we called out the Arab troops, put Hotchkiss round the central square, and imposed peace in three hours, after inflicting about twenty casualties.

The part played by the Druses was an ignoble one. We had never expected them to join the Sherif, and had therefore excluded them from our calculations of war-wages. After the British victory in Palestine they began to believe that perhaps they were on the wrong side: so when we came forward the second time to Deraa they all collected round Sultan el-Atrash and Husein abu Naif, our two firm friends in Jebel Druse, clamouring for military service. Sultan believed them, and marched to Ghazale to join us with about one thousand five hundred of them, all mounted. They hung round behind our horse, never entering the fight, and waited till Damascus was taken. They then paraded before the Sherif, and began to loot the inhabitants. After the Arabs checked them at this and drove them out of the town to Jaraman, they came to me, and said that their real feelings were pro-British. As they were the only people in all Syria to volunteer for service against Egypt in 1914, this was hard to credit, and I gave them little satisfaction. They are greedy braggarts who soon knock under to a show of force.

Supplementary Despatches

By or about T. E. Lawrence from the Arab Bulletin

I. Distribution List
6 June 1916

Arab Bureau Summaries will deal with any political events in Turkey or else-where that affect the Arab movement.

They will be issued irregularly, with a serial number. Distribution as under.

The contents are to be treated as strictly secret, and extracts from them should not be made (even for other confidential summaries) until Intrusive, Cairo has been informed. They should not be shown except to officers actually concerned.

The Residency	5 (3 for FO)
GOC.-in C., EEF	1
HE the Sirdar, Khartoum	1
DID, Admiralty, London	1
Lt-Col. O'Sullivan, RM, Navy House, Port Said (for Naval C.-in-C.)	1
DMI, War Office, London	1
GOC, Nairobi, BEA	1
CGS, Army Headquarters, India	1
Brig.-Gen. Clayton	1
Lt-Col. Sir Mark Sykes, c/o DMI, London	1
Lt-Col. Parker	1
Secretary, Foreign Dept, Simla	1
Sir P. Z. Cox, Basra	1
CPO, Aden	1
HBM Minister, Adis Abeba	1
Commissioner, Somaliland	1
HE the High Commissioner, Cyprus	1
ADI, Khartoum	1
R. Storrs, Esq.	1
Colonel Wilson	1
Arab Bureau	2
Col. Murphy	1

Fforde	I
Lawrence	I
Col. Watson	I

II. Hejaz News
9 July 1916

The blockade on the Hejaz coast has been raised, so far as Jidda and Lith are concerned, and dhows are again trading there with stores from Egypt and the Sudan. Telegraphic and telephonic communication between Jidda and Mecca is re-established, and it is hoped to repair the cable from Jidda to Suakin. The Sherif has asked for the restoration of a postal service, and passenger facilities. Lith surrendered on 23 June. The Sherif has decided to retain in his own hands the prisoners he has taken, and he has sent a wire for the President of the United States, begging him to inform Enver, Talaat, and Jemal that if his brother, Sherif Nasir, in Constantinople, or any of his relations in Turkish hands is ill-treated, he will retaliate on the civil and military prisoners he holds. A vigorous press propaganda directed in Constantinople by Shawish, and in Syria by Shekib Arslan (a Druse who turned Mohammedan some years ago) is being worked by the Turkish government against the Sherif. In Syria this will probably not be very effective as the Sherif has ninety per cent of the sheikhs firmly on his side.

The Sherif seems to have raised some 15,000 men to date. The Turks had the old Hejaz (22nd) Division in garrison in the province, and a new division, not yet brought up to establishment, in Medina. The latter is under Fakhri Pasha, commander of the 12th Army Corps and second in command in Syria. He is ruthless, vigorous, and clear-headed, with a knowledge both of administration and of war. News from the Syrian coast is that ten battalions have been sent down the Hejaz line to reopen communications with Medina, and reinforce Fakhri. The Sherif has captured two trains, somewhere on the line north of Medina, but we have little information as to how much the line has been torn up. He is asking for native sappers to use explosives.

The Sherif on 8 June, betrayed that he was getting anxious about the position of Medina. The carriage of supplies has broken down, his forces are short of food, and are deserting him for the Turks, who can feed them. So long as this does not go too far there would be no harm in the Sherif suffering a mild check. He will be more modest and accommodating if he realises more closely that he is dependent on our help for success. Medina is too strongly held for him to assault it, and there is abundant food in it, for a longer seige than the Sherif desires. He is asking for howitzers, and more mountain-guns. Since the evening of 25 June, the Turks have not sent any wireless messages to Medina, though they still receive reports from Fakhri. It is, therefore, probable that the land line is restored. One Turkish message of 21 June, mentioned that a squadron of battle-planes was leaving Constantinople for Medina.

Captain T. E. Lawrence, February 1917: an early picture of him in Arab clothes, probably taken during the weeks spent in the Red Sea port of Wejh

The iconic image that would become a trademark: Lawrence mounted on a camel, photographed at Akaba, 1917–18

Emir Abdullah *(centre left)* with Emir Ali *(to Abdullah's right)*, photographed by Lawrence. Ali and Abdullah were the eldest of the four sons of Sherif Hussein of Mecca, who launched the Arab Revolt. Although he failed to impress Lawrence in 1916, Abdullah had an important future in the post-war Middle East

Emir Feisal, junior to Ali and Abdullah, was the son seen by Lawrence as the Arabs' most capable and inspiring commander, 'the leader who would bring the Arab Revolt to full glory'. Lawrence served as his liaison officer and adviser throughout the subsequent campaign. Feisal later became King of Iraq

Sherif Nasir of Medina, leader of the Akaba expedition, photographed by Lawrence in 1917. Praising him for his courage and his commitment to the revolt from start to finish, Lawrence wrote: 'All that could be told of him was good'

Auda abu Tayi *(left)* and kinsmen, photographed by Lawrence on the first day of the Akaba expedition, 9 May 1917. Lawrence was hugely impressed by Auda, veteran chief of the Howeitat tribe, seeing him as one of the heroic figures of the campaign

Lawrence in major's uniform with D. G. Hogarth in the uniform of a commander of the Royal Navy, Cairo, 1918. Hogarth had encouraged and supported Lawrence from his Oxford days; now they found themselves collaborating in time of war

General Sir Edmund Allenby, Commander-in-Chief, Egyptian Expeditionary Force, from June 1917; later Special High Commissioner for Egypt, 1919–25. Lawrence described him as 'the nearest to my longings for a master'. The two quite different men formed an unlikely but mutually profitable partnership

Attacks on the Hejaz Railway: Lawrence's own photograph of a station blown up during one of his railways raids, with a wrecked truck in the foreground – a symbol of 'tip-and-run' guerrilla warfare at its most effective

The Battle of Tafileh, January 1918: Lawrence's own photograph, captioned by him 'Tafileh, Turkish prisoners defiling'. This was the one conventional action in which he took part; although it was successful, he was dismayed by its high count in casualties

Lawrence with his bodyguard, Akaba, 1918,
photographed by Lawrence's Akaba base officer,
Captain Raymond Goslett. Lawrence wrote of
them: 'My bodyguard of fifty Arab tribesmen . . .
are more splendid than a tulip garden'

Sherif Shakir's army, March 1917, photographed by Lawrence when returning from the raid described in 'Raids on the Railway' (pp. 111–21). Using a 120 camera, almost certainly a Kodak, Lawrence developed a remarkable skill in photography at speed or on the move. He was not only a key performer in the Arab Revolt, he was also its leading photographer

In the later stages of the desert campaign, motorised combat – what Lawrence called 'fighting *de luxe*' – increasingly became the norm. The photograph shows Lawrence in his Rolls-Royce tender *Blue Mist*, which suffered only one breakdown during more than a year of use, in the streets of Damascus in early October 1918. The photograph suggests a Lawrence more exhausted than elated with the strain of two years of continuous active service

Colonel Lawrence embattled, a post-war photograph taken in Paris, 1919. Note that the photograph was issued by an American agency, an indication of the rapid spread of his fame

At the Paris Peace Conference, January 1919: a famous image showing Emir Feisal *(centre)*, with Lawrence in the Arab headdress which he affected to publicise the Arab cause. Gertrude Bell described him as the conference's 'most picturesque figure'. Another commentator remarked that to get their way 'people of his kind used themselves as they would use an animal or an instrument'. Stories of what he had said to France's most senior soldier, Marshal Foch, were circulated among the delegates, but unfortunately, however well presented, the Arab case failed to impress the conference's leading statesmen. The other figures are *(from left)*: Rustum Haider, Feisal's personal secretary; Nuri Said, later to serve with Feisal in Iraq; Captain Pisani, commander of the French gunnery detachment with Feisal's army; Feisal's slave; and Captain Hassan Kadri

THE EVOLUTION OF A REVOLT

By T. E. Lawrence (late Lieut.-Colonel General Staff, E.E.F.)

The Arab Revolt began in June, 1916, with an Arab offensive, a surprise attack by the half-armed and inexperienced tribesmen upon the Turkish garrisons in Medina and about Mecca. They had no success, and after a few days' effort they withdrew out of range of the fort artillery, and began a blockade. This method forced the early surrender of Mecca, whose road communications were too long and rough to be held by the Turks. Medina, however, was linked by railway to the Turkish main Army in Syria, and, thanks to their superior numbers and equipment, the Turks were able in a week's fighting to restore the line and reinforce the temporarily-besieged garrison there. The Arab forces which had attacked it fell back gradually as the Turks became more offensive, and at last moved fifty miles south-west into the hills, and there took up a position across the main road to Mecca.

At this point the campaign stood still for many weeks, while both sides breathed, and the Turks prepared to take the initiative, by sending an expeditionary force to Mecca, to crush the revolt where it had started. They moved an army corps to Medina by rail, and strengthened it beyond establishment with guns, cars, aeroplanes, machine guns, and quantities of horse, mule and camel transport. Then they began to advance down the main western road from Medina to Mecca. The total distance was about two hundred and fifty miles. The first fifty miles were easy : then came a belt of hills twenty miles wide, in which were Feisal's tribesmen standing on the defensive : after the hills was a level stretch, for seventy miles along the coastal plain to Rabegh, rather more than half-way. Rabegh is a little port on the Red Sea, with good anchorage for ships. In it was Sherif Ali, Feisal's eldest brother, with more tribal forces, and the beginnings of an Arab Regular Army, recruited men of Arab blood, who had served in the Turkish now willing to fight against their old masters for freedom.

55

THE

ARMY QUARTERLY

With which is incorporated

The United Service Magazine

Edited by
Major-General G. P. DAWNAY
C.B., C.M.G., D.S.O., M.V.O.

Assistant Editor
CUTHBERT HEADLAM, D.S.O., O.B.E.
(late Lieut.-Colonel, General Staff, B.E.F.)

VOLUME I.
(OCTOBER, 1920 and JANUARY, 1921.)

London :
WILLIAM CLOWES & SONS, LTD.
94, Jermyn Street, St. James's, S.W.

'The Evolution of a Revolt', Lawrence's first account of his philosophy of guerrilla warfare, October 1920. It was published in, *right*, the first edition of the *Army Quarterly*. Much of the text later went into *Seven Pillars of Wisdom*

The Cairo Conference, March 1921: an outing to the Sphinx and the Pyramids, with *(from left, mounted)* Mrs Clementine Churchill, Colonial Secretary Winston Churchill, the famous traveller and writer Gertrude Bell, and Lawrence, in suit and trilby hat. Churchill was thrown by his camel and hurt his hand, but insisted on riding back to Cairo side by side with Lawrence

Delegates from Cairo during a visit to Amman, including Gertrude Bell *(left)*, Lawrence *(centre)*, Sir Herbert Samuel, High Commissioner of Palestine *(centre right)*, and Emir Abdullah *(right)*, shortly to become ruler of Transjordan and, ultimately, King of Jordan. Lawrence looked so unlike his now well-known image in his civilian clothes that he was taken by one observer to be a junior secretary to one of the conference's lesser lights

Lawrence as Aircraftman T. E. Shaw on one of his Brough Superior motorcycles, photographed at RAF Cranwell after his return to the RAF in 1925. It was on a later model that he had his fatal accident in May 1935

Aircaftman Shaw photographed in India, December 1928. One of several studies taken by his commanding officer at RAF Miranshah, Flight Lieutenant S. J. Smetham

A late photo-portrait of Lawrence, February 1935, by Wing Commander R. G. Sims. A more mature Lawrence, all passion spent; or perhaps not

for wit is more dignified than humour. Do not cause a laugh at a Sherif except amongst Sherifs.

13. Never lay hands on an Arab; you degrade yourself. You may think the resultant obvious increase of outward respect a gain to you: but what you have really done is to build a wall between you and their inner selves. It is difficult to keep quiet when everything is being done wrong, but the less you lose your temper the greater your advantage. Also then you will not go mad yourself.

14. While very difficult to drive, the Bedu are easy to lead, if you have the patience to bear with them. The less apparent your interferences the more your influence. They are willing to follow your advice and do what you wish, but they do not mean you or anyone else to be aware of that. It is only after the end of all annoyances that you find at bottom their real fund of good will.

15. Do not try to do too much with your own hands. Better the Arabs do it tolerably than that you do it perfectly. It is their war, and you are to help them, not to win it for them. Actually also; under the very odd conditions of Arabia, your practical work will not be as good as perhaps, you think it is.

16. If you can, without being too lavish, forestall presents to yourself. A well placed gift is often most effective in winning over a suspicious sheikh. Never receive a present without giving a liberal return, but you may delay this return (which letting its ultimate certainty be known) if you require a particular service from the giver. Do not let them ask you for things, since their greed will then make them look upon you only as a cow to milk.

17. Wear an Arab headcloth when with a tribe. Bedu have a malignant prejudice against the hat, and believe that our persistence in wearing it (due probably to British obstinacy of dictation) is founded on some immoral or irreligious principle. A thick headcloth forms a good protection against the sun, and if you wear a hat your best Arab friends will be ashamed of you in public.

18. Disguise is not advisable. Except in special areas let it be clearly known that you are a British officer and a Christian. At the same time if you can wear Arab kit when with the tribes you will acquire their trust and intimacy to a degree impossible in uniform. It is however dangerous and difficult. They make no special allowances for you when you dress like them. Breaches of etiquette not charged against a foreigner are not condoned to you in Arab clothes. You will be like an actor in a foreign theatre, playing a part day and night for months, without rest, and for an anxious stake. Complete success, which is when the Arabs forget your strangeness and speak naturally before you, counting you one of themselves, is perhaps only attainable in character: which half success (all that most of us will strive for — the other costs too much) is easier to win in British things, and you yourself will last longer, physically and mentally, in the comfort that they mean. Also then the Turks will not hang you, when you're caught.

19. If you wear Arab things wear the best. Clothes are significant among the tribes, and you must wear the appropriate, and appear at ease in them. Dress like a Sherif — if they agree to it.

A key page from Lawrence's 1917 document 'Twenty-Seven Articles' (pp. 142–7), in his original handwriting: seen in the Iraq insurgency of 2003 and after as a vital message for our times

The news of a rising in Syria caused great relief to the Sherif. Rumour (which we believe greatly exaggerated) said that the Hauran Druses had rebelled, and that Nuri Shaalan with 15,000 Ruwalla had invaded the Damascus Vilayet, with the help of Arab officers, and the Fedaan. The Sherif appears at once to have foreseen a rapid invasion of Syria by his forces, and told us that further destruction of the Hejaz line was undesirable, as he would shortly need it himself. At Taif, Sherif Abdalla has captured a gun and 200 Turks. At Mecca the Egyptian artillery on 3 and 4 July , breached the small fort, which promptly surrendered. The barracks are still holding out, and the Sherif hopes to persuade them to surrender without violence. He is obviously very averse to fighting in the Holy City itself. The fort, however, had been bombarding the city, and was responsible for the shots which struck the Kaaba, and that which burned the Kiswa.

The Sherif has asked for recognition by the Allied governments, and that the pilgrimage shall take place as usual. He has suggested a radical reduction in pilgrimage dues, to celebrate the opening of the new regime. His military programme contemplates the formation of a disciplined army, with the help of Arab troops from the Turkish forces and Syrian and Mesopotamian officers. With these he intends to invade Syria, but the moment when he can undertake an offensive is so remote and his powers of an offensive without our co-operation so slight that we need hardly expect anything from him inconvenient to our plans. The Sherif estimates the Turkish forces in Syria at 38,000 but his information is not good.

At Jidda there is an entire lack of organisation. The townsmen are (as ever) afraid of the Arabs, and hope for control by us. The Ashraf are intriguing against one another, and have no administrative experience. The hold of the Sherif on the Arabs of the coast is not strong, and Turkish influence still exists at Yambo. There is great dislike of Egyptians, of course. Sherif Mehsin, the Sherif's representative in Jidda seems good, but knows little. The Sherif and his family show personal courtesy to our representatives, but others obviously distrust us. Public security is well maintained.

A draft proclamation from the Sherif, intended by him for publication is appended. It has not yet been distributed, and has only been submitted for our approval.

Idrissi on 30 June, said that he intended about 10 July, to attack Kunfida and Mahail to cut communications on the north and join up with the Sherif. He has written a friendly letter to the Sherif, in which he called himself his servant, and asked for Emir Feisal to be sent to command him and his forces. He mobilised on 29 June, but found some difficulty in persuading some of his tribes to take up arms. He considers that the Imam is unfriendly, and is watching him, and he will not attack Lobeia until he has cleared his northern frontier. The Hashid and Bakhil tribes will remain neutral, unless we take special measures.

On 30 June, news was brought to Birk that the Sherif's forces were advancing on Kunfida. The news seems to have been exaggerated; and no confirmation has been received as yet. Kunfida is debateable land on the borders of the Sherif and the Idrissi. It is doubtful whether the relations between the Sherif and the Idrissi are good enough to make combined operations possible. The old ill-feeling might revive if there was disappointment or some booty to be shared. We have represented to each side how undesirable collision would be and ships were sent to supervise the operations, with the result that Kunfida surrendered to us on 8 July. The Idrissi flag was hoisted. The garrison composed of eight officers and 190 men, were taken prisoners.

III. Note by Cairo on Arab Labour
5 September 1916

The success or failure of Arab labour depends almost entirely on the treatment the individual man receives from his employer. The tribesman is not sufficiently advanced to be directed by economic laws: nor is there anywhere in the provinces of Turkey a population dense enough to supply a large floating class of casual workmen.

Cant phrases of the dignity of labour are not yet current in Arabic, and unskilled labour, far from receiving the tribute of uncomprehending respect accorded it in the rare atmosphere of unions, is still held more degrading than honest beggary. It is worthier to starve on your own tiny plot, than to hire out your body for a wage, and in consequence the Arab day labourer is most often drawn from the worst class, and performs his task by rote, neither thinking nor caring about it. Such men are everywhere irremediably unskilled.

A way of bettering this case in country districts, is by enlisting the help of the peasant farmer or his sons; but this is precisely what is most difficult to do. Their labour (when you get it) compares well with almost any other in quantity and in quality. Their intelligence is very quick, and ready to adapt itself to new occupations. Often they do not work well side by side with the lowest class, and sometimes are only to be attracted by establishing a fictitious hierarchy among the workmen, and sowing the superstition that certain jobs are more honourable, and therefore to be reserved for better families. If this desirable job can be one that sets the pace for the rest (as the pick in a digging gang) the ordinary workman will be pulled up to the level of his leaders.

In course of time the rise of the standard of living will probably throw out the smallest holders, and make them dependent on a day wage. They will then form a skilled-labourer class.

The actual handling of the men is not easy. It is usually successful in proportion as the men are in closer touch with their employer, and, therefore, a large European supervising staff is advisable. The happiest master is he who knows the names and relationship of all his men, for under such conditions the feudalism latent in the sedentary tribes attaches them to him; his ascendancy becomes not only personal, but almost instinctive, if he has a gift of humour to temper the necessary firmness, and enough humanity to be interested in his men off the works. In such case there is little they will not do for him.

Ridicule is the greatest weapon in the Europeans' armoury. To insult or to lay hands on a workman spoils the gang – and as fatal in the long run is a machine-made system, or anything approaching a 'coolie' standpoint. British private firms in the Arab provinces of Turkey have generally been conspicuous for the good relations existing between them and their employés – and the Germans have been at the other end of the scale. Indeed, it has often been due only to their assiduous cultivation of consular or government protection that the latter have been able to achieve large undertakings.

The actual figures of day-work in Mesopotamia seem good. In North Syria, under easier conditions, the Baghdad line used to reckon to get a cubic metre of cut and carry per man per day in normal to stiff soil. A British undertaking, under close supervision, in the same district, with 300 men and a thirty-yard carry, used to average a total of 700 cubic metres per day; but the majority of its men were of the landed peasant class.

Kurd labour, while more robust, proved rather stupid, and is more difficult to keep good-tempered. Large bodies of Kurds are almost sure to fall out with someone, or among themselves. They are less fastidious than the Arabs in a dirty job – like coaling. Turkish labour performs its daily duty, but in a hopeless way, and mechanically. It is very hard, indeed, to persuade it to an interest in what it does.

IV. Hejaz Narrative
5 September 1916

There has been practically no news from the Hejaz since 30 August. Steps are being taken to deal with Hussein ibn Mabeirig of Rabegh, who has been holding up stores and arms landed there, for the forces under Sherif Feisal.

Three deserters from the Turkish forces at Medina, who left there about a month ago report that they belonged to the Yemen Mofraza, a batch of recruits formed into the shape of a regiment (under Khaira Bey, an Arab), and sent from Constantinople to Damascus for the Yemen AC. Their route from Damascus (where they stayed for four months) was to have been Medina, Mecca, and then by land to the Yemen. They did not know where the Yemen was. There was a preponderance of Turks among the recruits when they started, but they went sick with the heat all along the way. One 'company' which left Damascus 130 strong, marched out of Medina to fight only eighty strong. The remaining fifty were Turks down with heat in the hospital at Medina.

The railway journey from Damascus took four days and four nights continuous travelling, with no longer stop than three hours, and generally not stopping more than ten or fifteen minutes. They had two engines from Deraa to Maan, and one afterwards. (This would be accounted for by the Amman gradients.) The train was of from ten to fifteen box-wagons, and two companies (about 300 men) with their baggage, and officers filled it. The wood fuel was carried mostly on the tender, from stores filled in various stations. Besides the main supplies from the Amanus and Taurus Wood Contract Company (Saghiz and Co.), local fuel was being collected by the Beduin. This consisted of the thicker stem of the thorn, broom, tamarisk and acacia of the desert. (Miserable fuel for an engine, and not much of it.)

On most stations were about ten men guarding the line: other soldiers were in working gangs, doing repairs and improvements. There was a larger garrison at Maan, and at Tebuk. When they reached Medina (which was just before the war there began, presumably at the end of May) there were few men there, only some battalions long in the Hejaz (probably two battalions of the 130th Regiment and a train battalion). Basri Pashi was military governor. Fakhri Pasha came down later.

After hostilities began between Sherif Feisal and the Turks many more troops came down. They thought they were perhaps as many as 10,000 in all, but none of them knew how big a number above 1,000 is, and could not judge.

They were in Awali themselves, and orders came to withdraw from it at night. They then presumably deserted in the dark. They were captured by Arabs and kept for a fortnight, robbed of all they had, and threatened with death to persuade them to join the Sherif's forces. They refused. One of them liked the Turks, and the others said 'Our four brothers are in the Turkish Army at Medina. We do not want to make them run the danger of killing us.' So they refuse to do anything, and were sent down to Yanbo where they got on board a cruiser.

V. Note on the Garrison of Medina
14 September 1916

Cairo information, based on the interrogation of prisoners, and not yet well-established, is to the effect that the force in Medina consists of two battalions of the 130th Regiment, three battalions of the Yemen Mofraza, probably three battalions of the 42nd Regiment, and possibly part of 162nd Regiment. There are besides camelry, cavalry, and the Mohafiz tabur, some artillery units of the 3rd and 43rd Divisions, and perhaps some drafts from the units of the XIIth Army Corps. Total 11,000 men at least, and possibly more.

VI. Note on the Hejaz Military Situation
16 October 1916

The failure of the Turks to effect an advance on Mecca before or during the pilgrimage has ensured the safety and success of the Egyptian and other pilgrimages which attended the annual ceremonies under the Sherif's protection. The moral effects of this should be to enhance very considerably the prestige of the Sherif among all those peoples who sent representatives to the Holy City.

The military situation, must, however, remain critical as long as so large a Turkish force remains intact south of Medina, and as long as this force can obtain reinforcements and supplies from Syria by means of the Hejaz railway.

For the moment the holding of Rabegh contributes an effective bar to any contemplated advance on Mecca, as the Sultani road still represents the only practicable road along which there is sufficient water for a large force. Very soon, however, the autumnal rains will render the inland route or routes possible for the advance of a flying column.

The Turks are not likely to abandon their attempts to re-take Mecca until they are either effectively cut off from Syria or utterly defeated in the field. They naturally regard the possession of Mecca as indispensable to their otherwise shadowy claim to the Khalifate, and are certain to sacrifice strategic consideration to the attainment of what they regard as a paramount political objective. The denial of Mecca to the Turks is a vital blow to the position and pretentions of the CUP, as well as an essential to the growing prestige of the Sherif.

The maintenance of the Sherif's present position has, in addition, the military importance of preventing the Turks reinforcing or maintaining their three immobilised divisions in the Asir and the Yemen. It prevents the Turks moving on the flank of the Suez Canal by using the Arabian coast as a base of either operations or propaganda, and engages a Turkish force badly needed elsewhere by its German masters in a theatre where the very existence of hostilities is a menace to their moral and political authority in Syria and Mesopotamia, as well as in Arabia.

VII. The Turkish Hejaz Forces and Their Reinforcement
By T. E. Lawrence and P. P. Graves
26 November 1916

The other Turkish armies may be dismissed more briefly. The force in Mesopotamia and Persia will not be wantonly brought back while Baghdad is in danger, or until a further Russian advance in Armenia threatens its communications. The Turkish forces in Armenia, over the 500 mile front from the Black Sea to Rowanduz, amount to no more than 102,000 rifles, and while Russia maintains her hold can hardly acquit themselves of their own task, much less spare men for Medina. The army in Europe, available for active service, is infinitesimal.

It will, therefore, be hard for Turkey either to form new units or spare old ones, for the comparative luxury of a campaign in the Hejaz; and so the appearance of the overwhelming force which would put an immediate end to the Arab rising is improbable. On the other hand the warfare in Arabia is on a pigmy scale, and so little turns the difference that the Turks may think it cheaper to strike than to defend. They could spare a division from North Syria, if the transport problem is soluble, if they can overcome the reluctance of their German staff to side-shows, and if they can feel assured that the Allies appear to have abandoned any idea of striking by sea at Syria. Of these three difficulties the problem of transport is perhaps the greatest.

VIII. Intelligence Report
4 January 1917

Later information, received from Sherif Feisal, states that the Subh, although they have detached themselves from Sherif Ali, have not gone over to the Turks, but are scattered among the hills. Feisal, who was at Nakhl Mubarek on 29 December, with some Juheinah, is in no way depressed by the situation. The Turks are still consolidating their positions along the line Kheif, Hamra, Bir Said, where the bulk of the 55th Regiment still appears to be. They are reported as far south as Huseiniyah, below Wasta, in Wadi Safrah, but only on reconnaissance. There are reasons for believing that the evacuation by the Turks of the Ghayir district recently reported by aeroplane observers is incorrect, and that the Turks are still in that neighbourhood. They are still endeavouring to get supplies from central Arabia. An Arab NCO deserter from the Turks, who had reached Yambo, states that forage is short, but that food is adequate; also that there is an average of two short trains (ten trucks in all) a day into Medina, but on some days no train arrives. The Turks had, in September, a company of infantry at Tebuk and one at Medain Salih, and a German doctor at the latter place. The railway in the Medina section is guarded by 1,500 Muhafza Tabur under El-Rahman. He says Fakhri Pasha, the GOC of the Expeditionary Force, is returning to Medina shortly, after visiting Nakhl Mubarek, Hamrah and Ghayir, leaving Ghalib Bey in command at Hamrah. At Nakhl Mubarek he found our seaplanes too active, and withdrew to Bir Said. The Turks have a large supply-dump at Bir Derwish. Feeling among the Turks runs strongly against the Sherif, and a reward has been offered for the capture of the British officer (Capt. Lawrence) who is with Feisal.

IX. Hejaz: The Present Situation
11 April 1917

Military operations in Hejaz seem to be somewhat hanging fire; but this appearance is due partly to defects in our information. Owing to the distance inland at which the forces of all four emirs are operating, we get news less constantly and rapidly than we did before Medina itself and the railway became their immediate objectives. Moreover, while the weak wireless set at Wejh has not much improved the situation, several patrol ships have been withdrawn; and the RFC flight, recently transferred to Wehj, has only just got going again, after finding a satisfactory advanced landing ground at Beidha on the northern road to El-Ala . . . We do know, however, that a considerable detachment from Abdullah's force in Wadi Ais, with which Capt. Lawrence is at present, has attacked Abul Naim station, under the lead of Sherif Shakir. The latter reports that he destroyed the station and also a train of seven wagons, and that he killed forty Turks. Details will follow later. On 16 and 17 March some 45 culverts and main rails were wrecked just south of el-Ala by one of Feisal's detachments which also burned telegraph poles. Colonel Newcombe reports a second raid made between Khishm Sana and Dar el-Hamra stations, in which 110 rails and much telegraph wire were destroyed; twenty-one prisoners were taken, presumably from repair-gangs, and a Turk was killed. No train from the north had passed that point between 24 March and the date of Newcombe's despatch. But the Turks, if not interfered with, seem able to repair about a kilometre of double track per diem. Lieutenant Garland has returned to resume his operations and has gone inland from Wejh. The section of the line from Medain Salih to Tebuk is reported held by 600 Turks, who have three aeroplanes. At Medain Salih itself are 300 infantry, of whom two-thirds are Syrians. At el-Ala are 500 men, similarly divided between Turks and Syrians, as well 60 camel corps and a small cavalry force. The whole enemy composite force, based on Tebuk, is about 5,000 strong.

X. Note: Wejh Map (Provisional Sheet)
31 May 1917

It is to be regretted that we were obliged to publish, in our Nos. 50, 51, Captain Lawrence's detailed and intricate route-reports without any accompanying chart; but his sketch-map did not accompany the reports, and was so long delayed that we began to fear it lost. It has, however, now come to hand, and been re-drafted at the Survey of Egypt, for inclusion in the revised edition of the Wejh 1:500,000 Provisional Sheet, now in active preparation. This will embody also Colonel Newcombe's route-traverses from Wejh to Muadhdham, and the excellent chart of the lower basin of Wadi Hamdh from Wejh to Ugla (Akila), furnished by the RFC from observations taken both by flying officers and those who have gone up with motor cars. The last report from the latter shows that, where sand and brushwood become thick, the Crossley tender can progress where the Ford cannot.

This fresh material will greatly improve the sheet, not only filling in several areas which were sketchy or blank, but altering the positions assigned to the railway and to several important road-stations. It will leave, however, a considerable blank area between the Wadi Hamdh and Colonel Newcombe's routes, and will not alter either the northern plotting, which must still depend on Burton's chart, or that of the region east of the railway. For the latter, however, we have hopes from the re-plotting of Huber's *data*, which, we are informed, has been carried out recently with great care by RGS drafts-men under the supervision of Mr Douglas Carruthers. The latter has been reconsidering also Guarmani's route-notes, and has supplied us with an English translation of the *Neged Settentrionale* (with valuable introduction), which the Arab Bureau proposes to issue in the same form as Rannkiaer's book, issued last year.

XI. Intelligence Report: The Northward Move
9 July 1917

Report reaches us from Wejh, under date June 30, as follows:

'Audeh abu Tayyeh arrived at Kasr el Azrak, and many Arabs have come to him to submit loyalty and to fight under the flag which was given to him by HE Sherif Feisal with Sherif Nasir, Nasib el Bakry and Captain Lawrence.

'The Turkish Government hearing the Audeh had joined the Sherif's army, sent a force and destroyed El Gifa wells (Wells east of Maan) knowing that Audeh will make this place his headquarters.'

This is the first news we have had of the doings of Abu Tayyeh since he started north with Captain Lawrence, Sherif Nasir and Nasib el-Bakry. Kasr el-Azrak is east of Salt, about 120 miles north of the Jafar depression (El Gifa, above). It is doubtful whether we should understand that Captain Lawrence is with him there, or whether in fact the party, after showing itself in the north, has returned to the Maan district and is now directing the oper-ations of the Howeitat, elsewhere reported, whose activity without this direction it is difficult to account for.

XII. Extract from an Intelligence Report under Heading 'Arabia/Hejaz'
24 July 1917

An explanation of the recent activity of the tribes round Maan, referred to in the last bulletin, has reached us in the person of Capt. Lawrence, after coloured adventures in that district. The results achieved may be summarised as follows: he left Wejh on 9 May with Sherif Nasir ibn Husein as OC Expedition, and Nesib Bey el Bakri as Political Officer, picked up thirty-six men and also Auda Abu Tayi (of whom more below) and he arrived at Akaba on 8 July with an army of 2,000 Arabs, and a tally to their credit of 700 dead Turks and 600 prisoners. The Arab concentration, which, to produce these results, they had busied themselves in forming, took place at El Bair to the NE of Maan and was under the general command of Sherif Nasir. The main force moved to El Jafar on 30 June, clearing one well, and thence to kil. 479 where the line was destroyed on a large scale, while a column was attacking N of Maan near Aneyza. The Arabs then marched towards Fuweilah, where the gendarme post had been destroyed by an advance column. They were met with the news of the re-occupation of Fuweilah by a belated relief expedition of the 4th Battn of the 174th Regt from Maan. This was completely defeated on 2 July at Abu Lissan, the OC, 160 men and a mountain-gun being captured, and the rest of the battalion annihilated. At the same time, a flying column was sent north which defeated the Turkish post at Hisha (railhead five miles E of Shobak) and occupied Wadi Musa, Shobek and Tafileh.

From Fuweilah the main force advanced and captured the post of Mreigha and then moved to Guweira, where it was reinforced by Ibn Jad of the Akaba Howeitat, and took 100 men and five officers. From Guweira it marched on El Kethira (wiping out a post of three officers and 140 men) and thence to El Khadra, in the north of Wadi Ithm, where the Akaba garrison surrendered at discretion. Akaba was entered on 6 July with 600 prisoners, about forty officers and a German Unter-Offizier well-borer. Of these, the German, twenty-five Turkish officers and 360 rank and file have been sent to Egypt, while the remainder, being Arabs or Syrians, have volunteered and been incorporated into the Arab army. The Turkish dead are estimated at 700.

The forces which accomplished these remarkably successful operations were mainly Abu Tayyi Howeitat under Sheikh Auda Abu Tayi, Rualla Anazeh under Sheikh ibn Dughini and Sherarat. Their losses were only four men killed and five men wounded in the actual fighting, though an old man, six women and seven children were surprised in their tents by a Turkish cavalry patrol and slaughtered.

At present some 5,000 Arabs are in arms in the Maan area. Reports show that the Turks fully realise the danger of the threat and are likely to attempt strong measures. They are already reported to have brought down some mule mounted companies to Maan and to have enlisted the help of 500 Beni Sakhr Arabs, 250 from Kerak and fifty of the Khoreisha Howeitat. Sheikh Fawwaz ibn Faiz of the Beni Sakhr, who was one of their chief supports, has died within the last few weeks. Sheikh Mishkal is mentioned as his successor and they can count on Sheikh Hamed el Arar, but the Trad and Zebn elements of the Beni Sakhr, as well as the larger portion of the Ibn Jazi section, are on the side of the Sherif. From all that Capt. Lawrence could hear, the disposition of the northern tribes is increasingly anti-Turk and favourable to the Sherif of Mecca. Sheikh Nuri Shaalan and his son Nawwaf have re-affirmed their loyalty. The Druses are deeply incensed against the Turks and the same feeling exists among the Serdivah, the Jebeliyah and the Metawala of Anti Lebanon and the Orontes valley. Sheikh Fahad ibn Hadhdhal of the Amarat has come in to Bagdad and offered the wholehearted support of himself and his tribes and there is reason to believe that the Western Bishr and border tribes from Homs to Aleppo are equally ready to cut loose from the Turks should a favourable occasion arise.

XIII. News of Anazeh Tribes
8 October 1917

Two satisfactory signs of Nuri Shaalan's attitude towards the king of the Hejaz and ourselves have come to hand during the past week. One is an agreement, authoritatively reported, that, during Nuri's absence from Jauf on business of the king's a Sherifian artillery detachment shall guard the oasis against Rashidite attack. Ceylon mountain-guns are asked for as the armament of the detachment. The other sign is a request from Nuri, transmitted through Major Lawrence, that half his tribe, the Ruwallah, should be allowed to supply itself from some Mesopotamian market, controlled by us. He states that the usual supplies of Hauran corn have been headed off, presumably by the Turks, from his tribesmen, owing to the latter showing their hand too soon. Nuri's request has been referred to Baghdad.

XIV. Report: Railway Raids Northern Section
27 November 1917

We have received news through Akaba, that, on 7 November, a party under Major Lawrence and Sherif Ali ibn Husein blew up a two-engined train somewhere on the line west of Deraa. The casualties of the enemy are stated to have been considerable.

The original objective of this party was found impossible to attain, and it seems to have retraced its steps to Kasr el-Azrak, and from there to have undertaken certain operations against the Hejaz railway in conjunction with other parties. The whole stretch from Zerka to el-Hasa has been attacked at various points. The same Akaba information states that a Beni Sakhr party, under Sherif Husein Shakrani, has broken 'an important bridge' north of el-Hasa, taking forty-five prisoners, including Sami Bey, Kaimmakam of Maan, and a Bimbashi of the Medical Corps, and fifty-six rifles and much other booty. This, no doubt, is the bridge guessed . . . to have been south of the el-Hasa station and broken on 11 or 12 November. It is probably the stone bridge of six twenty-five foot arches about thirty kilometres up the line under Jebel Hafira. The raid south of Maan . . . on or about 17 November, took place at kil. 510, north of Akabat el-Hejazia. It resulted in the destruction of a dozen rails, and the cutting of the telegraph wires. Lieut. Pisani was with this party which has now returned to Akaba.

XV. Notes: Northern Section and Late News
5 December 1917

Northern Section. A later report, which puts the train-demolition effected by Major Lawrence's party on 11 November, instead of 7 November . . . makes it certain that this is the same event as that . . . at Khirbet es-Sumra. There has, therefore, been only one two-engined train affected, and the locality of Major Lawrence's feat was south, not west, of Deraa. He lost eight men killed.

Late News. Up to 3 December no further suspected case of cholera or para-cholera at Akaba since 19 November, but one of true Asiatic cholera from there landed at Suez in the interval. According to Arab report, sent late last month, by Sherif Ali to King Husein, Fakhri has had the railway buildings outside the walls blown up; this if true, looks like concentration in the town preparatory to some measure of evacuation. Scurvy is serious at Medain Salih. Major Lawrence returned to Akaba at the beginning of December.

XVI. Extract from an Intelligence Report on Arabia
4 June 1918

Dr Weizmann, the leader of the Zionist Commission, accompanied by Major Ormsby-Gore, is to pay a flying visit to Emir Feisal at, or inland from, Akaba, and left Suez for that port on 1 June. It is hoped that Lieut.-Colonel Lawrence may be able to meet him on arrival and introduce him to the emir.

XVII. Note: Feisal and Weizmann
28 June 1918

The meeting between the Emir Feisal and Dr Weizmann . . . duly took place on June 4 at Uheida, Lieut.-Colonel Joyce, DSO, being present and acting as interpreter. Lieut.-Colonel Lawrence was absent in the northern area of operations at the time, and Major Ormsby-Gore had been prevented by an illness, developed on the voyage, from going up-country. The meeting was cordial and appears to have given mutual satisfaction. Both principals agreed that the close co-operation of Jews and Arabs was necessary in the interests of each, if there was to be any stable independence in the Arab-speaking lands, but Feisal declined to enter upon a statement of the precise political arrangements which he contemplated, pleading that his father alone was competent to make such a statement. Dr Weizmann told him that the Jews do not propose to set up any government of their own, but wish to work, under British protection, to colonise and develop Palestine with all consid-eration for legitimate vested interests. Feisal replied, that in view of the dan-gerous use that enemy propaganda could make of any pronouncement of his in favour of an Arab territory being controlled by non-Arab hands, he would only state his personal opinion that Dr Weizmann's wish was not incapable of realisation; and he welcomed cordially the latter's offer to represent Arab as well as Jewish aims in America. Feisal hoped for another meeting later on. The practical outcome of this interview is not much more, of course, than the formation of mutual acquaintance between the leader of Entente Zionism and the Arab who is likely to have as much say as anyone in shaping Syrian destinies; but some mutual esteem has resulted, and when the time for bargaining comes, the two principals will start with some idea of what each is worth and to what end each is working.

XVIII. Notes on Camel-Journeys
With Accompanying Comment by 'G. Harland'
24 May 1919

I have been several times lately asked for figures of camel-journeys, both for speed and for endurance, and no doubt therefore the following notes on the subject will be of interest. In all cases she-camels only are concerned.

For speed, the best performance I know was the 39 hours' ride of Sherif Barakat ibn Smeiyah, from Medina to Mecca, by the Rabegh road a few years ago. It was a race, and camels were changed at Rabegh, 154 miles from Medina. The total distance works out at about 280 miles, and it was covered practically without a stop, except for a few minutes at Rabegh. The average speed was thus over seven miles per hour. A race of this sort is a test of the man's endurance, rather than that of the camel. Another equally fine ride was that of Aissa, a Harb tribesman, who came from Zilfi in Qasim to Yenbo in three days, and returned to Zilfi in four more, making a total of seven days for the round trip of 900 miles, an average of 130 miles a day. Aissa used four camels.

Rides on single camels are more interesting as records. One of the Atram family of Fitenna Abu Tayi Howeitat, on a home-bred pedigree camel, rode between sunset and sunset from Nebk abu Gasr to Bair and Jefer, a distance of 143 miles. He rested in Jefer one day and returned on the third day to Nebk on the same camel. I owned this camel some years later, and found by experience that it would keep up a comfortable and steady trot of seven and a half miles per hour for hour after hour without special urging: but I never had need to do a trotting journey of greater length than from Rum to Akaba (39 miles) on it. It did this in a little under five hours, carrying a good deal of kit besides myself. Mesnid, a Sherari, took a message from Jefer to Akaba for me. He left Jefer at noon, and returned with the reply two days later at noon, doing 220 miles, and his errand also, in the 48 hours. He rode a Sherari four-year-old.

The fast time for a camel-postman from Medina to Mecca is three days. This is an average of about 95 miles a day.

With one servant I rode from Azrak through Jefer, Shedia, and Rum to Akaba (290 miles) in three days and a half. This is an average of about 84 miles a day. We rode Beni Sakhr camels.

One of the Harith Sherifs of Modhig rode from Akaba to Mecca in nine days. The total distance is about 690 miles, which gives him an average of 77 miles a day. He rode a Sherari camel, and the trip is one of the finest I have heard of.

Exceptional performances of this sort cannot be expected of the ordinary camel in ordinary condition. When riding *ghazzu* with the Howeitat or Beni

Sakhr I found that for long journeys camels were never permitted to trot, since it interrupts the chances of grazing on the march. They do a steady walk of nearly four miles an hour, and keep this up for from sixteen to twenty hours daily, giving them an average mileage of from 64 to 80 miles. The smaller of these distances can be counted on as an average for perhaps ten or twelve days. For a month's riding day by day, it would be unwise to expect more than 50 miles a day from a camel in good condition. Weak camels cannot be expected to do more than about 40 miles a day average. With strong camels my experience has been that the man gives in sooner than the camel. My longest month was 1,400 miles, and I found it very difficult. A bad or inexperienced rider will wear out a camel very quickly. Arabs mostly ride light, about eight or nine stone, and their clothes and kit are usually less than we can do with. I carried little, and yet managed to use twice as many camels as my men.

For a disciplined camel corps, forty miles a day is a fair march, and that this average was passed for three days on end by Colonel Buxton's column of ICC when going north from Bair speaks very well for the riders and the animals. The latter (and indeed the former) were all male, were all unaccustomed to desert conditions, and were carrying heavy loads. A column marching in the Arab formation of small independent groups of ten or twelve will make better way than a column that tries to keep in regular line. An Arab party of 20 men (my servants) marched once with all their kit from Abu el Lissan to Akaba (60 miles) in just over five hours, as the last stage of a journey of five 50-mile marches. The camels were all fit to start the next day. Needless to say they were all pushing their camels on this last occasion. A stripped camel, racing, will do something like twenty miles an hour for nearly two hours. For a short burst I have timed them trotting at 22 and cantering at 26 miles per hour.

TEL

The performances described by Colonel Lawrence are exceptional ones made on the best camels. During my experience in the southern Hejaz I found that either the incentive had to be very strong, or the remuneration most lavish, to induce a Bedou to cover more than 30 or 40 miles a day. The fastest rate for the emir's *neggabs* from Mecca to the Arab camps on the outskirts of Medina, and from the camps to the coast at Yenbo, was 50 miles a day, but the payment worked out at £2 10s. per diem.

On raids, the rate of progress was generally 15 miles a day and never more than 25. This was done at walking pace and the Bedouin intensely disliked travelling more than eight hours out of the twenty-four, or more than three hours without rest. It was my experience that for endurance in camel riding though not for speed the Britisher could easily outstrip the Bedou, and during my different journeys my Arab companions were, in every case, the first to suggest halting for rest.

The camels of the southern Hejaz are, in general, poor beasts, and ten hours' continuous marching as a rule exhausts them. I have known several cases where the mounts of postmen, after doing a trip from Yenbo to the emirs' camps and back (about 200 miles) in 5 days, have simply dropped dead at the end of the journey.

Baggage caravans march at the rate of about two miles an hour only, and to accompany such a caravan is probably the most tiring and uncomfortable form of travelling that exists. The camels are tied together in a long string and usually travel during the night only. A march generally extends to 10 or 12 hours. Except for the man on the leading camel, the Arabs arrange comfortable places on which to lie down on top of the camel loads and sleep the whole night.

G. HARLAND

Part Two
In Time of Peace

Introduction

Peace was not the term that would spring easily to Lawrence's mind when he looked back on the period that followed his return to England in October 1918. It might apply to a world in which, give or take a number of ongoing conflicts, some minor, some serious and prolonged, the horizon was no longer dominated by the flash of the guns, but to his closer focus he was caught up in what he would caustically label a 'dog fight in the corridors of Downing Street' that went on for almost three years. This was scarcely less of an ordeal than the one he had just come through; if anything it was more draining, because it was beset with more frustrations and lightened by fewer successes.

The mix of documents, articles and letters that make up this section – bar one – date from these difficult and challenging years. In the majority of cases we see here a campaigner strenuous in combat, fighting with words rather than weapons for the cause with which he had identified himself from the moment he set foot in Arabia: justice for the Arabs. There is a more relaxed, almost breezy mood in one text, 'Demolitions under Fire', in which he is writing about the practicalities of guerrilla warfare, and a more upbeat historian's confidence in another, 'The Evolution of a Revolt', where he expounds his philosophy of insurgent warfare. Even in these cases he is, of course, implicitly making his case, by the very fact of portraying the Arab Revolt as serious business. Mostly, however, he is more or less overtly promoting his special cause. Sometimes he writes with irony and anger, as in his letters on the Iraq crisis of 1920; sometimes he takes a larger, more benign view, as in his essay 'The Changing East', in which, among other things, he seems to be advocating a process of de-imperialisation decades ahead of its time.

The one text from outside the dog-fight years is the final item, which first appeared in 1929. It is well worthy of reprinting in this anthology but with the gloss that Lawrence was its author at second hand, since (as is explained on p. 274) it was basically a compilation of evidence taken from his writings on guerrilla warfare by a trusted military expert, though bearing the special cachet of being the last piece of serious prose bearing his name (if in abbreviated form) to be published in his lifetime.

What was his mindset at the end of all this effort, first in two years of war, subsequently in three years of (alleged) peace? As is explained at some length elsewhere, in the introduction to 'The Changing East' (pp. 248–9), his collaboration with Winston Churchill at the Colonial Office in 1921–2 allowed him to feel, or at least to claim, that he had achieved as much as was possible of his political aims. Thereafter, he left the public stage, seeking the anonymity of the ranks, first in the Royal Air Force, then in the Army, and then again in the Air Force. Plagued by a celebrity he had initially cultivated but then came to loathe, he became a man effectively on the run, changing his name not once but twice as he did so. If 1929 was the date of his last published testimony before his death, it was also almost certainly the year of an undated statement by him that struck David Garnett, editor of the magisterial volume of Lawrence's letters published in 1938, so forcibly that he gave it a special place in his sections on the post-war years. It came from a letter to an unknown correspondent of which only one incomplete paragraph has survived. I offer its keynote sentences here, since they seem to me to have a direct bearing on the massive effort of brain and hand represented by the writings republished in this book: 'I have done with politics, I have done with the Orient, and I have done with intellectuality. O Lord, I am so tired! I want so much to lie down and sleep and die. Die is best, because there is no reveille . . .'

He continued to write, above all letters, though also some literary criticism; he also produced a new prose translation of Homer's *Odyssey* that has been much reprinted, but the years of passionate advocacy were over. He would later achieve, almost, a kind of peace, but his death in 1935 at the age of forty-six, while facing an uncertain future following his discharge from his much loved Royal Air Force, would leave the question unanswered as to whether this was a peace that would have endured.

I

Reconstruction of Arabia

4 November 1918

What makes this document particularly interesting is its date, its authorship and the forthrightness of its argument. It is dated 4 November, i.e. a calendar month after Lawrence's hurried departure from Damascus on 4 October – just four days after that city's dramatic fall – while its authorship is given as T. E. LAURENCE, *Lieut.-Colonel*, the incorrect spelling suggesting that whoever typed his text, presumably written by hand, had not realised that this was the submission of an officer already making a notable name in London's inner political circles.

As early as 21 October he had launched his one-man pro-Arab campaign when he appeared before the War Cabinet's Eastern Committee, whose chairman was the former Viceroy of India, Lord Curzon, now serving under Prime Minister David Lloyd George as Lord President of the Council. Curzon had opened proceedings by stating that 'he and every member of His Majesty's Government had for some time watched with interest and admiration the great work which Colonel Lawrence had been doing in Arabia, and felt proud that [he] had done so much to promote the successful progress of the British and the Arab arms'. Invited to give his own views, Lawrence did so without prevarication, proposing positions of power for the three sons of the founder of the Arab Revolt, Grand Sherif Hussein, who had fought to greatest effect in the field. In the words of the official minutes of the meeting: 'Colonel Lawrence's own idea was the establishment of Abdullah as ruler of Baghdad and Lower Mesopotamia, Zeid in a similar position in Upper Mesopotamia, with Feisal in Syria.'

The minutes of a later meeting on 27 October included the following comment on him: 'He is a man with a remarkable career and of great ability, and he represented to us what we may call the extreme Arab point of view, the kind of thing Faisal would have said if he had been at our table that afternoon.' The official reaction to his advocacy can be gauged from the keyword 'extreme' in this distinctly 'Whitehall' sentence. Remarkable proposals: pity about the small chance of their being carried out.

Yet the case was still there to be made, as this document shows. David Garnett, who printed it in his 1938 collection of letters, described it somewhat blandly as having been 'written by Lawrence for the information of the British Cabinet on his return to England', adding, 'Although a secret document I have been allowed to copy it and to include it here.' The minutes quoted above, to which it must be presumed Garnett did not have access, arguably put the document in a different light. He was not so much stating a case as re-stating it with extra forcefulness, using not only the power of argument but also a hint of mockery to hammer home his message. His final paragraph pointedly attacks the so-called Sykes–Picot Treaty, which, dating back as far as May 1916, i.e. *before* the Arab Revolt, had proposed a partition of the territories of the Ottoman Empire (assuming that power's defeat in the war) between the major Allies, with Russia, France and Britain as the beneficiaries. Russia's exit from the scene following the Bolshevik Revolution took out one player from this political chess game entirely, while to Lawrence a further factor rendering the Treaty obsolete was the doctrine of self-determination newly advocated by the American president, Woodrow Wilson, a towering figure on the world stage since the USA's entry into the war in April 1917. More important still, Lawrence believed that the contribution of the Arabs to the recent military success in the Middle East made the post-war position of the French and the British as envisaged by the Sykes–Picot Treaty unsustainable. Hence Lawrence's demand that no 'second edition' of it should be attempted, since the 'geographical absurdities of the present Agreement will laugh it out of court'.

Knowing what we now know of Lawrence, we might see nothing extraordinary in his approach. But effectively this was a 'hostilities only' officer hectoring the leading Allied powers without fear or favour, while blatantly accusing them of moral duplicity. Unsurprisingly, not everybody saw the situation as he did. The outflow from the Sykes–Picot Treaty would pollute relations between Arab and Allied authorities into and far beyond the peace conference which opened in Paris two months later in January 1919.

The document appears as item 107 in David Garnett, *The Letters of T. E. Lawrence* (Jonathan Cape, London, 1938), though with the mistaken attribution to 'T. E. Laurence' corrected.

Reconstruction of Arabia
4 November 1918

The wish of the last generation of British statesmen (expressed in many ways beside the Bagdad Railway Agreements and the Alexandretta negotiations of 1915) to withdraw from their imperial position in the Middle East, made it desirable to find indirect means of keeping intact our 'Monroe' area, the quadrangle of land between Egypt, Alexandretta, Persia and the Indian Ocean. When war broke out an urgent need to divide Islam was added, and we became reconciled to seek for allies rather than subjects. We therefore took advantage of the dissatisfaction felt by the Arabic-speaking peoples (formerly voiced by Abbas Hilmi) with their alien rulers, and of the tendency, each day more visible, of the subject eastern peoples to demand a share in the dangers of government. We hoped by the creation of a ring of client states, themselves insisting on our patronage, to turn the present and future flank of any foreign power with designs on the three rivers.

The greatest obstacle, from the war standpoint, to an Arab movement, was its greatest virtue in peace time – the lack of solidarity between the various Arabic movements. The local jealousies in Syria, in Mesopotamia, in Arabia and in Egypt made it hard to know where or with whom to begin. There were abortive attempts with Sayid Taleb and with Aziz el Masri before we made up our minds to concentrate on the Sherif of Mecca. The Sherif was ultimately chosen because of the rift he would create in Islam, because his geographical position gave him a fair chance of surviving, and because his pre-eminence amongst Arabs was based on the arbitrary and empiric, but in the East unassailable, ground of family prestige.

Negotiations began between the Sherif and Sir Henry MacMahon, who was given discretion by the British government to conclude an agreement that would bring him in. Sir Henry was unfortunately not informed of the Sykes–Picot Agreement then in proof. The Sherif had no idea that we wanted him only as a figure-head; throughout the correspondence he spoke as the mandatory of the Arabs – meaning everyone under Turkish rule who spoke Arabic.

His first season as a rebel was not fortunate, and his chances were not improved by the dismissal of Sir Henry MacMahon and the substitution of Sir Archibald Murray, Sir Reginald Wingate and Colonel Brimond as his advisers. Nevertheless he was able eventually to carry all western Arabia with him from Mecca northwards, until the occupation of Akaba by Feisul in August 1917, closed the Sherifian military movement.

Feisul now undertook for his father (who had aged very fast) the liberation of Syria. His status for so doing was as a sealed member of the Syrian Revolutionary Committee. He remained in constant touch with his fellow-members in Egypt, with him in the field, and in undelivered Syria, treating them as colleagues. For his instrument he formed a regular army of Syrians and Mesopotomians, and returned to the Hejaz all his Arabians. As a detail of interest I may mention that only eight Hejazis shared in the entry in to Damascus.

Feisul's military operation could not be independent: he made himself the handmaid of General Allenby, the Allied Commander-in-Chief. I hope that in dividing the common spoils we will not descend to commercial arguments of the exact participating contingents of British, French, Indian, Arab, Jew, or Armenian troops. The Commander-in-Chief's Arab alliance enabled him to throw his cavalry, without lines of communication or the usual precautions, from Jaffa to Aleppo in pursuit of the Turks through country nominally hostile, but really our own. General Allenby reversed the old policy towards the Arabs, and helped them in every way he could in materials, advice and men. Their rapid success is due to him.

The war work of the ruling family of Mecca is now completed. We can hardly question the courage of King Hussein, who joined us, against Feisul's advice, soon after the fall of Kut, with the example of our other small friends before his eyes. It is also easy to see the moral ordeal it has been for the oldest, most holy, and most powerful family of the Arabs (a people who lay more stress on faith and pedigree than others), to cast off the friends and allegiance of a lifetime and to incur, on behalf of their national freedom, the unmeasured abuse of India, Turkey, Afghanistan and Egypt. The physical dangers and sufferings of the four princes in the very difficult campaigns of 1916, 1917 and 1918 must be reckoned to their credit. The loyalty to their word and allies of the old king and his sons, who have refused from the Turks successive offers of autonomy in Arabia, independence in Arabia with autonomy in Syria, and of the Khalifate, with independence in Arabia and autonomy in all the Arabic provinces, may be recommended as an example to the Power which persuaded him to revolt, but which was ready, without his knowledge, to hand him over, with the people for whom he stood guardian, to the Turks on much worse terms.

The Present Intention of the Arab Governments

(a) In Arabia, meaning the peninsula proper, the old man of Mecca intends to be the unquestioned head. If he has patience, he will become so by slow processes of time and pilgrimage. As, however he is foolish, it would be well if one of his sons joined him soon at Mecca. In Yemen the Sherif has no concrete aims. Ibn Rashid and Kuweit are already in touch with him. In Nejd, the situation created by the indirect conflict of India and Egypt over Ibn Saud and the Idrisi presents no real difficulties. Both men are fortunately heretics in Islam, not much better than the Agha Khan in orthodox opinion. Idrisi tried to graft elements of African fetishism on the abstract creeds of Arabia, and is failing. His disappearance is only a question of years. Ibn Saud is now striving to limit the puritan revival becoming too strong for him. If he is carried away by it, and attacks the Holy Places, the orthodox Islam will deal with him, as with his ancestor. If he can control it he will remain Emir of Nejd after military failure has warned him to recognise the Sherif as his overlord. I think Ibn Saud is friendly to us and that he is the only person so minded in his dominions.

I would like to suggest that the experience of the last four years has shown the undesirability of allowing Arabia to be controlled by any or by all of the present authorities in Cairo, Bagdad, Damascus or Simla. We have been provincial, if not parochial, in view.

(b) In Syria the Arab movement becomes really important, since its origin was to prevent the man-power and strategic advantages of that country falling into the hands of any Continental power. For this purpose the Arabs require equal rights with any other power in the Gulf of Alexandretta, the coastline from there to Tripoli, the port of Tripoli and its railway to Homs, the Bukaa from Homs to Lake Huleh, access by treaty to Haifa, and all the country east of this line and the Jordan. Further, Feisul requires to be sovereign in his dominions, with complete liberty to choose any foreign advisers he wants of any nationality he pleases. These advisers will be part of the Arab government and will draw their executive authority from it and not from their own government. It may be possible to secure Arab recognition of the

Turkish Dette in return for an equitable share of the Beyrout and Haifa Customs receipts. Feisul will, however, not consider himself bound by any agreement to which he is not a party.

His assets in Syria are not small. He controls most of the good corn land and the four industrial towns. He has 80 per cent of the Moslems (including all the fighting men) on his side, all the Ansariya, all the Jews. He has inherited the old Turkish civil service, all whose lower ranks, and many of whose upper ranks, are Arab. He himself is clear-sighted and well educated, and is capable of satisfying the needs of Syria in local self-government. If he fails the responsibility will lie at the door of the European Powers, in whose word he shows an undue simplicity of trust.

(c) In Palestine the Arabs hope that the British will keep what they have conquered. They will not approve Jewish independence in Palestine, but will support so far as they can Jewish infiltration, if it is behind a British, as opposed to an international, façade. If any attempt is made to set up the international control proposed in the Sykes–Picot Agreement, Feisul will press for self-determination in Palestine, and give the moral support of the Arab government to the peasantry of Palestine, to resist expropriation.

(d) In Irak the Arabs expect the British to keep control. The Sherif, relying on his agreement with us, hopes for a nominal Arab administration there.

(e) In Jezireh there are very vivid Arab nationalists, but they are in an unsatisfactory geographical position until a proportion of the nomadic and settled Kurds can be persuaded to join hands with the local government required there.

I would suggest that areas (d) and (e) should be kept quite separate, at least administratively. The problems of Irak are those of great public works and of a highly developed agriculture. The problems of Jezireh are those of turbulent mountain villagers, and semi-nomadic tribes.

The Kurdish question is likely to be much larger and more difficult than the Armenian one.

If representations of small nations are admitted to the Peace Conference the cry of self-determination is likely to be raised, and agreements made semi-secretly between the Powers previously may be regarded with some suspicion. For this reason I would suggest that no second edition of the Sykes–Picot Treaty be produced. The geographical absurdities of the present Agreement will laugh it out of court, and it would be perhaps as well if we spared ourselves a second effort on the same lines. If we do not, I hope that we will at least recognise our official inclusion of the Arabs among the belligerents, and make them a party to any decisions affecting Arab areas conquered by themselves.

T. E. LAURENCE, Lieut.-Colonel

2

Three Articles from *The Times*

26–28 November 1918

If the previous document shows Lawrence attempting to influence events from behind closed doors, the three items that follow are the product of his decision to further the Arab cause by going public. He wrote the account from which they were taken at a sitting, and they appeared as major articles on successive days: 26, 27 and 28 November.

This was a mere fortnight after the armistice of 11 November which brought to an end the almost four-and-a-half-year nightmare known to history as the First World War. Britain was still almost totally absorbed in the struggle which had ravaged the European continent, producing psychological and economic meltdown and toppling monarchies and empires. Lenin and the Bolsheviks ruled in Moscow, the Kaiser was in exile, Germany was a republic and the casualty lists from the final battles fought on the notorious Western Front were still filling the columns of the newspapers and would do so for many days yet. Out of the Middle East comes a lone voice demanding justice for a people involved in a struggle so distant, so low on the list of priorities at that time, that it required all the eloquence Lawrence could muster to gain a hearing: a voice, almost literally, crying from a wilderness. That he was prepared to buck the popular trend, to jab at the conscience of the nation however unpropitious the circumstances, says much about his commitment to the cause he had taken as his own.

'Going public' in *The Times*, however, was doing so with a difference. This was Britain's most famous and influential newspaper, still sustained by its reputation gained in the previous century as 'The Thunderer', but by long tradition its contributors, however distinguished, were anonymous. As it happened, this suited Lawrence well. At this stage the description 'a correspondent who was in close touch with the Arabs throughout their campaign against the Turks' (or similar variants) would carry greater weight than the mere name of an officer known at this time only within the reaches of Whitehall and the War Office.

His letter to the Editor of *The Times*, Geoffrey Dawson, is remarkable for the vehemence with which he presses the Arabs' case:

They never had a press agent, or tried to make themselves out a case, but fought as hard as they could (I'll swear to that) and suffered hardships in their three campaigns and losses that would break up seasoned troops. They fought with ropes around their necks (Feisul has £20000 live and £10000 dead on him) I the same: Nasir £10000 live, and Ali el-Harith (£8000) and did it without, I believe, any other very strong motive than a desire to see the Arabs free.

Without question these letters are a fast, exciting read, yet strangely we see here, perhaps for the first time, signs of that diffidence as a writer that would make Lawrence condemn so much of his writing as unworthy. If the 'putrid stuff' syndrome, that tendency to loathe what he had written the moment he laid down his pen, has a beginning, it is here. Thus in his covering letter he suggests that the speed with which he had written had affected his style: 'It's a pity, because it begins decently, and drivels off into incidents. Please burn it.' Fortunately Dawson did not heed Lawrence's advice, but published instead, giving the articles, in the context, a remarkably high profile.

It is noteworthy that Lawrence deliberately left himself out of the picture, giving maximum credit to the Arabs. Even in areas where he had been a prime mover, he masked his own involvement. As is now well known, after the seizure of Akaba in June 1917 he rushed at once to Cairo to be first with the good news. Here he refers to 'messengers . . . sent off hastily to Egypt', with no indication of any British participation, let alone that the principal messenger was himself.

He also gives considerable credit to the Royal Navy for its contribution; but then there could be no discredit in the Arabs accepting aid from the sea, while he felt it important to accentuate their role as a land force. The naval role would be discreetly diminished in *Seven Pillars of Wisdom*, while the British role, and of course his own, would be considerably increased.

With all their limitations, however, these are powerful polemics, and, in spite of the spin, not bad history. If there had been no *Seven Pillars*, the Arab Revolt would still have had an outstanding barrister presenting the case for the defence.

The letters were reprinted in Stanley and Rodelle Weintraub, *Evolution of a Revolt* (The Pennsylvania State University Press, University Park, PA, and London, 1968), and in my *Secret Despatches from Arabia and Other Writings by T. E. Lawrence*, 1991 (see Preface, p. 20).

I. The Arab Campaign
26 November 1918

The Arab Campaign
Land and Sea Operations

British Navy's Help

We print below the first of a series of articles from a correspondent who was in close touch with the Arabs throughout their campaign against the Turks after the revolt of the Sherif of Mecca. This article describes the first stage of the campaign – the successful revolt at Mecca; the abortive Arab attack on Medina; and the seizure of the port of Wejh by the British Navy – acting in close contact with Sherif Feisul – as a base for operations against the vital section of the Hedjaz Railway.

(From a correspondent)

Soon after he heard the news of the surrender of Kut by General Townshend, Hussein ibn Ali, Grand Sherif and Emir of Mecca, sent word to the British government that he could no longer stand by and witness the continued subjection of the Arabs to the Turks. He asked for pay, arms, and food for his troops, and before they had been promised him broke out into rebellion against the Young Turk Party and their German masters.

The Sherifs of Mecca have long been *de facto* rulers of Mecca and its province, and the immense prestige of the family amongst the Arabs (Hussein ibn Ali is the senior descendant of Mahomed, and as such head of the Sherifs, the Prophet's family) carried all the Arabs of the Hedjaz with them in their revolt. They easily crushed the Turkish garrisons of Taif, Mecca and Jedda, and opened up communication with the British Fleet in the Red Sea, so that the arms and food they needed for the further extension of their rising might be brought to their coasts.

The Attack on Medina

At Medina, where Sherifs Feisul and Ali (third and eldest sons of the Sherif of Mecca) raised their father's flag on 13 June 1916, the eventful day of the Mecca revolt, events were less fortunate. The Turks had expected hostilities, and had brought down large forces from Syria to anticipate events. Feisul raised all the tribesmen and villagers about Medina, and occupied the suburbs, but shrank from an attack on the Holy City itself. The Tomb of Mahomed makes Medina very sacred to all Moslems, and especially to members of the Prophet's own family; and the Arabs were new to warfare, and had not got before them the example of the Turks who shelled at Mecca the Kaaba, the centre of Moslem interest in things of this world. Whatever the cause, they lost their opportunity. They cut the railway to Syria, tearing up lengths of the metals with their bare hands and throwing them down the bank (for they had no explosives), but they refused to cut the precious water conduit, or to clear their way by fighting through the streets. The Turks, encouraged by their inactivity, sallied out at dawn, surprised the garden suburb of Awali, massacred in it hundreds of women and children and burned the rest – putting machine-guns at the gates and setting fire in many places to the flimsy houses.

Feisul dashed up with his Arab camel-men to the rescue, but was in time only to harry the last files of the retreating Turks. The Arabs now clamoured for an assault on the great citadel that stood without the walls, and when he tried to hold them back plunged forward without him. The Turks had, however, a formidable armament collected there, and the Arabs had never before met artillery fire. The assaulting column swerved aside and took refuge in the broken lava slopes of a low hill outside the north-east angle of the town. The Turks saw their weakness, and set out an enveloping force to cut off and destroy them. Feisul, with the rest of the Arabs, a mile back on the flank, saw the danger of their fellows, and started out to help them. The Turks opened with all their guns from the town wall, covering the open ground with bursting shrapnel, and after their first losses the Arabs wavered, and then took cover in the gardens. Feisul rode up to their front line on his horse, and called to them to follow him. Their chief refused, saying that it was death to cross the plain. Feisul laughed, and turning his horse forced it at a walk through the Turkish fire till he had gained the shelter of the opposite gardens. Then he waved to the men behind him, who charged across to him at a wild gallop, losing only about twenty men on the way.

The combined forces now engaged the sallying Turks, and a costly fight was maintained till dark, when Feisul found himself nearly without ammunition, and without reserves of men, food, or arms for the morrow. He had therefore to change all his plans, abandon hope of an immediate victory in the north, and instead endeavour to hold his disheartened army together till he could obtain new supplies from the coast, where Rabegh, half-way to Mecca, had been promised him as a base. The siege of Medina indeed made little progress after this, and the town still holds out, and may continue to do so for long after the rest of the world is at peace. It has been cut off from Turkey for long enough; but so have the Turkish garrisons of Asir and Yemen. It is a Holy City, so that the Arabs have never fired, and will never fire, a shot against it (ideal conditions for a besieged army). The Turks have deported every civilian, and scattered them, without record, or means, or hope of return, over all the Ottoman Empire. We found Medina refugees in Jerusalem, in Kerak, in Damascus. Some are in Konia, some in Angora, some in Constantinople itself; their only common touch to-day is destitution. Their gardens have fallen to the Turkish garrison, just as the jewels and splendid offerings of the Prophet's Tomb have fallen to the Turkish governors. The soldiers spend their days in husbandry, and at night withdraw to the sheltering walls of the town.

Arab Tactics
In the first days of the Arab revolt, however, things were not so easy nor so idyllic. The army in Medina was as strong as the Arab tribesmen outside, and was equipped with guns and machine-guns and aeroplanes. As they collected transport, or received it from Syria by the now repaired railway, they pushed their lines farther and father afield, and by seizing the only wells in the countryside began to make a menacing advance towards Rabegh, the key of Mecca in the military sense. Feisul flung himself into a tangle of difficult sandstone hills that flanked the Turkish advance, and while his

brother Ali at Rabegh was striving to form the beginnings of a regular army, to add to the tribesmen that technical aid which alone could enable them to meet the Turks fairly in the field, Feisul set himself, with little bands of ravaging Beduin on camels, to make impossible a serious advance of the Turks by raiding their lines of communication. It was risky work, since the Arab parties – because of difficulties of water supply – could not exceed ten or fifteen men, and these had to dash in on the main road, kill or carry off what they could, and regain their camels and escape before the garrison of the blockhouses could turn out. Only men who could leap into the camel saddle at the trot with one hand while carrying a rifle with the other were chosen for this service.

The Arabs' best efforts at defence proved insufficient, and Feisul saw that a change of plan was necessary if the Turks were to be prevented from regaining Mecca and crushing the Arab movement in its infancy. After consulting the British naval authorities in the Red Sea, he determined that if they would support him to the utmost, he would risk leaving the Mecca road undefended and carry his whole force away from Yenbo to attack Wejh, two hundred miles farther north along the Hedjaz coast. He argued that by boldly taking the offensive against the Turkish communications with Syria – and Wejh covered a vital section of the Hedjaz railway, the life-cord of the Turkish forces in Arabia – he would force them to divert a considerable force to purely defensive purposes, and might so deceive them by his apparent careless confidence in the strength of Mecca as to persuade them to abandon their forward march against it. To take his place Feisul called up his younger brother Zeid, and gave him what men he thought not worth taking away, so that Zeid might make a semblance of resistance in the hills, while he also asked his elder brother Abdulla, who had been blockading Medina on the east, to move across the railway, north of Medina, and appear to threaten the Turkish line of communication directly. Abdulla had actually no force capable of doing anything very serious, but he made a fine start by cutting up some mobile Turkish units, and left between the metals of the railway a letter to the Turkish Commander-in-Chief in Medina, telling him of all, and much more than all, of what he meant to do.

A Flank March
Feisul's own operation consisted of a flank march of two hundred miles parallel to the Turkish front by an inferior fighting force, leaving behind it an open base and the only possible defence line of the Middle Hedjaz undefended. He embarked on the ships put at his disposal by the British Senior Navy Officer, Red Sea, all his arms and stores from Yenbo before he left the place. He divided his ten thousand men into nine sections, to move independently to Um Lejj, a little coastal village half-way, and ordered to concentrate there by 14 January 1917. At Um Lejj he issued them with fresh supplies (obtained, as agreed, from the ships), and sent on board a landing party to be used in the actual attack on Wejh in co-operation with the Navy. He had then

to contemplate a march of 150 miles, without a single spring of water and only a few weak wells to suffice for what was, for the desert, an exceptionally large army. To aggravate things, there was little grazing for the camels, and the scarcity of baggage animals made it impossible to carry forage. The Beduin, too, who guided us, had no short unit of time, such as the hour, to inform us of distance, and no longer measure of space than the span. They had no realisation of numbers larger than ten, and could not tell us the roads, or the wells or how much capacity they had. Inter-communication between Beduin forces is always hindered because no man in the force can read or write. In the end, however, we got through, on 25 January, without losing a man from hunger or thirst. We lost many camels, but all our mules survived the trip, thanks to a Royal Indian Marine ship which put into an uncharted bay on the coast and supplied them with water in the middle of a dry march of seventy-five miles.

The actual business of Wejh was settled by the Navy and the landing party before the main army came up. Feisul was in time only to cut off some of the escaping garrison and capture all their reserves of arms and equipment. The naval force had a quite difficult fight, but eventually carried their points without undue loss by making free use of water communication to outflank the Turkish positions and by the very vigorous support given by the ship's guns to the various landing parties. The Turks entrenched themselves in the town, and fought from street to street, while the Arabs cleared the houses both of Turks and of all movable property. The whole place was taken in thirty-six hours, and the Navy set the seal on its work by taking up other Arab landing parties to Dhaba and Moweilah on 8 February and 9 February, by the action of which the whole of the northern end of the Red Sea, up to the Gulf of Akaba, was cleared of the enemy.

The naval side of the Sherifian operations, when the time comes to tell of it, will provide a most interesting case of the value of command of the sea as a factor in shore operations against an enemy depending entirely on land communications for his maintenance. This advantage over the enemy enabled a small, irregular, and very ill-equipped force of discordant tribesmen to checkmate a Turkish force nearly their equal in numbers, armed and supplied with the best materials the Turks possessed, composed in part of Dardanelles veterans and in part of almost the only units of the old Turkish first-line army which had escaped the slaughter-house, and led by two of their best generals. The Sherif was fortunate in having to deal with Admiral Wemyss and other senior officers, who took constant pains to understand the very difficult shore conditions, and as often suggested the means that would provide the most efficient contact with their ships.

II. The Arab Epic (1)
27 November 1918

The Arab Epic
Feisul's Battles in the Desert

On the Threshold of Syria

The following is the second article from a correspondent who accompanied the Arab army of the Grand Sherif of Mecca, led by his son, Sherif Feisul, through the campaign against the Turks. The first article appeared in The Times *yesterday.*

After the occupation of Wejh, the Arab operations had to take a new phase. The Turks who had been advancing on Mecca at once fell back on Medina, and began to defend their pilgrim railway seriously. This gave the Arab Sherif Feisul the time and leisure he so much needed to construct his army of regular troops. It need hardly be said that Arabia provided no recruitable population. The Beduin is hostile to discipline, and unfit for regular service; though on his own day, in his own country, and in his own style, he will dispose of many times his number of any troops that can be brought against him. Feisul's regular army was composed of peasantry from Syria and from Mesopotamia. In part, they came from their own districts secretly to him. Many were deserters from the Turkish army, for the Turks when war broke out had pressed 150,000 Arab-speaking subjects into their army, and these men, when the Sherif revolted, all knew that the day of reckoning with their masters was approaching.

Besides the labour of forming a regular army Sherif Feisul at Wejh devoted himself day and night to securing desert power, to take the place of the British sea power that henceforward could serve him only indirectly. In this he succeeded, thus gaining a means of approach and a line of communication for all enterprises he desired against the cultivated land of Palestine and Syria as ready and inviolable almost as the sea has proved to Britain. It took him months to obtain the suffrage of all the tribes, and the expenditure of as much tact and diplomacy as would suffice for years of ordinary life. What he achieved, however, is little short of wonderful. From time immemorial the desert has been a confused and changing mass of blood-feuds and tribal jealousies. To-day there are no blood-feuds among the Arabs from Damascus to Mecca; for the first time in the history of Arabia since the seventh century there is peace along all the pilgrim road.

While forming his army and developing his policy, Feisul kept the Turks busy by frequent railway raids. He cut the line in dozens of places, and did each time what damage he could. But the construction of the Hedjaz railway is primitive and there are no great bridges or elaborate constructions which can be destroyed, to interrupt the line for a sensible period. His work had to be done and redone continually, and very heartbreaking work it was.

A Fighting Sheikh

By early May however, Feisul's propaganda in the north was crowned with success, by the adhesion to him of Sheikh Auda abu Tayi, the leading spirit of the Howeitat and the finest fighting man in the desert. He is over fifty now, but still tall and straight, and as active as a young man. He prides himself on himself, as being the quintessence of everything Arab. His hospitality is sweeping, often crushing: his generosity has reduced him many times to poverty, and swallowed the profits of a hundred successful raids. He has married twenty-eight times, been wounded thirteen times, and in his battles has seen all his tribesmen hurt and most of his relations killed. His escape from wounds in the last eight years he ascribes to an amulet (the rarest and richest in the world, in his judgement), a complete copy of the Koran, pro-duced in photo-miniature by a Scotch firm. His private 'kill' in single fight is seventy-five since 1900 – Arabs, be it understood, for Turks are not entered in Auda's game-book. Under his hands the Howeitat had become the finest fighting men in the desert, and he has seen Aleppo, Basra, and Mecca in his raids. He is as hard-headed as he is hot-headed, has extreme patience, and ignores advice and abuse with the most charming smile. He talks abundantly, in a voice like a waterfall, of himself, and in the third person. His great pride is to tell tales against himself, or to tell in public fictitious, but appalling, stories of the private life of his host or guests.

Auda came to Wejh and swore allegiance to the Sherif in the picturesque Arab formula, on the book, and then sat down to dinner with Feisul. Half-way through the meal he rose with an apology, and withdrew from the tent. We heard a noise of hammering without, and saw Auda beating something between two great stones. When he came back he craved pardon of the Sherif for having inadvertently eaten his bread with Turkish teeth, and displayed the broken remains of his rather fine Damascus set in his hand. Unfortunately, he could hardly eat anything at all afterwards, and went very sorrowfully till in Akaba the High Commissioner sent him an Egyptian dentist, who refurnished his mouth.

From Wejh on 9 May Feisul sent off a small expedition of camel-men under Sherif Nasir, to take Akaba, three hundred miles farther north. They marched through the Hedjaz Hills, picking up a few adherents across a dreadful lava field, which foundered their camels, over the Hedjaz railway in a thunder of dynamite explosions, into the pathless central desert of Arabia, where they wandered for weeks in great pain of heat and hunger and thirst, losing many of their party and disheartening more. When they did reach water it was only to lose three more of their few men from snake-bite, for the Wadi Sirhan is venomous. However, at length they reached the Howeitat tents, and under the burden of the tribe's most insistent hospitality spent some uneasy days.

They had now marched some four hundred miles and were getting short of food. Some of the party rested here to gather recruits, while others went out north and west, to trouble the Turks by feints upon the railways of Syria and confuse them as to what they meant. They destroyed a bridge near Homs, and one near Deraa, and blew up a train near Amman.

A Rout

The Turks believed that they must be in Wadi Sirhan, and concentrated their available cavalry about the Hauran, and sent out all that could move into the desert after them. Nasir moved at once, south and west, and captured two stations near Katraneh. The Turks blew up the wells in the desert (Nasir had now learned to do with little water) and reinforced the threatened sector from Maan. This latter was, however, the area the Arabs really wanted, and a day later a section of the Howeitat, on 30 June, wiped out the first Turkish post on the new motor road from Maan to Akaba, after the Turks had won a first success and had cut the throats of thirteen Arab women and children. News of their attack reached Maan, and the mass of the garrison there set out to relieve the post. That day Nasir occupied the railway near Maan and blew up a series of bridges, and then threw himself between Maan and the Turkish relief column, which had reached its objective only to find the ground held by squadrons of wheeling vultures busy on their dead.

Throughout 2 July Nasir fought the Turks, in a heat that made movement torture. The burning ground seared the skin off the forearms of our snipers, and the camels went as lame as the men with the agony of the sun-burnt flints. The Turks were hemmed in to a gentle valley, with a large spring in the bottom. The Arabs were dry. They had rifles, and the Turks mountain-guns, with which they kept up the fight till evening. At dusk Auda collected our fifty horsemen in a crooked valley, about three hundred yards from the Turks, and suddenly burst at them over a rise, galloping into the brown of them, shooting from the saddle as he came. The Turks broke in panic, as Turks often will, and after one wild burst of musketry scattered in all directions, while the rest of the Arab force dashed down the hillsides into the hollow as fast as their cantering camels could take them. In five minutes it had become a massacre. Some of the Turks got away in the gathering darkness, but the Arabs took and killed more than their own total numbers.

Akaba Taken

There were still four Turkish garrisons between Nasir and the sea. The nearest was overrun in half-an-hour; the next but one surrendered, without a shot fired. The third was strongly placed, but the Arab leader announced that a sudden darkness at the third night hour would enable it to be rushed without loss – and the moon was good enough to be eclipsed that night. Fortified by such evident proof of ghostly alliance, the Arabs pressed on down the great road that the Turks had prepared for the invasion of Egypt. The fourth post fell back before our approach to the main position of Akaba, where the Howeitat tribesmen, before even we were near, clustered about them like hornets, sniping any head or body that showed, and cutting off all egress. They were six miles from the beach in the mouth of an immense ravine, impregnable from attack by the sea, as they knew, and we knew, but very open to a force taking them, as we were doing, unexpectedly from the east. When Nasir came up he tried to make them parley; the local Arabs fiercely refused. 'They tore our men in four pieces between yoked mules, why should we spare them?' . . . but the Sherif after a day and a night of earnest work regained control of his men. He then, with only one companion, advanced into the open between the Arabs and the Turks, so that his men had perforce to hold their fire, and sent in a prisoner with the white flag to tell the Turks that all was up. Fortunately the Turkish commander agreed and the Arabs swept through his camp into the village of Akaba in a mad rush of joy.

Our position, when we first arrived in Akaba, was miserable. We had no food, and hundreds of prisoners. They ate our riding camels (we killed them two a day), caught fish, and tried to cook the green dates, till the messengers, who had been sent off hastily to Egypt across the Sinai desert, could send help and food by sea. Unfortunately the camels by now had done a thousand miles in five weeks, and were all jaded, so that it took the men two days to get to Suez, where Admiral Wemyss at once ordered a man-of-war at top speed to Akaba, with all the food that was to be found on the quays. That ship is gratefully remembered in the desert, for it saved two thousand Arabs and one thousand Turks from starvation.

The Wilderness Road

Feisul came to Akaba in August, and once again his tactics and the colour of the Arab movement had to change. The abandon of the early days, when each man had his camel and his little bag of flour and his rifle, was over. The force had to be organised and become responsible. No longer could Feisul throw himself into the thickest of the doubtful fight and by his magnetic leadership, and still more wonderful snap-shooting, turn the day in our favour. No longer could the Sherifs in glowing robes, hurtle out in front of their men in heady camel charges and bring back *spolia opima* in their own hands. Even our wonderful Arab bodyguards – Central Arabia camel-men – dressed in all the colours of the rainbow, only one degree less gorgeous than their camel-trappings, had to be sacrificed. The Sherifian army now stood on the threshold of Syria, and its work was henceforward with the townsmen and the villagers – excellent people, but not the salt of the earth, as are the Arabs of the desert.

The desert was Feisul's; he had worked his miracle, and made the wilderness peace; but the wilderness was only our road, the means by which we could arrive at the cultivated places we wished to raise or occupy. Another sobering influence was the knowledge that we formed part of the army of General Allenby. Akaba was on his extreme right, and the Arab army formed his right wing. Our plans were only a part of his plans, instead of being joyous ventures of our own. The Arab army, however unorthodox its elements, tried its best to fulfil the wishes of the Commander-in-Chief and to contribute its uttermost to his plans. In return he gave it the materials, the advice, the advisers, and the help it needed, and enabled Feisul to transform what had been a mob of Beduin into a small but well-made force of all arms.

III. The Arab Epic (2)
28 November 1918

The Arab Epic
Doom of Turk Power in Syria

Wrecking the Hedjaz Railway

The correspondent who was with the army of the Grand Sherif of Mecca throughout the campaign against the Turks concludes his account of the campaign to-day. He does not deal with the Arab attack on Maan in April 1918, because this was included in General Allenby's last dispatch, nor with the final Arab advance on Damascus which was described in The Times *of 17 October. The two other articles of this series appeared on 26 November and yesterday.*

The new Arab army – now the right wing of General Allenby's army – was tried before the end of October 1917, when five hundred men of it, with two mountain-guns and four machine-guns, holding a selected position on the heights around Petra – the 'rose red city half as old as time', whose ruins make notable the Nabathaean hills – held them against four Turkish infantry battalions, a cavalry regiment, half a mounted infantry regiment, six mountain-guns, four field-guns, and two machine-gun companies. The Turks attacked in three columns, drove back the Arabs in one point, and captured one mountain-gun, but were counter-attacked and driven in flight back across the plain. The Arab losses were heavy, but they retook their lost gun.

The Arab regular army then fell back from the hill-tops, because of the heavy snowfall of 1917–18. The Turks also had to fall back to near the railway, and there was only fighting of the Beduin, till spring, when the Arab main army attacked Maan, between 13 April and 17 April, as their share of the British Amman attack. This phase of the operations has been dealt with by General Allenby in his last dispatch in full detail.

A Camel Charge
The winter was, however, not uneventful for us, since Feisul tried, by means of the local tribes and peasantry, to share in the British descent to the Dead Sea and Jordan valley. Sherif Nasir again led the forlorn hope, and again

Auda abu Tayi joined us. There came also some of the Beni Sakhr clan from Moab. The force moved about the desert east of Maan, uneasily for a time, and then suddenly, in the first days of January, made an attack on the third railway station north of Maan, called Jurf. The Turks held the station buildings strongly, and a covering knoll above it; but Nasir had with him a little mountain-gun, which knocked out the first Turkish gun, and so encouraged the Beduin that they got on their camels and again repeated the camel charge that had won us the fight for Akaba. Bullets have little immediate effect on a camel that is going at twenty-five miles an hour, and before the Turks could do anything the Arabs were over the trenches and among the station buildings. The survivors of the garrison, some two hundred in number, surrendered at discretion.

From Jurf Nasir marched to Tafileh and summoned it to surrender. The Turkish garrison of one hundred laughed at us; but Auda galloped up under their bullets to the east end of the town, where the market opens on to a little green place, and in his voice, which at its loudest carries above all the tumult of a *mêlée*, called on the dogs of villagers to hand over their Turks. All the Arab world knows Auda, and while they regard him as a most trying friend, love him as a national monument; so without more ado they surrendered themselves and their Turkish garrison.

Tafileh is a village of about six thousand inhabitants, and we looked, with the reinforcement of its men, to do great things. As a beginning our horse, with the help of Abu Irgeig and the Arabs of Beersheba, charged one night up the east bank of the Dead Sea from its south end, flying through the defiles between the hills and the lake and over the Turk patrols before they could give warning, till at dawn they passed over the root of the flat promontory called the Lissan and came gently through the bushes till they were within easy shot of the little harbour where half the Turkish Dead Sea fleet was moored by cables to the shore. The crews were on shore breakfasting, and the Arabs, by a swift cavalry charge, were able to capture the Turkish fleet with its crews, sink the ships, and get the officers and sailors away with them before the garrison on the bluffs above had realised that irregularities were being committed. The 'fleet' were of course only motor launches and fishing vessels; but there are few sea forces that have been captured by cavalry, and the disgust of the two very smart naval officers we took gave us great comfort.

Fighting at Tafileh

Meanwhile the Turks of Damascus had become alarmed at the Arab progress, and had sent down their GOC Amman, with a composite regiment of infantry, some cavalry, and two mountain howitzers, to turn us out of Tafileh. He came along delicately, laying his telephone lines and making his roads, and with him were the new civil staff for Tafileh and the equipment of the new post office there. We got in touch with him on 24 January 1918, and found him unpleasantly strong. In fact he pushed us nearly out of Tafileh that night. The flashes of the Turkish rifles at the crest of the great gorge in which Tafileh lies were very visible, and there ensued a great panic in the town. All the women screamed with terror, and threw their household goods and children out of their houses into the streets, through which came plunging mounted Arabs, shooting busily at nothing in particular. At dawn, however, we were still in the place, and were able to send up a few men with two automatic rifles to assist the peasantry. This improved things, but was obviously insufficient, and the fighting became very hot, with a good deal of shelling by the Turks and huge bursts of machine-gun fire from their twenty-seven machine-guns. A shell knocked out one of our automatic rifles, and the other finished its ammunition. So we chose out a second position about two miles in rear of the flint ridge we were actually holding, and sent back to collect all the men we could upon it.

As soon as they began to appear we sent back the thirty peasants (on foot) who were helping us in the forward position and held it for another fifteen minutes only by thirty Howeitat horsemen. By then things had become quite impossible, with the air thick with bullets and reply from our side nearly out of the question, so the horsemen mounted again and scampered back to the reserve line. The Turks occupied our old ridge a few minutes later, and were obviously astonished to see the second line in front of them, with a mob of men walking about on top of it. We had now about three hundred men, and showed them all we could.

Shortly afterwards Sherif Zeid joined us, with one mountain-gun, four machine-guns, and seven automatic rifles; also about two hundred more men. We sent the Arab horse away to the Turkish left to turn their distant flank, and a peasant force, with some automatics, to turn their right flank. Meanwhile in the centre we demonstrated, and fired our mountain-gun, and carried out some astonishing tactics, till the outflanking parties were in position. We then attacked boldly across the hollow between the two ridges direct at the Turkish centre. As we were only about half their strength, this amused them so much that they did not notice our outlying parties till they opened fire and shot down all the Turkish machine-gunners. At the same moment we charged (camels, horses, and men pell-mell) and carried their main position with its fifteen Maxims before sunset. The peasantry from miles round were rallying to us, and met the broken Turks falling back before our men, who were tired out and very hungry; since we had been fighting for thirty hours. The local people therefore relieved us of the duty of pursuit, and filled our place so satisfactorily that only about eighty of the Turks got away, and they lost the whole of their animals, carts, guns, and machine-guns.

A Hard Winter
After this affair we were in good spirits, and foresaw ourselves meeting the British shortly at Jericho. However, things went wrong. It was partly the reaction after a great effort, partly the stimulus we had given to the Turks,

partly the awful weather – for just after the end of January the winter broke for good, and we had days of drenching rain, which made the level ground one vast mud-slide, on which neither man nor camel could pass. When this cleared we had snow, and snow, and snow. The hills round Tafileh are five thousand feet high, and open on the east to all the winds that Arabia can send, and conditions soon became impossible. Snow lay on the ground for three weeks. If the camels were strong and fit they would march for one day or two days through a coating six inches thick; but in all the hollows were drifts a yard deep, and at these our unfortunate men had to dismount and dig a way through with their bare hands. The Beduin had never remained in these hills for winter before, and gradually quitted them this year also. It increased one's misery to see below one, in Wadi Arabah, the level land of the Dead Sea depression flooded with sunlight, and to know that down there was long grass sown with flowers, and the fresh milk and comfort of spring in the desert. The Arabs wear only a cotton shirt and a woollen cloak, winter and summer, and were altogether unfitted for weather like this; very many of them died of the cold.

One curious incident was when a party of 150 Arabs went out to raid the railway near Maan. They marched from Akaba, with its sweltering heat for sixty miles, and halted for the night. Next morning they climbed the escarpment, which looked, they said, like a negro with a white skull cap on, and marched through powdery snow till dark, which proved windy and with faint attempts at a blizzard. They then camped in a three-foot water-course, barracking their camels for protection against the wall of the gully, to save them from the pitiless wind. They themselves lay down on the other side of the gully and slept. It was a bitter night, and no one was lively enough to get up and look about him, as it snowed gently, and everyone shivered all the time with the cold. At dawn, however, they found the side of the gully where the camels were one smooth drift of snow, out of which, like dark islands, were sticking the humps and saddles of their beasts. They set to, with the large iron spoons in which coffee beans are roasted, and dug out many of them – but all except three were dead! The jest was our marching home those long miles barefooted and laden with all our baggage, while the local attempts at a blizzard became more and more realistic. On another occasion Sherif Feisal sent out a party of thirty-four camel riders, to carry money to his brother in Tafileh eighty miles away – and four days afterwards one solitary rider, the only one of the party, struggled in. After this we all gave up touring the hills of either Edom or Moab in winter.

Railway Raids

For many months whenever there was no operation in hand someone on the Arab front (which was four hundred miles long, and was held by some forty thousand Arabs) would say, 'Let us undertake a railway raid,' and something more or less exciting would happen. Unquestionably the greatest game of all railway work is blowing up trains. Once in September 1917, an Arab party marched out of Akaba with explosives to Rum, a spring in the most wonderful red sandstone cliffs, that look too regular to lie natural, and are yet far too overwhelming to be artificial. It is like an immense empty triumphal road, waiting for a procession or review greater than the world can bring it. At Rum we collected a raiding party of Howeitat. Though the very pick of the fighting men of Arabia, they were the most cranky, quarrelsome collection imaginable. In six days there had to be settled fourteen private feuds, twelve assaults with weapons, four camel-thefts, one marriage-portion, two evil eyes, and a bewitchment. It takes longer than making out company returns in triplicate.

We reached the line, and wandered up and down it, by day and night, keeping hidden, till we found a place that pleased us, and there we laid an electric mine. The line crossed a valley on a high bank five hundred yards long, pierced by three small bridges about two hundred yards from each other. We laid the mine over the southernmost, connected it electrically with the firing mechanism under the middle one, and arranged for two Lewis guns to take position under the northernmost one. From this northern bridge ran up a long transverse gully westward. It was about two feet deep, and sprinkled with broom brushes, behind which the men (on foot) and the Lewis guns hid till wanted.

On the first day no train came; on the second a water-train and a line patrol together. On the third, about 8 a.m., a train of twelve wagons came down from Maan and passed slowly over the embankment. The Beduin were all lying behind the bushes, the Lewis gunners were under their arch, and the firing party under theirs, dancing a wild war-dance as the train rumbled over their heads. One man was left right out in the open to give the signal to the firing party when to fire the mine; he looked a harmless enough Arab, and the officers in the train amused themselves by firing at him with their pistols. As soon, however, as the locomotive was over the mine he jumped up and waved his cloak, and instantly there was a shattering roar, a huge cloud of smoke and dust, the clanking of iron and the crushing of woodwork, and the whirring noise of the fragments of steel from the explosion sailing through the air.

Till the smoke cleared there was dead silence, and then the two Lewis guns which had come out to right and left at the edges of their abutments raked the troops as they leaped out of the derailed trucks. The Beduins opened a rapid fire also, and in six minutes the affair was over, as the Arabs charged home on the wreck. We found that we had more prisoners than we wanted, some seventy tons of foodstuffs, and many little things like carpets and military stores. The Beduin plundered at lightning speed, while we signed the duplicate way-bills and returned one copy to the wounded guard, whom we meant to leave in place. Then we fired the trucks and drove off our now overladen camels before the relief parties of Turks, who were hurrying up from north and south, could cut us off.

Raids did not always go so well, but many of them were very damaging to the Turk. Thus it took him months to repair the break in the line made by Sherif Nasir in one raid about seventy miles north of Maan on 18 May 1918. All his operations in the Maan area were delayed until General Allenby was ready to take the offensive in the autumn. Sheikh Auda did a good thing during that fighting, for the Turks sent down the last survivors of their last company of camel corps. They penned their camels in a yard of the station while they fought. Auda could not resist the temptation to loot, and dashed in on his mare with twelve of his tribe; and for the loss of one man and two horses they brought out the whole twenty-five riding camels from within one hundred yards of the Turkish machine-gun. It was a very wonderful sight.

3

Demolitions under Fire

January 1919

Lawrence was clearly exceptionally active in the weeks following his return from the East, since this article appeared in print, in issue No. XXIX of the *Royal Engineers' Journal*, as early as January 1919. He had to prepare for the peace conference in Paris, to which he was to go as aide and mentor to the Emir Feisal; he met Feisal at Marseilles on his arrival in Europe and subsequently accompanied him during a number of official visits in Britain, including an audience with King George V; yet he still found time to write a lucid, comprehensive account of the technical side of his desert campaign. At a period when it might have been assumed that he was far more absorbed in politics than in the practicalities of a war he had now put behind him, he seems to have turned to the subject with relish. It was perhaps a welcome change from harassing politicians to take time to describe at length and in detail how he attacked trains.

It would later emerge that he was not deemed by some at least of his fellow officers to be the most professional, or the most restrained, of saboteurs. In a BBC television documentary in 1962, one officer who served with him in 1918, Second Lieutenant, later Sir Alec Kirkbride, recalled that he 'liked to make as big a bang as possible, [thus wasting] a great deal of explosives that had been brought on camel back for hundreds of miles.' Present at an attack on a railway station, this officer, much his companion's junior in rank, saw that Lawrence had put a mass of explosive under a nearby bridge:

> Knowing his habits I said, 'Please sir, give me a bit of warning before you fire your charges and let me get my men away.' 'Oh yes, all right, don't fuss, don't fuss.' So we went down and I was quite happily putting my charges in, and suddenly there was a most terrific bang and the bridge flew into the air and fell all over the station. I was absolutely furious, as furious as a subaltern could be with a colonel, which had its limits. And he sat on a boulder and laughed at me.

Yet it should be remembered that Lawrence was no slouch as a mechanic, and that arguably the most satisfying phase of his life was the time in the early 1930s when he worked with a team of like-minded colleagues on the design and production of air–sea rescue boats for the RAF. One of the most memorable comments he ever made about his own life and career occurs in a letter to another former officer of the desert campaign, written in gentle self-deprecation in 1934 as he approached the end of his service career: 'After having dabbled in revolt and politics it is rather nice to have been mechanically useful.'

This article was later reprinted in David Garnett, *The Essential T. E. Lawrence* (Jonathan Cape, London, 1951), in Stanley and Rodelle Weintraub, *Evolution of a Revolt*, and in my *Secret Despatches from Arabia and Other Writings by T. E. Lawrence*.

Demolitions under Fire
January 1919

We were interested in the Hejaz railway, and spent nearly two years on it. The Turkish counter-measures were passive. They garrisoned each station (an average of fourteen miles apart) with half a company, entrenched, sometimes with guns, and put in between the stations a chain of small entrenched posts, usually about two thousand yards apart, and sited on small knolls or spurs within two hundred yards of the railway, so that each post could see its neighbours and command all the intermediate line. Extra posts were put on one or other bank of any large bridge. The fifteen or twenty men in the post had to patrol their section of line after dawn each day, and in the afternoon. There was no night activity on their part.

The Turks arrived at their system of defence after considerable experience of our demolition parties, but we were able, till the end of the war, to descend upon the railway when and where we pleased, and effect the damage we wished, without great difficulty. At the same time our ways and means had constantly to be improved. We began with small parties of ten or fifteen Beduins, and we ended with mobile columns of all arms, including armoured cars; nevertheless I believe that it is impossible for a purely passive defence, such as the Turkish, to prevent a daily interruption of the railway traffic by a decently equipped enemy. Railway defence, to be inviolable, would require a passive force, entrenched with continuous barbed wire fence, and day and night patrol, at a considerable distance from the line, on each side of it; mobile forces, in concentrations not more than twenty miles apart; and liberal air reconnaissance.

The actual methods of demolition we used are perhaps more interesting than our manners of attack. Our explosives were mainly blasting gelatine and guncotton. Of the two we infinitely preferred the former when we could get it. It is rather more powerful in open charges in direct contact, far better for indirect work, has a value of 5 to 1 in super-tamped charges, is quicker to use, and more compact. We used to strip its paper covering, and handle it in sandbags of fifty pounds weight. These sweated vigorously in the summer heats of Arabia, but did us no harm, beyond the usual headache, from which we never acquired immunity. The impact of a bullet may detonate a sack of it but we found in practice that when running you clasp it to your side, and if it is held on that furthest from the enemy, then the chances are that it will not be hit, except by the bullet that has already inflicted a mortal wound on the bearer. Guncotton is a good explosive, but inferior in the above respects to gelatine, and in addition, we used to receive it packed sixteen slabs (of fifteen ounces each) in a wooden box of such massive construction that it was nearly impossible to open peacefully. You can break these boxes with an entrenching tool, in about four minutes slashing, but the best thing is to dash the box, by one of its rope or wire beckets against a rock until it splits. The lid of the box is fastened by six screws, but even if there is time to undo all of these, the slabs will not come out, since they are unshakeably wedged against the four sides. I have opened boxes by detonating a primer on one corner, but regard this way as unnecessarily noisy wasteful and dangerous for daily use.

Rail Demolition. Guncotton in fifteen-ounce slabs is convenient for rail cutting. The usual method of putting a fused and detonated and primed slab against the web is quick and easy, but ineffective. The slab cuts a six-inch section out of the lie, leaving two clean fractured surfaces (Hejaz rails are of a mild Maryland or Cockerill steel). The steel chairs and sleepers are strong, and the enemy used to tap the broken rails again into contact with a sledge, and lay in a new piece whenever the combined fractures were important enough. New rails were ten metres long, but the line worked well on unbolted pieces two or three metres long. Two bolts are enough for a fish plate, and on straights the line will serve slow trains for a mile or two without fish plates, owing to the excellence of the chairs. For curves the Turks, after we had exhausted their curved rails, used short straights. These proved efficient even on 120-metre curves. The rate of repair of a gang one hundred strong, in simple demolition is about 250 cuts an hour. A demolition gang of twenty would do about six hundred cuts an hour.

A better demolition is to lay two successive slabs on the ballast beneath the bottom flange under the joint and fish plate, in contact with the line. This spoils the fish plate and bolts, and shortens each of two rails by a few inches, for the expenditure of two slabs and one fuse. It takes longer to lay than the simple demolition, but also takes longer to repair, since one or other rail is often not cut, but bent, and in that case the repair party has either to cut it, or to press it straight.

The best demolition we discovered was to dig down in the ballast beside a mid-rail sleeper between the tracks, until the inside of the sleeper (iron of course) could be cleared of ballast, and to lay two slabs in the bottom of the hole, under the sleeper, but not in contact with it. The excavated ballast should then be returned and the end of the fuse left visible over the sleeper for the lighting party. The expansion of air raises the middle of the sleeper eighteen inches from the ground, humps the two rails three inches from the horizontal, draws them six inches nearer together, and warps them from the vertical inwards by the twisting pull of the chairs on the bottom outer flange.

A trough is also driven a foot or more deep across the formation. This gives two rails destroyed, one sleeper or two, and the grading, for two slabs and one fuse. The repair party has either to throw away the entire track, or cut a metre out of each rail and re-grade. A gang of one hundred will mend about twenty pairs an hour, and a gang of forty will lay eighty an hour. The appearance of a piece of rail treated by this method is most beautiful, for the sleepers rise up in all manner of varied forms, like the early buds of tulips.

Simple demolitions can be lit with a twelve-inch fuse. The fish-plate-flange type should be lit with thirty-inch fuses, since the fragments of steel spray the whole earth. The 'tulips' may be lit with a ten-inch fuse, for they only scatter ballast. If however, the slabs have been allowed to get into contact with the metal of the sleeper they will throw large lumps of it about. With a ten-inch fuse most of these will pass over the head of the lighting man who will be only fifteen yards or so away when it goes off. To be further is dangerous. We were provided with Bickford fuse by Ordnance. The shiny black variety causes many accidents, owing to its habits of accelerating or smouldering. The dull black is better, and the white is very good. Our instantaneous fuse has an amusing effect if lit at night among friendly tents, since it jumps about and bangs; but it is not good for service conditions. The French instantaneous fuse is reliable. Detonators should always be crimped on to ready-cut fuses, and may be safely carried in the pocket or sandbag, since great violence is required to set them off. We generally used fuses for lighting.

Speaking as a rule rail demolitions are wasteful and ineffective unless the enemy is short of metal or unless they are only made adjuncts to bridge-breaking.

A pleasant demolition, of a hybrid type, is to cut both rails, and turn them over, so as to throw them on their face down the bank. It takes thirty men to start this, but a small gang can then pass up the line, bearing on the overturned part, and the spring of the rails will carry on the reversing process, until you have done miles of it. This is an effective demolition with steel sleepers, since you wreck the ballasting. We tried it once on about eight miles of a branch line, with a preponderance of spiked wooden sleepers, and it made such a mess of rails and sleepers that the Turks washed their hands of it.

The Hejaz line carried a minimum of traffic, so that there was no special virtue in destroying the points of crossing places.

Bridge Demolitions. The lightness of traffic affected the tactics of bridge demolition also, since a single break was met either by transport or deviation. As with the rails however, the methods we used are perhaps more important than why we did it. Most of the bridges are of dressed limestone masonry, in eighty- to one-hundred-pound blocks, set in lime mortar. The average spans were from four to seven metres, and the piers were usually fifteen feet wide and four feet six inches thick. It is of course better to shatter a bridge than to blow it sky-high, since you increase your enemy's labours.

We found that a charge of forty-eight pounds of guncotton, laid against the foot of the pier on the ground, untamped, was hardly enough, and that sixty-four pounds was often a little too much. Our formula was therefore about $\frac{1}{5}$ BT^2 for guncotton charges below one hundred pounds, untamped. In a pier fifteen feet broad, had the feet been marked off on it, we would have had no explosive between feet 1 and 3 and 12 and 15. The bulk would have been against 4, 5, and 10, 11, with a continuous but weaker band uniting 5 and 10. Dry guncotton is better than wet for such work; gelatine is about 10 per cent stronger for these open charges. With charges above one hundred pounds $\frac{1}{6}$ BT^2 or $\frac{1}{7}$ BT^2 is enough. The larger your object the smaller your formula. Under fire, the inside of the bridge is fairly safe, since enemy posts enfilade the line and not the bridge arches. It is however seldom leisurely enough to allow of tamping a pier charge by digging. When it is, a trench a foot deep is all that is possible, and this does not decrease a guncotton charge by more than 10 per cent. Gelatine profits rather more in proportion by simple tamping.

A quick and cheap method of bringing down the ordinary pier or abutment is by inserting small charges in the drainage holes that are usually present. In the Hejaz line these were in the splay of the arch, and a charge of five pounds of gelatine, or twenty-five of guncotton, in these would wreck the whole line. The depth and small size of the drainage holes tamp the explosive to an extreme degree. Where the bridge was of many spans we used to charge alternate drainage holes on either side. In the ordinary English abutment where the drainage holes are small and frequent, it would be wise to explode several simultaneously by electricity, since the effect is much greater than by independent firing. Necklacing and digging down from the crown or roadbed are methods too clumsy and slow for active service conditions.

In North Syria, where we came to bridges of great blocks of basalt, with cement joints, we had to increase our charges for untamped work to $\frac{1}{4}$ or even $\frac{1}{3}$ BT^2.

We found guncotton most convenient to handle when we knotted it up into thirty-slab blocks by passing cords through the round holes in the middle of the slabs. These large bricks are quick to lay and easy to carry. An armoured car is very useful in bridge demolition, to hold the explosive and the artist. We found in practice that from thirty to fourty seconds was time enough to lay a pier demolition charge, and that only one man was necessary. We usually used two-foot fuses.

Girder bridges are more difficult. In lattice bridges where the tension girder is below the roadway, it is best to cut both compression beams. If the tension girder is overhead, it is better to cut both tensions and one compression. It is impossible to do a bridge of this sort very quickly. We had not many cases, but they took ten minutes or more each. When possible we used to wedge the gelatine in the angles of meeting girders. The only quick way is to lay an enormous single charge on the top of the abutment and root it all away with the holdfasts. This may require one thousand pounds of gelignite, or more, and a multiplicity of porters complicates things. I never blew up a plate girder.

Mining trains pertains perhaps more to operations than to engineering, and is, anyway, a special study in itself. Automatic mines, to work on rail deflection always sounded better than they proved. They require very careful laying and to be efficient have to be four-charge compound. This involves electrical connection. The best mine action we had was made for us by Colonel R. E. M. Russell, RE, and we were about to give it extended use when the enemy caved in.

The ordinary mine was fired electrically by an observer. It is an infallible but very difficult way of destroying hostile rolling stock, and we made great profit from it. Our standard charge was fifty pounds of gelatine. Guncotton is very little use.

However mining is too large a subject to treat of. The army electrical gear is good, but the exploder seems needlessly heavy. By using a single strand insulated wire (commercial) we fired four detonators in parallel at five hundred metres; army multiple-stranded insulated cables will fire two at five hundred metres. In series I have never had occasion to fire more than twenty-five detonators (at 250 yards), but I see no reason why this number should not be greatly increased. The army electric detonators never failed us. A meter test might show that some of them were defective, but even the defective ones will fire on an exploder. It is usually unnecessary to insulate your joints. The exploder goes out of action quickly if knocked about in a baggage column, or slung on a trotting camel, so I usually carried two as reserve.

4

The Iraq Letters

July–August 1920

The three letters in this section were written to three different newspapers, *The Times*, the *Observer* and the *Sunday Times*, during a period of severe crisis in the Middle East in 1920.

Following the decisions made at the peace conference, Great Britain was awarded the mandate for Mesopotamia (increasingly known as Iraq). Not surprisingly, this produced an angry reaction among the un-consulted populace, and in July 1920 a rebellion broke out so difficult to contain that the British were forced to summon reinforcement troops from India.

Lawrence's first letter, published on 22 July in *The Times*, railed against the fact that the British were essentially setting up in Mesopotamia a government which is 'English in fashion and is conducted in the English language'. Quick with his condemnation, he was also forthright with his proposed solutions. He would make Arabic the government language, raise two divisions of local volunteer troops, all Arabs, whom he would entrust with the maintenance of order and 'would cause to leave the country every single British soldier, every single Indian soldier'. So far his advice might seem applicable to Iraq in the wake of the conflict begun in 2003, but then he added a suggestion that must have seemed strikingly implausible to most of his readers in 1920, that Mesopotamia should become a 'brown dominion', and that 'we should then hold of Mesopotamia exactly as much (or as little) as we hold of South Africa or Canada'. The 'only alternative' would seem to be 'conquest, which the ordinary Englishman does not want, and cannot afford'.

Britain was not the only power enjoying the mixed results of being awarded a mandate in the Middle East. In March 1920, following the failure of the victorious powers to award him the prize for which he and Lawrence had argued at the peace conference, Feisal had set himself up as ruler in Syria. But the mandate for Syria had been awarded to the French, who put paid to Feisal's self-elevation by ignominiously ousting him on 24 July. The result of this was that both European powers were simultaneously attempting to put down nationalist insurgency by resorting to a costly deployment of troops, artillery and air power.

In his second letter, which appeared on 8 August in the *Observer*, Lawrence rode to the attack against both the former allies, France as well as Britain. In fact if anything, as has been noted with approval by the eminent French Lawrencian scholar, Dr Maurice Larès, he gave greater validity to the French position than that of the British, stating:

> We have really no competence in this matter to criticise the French. They have only followed in very humble fashion, in their sphere of Syria, the example we set them in Mesopotamia . . . It would show a lack of humour if we reproved them for a battle near Damascus, and the blotting out of the Syrian essay in self-government, while we were fighting battles near Baghdad . . .

If he was prepared to rattle the dovecotes in his earlier letter, he was even more out-spoken in this one. For he went on to make a suggestion which has frequently raised shocked eyebrows among those who have failed to appreciate the deliberately ironic, indeed almost macabre, tone in which it was expressed. 'It is odd that we do not use poison gas on these occasions . . . By gas attacks the whole population of offending districts could be wiped out neatly; and as a method of government it would be no more immoral than the present system.'

Quite correctly in my view, Tabachnik and Matheson, in their book *Images of Lawrence*, describe this suggestion as 'Swiftian'. Well aware of the revulsion created by the use of poison gas in the First World War, Lawrence was approaching the problems of the Middle East as Jonathan Swift almost two centuries earlier had parodied the matter of widespread starvation in Ireland. In 1729 Swift published what he called 'A Modest Proposal', to the effect that the problem of feeding the children of the Irish poor could be solved by their being handed over to be eaten by the rich. Likewise Lawrence was proposing with tongue firmly in cheek that the kinsmen of the people he had fought with in the war should be gassed for objecting to an imperial suzerainty which he felt had no validity: a suggestion which, however, can now create ripples of dismay when we reflect that seven decades later the Iraqi dictator, Saddam Hussein, would adopt in reality the precise policy suggested by Lawrence in mockery.

However, a word of caution is required here. Poison gas might be anathema in terms of public perception following its use, by both sides, in the 1914–18 war, but it had not been not entirely excluded from military and even political considerations in the troubled post-war world. In the so-called Third Afghan War which began in 1919, the British found themselves confronted by warring tribesmen so difficult to subdue that they considered resorting to gas as being 'more merciful' than high explosive. Churchill wrote: 'If it is fair for an Afghan soldier to shoot down a British soldier behind a rock and cut him to pieces as he lies wounded . . . why is it not fair for a British artillery-man to fire a shell which makes the said native sneeze?' Any idea that this might con-flict with the ancient concept of chivalry in war was laughed to scorn, since in British officers' eyes the tribesmen were 'vermin fit only for extermination'. Not dissimilarly, in relation to Iraq in 1920, Churchill, anxious to limit the financial and human cost of a massive display of force, was prepared to resort to the use of asphyxiating gases dis-charged from aeroplanes, calculated to cause 'discomfort or illness but not death'. The Cabinet, however, was reluctant to sanction the employment of gas even of an (allegedly) non-lethal variety, and in the event gas bombs were never dropped by British policing aircraft.

Lawrence was a private citizen at this time, not in any way party to confidential discussions in Whitehall, and there is no hint in the letters printed here that he is in any way trying to help the government in its task of crushing 'native' disaffection. Moreover, no one was less likely than he to consider revolting tribesmen as 'vermin fit only for extermination', nor is there the slightest inkling that he was somehow trying to give support to Churchill's minimal gassing philosophy. The tone of voice of his suggestion that 'by gas attacks the whole population of offending districts could be *wiped out neatly*' (my italics) suggests the deadly logic of a Swift rather than an argument out of realpolitik.

In this context it is worth considering the leading paragraph of the third letter, published on 22 August in the *Sunday Times*, which has been powerfully quoted more than once during the Iraq emergency dating from 2003 as a statement applicable as much to these present times as to 1920:

> The people of England have been led in Mesopotamia into a trap from which it will be hard to escape with dignity and honour. They have been tricked into it by the steady withholding of information. The Baghdad communiqués are belated, insincere, incomplete. Things have been far worse than we have been told, our administration more bloody and inefficient than the public knows . . . We are to-day not far from a disaster.

The concepts of 'dignity and honour' referred to by Lawrence make uneasy bedfellows with poison gas.

Reading the above, many aficionados of *Seven Pillars of Wisdom* might recall a striking reference to Mesopotamia in its eloquent Introductory Chapter, which is standard in all modern editions, but which, on the advice of Bernard Shaw, was suppressed in the book's earliest versions, largely for political reasons, being first published in abbreviated form in David Garnett's volume of letters in 1938 (pp. 262–3). This quotation, too, might seem to have a strong contemporary resonance. Harking back to the consequences of the war, Lawrence commented:

> When we won, it was charged against me that the British petrol royalties in Mesopotamia were become dubious, and French Colonial policy ruined in the Levant.
>
> I am afraid I hope so. We pay for these things too much in honour and in innocent lives.

The verdict is not yet possible on the new intervention in the politics of the Middle East; it will perhaps not be arrived at for many years. Nor can it be said Lawrence was right on all the matters relating to the part of the world with which he has come to be associated; far from it. But his voice is pertinent on numerous aspects of the problems that plague the 'Changing East' (as he himself called it: see the next section) and is therefore worth hearing.

The letters appeared as items 127, 130 and 131 in David Garnett, *The Letters of T. E. Lawrence*; the letter of 22 August was included in *The Essential T. E. Lawrence*; all three are printed in Stanley and Rodelle Weintraub, *Evolution of a Revolt*.

I. To the Editor of *The Times*
22 July 1920

Sir, In this week's debate in the Commons on the Middle East a veteran of the House expressed surprise that the Arabs of Mesopotamia were in arms against us despite our well-meant mandate. His surprise has been echoed here and there in the press, and it seems to me based on such a misconception of the New Asia and the history of the last five years, that I would like to trespass at length on your space and give my interpretation of the situation.

The Arabs rebelled against the Turks during the war not because the Turk government was notably bad, but because they wanted independence. They did not risk their lives in battle to change masters, to become British subjects or French citizens, but to win a show of their own.

Whether they are fit for independence or not remains to be tried. Merit is no qualification for freedom. Bulgars, Afghans, and Tahitians have it. Freedom is enjoyed when you are so well armed, or so turbulent, or inhabit a country so thorny that the expense of your neighbour's occupying you is greater than the profit. Feisal's government in Syria has been completely independent for two years, and has maintained public security and public services in its area.

Mesopotamia has had less opportunity to prove its armament. It never fought the Turks, and only fought perfunctorily against us. Accordingly, we had to set up a wartime administration there. We had no choice; but that was two years ago, and we have not yet changed to peace conditions. Indeed, there are yet no signs of change. 'Large reinforcements', according to the official statement, are now being sent there, and our garrison will run into six figures next month. The expense curve will go up to £50 million for this financial year, and yet greater efforts will be called for from us as the Mesopotamian desire for independence grows.

It is not astonishing that their patience has broken down after two years. The government we have set up is English in fashion, and is conducted in the English language. So it has 450 British executive officers running it, and not a single responsible Mesopotamian. In Turkish days 70 per cent of the executive civil service was local. Our eighty thousand troops there are occupied in police duties, not in guarding the frontiers. They are holding down the people. In Turkish days the two army corps in Mesopotamia were 60 per cent Arab in officers, 95 per cent in other ranks. This deprivation of the privilege of sharing the defence and administration of their country is galling to the educated Mesopotamians. It is true we have increased prosperity – but who cares for that when liberty is in the other scale? They waited and welcomed the news of our mandate, because they thought it meant dominion self-government for themselves. They are now losing hope in our good intentions.

A remedy? I can see a cure only in immediate change of policy. The whole logic of the present thing looks wrong. Why should Englishmen (or Indians) have to be killed to make the Arab government in Mesopotamia, which is the considered intention of His Majesty's government? I agree with the intention, but I would make the Arabs do the work. They can. My little experience in helping to set up Feisal showed me that the art of government wants more character than brains.

I would make Arabic the government language. This would impose a reduction of the British staff, and a return to employment of the qualified Arabs. I would raise two divisions of local volunteer troops, all Arabs, from the senior divisional general to the junior private. (Trained officers and trained NCOs exist in thousands.) I would entrust these new units with the maintenance of order, and I would cause to leave the country every single British soldier, every single Indian soldier. These changes would take twelve months, and we should then hold of Mesopotamia exactly as much (or as little) as we hold of South Africa or Canada. I believe the Arabs in these conditions would be as loyal as anyone in the Empire, and they would not cost us a cent.

I shall be told that the idea of brown dominions in the British Empire is grotesque. Yet the Montague scheme and the Milner scheme are approaches to it, and the only alternative seems to be conquest, which the ordinary Englishman does not want, and cannot afford.

Of course, there is oil in Mesopotamia, but we are no nearer that while the Middle East remains at war, and I think if it is so necessary for us, it could be made the subject of a bargain. The Arabs seem willing to shed their blood for freedom; how much more their oil!

II. France, Britain, and the Arabs
8 August 1920

There is a feeling in England that the French occupation of Damascus and their expulsion of Feisal from the throne to which the grateful Syrians had elected him is, after all, a poor return for Feisal's gifts to us during the war: and the idea of falling short of an oriental friend in generosity leaves an unpleasantness in our mouths. Feisal's courage and statesmanship made the Mecca revolt spread beyond the Holy Cities, until it became a very active help to the Allies in Palestine. The Arab army, created in the field, grew from a mob of Bedouins into an organised and well-equipped body of troops. They captured 35,000 Turks, disabled as many more, took 150 guns, and a hundred thousand square miles of Ottoman territory. This was great service in our extreme need, and we felt we owed the Arabs a reward: and to Feisal, their leader, we owed double, for the loyal way in which he had arranged the main Arab activity when and where Allenby directed.

Yet we have really no competence in this matter to criticise the French.

They have only followed in very humble fashion, in their sphere of Syria, the example we set them in Mesopotamia. England controls nine parts out of ten of the Arab world, and inevitably calls the tune to which the French must dance. If we follow an Arab policy, they must be Arab. If we fight the Arabs, they must fight the Arabs. It would show a lack of humour if we reproved them for a battle near Damascus, and the blotting out of the Syrian essay in self-government, while we were fighting battles near Baghdad, and trying to render the Mesopotamians incapable of self-government, by smashing every head that raised itself among them.

A few weeks ago the chief of our administration in Baghdad* was asked to receive some Arab notables who wanted to urge their case for partial autonomy. He packed the delegation with some nominees of his own, and in replying, told them that it would be long before they were fit for responsibility. Brave words – but the burden of them has been heavy on the Manchester men this week at Hillah.

These risings take a regular course. There is a preliminary Arab success, then British reinforcements go out as a punitive force. They fight their way (our losses are slight, the Arab losses heavy) to their objective, which is meanwhile bombarded by artillery, aeroplanes, or gunboats. Finally, perhaps, a village is burnt and the district pacified. It is odd that we do not use poison gas on these occasions. Bombing the houses is a patchy way of getting the women and children, and our infantry always incur losses in shooting down the Arab men. By gas attacks the whole population of offending districts could be wiped out neatly; and as a method of government it would be no more immoral than the present system.

We realise the burden the army in Mesopotamia is to the Imperial Exchequer, but we do not see as clearly the burden it is to Mesopotamia. It has to be fed, and all its animals have to be fed. The fighting forces are now 83,000 strong, but the ration strength is three hundred thousand. There are three labourers to every soldier, to supply and serve him. One in ten of the souls in Mesopotamia to-day belongs to our army. The greenness of the country is being eaten up by them, and the process is not yet at its height. To be safe they demand that we double our existing garrison. As local resources are exhausted this increase of troops will increase the cost by more than an arithmetical progression.

These troops are just for police work to hold down the subjects of whom the House of Lords was told two weeks ago that they were longing for our continued presence in their country. No one can imagine what will be our state there if one of Mesopotamia's three envious neighbours (all nursing plans against us) attack us from outside, while there is still disloyalty within. Our communications are very bad, our defence positions all have both flanks in the air, and there seem to have been two incidents lately. We do not trust our troops as we did during the war.

* Colonel A. T. Wilson, the Acting Civil Commissioner.

Then there are the military works. Great barracks and camps have had to
be constructed, and hundreds of miles of military roads. Great bridges, to
carry motor-lorries, exist in remote places, where the only local transport is
by pack. The bridges are made of temporary materials, and their upkeep is
enormous. They are useless to the civil government, which yet has to take
them over at a high valuation; and so the new state will begin its career with
an enforced debt.

English statesmen, from the premier downwards, weep tears over the
burden thrust on us in Mesopotamia. 'If only we could raise a local army,'
said Lord Curzon, 'but they will not serve' ('except against us,' his lordship
no doubt added to himself). 'If only we could find Arabs qualified to fill executive posts.'

In this dearth of local talent the parallel of Syria is illuminating. Feisal had
no difficulty in raising troops, though he had great difficulty in paying them.
However, the conditions were not the same, for he was arbitrarily deprived
of his Customs' revenue. Feisal had no difficulty in setting up an administration, in which the five leading spirits were all natives of Baghdad! It was
not a very good administration, but in the East the people are less exigent
than we are. Even in Athens Solon gave them not the best laws, but the best
they would accept.

The British in Mesopotamia cannot find one competent person – but I
maintain that the history of the last few months has shown their political
bankruptcy, and their opinion should not weigh with us at all. I know ten
British officials with tried and honourable reputations in the Sudan, Sinai,
Arabia, Palestine, each and all of whom could set up an Arab government
comparable to Feisal's, in Baghdad, next month. It also would not be a
perfect government, but it would be better than Feisal's, for he, poor man,
to pull him down, was forbidden foreign advisers. The Mesopotamian effort
would have the British government behind it, and would be child's play for
a decent man to run, so long as he ran it like Cromer's Egypt, not like the
Egypt of the Protectorate. Cromer dominated Egypt, not because England
gave him force, or because Egypt loved us, or for any outside reason, but
because he was so good a man. England has stacks of first-class men. The
last thing you need out there is a genius. What is required is a tearing up of
what we have done, and beginning again on advisory lines. It is no good
patching with the present system. 'Concessions to local feeling' and such like
rubbish are only weakness-concessions, incentives to more violence. We are
big enough to admit a fault, and turn a new page: and we ought to do it with
a hoot of joy, because it will save us a million pounds a week.

III. Mesopotamia: The Truth about the Campaign
22 August 1920

Waste of Life and Money
'We are to-day not far from a disaster'

Mr Lawrence, whose organisation and direction of the Hedjaz against the Turks was one of the outstanding romances of the war, has written this article at our request in order that the public may be fully informed of our Mesopotamian commitments.

The people of England have been led in Mesopotamia into a trap from which it will be hard to escape with dignity and honour. They have been tricked into it by a steady withholding of information. The Bagdad communiqués are belated, insincere, incomplete. Things have been far worse than we have been told, our administration more bloody and inefficient than the public knows. It is a disgrace to our imperial record, and may soon be too inflamed for any ordinary cure. We are to-day not far from a disaster.

The sins of commission are those of the British civil authorities in Mesopotamia (especially of three 'colonels') who were given a free hand by London. They are controlled from no Department of State, but from the empty space which divides the Foreign Office from the India Office. They availed themselves of the necessary discretion of wartime to carry over their dangerous independence into times of peace. They contest every suggestion of real self-government sent them from home. A recent proclamation about autonomy circulated with unction from Bagdad was drafted and published out there in a hurry, to forestall a more liberal statement in preparation in London. 'Self-determination papers' favourable to England were extorted in Mesopotamia in 1919 by official pressure, by aeroplane demonstrations, by deportations to India.

Cabinet's Responsibility
The Cabinet cannot disclaim all responsibility. They receive little more news than the public: they should have insisted on more, and better. They have sent draft after draft of reinforcements, without enquiry. When conditions became too bad to endure longer, they decided to send out as High Commissioner the original author of the present system,[*] with a conciliatory message to the Arabs that his heart and policy have completely changed.

Yet our published policy has not changed, and does not need changing. It is that there has been a deplorable contrast between our profession and our practice. We said we went to Mesopotamia to defeat Turkey. We said we stayed to deliver the Arabs from the oppression of the Turkish government,

---

[*] Sir Percy Cox, who it had been decided was to return as High Commissioner the following October to form a provisional government of Arab notables.

and to make available for the world its resources of corn and oil. We spent nearly a million men and nearly a thousand million of money to these ends. This year we are spending 92,000 men and fifty millions of money on the same objects.

Worse than Turks

Our government is worse than the old Turkish system. They kept 14,000 local conscripts embodied, and killed a yearly average of two hundred Arabs in maintaining peace. We keep ninety thousand men, with aeroplanes, armoured cars, gunboats, and armoured trains. We have killed about ten thousand Arabs in this rising this summer. We cannot hope to maintain such an average: it is a poor country, sparsely peopled; but Abd el Hamid would applaud his masters, if he saw us working. We are told the object of the rising was political, we are not told what the local people want. It may be what the Cabinet has promised them. A minister in the House of Lords said that we must have so many troops because the local people will not enlist. On Friday the government announce the death of some local levies defending their British officers, and say that the services of these men have not yet been sufficiently recognised because they are too few (adding the characteristic Bagdad touch that they are men of bad character). There are seven thousand of them, just half the old Turkish force of occupation. Properly officered and distributed, they would relieve half our army there. Cromer controlled Egypt's six million people with five thousand British troops; Colonel Wilson fails to control Mesopotamia's three million people with ninety thousand troops.

Our Military Commitments

We have not reached the limit of our military commitments. Four weeks ago the staff in Mesopotamia drew up a memorandum asking for four more divisions. I believe it was forwarded to the War Office, which has now sent three brigades from India. If the north-west frontier cannot be further denuded, where is the balance to come from? Meanwhile, our unfortunate troops, Indian and British, under hard conditions of climate and supply, are policing an immense area, paying dearly every day in lives for the wilfully wrong policy of the civil administration in Bagdad. General Dyer was relieved of his command in India for a much smaller error, but the responsibility in this case is not on the army, which has acted only at the request of the civil authorities. The War Office has made every effort to reduce our forces, but the decisions of the Cabinet have been against them.

The government in Bagdad have been hanging Arabs in that town for political offences, which they call rebellion. The Arabs are not rebels against us. They are still nominally Turkish subjects, nominally at war with us. Are these illegal executions to provoke the Arabs to reprisals on the three hundred British prisoners they hold? And, if so, is it that their punishment may be more severe, or is it to persuade our other troops to fight to the last?

Cui Bono?
We say we are in Mesopotamia to develop it for the benefit of the world. All experts say that the labour supply is the ruling factor in its development. How far will the killing of ten thousand villagers and townspeople this summer hinder the production of wheat, cotton, and oil? How long will we permit millions of pounds, thousands of imperial troops, and tens of thousands of Arabs to be sacrificed on behalf of a form of colonial administration which can benefit nobody but its administrators?

5

The Changing East

September 1920

This essay first appeared in a journal called *The Round Table* in September 1920, anonymously, in accordance with that publication's practice.

When, some years after his brother's death, the London publishers Williams & Norgate approached A. W. Lawrence with a view to publishing a miscellany of T. E. Lawrence's writings, A. W. responded by compiling a small but select anthology with a Middle Eastern theme which came out in 1939 under the title *Oriental Assembly*. He included 'The Changing East', plus the next item in this section, 'The Evolution of a Revolt', while also finding space for the first printing at full length of the Introductory Chapter of *Seven Pillars of Wisdom* (see introduction to 'The Iraq Letters', p. 240).

The date of this essay's first publication, September 1920, is highly significant, because Lawrence must have been engaged in writing it at the same time as he was contemplating or actually writing the letters of angry protest featured in the preceding section, of which two date from the previous month. By contrast with those letters, its tone throughout is meditative, at times almost elegiac, certainly more elegant, and there is not the slightest hint of any recourse to intemperate or violent means to force a pro-British or pro-Western solution on areas of conflict or disturbance. Indeed, what strikes home as its most memorable message on rereading it today is that someone who has often been accused of being, despite all suggestions to the contrary, a covert imperialist, could suggest that arguably the best policy to pursue in relation to subject nationalities was to give them their head, to let them go. In 1940, in one of his greatest speeches at a time of greatest danger, Winston Churchill as Prime Minister referred to the British Empire as possibly lasting a thousand years. Of course, the emphasis at that time was on the claim that this would be its 'finest hour', but the long-term endurance of the Empire was assumed, virtually, as not negotiable, as 'given'. Here, twenty years earlier, we have Lawrence arguing that although 'the British Empire is so much the largest concern in the world that it offers unrivalled inducements to small peoples to join it', it should also be conceded that, in regard to such 'small peoples', the British 'have to be prepared to see them doing things by methods quite unlike our own, and less well: but on principle it is better that they half-do it than that we do it perfectly for them'. He continues: 'In pursuing such courses we will find our best helpers not in our former most obedient subjects, but among those now most active in agitating against us, for it will be the intellectual leaders of the people who will serve the purpose, and these are not the philosophers nor the rich, but the demagogues and the politicians.' He then makes a truly remarkable statement: 'It seems a curious class to which to entrust the carefully begun edifices of our colonial governments – but in essence it will not be dissimilar to the members of our own House of Commons, whom we entrust with our own liberties.' It is still possible that some modern commentators might see these pronouncements as patronising in terms of their assumptions as to the capacity and competence of emergent peoples: but it can also be seen as in essence going beyond his already mentioned 'brown dominion' concept, and therefore as being astonishingly ahead of its time.

Both the letters and this article predated Churchill's 1921 Cairo conference, in which Lawrence was actively involved at Churchill's personal request, the aim of which was to sort out the unsatisfactory state of the Middle East created by the dispositions agreed in Paris. As a result of its findings Feisal was installed on the throne of Iraq while his brother Abdullah became ruler of Transjordan, later the kingdom of Jordan. The settlement thus achieved allowed Lawrence, as he stated in *Seven Pillars of Wisdom*, to conclude that he was 'quit of our wartime Eastern adventure with clean hands', and while writing in 1927 to his biographer Robert Graves he described it as 'the big achievement of my life'.

In the context of this present book, the mixed results of this settlement should perhaps be outlined. The kingdom of Jordan is still ruled by a descendant of Abdullah, bearing his great-grandfather's name with the title of King Abdullah II. In Iraq the monarchy was ended by a military coup in 1958, when King Feisal II, who had reigned since his father's death in 1933, and the rest of the royal family were brutally shot dead and the revolutionary Ba'ath Party took control. To a considerable extent the ongoing Iraq crisis could be said to have stemmed from that event.

The Changing East
September 1920

A picture-writer once coined a phrase, 'The Unchanging East', and Time has turned round and taken revenge upon him. The East is to-day the place of change – of changes so great and swift that in comparison with it our Europe is standing still. We have been much engaged lately, making wars and peaces, looking at our own hurts, and trying to restore the balance of the times, and so we have not always been able to spare attention to what Asia is doing or thinking. We have tried to deal with her on the old traditional lines, and to our dismay she has not reacted properly. There have been outbreaks, unrest, protestations, and we, lacking the knowledge of movements there, have missed the sequence and find ourselves reduced to force, as our last remedy and restoration.

Yet there is urgent need for comprehension, of a careful study of our possessions in Asia, in order that we may regain touch with their opinion. We

are all agreed as to the need of this stock-taking, though few of us will agree
later on the lessons of it. We sent out a commission to India, which considered reform in India; we sent out a commission to Egypt, to consider reform
in Egypt. We heard talk the other day in the House of Lords of a commission for Mesopotamia. Even Malta has had one. These all have been piece-
meal affairs, conducted by statesmen in blinkers, forbidden to see anything
except the political conditions of the province to which they were addressed.
None of them gave us a general survey of the new Asia: none of them
described the disease as well as the remedy. This disease is physical, material, moral, mental, all you will. It is the civilisation-disease, the inevitable
effect of too close contact with the West. The aborigines of Australia got it
when they met us, and they died of it. There were biological reasons why
their frames were too weak to stand contact with a body social so different
from their own. Asia is tougher, older, more numerous, and will not die of
us – but indubitably we have made her very ill. Europe is not a thing easily
digested.

We see the strain we have put on Asia soonest in the domain of matter. We
evolved our own machinery in long centuries of struggle and invention, years
in which the face of Europe gradually changed, without any too violent
misery, to suit the new ideas: we had pack-horses, solid wheels, springless
wagons, coaches, railways, motor cars, aeroplanes: we found the progress
indecently fast at times, and put men with red flags to walk before the
machines while we breathed – but what of Asia, which has stepped in a lifetime of thirty years from saddle-donkeys to Rolls-Royce cars, from blood-
mares to aeroplanes? We grew by slow stages of muskets from bows to
automatic guns: it took us five hundred years. The marauder of the desert
laid away his spear just before the war, and to-day goes out on his raids with
a Maxim. We invented the printing press four hundred years ago, and served
a long apprenticeship by way of wooden types, screw and lever presses,
steam presses, electric presses, to the cheap speed of the modern newspaper.
The East has side by side the old-fashioned scribe, making each year a poorer
living, and the linotype. The vernacular press came to them full-born. These
are the material sides. Asia has in thirty years leaped across a stage which
took us hundreds. She has not done it very well, perhaps, no better than parts
of Russia, parts of the Balkans, parts of South America: the important part
is that she has done it, and the Asia of Kinglake and Lamartine is wholly
gone. Our eyes show us this, and some of us, the mediaevalists, lament it.
However, that is just a pose. The clock has never been put back: but the sim-
plest thing in the world is to push its hands a little forward, and there are so
many people pushing Asia that it is rather difficult to realise what the un-
assisted speed of its own ticking is. We will hardly learn this till they stop tin-
kering at it: yet it is important for us to learn it, since the earth is just a track
along which countries and continents race with one another, and for all we
know Asia may be gaining on us mentally.

This mental and moral growth is so hard to measure. The material changes prepare our heads to note great change in other ways, but their apprehension stays uncertain. There has been a change in ideas: we hear the people of Asia talking about representative government and parliaments. In our fathers' days they were governed by theocrats and autocrats. We think how long it took England to conceive and bring forth a House of Commons, and we begin to be astonished at this headlong Asia. There are labour troubles in Cairo and Bombay, a general strike in Mecca, trades union congresses in Constantinople. This disease they have caught quickly. Self-determination – yes, they have adopted that: League of Nations – they care more for it than we do. Things must be moving. Before the war we saw their politics changing, as the old springs of action became exhausted, and new motives came into play. In our fathers' days the East, and especially the Middle East, this side of Afghanistan, was logical, similar and simple. These countries, Persia, Turkey, Egypt and the rest, were old-established governments, of sultans and princes ruling by right, often by divine right, basing their regulations on the dictates of the state religion. The men were Moslems first, or Christians, or infidels of some sort. Later on, if there was any reason for it, they might be Turks or Arabs, but about this they were not too certain: the important thing was the faith. We cannot sneer at them. Only too recently, in the manuscript and crossbow days, we were like them. About 1870, though, we began to see stirrings of a new idea, the sense of nationality, which had been invented in western Europe, and had moved slowly south and east, causing turmoil and wars in the separate countries as it passed. Nationality is a turbulent principle, and has cost probably as many lives as religion, in its much briefer reign. It grew most virulent in its old age: the Balkans and Ireland, the last places to catch it, have it gravely. We, the older sufferers, seem now nearly immune from it: we may be passing into an economic stage, in which wars and governments will be mainly businesses. It sounds a futile motive of disputes. The economic motive may yet rank with religion and nationality in destructiveness.

However, the Middle East is not as far as this yet. Its first symptoms of nationality were shown in Turkey, when Midhat Pasha began to use French words in government; and in Egypt when Arabi Pasha rose up in arms, and began to drive out the Khedive and his Turkish entourage. Both ideas were sternly discouraged. The English bolstered up the foreign dynasty in Egypt, and Abd el Hamid took up Pan-Islam, a hierarchic conception of Islam, as a corrective to the Midhat notions. He got it from a German book, which had been confusing the Khalifate and the mediaeval Papacy. However, the idea had a temporary success, and still holds some ground in India and Africa. For a few years there was peace in Asia, and Europe understood it again without having to change its way of thinking. This was better for Asia and for us, since, as a German pointed out, when we have to change our mind about a thing, we charge our inconvenience also to the account. The new ideas were not dead – indeed, they could not be, with the Balkans offering such a lively breeding ground of nationality-microbes at the gate of Asia:

and some twenty or thirty years later they were patent once more, this time not as agitations, but as conspiracies. Persia was full of them: in the end she broke out into disorder and obtained a constitution, whose precise use afterwards puzzled her. She knew that a constitution was the fashionable thing – everybody who was anybody in states had one – but it did not seem to be able to work, itself, and no one in Persia had learnt its habits. However, they still have it, and have had it for ten years.

Turkey then came out strongly, after the British had made some little adjustments in Egypt, as safety-valves for political vapours. Abd el Hamid was stiffer than our Lord Cromer or Sir Eldon Gorst, and so Turkey's nationalism got so pent up that at last it blew him quite off his seat. This was a short end to Pan-Islam: the spiritual and temporal master of Islam was put in prison, and then deposed in favour of a mental degenerate. The old cry would no longer work, as they all in one week took up the new one. Turkey announced the brotherhood of peoples. The Young Turks had forgotten their statistics when they made this statement, but events soon showed them their mistake. The Turks were a minority – perhaps only 30 or 35 per cent, in the Ottoman Empire. The subject races, Greeks, Armenians, Albanians, Kurds, Arabs, who formed the rest, could understand the idea of brotherhood, for they had been reading Herbert Spencer and his like for years, and saw at once that they were equal to the Turks, and that it was a sacred duty to go out and help them to establish this new era. So in their millions they began to join together, and think how best to carry on the common government.

Enver and his colleagues struck back in self-defence. They evolved a doctrine of Pan-Turanianism (a doctrine of mixed pedigree, out of a French book and a German book), which taught that the Ottoman Empire must become really Ottoman, and that to its boundaries of 1910 must be added all Turkish-speaking countries in the world. This gave them a broad domestic battle, and a projection later into Khiva and Russian Turkestan. The *irredenta* they decided to leave alone for the moment: first they would make these alien races inside the Empire one. It must be done quickly, for Europe was not looking kindly on them: so they took steps to lop the Greeks and Armenians to the proportions of their bedstead, and began to work upon the Arabs, to teach them Turkish as a first step, and to make them good Ottomans the second. They invented a sharp saying: 'A Turkish ass is better than an alien prophet,' to teach the people the relative worth of Islam and nationality. The subject races found Enver's little finger very heavy, and began to whisper to one another, in the strictest secrecy, that such things were contrary to the very principles of nationality in whose name they were done. These whisperings increased and became organised, till by 1914 there were healthy conspiracies, aiming to take local autonomy by force from Constantinople, afoot in Armenia, in Kurdistan, in Syria, and in Mesopotamia. Then the war came.

Even before the war we had all Turkey going shipwreck, by her own stupidity. The Turkish race have a fatal habit of obedience, unquestioning obedience, and an equally costly capacity for sacrificing themselves for their state. The first is demonstrated if in a crowded railway station in Turkey you say 'Sit down' firmly. At once they all sit down: and the second has been demonstrated times without number during the war in their dogged holding of entrenched positions. Two such qualities imply some innate stupidity in the Turk, and that the native-born possesses in a wonderful degree. He had been a great governor – when government was a crude affair of character and muscle. In these days of telegraphs and high taxation his standard of performance was poor: actually he was not worse than before: only we were better, and so he looked bad. Even at this level he could not find masters of his own: his rulers were Albanians, Bulgars, Circassians, Jews, Armenians, anything but old Turks.

Like his government, so his trade passed away from the Turk. It became scientific, complicated, and he gave it up to the clever races, Jews, Armenians, Arabs, who understood book-keeping and economics. The wealth of Turkey and the manufactures and machinery fell into non-Turk hands. In fact, of his former dominion the Turk kept only the sword – and he tried to change even his sword, which he handled as well or better than any race in Europe, for rifles and big guns and aeroplanes, and in such new-fangled things his factor of efficiency soon dropped. He found that they put a premium on brains, and accordingly the meaner races, who used their wits before their hands, gained steadily on him. In the old days a few rusty horse-men had held Tripoli and Albania, and Arabia and Syria, and Mesopotamia and Armenia in subjection. Now each province demanded a substantial gar-rison. These garrisons had to be real Turks – no others but Anatolians were loyal – and so the conscription every year took a larger and larger percent-age of the young generation. These were splendid rank and file, but the old classes were no longer fit for officers. An officer nowadays must read and write, and know a little mathematics, and study Von der Goltz: so they had to find them from the clerkly classes of the towns, sons of officials, and mer-chants' sons, and westernised young men. They were full of Byzantine vices, and utterly despised the peasant clods who were their soldiers. They neglected all such as did not minister to their pleasure; and with one disease and another, with bad sanitation, bad food, and casualties, the army began to eat up the youth of Turkey. The birth-rate in Anatolia fell, and we who were looking on could see Turkey shrivelling and dying of overstrain. The Italian war, the Balkan wars, were aggravations of an already hopeless state.

Then, when things were in this flux, thus came the war, and Asia, which had been moving fast for twenty years, put on a dizzy spurt, and left our expectations straining far behind. During the war Europe came bodily to Western Asia. On one side of the fence were the armies of the Germans, on this side the armies of the Allies. Each set great departments, fortified with all their resources, to work on the senses of the Orientals. We talked for and against Holy Wars, as finely as any Moslem dialectician. We preached of the rights of civilisation, of the laws of humanity, of international law, Geneva conventions, Hague conferences. We poured out leaflets, and picture papers, newspapers, films, all to convey an impression which should make the East understand us, and help us with conviction. Like other artists, the character we most illustrated in these productions was our own. The astonished peoples of Western Asia could not choose but hear us, and began, willingly or unwillingly, to see what we were like, and comprehend our least notions. They did not always like them, but they learned a lot. In particular they learned what each of us was fighting for (they heard it from all our mouths, and we all said much the same thing), and a thing sworn to by so many witnesses must surely be true. This liberty, this humanity, this culture, this self-determination, must be very valuable.

In the West, however crude and particular be the war-cry, there will always be an idea or principle behind: though in England you seldom drag the abstract word into the light: it is wiser to let those who think infer it from the illustration, while the vulgar worship the material image. In the East the people are more philosophical by nature, and often care more for the idea than the application. Anyway, they will insist on some abstraction to fill the vacant places of their minds. In the nineteenth century they had had religion, a creed with a body as well as a spirit, one which showed them their road by day as well as by night. They regulated their manners, their meals, their trades, their families, their politics, by its light. The attempt of Abd el Hamid to rationalise this, to make it logical as well as theological, smashed it. When he fell, so did the rule of faith in works. The East remained Moslem, but its public life turned national. People called themselves Egyptians, or Arabs, or Turks, and their newspapers, directed by men emancipated from formal Islam by the influence of Western ideas, carried this difference of motive, this new outlook, into the smallest points of life. The abstract standard by which politics and conduct were now judged was this new one of nationality. The nation became the rule of life, the modern creed – and as the war drew on Moslem learnt to go out and fight Moslem, and accept death gladly in battle for the new ideal. When England was at her greatest straits to defend her straggled holdings in the East, these feelings reached their height – and the best measure of their height is not that Indian Moslem fought Turkish Moslem to vindicate the place of India as a partner in our Empire, but that the people of Mecca, the centre of Islam, under its emir, the Sherif of Mecca, the senior descendant of the Prophet, rose in rebellion against the Khalif, the Sultan of Constantinople, and that this rebellion carried everyone of Arabic speech in Asia at least sympathetically to its side. This was the final triumph, the highest expression there can ever be in Western Asia of the principle of nationality as the foundation of political action, opposed to the principle of a world-religion, a supra-national creed. Not the Galilean but the politician had conquered.

The armistice came, but did not check this movement; it made adherence to it more safe and more rational. The original stalwarts who marched north under Feisal side by side with Allenby had staked their heads on their fervent belief in an Arab movement. Their victory made them fashionable, and

PACKING SLIP:
Amazon Marketplace Item: T. E. Lawrence In War And Peace: An Anthology
Of The Military Writings Of...
Listing ID: 0413W912905
SKU:
Quantity: 1

Purchased on: 08-May-2006
Shipped by: moyolawn@yahoo.com
Shipping address:

Ship to: Robert A. Silano
Address Line 1: 2122 Massachusetts Avenue, N.W. (Apt. 228)
Address Line 2:
City: Washington
State/Province/Region: DC
Zip/Postal Code: 20008
Country: USA

Buyer Name: Robert A. Silano

- -

Here are the details of your completed Amazon Marketplace sale:

http://us.f612.mail.yahoo.com/ym/ShowLetter?box=Inbox&MsgId=6841_1294045_46193_...   5/9/2006 removed the drawback of campaigning from their programme. Two months after the armistice Syria was nationalist in sentiment from south to north, Egypt was in arms against the British under a like banner, and the young officers of Turkey were banding together against the Sultan (thought to be out of date, silly, and too fond of Europe) to make a new Turkey out of the ruins of the old. They had lost their provinces in Europe – let them go: they had lost their Arabic provinces – let them go. They might lose an Armenian province in the north-east – let it go. They might lose Smyrna – let it go too. Their needs, in this new conception of their national future, were the body of Anatolia, from the Sea of Marmora through Cilicia, to Diarbekir, Erzeroum, Van, Azerbaijan, and even the Caspian. Some day they would cross the Caspian, and attract to their alliance the Turkomans of Turkestan, until all the Turk-speaking peoples to the borders of China were in their orbit. This was the logical Turanianism, the true figure of that which under Enver had been a distorted policy of suppression. Mustafa Kemal, a young, vain, clever, greedy soldier, made himself the leader of the new party, and speedily enrolled under his nominal guidance all the mass of Turks in Asia. His country is self-supporting, and he can sustain without danger the attacks of the Greek army, and the blockade of the Allies, if he can open friendly relations with Russia on his eastern front. He first tried to approach Italy, and then France, and then England, but found the one insufficient, the other too interested, the third legitimist. He is now blocked from the Aegean by Greek armies, and has to choose between surrender to them and friendship with Russia. The latter will probably mean his own personal downfall, for family reasons: but his followers will not hesitate to sacrifice him, if necessary, for the good of their state. Union with Russia will postpone the dream of an autonomous Turkestan for a generation, and will lock up Turkey in Anatolia proper for so long. Without foreign colonies, foreign wars, and foreign garrisons, she should meanwhile register a large increase of population.

The fate of the Arabs is more difficult to prophesy than that of the Turks, for they are a people of far higher mentality, subtle intellects capable of a depth of thinking, practical intellects capable of a degree of production, inflammable intellects capable of a deal of destruction. They lack system, endurance, organisation. They are incurably slaves of the idea, men of spasms, instable like water, but with something of its penetrating and flood-like character. They have been a government twenty times since the dawn of history, and as often after achievement they have grown tired, and let it fall: but there is no record of any force except success capable of breaking them. The history of their waves of feeling is significant in that the reservoir of all ideas, the birth of all prophecies are shown in the deserts. These empty spaces irresistibly drive their inhabitants to a belief in the oneness and omnipotence of God, by the very contrast of the barrenness of nature, the lack of every distraction and superfluity in life. Arab movements begin in the desert, and usually travel up the shortest way into Syria – for it is remarkable that whereas all prophets go to the desert, yet none of them are ever desert-born. It is the Semitic townsman or villager who receives the revelation. For this reason, for what seemed to be the immemorial finger-sign of history, this present Arab movement, the craving for national independence and self-government, was started in the desert. It, too, took the traditional road to Damascus, the traditional first centre of new movements, and with the successful establishment of Feisal there the second phase was finished. This is not, however, the proper end of the Arab movement: the weight and importance of the Semitic states have always lain in Bagdad, for very sound reasons of economics and population. Syria is a poor country, small and mountainous, dry, lacking in minerals and in arable land. There is no probability that her native population will ever be very dense. Mesopotamia has big rivers, and a huge area of irrigable land. Her wealth in grain and cotton will be very great, and nature may have bestowed on her abundance of cheap fuel. Should that be the case, she will inevitably take the headship of the Arab world in the future, as so often in the past. Damascus may hold an interim pre-eminence: Bagdad must be the ultimate regent, with perhaps five times the population of Syria, and many times its wealth. Mesopotamia will be the master of the Middle East, and the power controlling its destinies will dominate all its neighbours.

The question of a unity of the Arabic peoples in Asia is yet clouded. In the past it has never been a successful experiment, and the least reflection will show that there are large areas, especially of Arabia, which it would be unprofitable ever to administer. The deserts will probably remain, in the future as in the past, the preserves of inarticulate philosophers. The cultivated districts, Mesopotamia and Syria, have, however, language, race, and interests in common. Till to-day they have always been too vast to form a single country: they are divided, except for a narrow gangway in the north, by an irredeemable waste of flint and gravel: but petrol makes light of deserts, and space is shrinking to-day, when we travel one hundred miles an hour instead of five. The effect of roads, railways, air-ways and telegraph will be to draw these two provinces together, and teach them how like they are: and the needs of Mesopotamian trade will fix attention on the Mediterranean ports. The Arabs are a Mediterranean people, whom no force of circumstances will constrain to the Indian Ocean: further, when Mesopotamia has done her duty by the rivers, there will remain no part for water transport in her life – and the way by rail from Mosul or Bagdad to Alexandretta or Tripoli is more advantageous than the way to Basra. It may well be that Arab unity will come of an overwhelming conviction of the Mesopotamians that their national prosperity demands it.

The future of Persia is also clouded. In the days before the war she was judged for division between Great Britain and Russia. During the war she suffered occasional invasion from Turkey, and was the bed wherein German and British propagandist missions hunted one another. The Russian revolution delivered her from both these pains: England was left the only power capable or inclined to help her out of her bankruptcy and disorder on to the path of decent self-government. Unfortunately the statesmen of the two countries took rather a crude view of the situation, and concluded an agreement open to unfavourable interpretations, not only in the world outside (quite ready to take us at our worst), but in Persia itself. Consequently the advanced elements in Persia deserted us, and began to look across their northern frontier for Russian help. This was forthcoming in minute doses, and they, who included most of the militant spirits in Persia, took active measures against us. Our withdrawal gave them the prestige of a victory, and it seems possible that Persia will either be united under a national and unfriendly administration, or dismembered as before the war, and fought over by Russian and British partisans, nominally Persian subjects.

Egypt, another independent member of the group of new states that the war has sketched in the Middle East, has consolidated herself under pressure of the war and the riots since into the fair semblance of a single people. Her nationalists, who are in reality all the people of Egypt after their degree, have lost their former distinction of Moslem and Christian, and now find a common basis in their geographical situation and their daily speech. They have emancipated themselves from the clerical influence of the Azhar, the old-style Moslem University of Cairo, the former stronghold of pro-Turk or anti-British sentiment. The new nationalists envisage an attack upon this hoary institution, to bring its character and curriculum more into the trend of the present need of Egypt. In questions regarding the position of women and public education they are as advanced as the nationalists of Turkey. Politically their horizon is still very narrow, hardly leaving the banks of the Nile: but there is little doubt that the pressure of surplus population and excess of wealth will soon lead their eyes into larger enterprises, and then the North African question, at present easy to handle in sharply opposed compartments, will become a burning one. Egypt is so much the strongest component of this new North Africa that its government will be able to play in it something of the decisive rôle which the future Mesopotamian government will play in the Arab confederation.

Two new elements of some interest have just set foot in Asia, coming rather as adventurers by sea – the Greeks in Smyrna, and the Jews in Palestine. Of the two efforts the Greek is frankly an armed occupation – a desire to hold a tit-bit of Asiatic Turkey, for reasons of trade and population, and from it to influence affairs in the interior. It appears to have no constructive possibilities so far as the New Asia is concerned. The Jewish experiment is in another class. It is a conscious effort, on the part of the least European people in Europe, to make head against the drift of the ages, and return once more to the Orient from which they came. The colonists will take back with them to the land which they occupied for some centuries before the Christian era samples of all the knowledge and technique of Europe. They propose to settle down amongst the existing Arabic-speaking population of the country, a people of kindred origin, but far different social condition. They hope to adjust their mode of life to the climate of Palestine, and by the exercise of their skill and capital to make it as highly organised as a European state. The success of their scheme will involve inevitably the raising of the present Arab population to their own material level, only a little after themselves in point of time, and the consequences might be of the highest importance for the future of the Arab world. It might well prove a source of technical supply rendering them independent of industrial Europe, and in that case the new confederation might become a formidable element of world power. However, such a contingency will not be for the first or even for the second generation, but it must be borne in mind in any laying out of foundations of empire in Western Asia. These to a very large extent must stand or fall by the course of the Zionist effort, and by the course of events in Russia.

It is curious how with each modification of the condition of Russia her potential influence has steadily increased in south-western Asia. Since the Czarist days Russia has been sole arbiter of northern Asia, from the Black Sea to the China Sea, and so large a proportion of her bulk lies in Asia that there is real reason for considering her revolution an Asiatic phenomenon. It has at least a very strong Asiatic importance, and may well yet do for Asia what the kindred revolution in France did for Europe, after a parallel cycle of some sixty years. It is not that the doctrines of Lenin find a ready echo in the minds of the peasantry of Asia – they have not found their warmest adherents in the peasantry of Russia: but the Bolshevist success has been a potent example to the East of the overthrow of an ancient government, depending on a kind of divine right, and weighing on Asia with all the force of an immense military establishment. Its fall has not affected the division of Asia, north to Russia and south to England: it has changed the Russian area from an area of effective domination to an area of influence, a base of preaching or action for the advanced members of every society. Further, it will provide a frontier permanently open, and an unlimited source of armament. In the old days the Russian imperial government kept their southern frontier along the hill-crests of central Asia strictly to themselves, and thus there was little coming or going between our half and theirs. This is now changed, and the progressive part of Asia has become the north and not the south. Upon the action, not of the Russian government, but of private individuals sharing the anti-imperialist views of the Russian state, and willing to work as private individuals to spread their beliefs in southern Asia, depends much of the future of Persia, of Anatolia, and to a lesser degree of Syria and Mesopotamia. The two temporary republics of Armenia and Georgia, may be said to be Russian in a more direct fashion.

This new condition, of a conscious and logical political nationalism, now the dominant factor of every indigenous movement in Western Asia, is too universal to be extinguished, too widespread to be temporary. We must prepare ourselves for its continuance, and for a continuance of the unrest produced by it in every contested district, until such time as it has succeeded and passed into a more advanced phase. It is so radical a change in the former complexion of Western Asia as to demand from us a revision of the principles of our policy in the Middle East, and an effort to adjust ourselves, that the advantage of its constructive elements may be on our side.

This new imperialism is not just withdrawal and neglect on our part. It involves an active side of imposing responsibility on the local peoples. It is what they clamour for, but an unpopular gift when given. We have to demand from them provision for their own defence. This is the first stage towards self-respect in peoples. They must find their own troops to replace our armies of occupation which we are going to withdraw. For this they must be armed, and must learn by having arms not to misuse them. We can only teach them how by forcing them to try, while we stand by and give advice. This is not for us less honourable than administration: indeed, it is more exacting, for it is simple to give orders, but difficult to persuade another to take advice, and it is the more difficult which is most pleasant doing. We have to be prepared to see them doing things by methods quite unlike our own, and less well: but on principle it is better that they half-do it than that we do it perfectly for them. In pursuing such courses we will find our best helpers not in our former most obedient subjects, but among those now most active in agitating against us, for it will be the intellectual leaders of the people who will serve the purpose, and these are not the philosophers nor the rich, but the demagogues and the politicians. It seems a curious class to which to entrust the carefully begun edifices of our colonial governments – but in essence it will not be dissimilar to the members of our own House of Commons, whom we entrust with our own liberties. They will not wish to take charge, but we can force their hand by preparing to go. We do not risk losing them to another power – for the Englishman is liked by everyone who has not too much to do with him, and the British Empire is so much the largest concern in the world that it offers unrivalled inducements to small peoples to join it. Egypt, Persia and Mesopotamia, if assured of eventual dominion status, and present internal autonomy, would be delighted to affiliate with us, and would then cost us no more in men and money than Canada or Australia. The alternative is to hold on to them with ever-lessening force, till the anarchy is too expensive, and we let go.

6

The Evolution of a Revolt

October 1920

If 'Demolitions under Fire' appeared in the twenty-ninth edition of one military journal, that of the Royal Engineers, this piece had the distinction of appearing in the first number of another: *The Army Quarterly*, published in October 1920.

As stated in the introduction to the previous item, the article was reprinted in A. W. Lawrence's 1939 anthology, *Oriental Assembly*. In his Editor's Note, A.W. acknowledged its source and added: 'Some of contents were subsequently used in Chapter XXXIII of *Seven Pillars of Wisdom*.' (Readers of the 1922 Oxford Edition of *Seven Pillars of Wisdom*, published by Castle Hill Press in 1997, should note that the relevant chapter is number 35.) This is the chapter in which Lawrence, taken ill while visiting the camp of Emir Abdullah in Wadi Ais in March 1917, lies in his tent thinking through the strategy of the coming campaign. To some extent this is, I believe, a dramatic device, typical of the unique style of *Seven Pillars of Wisdom*, in which – as we have seen from this book's Introduction – concepts dating from the start of his involvement, or even earlier, are brought together to form a kind of thesis, in which Lawrence expounds at eloquent length his philosophy of warfare. Since the publication of 'The Evolution of a Revolt' coincided with his writing of *Seven Pillars of Wisdom* – though his labours on the latter would continue for the next six years – it is not surprising that the two works reflect each other.

One curious literary consequence perhaps not widely known is that somehow the article came to the notice of the historian and novelist John Buchan, who read it with the greatest interest. Writing to Basil Liddell Hart in October 1927, he stated: 'I should greatly like to see Lawrence's article on Guerrilla Warfare reprinted.' In the event its influence on Buchan was such that, when his novel *The Courts of the Morning* appeared in 1929, his remarkable literary creation Sandy Arbuthnot, hero of a number of his earlier adventures, had mutated into a recognisably Lawrencian figure. Previously there had been more than a hint of that remarkable adventurer, the Hon. Aubrey Herbert – a friend of Lawrence as well as of Buchan – in Sandy, to whom the novelist had given the extra panache of being an aristocrat, with the title, lightly worn, of Lord Clanroyden. In his new yarn, although he set it in South America, Buchan describes Sandy as 'crazed by the spell of far Arabia', as 'a dweller in tents', and as short, lithe and with steady, glowing eyes: Lawrence to the life. Ready to share his enthusiasm for the source which had inspired him, Buchan hoped to see its wider circulation. As a long-time admirer of Buchan, I am happy to see his wishes granted once more in this book.

One of Lawrence's most famous descriptions of the Arab Revolt was that it was a 'side-show of a side-show' (see p. 272). Here also we find, on p. 265, the first use of the concept now increasingly publicised that 'war upon rebellion is messy and slow, like eating soup with a knife'.

In addition to the sources indicated, this article appeared in shortened form in David Garnett, *The Essential T. E. Lawrence*, 1951, and in full in Stanley and Rodelle Weintraub, *Evolution of a Revolt*, where it supplied the title to the whole collection.

The Evolution of a Revolt
October 1920

The Arab revolt began in June 1916, with an Arab offensive, a surprise attack by the half-armed and inexperienced tribesmen upon the Turkish garrisons in Medina and about Mecca. They had no success, and after a few days' effort they withdrew out of range of the fort artillery, and began a blockade. This method forced the early surrender of Mecca, whose road communications were too long and rough to be held by the Turks. Medina, however, was linked by railway to the Turkish main army in Syria, and, thanks to their superior numbers and equipment, the Turks were able in a week's fighting to restore the line and reinforce the temporarily-besieged garrison there. The Arab forces which had attacked it fell back gradually as the Turks became more offensive, and at last moved fifty miles south-west into the hills, and there took up a position across the main road to Mecca.

At this point the campaign stood still for many weeks, while both sides breathed, and the Turks prepared to take the initiative, by sending an expeditionary force to Mecca, to crush the revolt where it had started. They moved an army corps to Medina by rail, and strengthened it beyond establishment with guns, cars, aeroplanes, machine-guns, and quantities of horse, mule and camel transport. Then they began to advance down the main western road from Medina to Mecca. The total distance was about 250 miles. The first fifty miles were easy: then came a belt of hills twenty miles wide, in which were Feisal's tribesmen standing on the defensive: after the hills was a level stretch, for seventy miles along the coastal plain to Rabegh, rather more than half-way. Rabegh is a little port on the Red Sea, with good anchorage for ships. In it was Sherif Ali, Feisal's eldest brother, with more tribal forces, and the beginnings of an Arab regular army, recruited from officers and men of Arab blood, who had served in the Turkish army, and were now willing to fight against their old masters for their national freedom.

Our military advisers had told us that Rabegh was the key of Mecca, since no hostile force could pass along the main road without occupying it and watering at its wells under the palm trees. Its defence was therefore of the main importance. The Navy could co-operate effectively from the harbour, and the circle of the palm-groves must be laid out as an entrenched position, and held by regular troops. They thought that Beduin tribesmen would never be of any value in a fixed position, and that therefore an Arab regular force must be formed and trained as soon as possible to undertake this duty. If the Turks advanced before the new force was ready, the British would have to lend a brigade, of British or Allied troops, to save the Sherif in his extremity, by maintaining this stop-block.

A personal reconnaissance of the Arab positions, here and in the hills where Feisal was, caused me to modify the views of the experts slightly. Feisal had some thousands of men, all armed with rifles, rather casual, distrustful fellows, but very active and cheerful. They were posted in hills and defiles of such natural strength that it seemed to me very improbable that the Turks could force them, just by their superior numbers: for in some ways it is easier to defend a range of hills against nine or ten thousand men than against nine or ten. Accordingly, I reported that the tribesmen (if strengthened by light machine-guns, and regular officers as advisers) should be able to hold up the Turks indefinitely, while the Arab regular force was being created. As was almost inevitable in view of the general course of military thinking since Napoleon, we all looked only to the regulars to win the war. We were obsessed by the dictum of Foch that the ethic of modern war is to seek for the enemy's army, his centre of power, and destroy it in battle. Irregulars would not attack positions and so they seemed to us incapable of forcing a decision.

While we were training the regulars (of course not sending officers or light machine-guns to Feisal in the hills meanwhile), the Turks suddenly put my appreciation to the test by beginning their advance on Mecca. They broke through my 'impregnable' hills in twenty-four hours, and came forward from them towards Rabegh slowly. So they proved to us the second theorem of irregular war – namely, that irregular troops are as unable to defend a point or line as they are to attack it.

This lesson was received by us quite without gratitude, for the Turkish success put us in a critical position. The Rabegh force was not capable of repelling the attack of a single battalion, much less of a corps. It was nearly impossible to send down British troops from Egypt at the moment: nor do I think that a single British brigade would have been capable of holding all the Rabegh position: nor was the Rabegh position indispensable to the Turks: nor would a single Arab have remained with the Sherif if he introduced British troops into the Hejaz.

In the emergency it occurred to me that perhaps the virtue of irregulars lay in depth, not in face, and that it had been the threat of attack by them upon the Turkish northern flank which had made the enemy hesitate for so long. The actual Turkish flank ran from their front line to Medina, a distance of some fifty miles: but, if we moved towards the Hejaz railway behind Medina, we might stretch our threat (and, accordingly, their flank) as far, potentially, as Damascus, eight hundred miles away to the north. Such a move would force the Turks to the defensive, and we might regain the initiative. Anyhow, it seemed our only chance, and so, in January 1917, we took all Feisal's tribesmen, turned our backs on Mecca, Rabegh and the Turks, and marched away north two hundred miles to Wejh, thanks to the help of the British Red Sea Fleet, which fed and watered us along the coast, and gave us gun-power and a landing party at our objective.

This eccentric movement acted like a charm. Clausewitz had said that rearguards modulate the enemy's action like a pendulum, not by what they do, but by their mere existence. We did nothing concrete, but our march recalled the Turks (who were almost into Rabegh) all the way back to Medina, and there they halved their force. One half took up the entrenched position about the city, which they held until after the armistice. The other half was distributed along the railway to defend it against our threat. For the rest of the war the Turks stood on the defensive against us, and we won advantage over advantage till, when peace came, we had taken 35,000 prisoners, killed and wounded and worn out about as many, and occupied a hundred thousand square miles of the enemy's territory, at little loss to ourselves.

However, we were not then aware that Wejh was our turning-point. We thought we had come to it to cut the railway, and I was at once sent up-country to do this, as a means to take Medina, the Turkish headquarters and main garrison. On the way up I fell ill, and spent ten days on my back in a tent, without anything to do except to think about war and analyse our hitherto empirical practice for its real import.

I was unfortunately as much in charge of the campaign as I pleased, and had had no training in command to fit me for such a work. In military theory I was tolerably read, for curiosity in Oxford years before had taken me past Napoleon to Clausewitz and his school, to Caemmerer and Moltke, Goltz and the recent Frenchmen. These had seemed very partial books, and after a look at Jomini and Willisen I had found broader principles in the eighteenth century, in Saxe, Guibert and their followers. However, Clausewitz was intellectually so much the master of them all that unwillingly I had come to believe in him. Tactically the only campaigns I had studied step by step were the ancient affairs of Hannibal and Belisarius, Mohammed and the Crusades! My interests were only in pure theory and I looked everywhere for the metaphysical side, the philosophy of war, about which I thought a little for some years. Now I was compelled suddenly to action, to find an immediate equation between my book-reading and our present movements.

However, the books gave me the aim in war quite pat, 'the destruction of the organised forces of the enemy' by 'the one process battle'. Victory could only be purchased by blood. This was a hard saying for us, as the Arabs had no organised forces, and so a Turkish Foch would have no aim: and the Arabs would not endure casualties, so that an Arab Clausewitz could not buy his victory. These wise men must be talking metaphors, for we were indubitably winning our war . . . and as I thought about it, it dawned on me that we had won the Hejaz war. We were in occupation of 99 per cent of the Hejaz. The Turks were welcome to the other fraction till peace or doomsday showed them the futility of clinging to our window pane. This part of the war was over, so why bother about Medina? It was no base for us, like Rabegh, no threat to the Turks, like Wejh: just a blind alley for both. The Turks sat in it on the defensive, immobile, eating for food the transport animals which were to have moved them to Mecca, but for which there was no pasture in their now restricted lines. They were harmless sitting there; if we took them prisoner, they would cost us food and guards in Egypt: if we drove them out northward into Syria, they would join the main army blocking us in Sinai. On all counts they were best where they were, and they valued Medina and wanted to keep it. Let them!

This seemed unlike the ritual of war of which Foch had been priest, and so I began to hope that there was a difference of kind between us and him. He called his modern war 'absolute'. In it two nations professing incompatible philosophies set out to try them in the light of force. A struggle of two immaterial principles could only end when the supporters of one had no more means of resistance. An opinion can be argued with: a conviction is best shot. The logical end of a war of creeds is the final destruction of one, and Salammbo the classical textbook-instance. These were the lines of the struggle between France and Germany, but not, I thought, between Germany and England, for all efforts to make our men hate the enemy just made them hate war, and later on by the armistice we made the Great War fall short of the Foch ideal. To me it seemed only a variety of war: and I could then see other sorts, as Clausewitz had numbered them, personal wars for dynastic reasons, expulsive wars for party reasons, commercial wars for trading reasons.

Then I thought of the Arab aim, and saw that it was geographical, to occupy all Arabic-speaking lands in Asia. In the doing of it we might kill Turks: we disliked them very much. Yet 'killing Turks' would never be an excuse or aim. If they would go quietly, our war would end. If not, we would try to drive them out: in the last resort we would be compelled to the desperate course of blood, on the maxim of 'murder' war, but as cheaply as possible for ourselves, since the Arabs were fighting for freedom, a pleasure only to be tasted by a man alive.

My own personal duty was command, and I began to unravel command and analyse it, both from the point of view of strategy, the aim in war, the synoptic regard which sees everything by the standard of the whole, and from the point of view called tactics, the means towards the strategic end, the steps of its staircase. In each I found the same elements, one algebraical, one biological, a third psychological. The first seemed a pure science, subject to the laws of mathematics, without humanity. It dealt with known invariables, fixed conditions, space and time, inorganic things like hills and climates and railways, with mankind in type-masses too great for individual variety, with all artificial aids, and the extensions given our faculties by mechanical invention. It was essentially formulable.

In the Arab case the algebraic factor would take first account of the area we wished to conquer, and I began idly to calculate how many square miles . . . perhaps 140,000 . . . and how would the Turks defend all that . . . no doubt by a trench line across the bottom, if we were an army attacking with banners displayed . . . but suppose we were an influence (as we might be), an idea, a thing invulnerable, intangible, without front or back, drifting about like a gas? Armies were like plants, immobile as a whole, firm-rooted, nourished through long stems to the head. We might be a vapour, blowing where we listed. Our kingdoms lay in each man's mind, and as we wanted nothing material to live on, so perhaps we offered nothing material to the killing. It seemed a regular soldier might be helpless without a target. He would own the ground he sat on, and what he could poke his rifle at.

Then I estimated how many posts they would need to contain this attack in depth, sedition putting up her head in every unoccupied one of these hundred thousand square miles. I knew the Turkish army inside and out, and allowing for its recent extension of faculty by guns and aeroplanes and armoured trains, still it seemed it would have need of a fortified post every four square miles, and a post could not be less than twenty men. The Turks would need six hundred thousand men to meet the combined ill wills of all the local Arab people. They had one hundred thousand men available. It seemed the assets in this part of command were ours, and climate, railways, deserts, technical weapons could also be attached to our interests, if we realised our raw materials and were apt with them. The Turk was stupid and would believe that rebellion was absolute, like war, and deal with it on the analogy of absolute warfare. Analogy is fudge, anyhow, and to make war upon rebellion is messy and slow, like eating soup with a knife.

So much for the mathematical element, which I annoyed the others by calling hecastics. The second factor was biological, the breaking-point, life and death, or better, wear and tear. Bionomics seemed a good name for it. The war-philosophers had properly made it an art, and had elevated one item in it, 'effusion of blood', to the height of a principle. It became humanity in battle, an art touching every side of our corporal being, and very warm. There was a line of variability (man) running through all its estimates. Its components were sensitive and illogical, and generals guarded themselves by the device of a reserve, the significant medium of their art. Goltz had said that when you know the enemy's strength and he is fully deployed, then you know enough to dispense with a reserve. But this is never. There is always the possibility of accident, of some flaw in materials, present in the general's mind: and the reserve is unconsciously held to meet it. There is a 'felt' element in troops, not expressible in figures, guessed at by the equivalent of δόξα* in Plato, and the greatest commander is he whose intuitions most

* Doxa (opinion), empirical knowledge of everyday facts and events, or of philosophical reality.

nearly happen. Nine-tenths of tactics are certain, and taught in books: but the irrational tenth is like the kingfisher flashing across the pool, and that is the test of generals. It can only be ensued by instinct sharpened by thought practising the stroke so often that at the crisis it is as natural as a reflex.

Yet to limit the art to humanity seemed to me an undue narrowing down. It must apply to materials as much as to organisms. In the Turkish army materials were scarce and precious, men more plentiful than equipment. Consequently our cue should be to destroy not the army but the materials. The death of a Turkish bridge or rail, machine or gun, or high explosive was more profitable to us than the death of a Turk. The Arab army just now was equally chary of men and materials: of men because they being irregulars were not units, but individuals, and an individual casualty is like a pebble dropped in water: each may make only a brief hole, but rings of sorrow widen out from them. We could not afford casualties. Materials were easier to deal with and put straight. It was our obvious duty to make ourselves superior in some one branch, guncotton or machine-guns, or whatever could be made most decisive. Foch had laid down the maxim, applying it to men, of being superior at the critical point and moment of attack. We might apply it to materials, and be superior in equipment in one dominant moment or respect.

For both men and things we might try to give Foch's doctrine a negative twisted side, for cheapness' sake, and be weaker than the enemy everywhere except in one point or matter. Most wars are wars of contact, both forces striving to keep in touch to avoid tactical surprise. Our war should be a war of detachment: we were to contain the enemy by the silent threat of a vast unknown desert, not disclosing ourselves till the moment of attack. This attack need be only nominal, directed not against his men, but against his materials: so it should not seek for his main strength or his weaknesses, but for his most accessible material. In railway cutting this would be usually an empty stretch of rail. That was a tactical success. We might turn the average into a rule (not a law – war is antinomian, said Colin), and at length we developed an unconscious habit of never engaging the enemy at all. This chimed with the numerical plea of never giving the enemy's soldier a target. Many Turks on our front had no chance all the war to fire a shot at us, and correspondingly we were never on the defensive, except by rare accident. The corollary of such a rule was perfect 'intelligence', so that we could plan in complete certainty. The chief agent had to be the general's head (de Feuquière said this first), and his knowledge had to be faultless, leaving no room for chance. We took more pains in this service than any other staff I saw.

The third factor in command seemed to be the psychological, that science (Xenophon called it diathetic) of which our propaganda is a stained and ignoble part. Some of it concerns the crowd, and adjustment of spirit to the point where it becomes fit to exploit in action, the prearrangement of a changing opinion to a certain end. Some of it deals with individuals, and then it becomes a rare art of human kindness, transcending, by purposeful emotion, the gradual logical sequence of our minds. It considers the capacity for mood of our men, their complexities and mutability, and the cultivation of what in them profits the intention. We had to arrange their minds in order of battle, just as carefully and as formally as other officers arranged their bodies: and not only our own men's minds, though them first: the minds of the enemy, so far as we could reach them: and thirdly, the mind of the nation supporting us behind the firing line, and the mind of the hostile nation waiting the verdict, and the neutrals looking on.

It was the ethical in war, and the process on which we mainly depended for victory on the Arab front. The printing press is the greatest weapon in the armoury of the modern commander, and we, being amateurs in the art of command, began our war in the atmosphere of the twentieth century, and thought of our weapons without prejudice, not distinguishing one from another socially. The regular officer has the tradition of forty generations of serving soldiers behind him, and to him the old weapons are the most honoured. We had seldom to concern ourselves with what our men did, but much with what they thought, and to us the diathetic was more than half command. In Europe it was set a little aside and entrusted to men outside the General Staff. In Asia we were so weak physically that we could not let the metaphysical weapon rust unused. We had won a province when we had taught the civilians in it to die for our ideal of freedom: the presence or absence of the enemy was a secondary matter.

These reasonings showed me that the idea of assaulting Medina, or even of starving it quickly into surrender was not in accord with our best strategy. We wanted the enemy to stay in Medina, and in every other harmless place, in the largest numbers. The factor of food would eventually confine him to the railways, but he was welcome to the Hejaz railway, and the Trans-Jordan railway, and the Palestine and Damascus and Aleppo railways for the duration of the war, so long as he gave us the other nine hundred and ninety-nine thousandths of the Arab world. If he showed a disposition to evacuate too soon, as a step to concentrating in the small area which his numbers could dominate effectively, then we would have to try and restore his confidence, not harshly, but by reducing our enterprises against him. Our ideal was to keep his railway just working, but only just, with the maximum of loss and discomfort to him.

Accordingly, I put in a few damages to the line, enough to annoy the enemy without making him fear its final destruction, and then rode back to Wejh, to explain to my chiefs that the Arab war was geographical, and the Turkish army for us an accident, not a target. Out aim was to seek its weakest link, and bear only on that till time made the mass of it fall. Our largest available resources were the tribesmen, men quite unused to formal warfare, whose assets were movement, endurance, individual intelligence, knowledge of the country, courage. We must impose the longest possible passive defence on the Turks (this being the most materially expensive form of war) by extending our own front to its maximum. Tactically we must develop a highly mobile, highly equipped type of army, of the smallest size, and use it successively at distributed points of the Turkish line, to make the Turks reinforce their occupying posts beyond the economic minimum of twenty men. The power of this striking force of ours would not be reckoned merely by its strength. The ratio between number and area determined the character of the war, and by having five times the mobility of the Turks we could be on terms with them with one-fifth their number.

Our success was certain, to be proved by paper and pencil as soon as the proportion of space and number had been learned. The contest was not physical, but mineral, and so battles were a mistake. All we won in a battle was the ammunition the enemy fired off. Our victory lay not in battles, but in occupying square miles of country. Napoleon had said it was rare to find generals willing to fight battles. The curse of this war was that so few could do anything else. Napoleon had spoken in angry reaction against the excessive finesse of the eighteenth century, when men almost forgot that war gave licence to murder. We had been swinging out on his dictum for a hundred years, and it was time to go back a bit again. Battles are impositions on the side which believes itself weaker, made unavoidable either by lack of land-room, or by the need to defend a material property dearer than the lives of soldiers. We had nothing material to lose, so we were to defend nothing and to shoot nothing. The precious element of our forces were the Beduin irregulars, and not the regulars whose rôle would only be to occupy places to which the irregulars had already given access. Our cards were speed and time, not hitting power, and these gave us strategical rather than tactical strength. Range is more to strategy than force. The invention of bully-beef has modified land-war more profoundly than the invention of gunpowder.

My chiefs did not follow all these arguments, but gave me leave to try my hand after my own fashion. We went off first to Akaba, and took it easily. Then we took Tafileh and the Dead Sea: then Azrak and Deraa, and finally Damascus, all in successive stages worked out consciously on these sick-bed theories. The process was to set up ladders of tribes, giving us a safe and comfortable route from our sea-bases (Yenbo, Wejh or Akaba) to our advanced bases of operation. These were sometimes three hundred miles away, a long distance in lands without railways or roads, but made short for us by an assiduous cultivation of desert-power, control by camel parties of the desolate and unmapped wilderness which fills up all the centre of Arabia, from Mecca to Aleppo and Bagdad.

In character these operations were more like naval warfare than ordinary land operations, in their mobility, their ubiquity, their independence of bases and communications, their lack of ground features, of strategic areas, of fixed directions, of fixed points. 'He who commands the sea is at great liberty, and may take as much or as little of the war as he will': he who commands the desert is equally fortunate. Camel raiding parties, as self-contained as ships, could cruise without danger along any part of the enemy's land frontier, just out of sight of his posts along the edge of cultivation, and tap or raid into his lines where it seemed fittest or easiest or most profitable, with a sure retreat always behind them into an element which the Turks could not enter. We were fortified in our freedom of movement by an intimate knowledge of the desert-front of Syria, a country peculiarly and historically indefensible against attack from the east. I had traversed most of it on foot before the war many times, working out the movements of Saladin or Ibrahim Pasha, and, as our war experience deepened, we became adepts at that form of geographical intuition, described by Bourcet as wedding unknown land to known in a mental map.

Our tactics were always tip and run, not pushes, but strokes. We never tried to maintain or improve an advantage, but to move off and strike again somewhere else. We used the smallest force, in the quickest time, at the farthest place. If the action had continued till the enemy had changed his dispositions to resist it, we would have been breaking the spirit of our fundamental rule of denying him targets.

The necessary speed and range were attained by the extreme frugality of the desert men, and their high efficiency when mounted on their she-riding-camels. The camel is an intricate animal, and calls for skilled labour in the handling: but she yields a remarkable return. We had no system of supply: each man was self-contained and carried on the saddle, from the sea-base at which the raid started, six weeks' food for himself. The six-weeks' ration for ordinary men was a half-bag of flour, forty-five pounds in weight. Luxurious feeders carried some rice also for variety. Each man baked for himself, kneading his own flour into unleavened cakes, and warming it in the ashes of a fire. We carried about a pint of drinking water each, since the camels required to come to water on average every three days, and there was no advantage in our being richer than our mounts. Some of us never drank between wells, but those were hardy men: most of us drank a lot at each well, and had a drink during the intermediate dry day. In the heat of summer Arabian camels will do about 250 miles comfortably between drinks: and this represented three days' vigorous marching. The country is not so dry as it is painted, and this radius was always more than we needed. Wells are seldom more than one hundred miles apart. An easy day's march was fifty miles: an emergency march might be up to 110 miles in the day.

The six weeks' food gave us a range of over a thousand miles out and home, and that (like the pint of water) was more than ever we needed, even in so large a country as Arabia. It was possible (for me, the camel-novice in the army, 'painful' was a better word) to ride 1,500 miles in the month without re-victualling, and there was never a fear of starvation, for each of us was riding on two hundred pounds of potential meat, and when food lacked we would stop and eat the weakest of our camels. Exhausted camel is poor food, but cheaper killing than a fat one, and we had to remember that our future efficiency depended on the number of good camels at our disposal. They lived on grazing as we marched (we never gave them grain or fodder), and after their six weeks on the road they would be worn thin, and have to be sent to pasture for some months' rest, while we called out another tribe in replacement, or found fresh riding-beasts.

We did not hamper ourselves with led-camels. The men carried with them a hundred rounds of ammunition and a rifle, or else two men would be an 'automatic' team, dividing the gun and its drums between them. They slept as they were, in their riding cloaks, and fared well enough till the winter of 1917–18, which caught us on the five thousand foot-hills of Edom behind the Dead Sea. Then we lost many men and camels frozen to death, or trapped in the snow, which lay over all the high lands in deep drifts for weeks, while we vainly appealed to Egypt for tents and boots and blankets. In reply we were advised that Arabia was a tropical country!

The equipment of the raiding parties aimed at simplicity, with neverthe-less a technical superiority over the Turks in the most critical department. We had great quantities of light machine-guns, used not as machine-guns, but as automatic rifles, snipers' tools, by men kept deliberately in ignorance of their mechanism, so that the speed of action would not be hampered by attempts at repair. If a gun jammed, the gunner had to throw it away and go on with his rifle. We made another special feature of high explosives, and nearly everyone in the revolt was qualified by rule of thumb experience in demolition work. We invented special methods of our own, for rapid work under fire, in the course of our months of practice, and before the end were dealing with any quantity of track and bridges economically and safely.

On some occasions we strengthened tribal raids by armoured cars, manned by Englishmen. Armoured cars, once they have found a possible track, can keep up with a camel party. They are, however, cumbrous and shorter-ranged, because of the difficulty of carrying petrol. Therefore we seldom used them more than a hundred miles from home. On the march to Damascus, when we were nearly four hundred miles off our base, we first maintained them by a baggage train of petrol-laden camels, and afterwards by the help of the Air Force were able to give them further supplies by Handley-Page. Cars are magnificent fighting machines, and decisive when-ever they can come into action on their own conditions. But though each has for main principle that of 'fire in movement', yet the tactical employments of cars and camel corps are so different that I do not recommend their being used in joint operations, except in very special circumstances. We found it demoralising to both to use armoured and unarmoured cavalry together.

The distribution of the raiding parties was unorthodox. It was impossible to mix or combine tribes, since they disliked or distrusted one another. Likewise we could not use the men of one tribe in the territory of another. In consequence, we aimed at the widest distribution of forces, in order to have the greatest number of raids on hand at once, and we added fluidity to their ordinary speed by using one district on Monday, another on Tuesday, a third on Wednesday. This much reinforced their natural mobility. It gave us priceless advantages in pursuit, for the force renewed itself with fresh men in every new tribal area, and gave us always our pristine energy. Maximum disorder was in a real sense our equilibrium.

The internal economy of the raiding parties was equally curious. We aimed at maximum articulation. We were serving a common ideal, without tribal emulation, and so we could not hope for any *esprit de corps* to reinforce our motives. Soldiers are made a caste either by being given great pay and rewards in money, uniform, or political privileges; or, as in England, by being made outcasts, cut off from their fellows by contempt. We could not knit man to man, for our tribesmen were in arms willingly, by conviction. There have been many armies enlisted voluntarily: there have been few armies serving voluntarily under such trying conditions, for so long a war as ours. Any of the Arabs could go home whenever the conviction failed him. Our only contract was honour.

Consequently we had no discipline, in the sense in which it is restrictive, submergent of individuality, the lowest common denominator of men. In regular armies in peace it means the limit of energy attainable by everybody present: it is the hunt not of an average, but of an absolute, a 100-per-cent standard, in which the ninety-nine stronger men are played down to the level of the worst. The aim is to render the unit a unit, and the man a type, in order that their effort shall be calculable, their collective output even in grain and in bulk. The deeper the discipline, the lower the individual efficiency, and the more sure the performance. It is a deliberate sacrifice of capacity in order to reduce the uncertain element, the bionomic factor, in enlisted humanity, and its accompaniment is *compound* or social war, that form in which the man in the fighting line has to be the product of the multiplied exertions of the long hierarchy, from workshop to supply unit, which maintains him in the field.

The Arab war was *simple* and individual. Every enrolled man served in the line of battle, and was self-contained. We had no lines of communication or labour troops. The efficiency of each man was his personal efficiency. We thought that in our condition of warfare the sum yielded by single men would be at least equal to the product of a compound system, and it was certainly easier to adjust to tribal life and manners, given elasticity and understanding on the part of the commanding officers. Fortunately for our chances nearly every young Englishman has the roots of eccentricity in him, and so we got on well enough. Of course we used very few Englishmen in the field, not more than one per thousand of the Arab troops. A larger proportion would have created friction, just because they were foreign bodies (pearls if you please) in the oyster: and those who were present controlled by influence and advice, by their superior knowledge, not by an extraneous authority.

In practice we did not employ in the firing line the greater numbers which the adoption of a 'simple' system put theoretically at our disposal. We preferred to use them in relay: otherwise our attack would have become too extended. Each man had to have liberal work-room. In irregular war if two men are together one is being wasted. The moral strain of isolated action makes this simple form of war very exacting on the individual soldier, and demands from him special initiative, endurance and enthusiasm. Our ideal was to make action a series of single combats. Napoleon, in his pregnant valuation of the Mamelukes in terms of French soldiers, first gave me the idea: Ardant du Picq widened its application: the prejudices of historians are generally the richest part of their histories. Our value depended entirely on our quality, not on our quantity. We had to keep always cool, for the excitement of a blood-lust would impair the science of our combatants, and our victory depended on our just use of speed, concealment, accuracy of fire. Irregular war is far more intellectual than a bayonet charge.

The illiteracy of our forces was not harmful, since we worked intentionally in these small numbers and explained our plan verbally to every one. Their very illiteracy has trained them to a longer memory and a closer hearing of the news. Nor were our tactics too subtle, for they had to be translated into independent action through the heads of our followers, and success was impossible unless most of them used their intelligence to forward our conception against the moral and material accidents of the path. This dilution of tactical ability to the level of the lowest interpreter was regrettable, but not all loss. The only alternative would be independent enterprise, and a mediocre design, persisted in, is grander than a series of brilliant expedients and will overcome them in the end.

By careful persistence, kept strictly within our strength and following the spirit of our theories, we were able eventually to reduce the Turks to helplessness, and complete victory seemed to be almost within our sight when General Allenby by his immense stroke in Palestine threw the enemy's main forces into hopeless confusion and put an immediate end to the Turkish war. We were very happy to have done with all our pains, but sometimes since I have felt a private regret that his too-greatness deprived me of the opportunity of following to the end the dictum of Saxe that war might be won without fighting battles. It was an irony of fate to entrust this side-show of a side-show, with its opportunity of proving or disproving the theory, to an outsider like myself, not qualified technically to make the best of it. I would have given so much to show that Saxe was the greatest master of his kind of war, but now all I can say is that we worked by his light for two years, and the work stood. This is a pragmatic argument that cannot be wholly derided.

Unfortunately our campaigns lacked a historian as much as an executant. Now that I try to write down what we did, and why, some of our principles look truisms (mankind would so rather believe a sophism) and some look contradictory. The fault must be either in my exposition or in my observation. Savage warfare seems never to have been thought out in English from the savage point of view, and the Arab revolt would have been a great opportunity for a thinker to test its possibilities on a grand scale. Our war was so odd and so far away that coy Authority left us to ourselves. We had no base machinery, no formal staff, no clerks, no government, no telegraphs, no public opinion, no troops of British nationality, no honour, no conventions.

The experiment was a thrilling one, which took all our wits. We believed we would prove irregular war or rebellion to be an exact science, and an inevitable success, granted certain factors and if pursued along certain lines. We did not prove it, because the war stopped: but here the thesis is:

It seemed that rebellion must have an unassailable base, something guarded not merely from attack, but from the fear of it: such a base as we had in the Red Sea ports, the desert, or in the minds of the men we converted to our creed. It must have a sophisticated alien enemy, in the form of a disciplined army of occupation too small to fulfil the doctrine of acreage: too few to adjust number to space, in order to dominate the whole area effectively from fortified posts. It must have a friendly population not actively friendly, but sympathetic to the point of not betraying rebel movements to the enemy. Rebellions can be made by 2 per cent active in a striking force, and 98 per cent passively sympathetic. The few active rebels must have the qualities of speed and endurance, ubiquity and independence of arteries of supply. They must have the technical equipment to destroy or paralyse the enemy's organised communications, for irregular war is fairly Willisen's definition of strategy, 'the study of communication' in its extreme degree, of attack where the enemy is not. In fifty words: granted mobility, security (in the form of denying targets to the enemy), time, and doctrine (the idea to convert every subject to friendliness), victory will rest with the insurgents, for the algebraical factors are in the end decisive, and against them perfections of means and spirit struggle quite in vain.

7

Science of Guerrilla Warfare

1929

This item, if nothing else, is a fascinating literary curiosity, in that it is the product of the work of two authors, not one: or, more correctly, of one author and one perceptive editor. Asked to contribute an article to the fourteenth edition of the *Encyclopædia Britannica* (to be published in 1929), on a subject of which he was an acknowledged expert, Lawrence refused but was content that the task should be undertaken by the encyclopaedia's Military Editor, Captain Basil Liddell Hart, with carte blanche to compile an article out of his, Lawrence's, already published writings. Liddell Hart, an admirer of Lawrence, and also a future biographer, set to with a will and produced a piece of such clarity, readability and style that it merits greater exposure than it has hitherto received. Hence its inclusion here; although not formally recognised in the canon of Lawrence's writings it bears his hallmark none the less, and is an excellent summation of his views on the subject. Necessarily it repeats material that appears elsewhere in this volume, but this if anything makes it more rather than less interesting, in that it shows how the thoughts of one man were sifted and reshaped by the sharp mind of another.

By the time it was published T. E. Lawrence had changed his name by deed poll to T. E. Shaw, but clearly the encyclopaedia's editors, if they were aware of this, wanted a more recognisable attribution at its conclusion, hence the authorial formula at the end of the essay: T. E. L.A.

The article was preceded by a short piece under the title 'Guerrilla', written by 'TB', i.e. Sir Thomas Barclay, Vice President of the International Law Association and author of various works including the important book *International Law and Practice*.

Both the article and the introductory paragraph were reprinted in an anthology entitled *The Treasury of the Encyclopædia Britannica*, subtitled 'more than two centuries of facts, curiosities, and discoveries from the most distinguished reference work of all time' (Viking, New York, 1992). The editors commented that 'the element of personal experience that pervades the article is unusual in encyclopaedias but must have been the chief reason that this particular author was sought.'

The introductory piece by 'TB' is included here as it was in both earlier publications.

☞ U.S.ENGLISH wants YOU! Become a Guardian of Official English and join the ranks of our most dedicated members. Find out how you can make a difference on the local, state, and national level.

☐ **YES! I want to become a Guardian of Official English so that I can champion the cause.**

Credit Card Payment Option

Type of Card: ☐ VISA   ☐ MasterCard   ☐ American Express

Name as it Appears on Card: _____

Credit Card Number: _____

Exp. Date: _____ Amount: $ _____ Zip Code: _____

Signature: _____

Because U.S.ENGLISH, Inc. is a 501 (c) (4) nonprofit lobbying organization, contributions are not tax-deductible.

Paid for and copyrighted 2006, by U.S.ENGLISH, Inc.
www.usenglish.org

![U.S. ENGLISH, INC. logo]

U.S.ENGLISH, INC.

1747 Pennsylvania Ave., NW • Washington, DC 20006

CAST YOUR VOTE TODAY!

FOR AN OFFICIAL ENGLISH CONSTITUTIONAL AMENDMENT

INSTRUCTIONS: Please indicate whether you believe U.S.ENGLISH, Inc. should allocate our resources to support a constitutional amendment to establish English as the official language of the United States of America. Our course of action will be based on the tabulated results of this confidential, members-only Proxy Ballot. Thank you for your participation and your strong support.

[X] **Ballot No.:** 06G13D   [X] **Member No.:** 108742745

Signed: _____   **Date:** _____

Return by: June 3, 2006

108742745 XX06613D 2105010003

[X] **Ballot Issued To:**

Mr. Robert Silano
Apt. 228
2122 Massachusetts Ave. NW
Washington, DC 20008-2833

|..|.|||..||..|.|..|..||..||..|.|..|.|.|..|.|.|..||.|

[ ] **YES,** I fully agree, the politicians have failed to act for way too long. We must now take the strongest of all measures to preserve our national unity — **a constitutional amendment** establishing English as the official language of America forevermore. To help U.S.ENGLISH, Inc. dramatically expand this Official English campaign, I've enclosed my generous contribution of:

[ ] **$225**   [ ] **$150**

this amount would really help!

[ ] **$300**   [ ] **Other $** ___

[ ] NO, Mauro, I can't support a constitutional amendment at this time. But, to support U.S.ENGLISH, Inc.'s other vital Official English initiatives at the federal, state, and local levels, I've enclosed my special donation of:

[ ] **Other $** ___

Please make your check payable to U.S.ENGLISH, Inc. or complete the credit card information on back.

THIS PROXY BALLOT IN THE PRIORITY RETURN ENVELOPE

...make your contribution online, please visit our website at www.usenglish.org. U.S.ENGLISH,

GUERRILLA, a term currently used to denote war carried on by bands in any irregular and unorganised manner; erroneously written 'guerilla', being the diminutive of the Span[ish], *guerra*, war. The position of irregular combatants was one of the subjects dealt with at the Peace Conference of 1899, and the rules there adopted were reaffirmed at the conference of 1907. They provide that irregular bands in order to enjoy recognition as belligerent forces shall (a) have at their head a person responsible for his subordinates, (b) wear some fixed distinctive badge recognisable at a distance, (c) carry arms openly and (d) conform in their operations to the laws and customs of war. The rules, however, also provide that in case of invasion the inhabitants of a territory who on the approach of the invading enemy spontaneously take up arms to resist it, shall be regarded as belligerent troops if they carry arms openly and respect the laws and customs of war, although they may not have had time to become organised in accordance with the above provisions. These rules were borrowed almost word for word from the project drawn up at the Brussels international conference of 1874, which, though never ratified, was practically incorporated in the army regulations issued by the Russian government in connection with the war of 1877–8. (TB)

Science of Guerrilla Warfare
1929

This study of the science of guerrilla, or irregular, warfare is based on the concrete experience of the Arab revolt against the Turks 1916–18. But the historical example in turn gains value from the fact that its course was guided by the practical application of the theories here set forth.

The Arab revolt began in June 1916, with an attack by the half-armed and inexperienced tribesmen upon the Turkish garrisons in Medina and about Mecca. They met with no success, and after a few days' effort withdrew out of range and began a blockade. This method forced the early surrender of Mecca, the more remote of the two centres. Medina, however, was linked by railway to the Turkish main army in Syria, and the Turks were able to reinforce the garrison there. The Arab forces which had attacked it then fell back gradually and took up a position across the main road to Mecca.

At this point the campaign stood still for many weeks. The Turks prepared to send an expeditionary force to Mecca, to crush the revolt at its source, and accordingly moved an army corps to Medina by rail. Thence they began to advance down the main western road from Medina to Mecca, a distance of about 250 miles. The first fifty miles were easy, then came a belt of hills twenty miles wide, in which were Feisal's Arab tribesmen standing on the defensive: next a level stretch, for seventy miles along the coastal plain to Rabegh, rather more than half-way. Rabegh is a little port on the Red Sea, with good anchorage for ships, and because of its situation was regarded as the key to Mecca. Here lay Sherif Ali, Feisal's eldest brother, with more tribal forces, and the beginning of an Arab regular army, formed from officers and men of Arab blood who had served in the Turkish army. As was almost inevitable in view of the general course of military thinking since Napoleon, the soldiers of all countries looked only to the regulars to win the war. Military opinion was obsessed by the dictum of Foch that the ethic of modern war is to seek for the enemy's army, his centre of power, and destroy it in battle. Irregulars would not attack positions and so they were regarded as incapable of forcing a decision.

While these Arab regulars were still being trained, the Turks suddenly began their advance on Mecca. They broke through the hills in twenty-four hours, and so proved the second theorem of irregular war – namely, that irregular troops are as unable to defend a point or line as they are to attack it. This lesson was received without gratitude, for the Turkish success put the Rabegh force in a critical position, and it was not capable of repelling the attack of a single battalion, much less of a corps.

In the emergency it occurred to the author that perhaps the virtue of irregulars lay in depth, not in face, and that it had been the threat of attack by them upon the Turkish northern flank which had made the enemy hesitate for so long. The actual Turkish flank ran from their front line to Medina, a distance of some fifty miles: but, if the Arab force moved towards the Hejaz railway behind Medina, it might stretch its threat (and, accordingly, the enemy's flank) as far, potentially, as Damascus eight hundred miles away to the north. Such a move would force the Turks to the defensive, and the Arab force might regain the initiative. Anyhow, it seemed the only chance, and so, in Jan. 1917, Feisal's tribesmen turned their backs on Mecca, Rabegh and the Turks, and marched away north two hundred miles to Wejh.

This eccentric movement acted like a charm. The Arabs did nothing concrete, but their march recalled the Turks (who were almost into Rabegh) all the way back to Medina. There, one half of the Turkish force took up the entrenched position about the city, which it held until after the armistice. The other half was distributed along the railway to defend it against the Arab threat. For the rest of the war the Turks stood on the defensive and the Arab tribesmen won advantage over advantage till, when peace came, they had taken 35,000 prisoners, killed and wounded and worn out about as many, and occupied one hundred thousand square miles of the enemy's territory, at little loss to themselves. However, although Wejh was the turning-point its significance was not yet realised. For the moment the move thither was regarded merely as a preliminary to cutting the railway in order to take Medina, the Turkish headquarters and main garrison.

Strategy and Tactics

However, the author was unfortunately as much in charge of the campaign as he pleased, and lacking a training in command sought to find an immediate equation between past study of military theory and the present movements as a guide to, and an intellectual basis for, future action. The text books gave the aim in war as 'the destruction of the organised forces of the enemy' by 'the one process battle'. Victory could only be purchased by blood. This was a hard saying as the Arabs had no organised forces, and so a Turkish Foch would have no aim: and the Arabs would not endure casualties, so that an Arab Clausewitz could not buy his victory. These wise men must be talking metaphors, for the Arabs were indubitably winning their war . . . and further reflection pointed to the deduction that they had actually won it. They were in occupation of 99 per cent of the Hejaz. The Turks were welcome to the other fraction till peace or doomsday showed them the futility of clinging to the window pane. This part of the war was over, so why bother about Medina? The Turks sat in it on the defensive, immobile, eating for food the transport animals which were to have moved them to Mecca, but for which there was no pasture in their now restricted lines. They were harmless sitting there; if taken prisoner, they would entail the cost of food and guards in Egypt: if driven out northward into Syria, they would join the main army blocking the British in Sinai. On all counts they were best where they were, and they valued Medina and wanted to keep it. Let them!

This seemed unlike the ritual of war of which Foch had been priest, and so it seemed that there was a difference of kind. Foch called his modern war 'absolute'. In it two nations professing incompatible philosophies set out to try them in the light of force. A struggle of two immaterial principles could only end when the supporters of one had no more means of resistance. An opinion can be argued with: a conviction is best shot. The logical end of a war of creeds is the final destruction of one, and Salammbô the classical textbook-instance. These were the lines of the struggle between France and Germany, but not, perhaps, between Germany and England, for all efforts to make the British soldier hate the enemy simply made him hate war. Thus the 'absolute war' seemed only a variety of war; and beside it other sorts could be discerned, as Clausewitz had numbered them, personal wars for dynastic reasons, expulsive wars for party reasons, commercial wars for trading reasons.

Now the Arab aim was unmistakably geographical, to occupy all Arabic-speaking lands in Asia. In the doing of it Turks might be killed, yet 'killing Turks' would never be an excuse or aim. If they would go quietly, the war would end. If not, they must be driven out: but at the cheapest possible price, since the Arabs were fighting for freedom, a pleasure only to be tasted by a man alive. The next task was to analyse the process, both from the point of view of strategy, the aim in war, the synoptic regard which sees everything by the standard of the whole, and from the point of view called tactics, the means towards the strategic end, the steps of its staircase. In each were found the same elements, one algebraical, one biological, a third psychological. The first seemed a pure science, subject to the laws of mathematics, without humanity. It dealt with known invariables, fixed conditions, space and time, inorganic things like hills and climates and railways, with mankind in type-masses too great for individual variety, with all artificial aids, and the extensions given our faculties by mechanical invention. It was essentially formulable.

In the Arab case the algebraic factor would take first account of the area to be conquered. A casual calculation indicated perhaps 140,000 square miles. How would the Turks defend all that – no doubt by a trench line across the bottom, if the Arabs were an army attacking with banners displayed . . . but suppose they were an influence, a thing invulnerable, intangible, without front or back, drifting about like a gas? Armies were like plants, immobile as a whole, firm-rooted, nourished through long stems to the head. The Arabs might be a vapour, blowing where they listed. It seemed that a regular soldier might be helpless without a target. He would own the ground he sat on, and what he could poke his rifle at. The next step was to estimate how many posts they would need to contain this attack in depth, sedition putting up her head in every unoccupied one of these hundred thousand square miles. They would have need of a fortified post every four square miles, and a post could not be less than twenty men. The Turks would need six hundred thousand men to meet the combined ill wills of all the local Arab people. They had one hundred thousand men available. It seemed that the assets in this sphere were with the Arabs, and climate, railways, deserts, technical weapons could also be attached to their interests. The Turk was stupid and would believe that rebellion was absolute, like war, and deal with it on the analogy of absolute warfare.

Humanity in Battle

So much for the mathematical element; the second factor was biological, the breaking-point, life and death, or better, wear and tear. Bionomics seemed a good name for it. The war-philosophers had properly made it an art and had elevated one item in it, 'effusion of blood', to the height of a principle. It became humanity in battle, an art touching every side of our corporal being. There was a line of variability (man) running through all its estimates. Its components were sensitive and illogical, and generals guarded themselves by the device of a reserve, the significant medium of their art. Goltz had said that when you know the enemy's strength, and he is fully deployed, then you know enough to dispense with a reserve. But this is never. There is always the possibility of accident, of some flaw in materials, present in the general's mind: and the reserve is unconsciously held to meet it. There is a 'felt' element in troops, not expressible in figures, and the greatest commander is he whose intuitions most nearly happen. Nine-tenths of tactics are certain, and taught in books: but the irrational tenth is like the kingfisher flashing across the pool and that is the test of generals. It can only be ensued by instinct, sharpened by thought practising the stroke so often that at the crisis it is as natural as a reflex.

Yet to limit the art to humanity seemed an undue narrowing down. It must apply to materials as much as to organisms. In the Turkish army materials were scarce and precious, men more plentiful than equipment. Consequently the cue should be to destroy not the army but the materials. The death of a Turkish bridge or rail, machine or gun, or high explosive was more profitable than the death of a Turk. The Arab army just then was equally chary of men and materials: of men because they being irregulars were not units, but individuals, and an individual casualty is like a pebble dropped in water: each may make only a brief hole, but rings of sorrow widen out from them. The Arab army could not afford casualties. Materials were easier to deal with. Hence its obvious duty to make itself superior in some one branch, guncotton or machine-guns, or whatever could be more decisive. Foch had laid down the maxim, applying it to men, being superior at the critical point and moment of attack. The Arab army might apply it to materials, and be superior in equipment in one dominant moment or respect.

For both men and things it might try to give Foch's doctrine a negative twisted side, for cheapness' sake, and be weaker than the enemy everywhere except in one point or matter. Most wars are wars of contact, both forces striving to keep in touch to avoid tactical surprise. The Arab war should be a war of detachment to contain the enemy by the silent threat of a vast unknown desert, not disclosing themselves till the moment of attack. The attack need be only nominal, directed not against his men, but against his materials: so it should not seek for his main strength or his weaknesses, but for his most accessible material. In railway cutting this would be usually an empty stretch of rail. This was a tactical success. From this theory came to be developed ultimately an unconscious habit of never engaging the enemy at all. This chimed with the numerical plea of never giving the enemy's soldier a target. Many Turks on the Arab front had no chance all the war to fire a shot, and correspondingly the Arabs were never on the defensive, except by rare accident. The corollary of such a rule was perfect 'intelligence', so that plans could be made in complete certainty. The chief agent had to be the general's head (de Feuquière said this first), and his knowledge had to be faultless, leaving no room for chance. The headquarters of the Arab army probably took more pains in this service than any other staff.

The Crowd in Action

The third factor in command seemed to be the psychological, that science (Xenophon called it diathetic) of which our propaganda is a stained and ignoble part. It concerns the crowd, the adjustment of spirit to the point where it becomes fit to exploit in action. It considers the capacity for mood of the men, their complexities and mutability, and the cultivation of what in them profits the intention. The command of the Arab army had to arrange their men's minds in order of battle just as carefully and as formally as other officers arranged the bodies: and not only their own men's minds, though them first: the mind of the enemy, so far as it could reach them: and thirdly the mind of the nation supporting it behind the firing line, and the mind of the hostile nation waiting the verdict, and the neutral looking on.

It was the ethical in war, and the process on which the command mainly depended for victory on the Arab front. The printing press is the greatest weapon in the armoury of the modern commander, and the commanders of the Arab army being amateurs in the art, began their war in the atmosphere of the twentieth century, and thought of their weapons without prejudice, not distinguishing one from another socially. The regular officer has the tradition of forty generations of serving soldiers behind him, and to him the old weapons are the most honoured. The Arab command had seldom to concern itself with what its men did, but much with what they thought, and to it the diathetic was more than half command. In Europe it was set a little aside and entrusted to men outside the General Staff. But the Arab army was so weak physically that it could not let the metaphysical weapon rust unused. It had won a province when the civilians in it had been taught to die for the ideal of freedom: the presence or absence of the enemy was a secondary matter.

These reasonings showed that the idea of assaulting Medina, or even of starving it quickly into surrender, was not in accord with the best strategy. Rather, let the enemy stay in Medina, and in every other harmless place, in the largest numbers. If he showed a disposition to evacuate too soon, as a step to concentrating in the small area which his numbers could dominate effectively, then the Arab army would have to try and restore his confidence, not harshly, but by reducing its enterprises against him. The ideal was to keep his railway just working, but only just, with the maximum of loss and discomfort to him.

The Turkish army was an accident, not a target. Our true strategic aim was to seek its weakest link, and bear only on that till time made the mass of it fall. The Arab army must impose the longest possible passive defence on the Turks (this being the most materially expensive form of war) by extending its own front to the maximum. Tactically it must develop a highly mobile, highly equipped type of force, of the smallest size, and use it successively at distributed points of the Turkish line, to make the Turks reinforce their occupying posts beyond the economic minimum of twenty men. The power of this striking force would not be reckoned merely by its strength. The ratio between number and area determined the character of the war, and by having five times the mobility of the Turks the Arabs could be on terms with them with one-fifth their number.

Range over Force

Success was certain, to be proved by paper and pencil as soon as the proportion of space and number had been learned. The contest was not physical, but moral, and so battles were a mistake. All that could be won in a battle was the ammunition the enemy fired off. Napoleon had said it was rare to find generals willing to fight battles. The curse of this war was that so few could do anything else. Napoleon had spoken in angry reaction against the excessive finesse of the eighteenth century, when men almost forgot that war gave licence to murder. Military thought had been swinging out on his dictum for a hundred years, and it was time to go back a bit again. Battles are impositions on the side which believes itself weaker, made unavoidable either by lack of land-room, or by the need to defend a material property dearer than the lives of soldiers. The Arabs had nothing material to lose, so they were to defend nothing and to shoot nothing. Their cards were speed and time, not hitting power, and these gave them strategical rather than tactical strength. Range is more to strategy than force. The invention of bully-beef had modified land-war more profoundly than the invention of gunpowder.

The British military authorities did not follow all these arguments, but gave leave for their practical application to be tried. Accordingly the Arab forces went off first to Akaba and took it easily. Then they took Tafileh and the Dead Sea; then Azrak and Deraa, and finally Damascus, all in successive stages worked out consciously on these theories. The process was to set up ladders of tribes, which should provide a safe and comfortable route from the sea-bases (Yenbo, Wejh or Akaba) to the advanced bases of operation. These were sometimes three hundred miles away, a long distance in lands without railways or roads, but made short for the Arab army by an assiduous cultivation of desert-power, control by camel parties of the desolate and unmapped wilderness which fills up all the centre of Arabia, from Mecca to Aleppo and Baghdad.

The Desert and the Sea

In character these operations were like naval warfare, in their mobility, their ubiquity, their independence of bases and communications, in their ignoring of ground features, of strategic areas, of fixed directions, of fixed points. 'He who commands the sea is at great liberty, and may take as much or as little of the war as he will': he who commands the desert is equally fortunate. Camel raiding parties, self-contained like ships, could cruise securely along the enemy's land-frontier, just out of sight of his posts along the edge of cultivation, and tap or raid into his lines where it seemed fittest or easiest or most profitable, with a sure retreat always behind them into an element which the Turks could not enter.

Discrimination of what point of the enemy organism to disarrange came with practice. The tactics were always tip and run; not pushes, but strokes. The Arab army never tried to maintain or improve an advantage, but to move off and strike again somewhere else. It used the smallest force in the quickest time at the farthest place. To continue the action till the enemy had changed his dispositions to resist it would have been to break the spirit of the fundamental rule of denying him targets.

The necessary speed and range were attained by the frugality of the desert men, and their efficiency on camels. In the heat of summer Arabian camels will do about 250 miles comfortably between drinks: and this represented three days' vigorous marching. This radius was always more than was needed, for wells are seldom more than one hundred miles apart. The equipment of the raiding parties aimed at simplicity, with nevertheless a technical superiority over the Turks in the critical department. Quantities of light machine-guns were obtained from Egypt for use not as machine-guns, but as automatic rifles, snipers' tools, by men kept deliberately in ignorance of their mechanism, so that the speed of action would not be hampered by attempts at repair. Another special feature was high explosives, and nearly everyone in the revolt was qualified by rule of thumb experience in demolition work.

Armoured Cars

On some occasions tribal raids were strengthened by armoured cars, manned by Englishmen. Armoured cars, once they have found a possible track, can keep up with a camel party. On the march to Damascus, when nearly four hundred miles off their base, they were first maintained by a baggage train of petrol-laden camels, and afterwards from the air. Cars are magnificent fighting machines, and decisive whenever they can come into action on their own conditions. But though each has for main principle that of 'fire in movement', yet the tactical employments of cars and camel corps are so different that their use in joint operations is difficult. It was found demoralising to both to use armoured and unarmoured cavalry together.

The distribution of the raiding parties was unorthodox. It was impossible to mix or combine tribes, since they disliked or distrusted one another. Likewise the men of one tribe could not be used in the territory of another. In consequence, another canon of orthodox strategy was broken by following the principle of the widest distribution of force, in order to have the greatest number of raids on hand at once, and fluidity was added to speed by using one district on Monday, another on Tuesday, a third on Wednesday. This much reinforced the natural mobility of the Arab army, giving it priceless advantages in pursuit, for the force renewed itself with fresh men in every new tribal area, and so maintained its pristine energy. Maximum disorder was, in a real sense, its equilibrium.

An Undisciplined Army

The internal economy of raiding parties was equally curious. Maximum irregularity and articulation were the aims. Diversity threw the enemy intelligence off the track. By the regular organisation in identical battalions and divisions information builds itself up, until the presence of a corps can be inferred on corpses from three companies. The Arabs, again, were serving a common ideal, without tribal emulation, and so could not hope for any *esprit de corps*. Soldiers are made a caste either by being given great pay and rewards in money, uniform or political privileges; or, as in England, by being made outcasts, cut off from the mass of their fellow-citizens. There have been many armies enlisted voluntarily: there have been few armies serving voluntarily under such trying conditions, for so long a war as the Arab revolt. Any of the Arabs could go home whenever the conviction failed him. Their only contract was honour.

Consequently the Arab army had no discipline, in the sense in which it is restrictive, submergent of individuality, the lowest common denominator of men. In regular armies in peace it means the limit of energy attainable by everybody present: it is the hunt not of an average, but of an absolute, a 100-per-cent standard, in which the ninety-nine stronger men are played down to the level of the worst. The aim is to render the unit a unit, and the man a type, in order that their effort shall be calculable, their collective output even in grain and in bulk. The deeper the discipline, the lower the individual efficiency, and the more sure the performance. It is a deliberate sacrifice of capacity in order to reduce the uncertain element, the bionomic factor, in enlisted humanity, and its accompaniment is *compound* or social war, that form in which the fighting man has to be the product of the multiplied exertions of long hierarchy, from workshop to supply unit, which maintains him in the field.

The Arab war, reacting against this, was *simple* and individual. Every enrolled man served in the line of battle, and was self-contained. There were no lines of communication or labour troops. It seemed that in this articulated warfare, the sum yielded by single men would be at least equal to the product of a compound system of the same strength, and it was certainly easier to adjust to tribal life and manners, given elasticity and understanding on the part of the commanding officers. Fortunately for its chances nearly every young Englishman has the roots of eccentricity in him. Only a sprinkling were employed, not more than one per thousand of the Arab troops. A larger proportion would have created friction, just because they were foreign bodies (pearls if you please) in the oyster: and those who were present controlled by influence and advice, by their superior knowledge, not by an extraneous authority.

The practice was, however, not to employ in the firing line the greater numbers which the adoption of a 'simple' system made available theoretically. Instead, they were used in relay: otherwise the attack would have become too extended. Guerrillas must be allowed liberal work-room. In irregular war if two men are together one is being wasted. The moral strain of isolated action makes this simple form of war very hard on the individual soldier, and exacts from him special initiative, endurance and enthusiasm. Here the ideal was to make action a series of single combats to make the ranks a happy alliance of commanders-in-chief. The value of the Arab army depended entirely on quality, not on quantity. The members had to keep always cool for the excitement of a blood-lust would impair their Science, and their victory depended on a just use of speed, concealment, accuracy of fire. Guerrilla war is far more intellectual than a bayonet charge.

The Exact Science of Guerrilla Warfare

By careful persistence, kept strictly within its strength and following the spirit of these theories, the Arab army was able eventually to reduce the Turks to helplessness, and complete victory seemed to be almost within sight when General Allenby by his immense stroke in Palestine threw the enemy's main forces into hopeless confusion and put an immediate end to the Turkish war. His too-greatness deprived the Arab revolt of the opportunity of following to the end the dictum of Saxe that a war might be won without fighting battles. But it can at least be said that its leaders worked by his light for two years, and the work stood. This is a pragmatic argument that cannot be wholly derided. The experiment, although not complete, strengthened the belief that irregular war or rebellion could be proved to be an exact science, and an inevitable success, granted certain factors and if pursued along certain lines.

Here is the thesis: rebellion must have an unassailable base, something guarded not merely from attack, but from the fear of it: such a base as the Arab revolt had in the Red Sea ports, the desert, or in the minds of men converted to its creed. It must have a sophisticated alien enemy, in the form of a disciplined army of occupation too small to fulfil the doctrine of acreage: too few to adjust number to space, in order to dominate the whole area effectively from fortified posts. It must have a friendly population, not actively friendly, but sympathetic to the point of not betraying rebel movements to the enemy. Rebellions can be made by 2 per cent active in a striking force, and 98 per cent passively sympathetic. The few active rebels must have the qualities of speed and endurance, ubiquity and independence of arteries of supply. They must have the technical equipment to destroy or paralyse the enemy's organised communications, for irregular war is fairly Willisen's definition of strategy, 'the study of communication', in its extreme degree, of attack where the enemy is not. In fifty words: granted mobility, security (in the form of denying targets to the enemy), time, and doctrine (the idea to convert every subject to friendliness), victory will rest with the insurgents, for the algebraical factors are in the end decisive, and against them perfections of means and spirit struggle quite in vain.

(T. E. L.A.)

Appendix A

The *Arab Bulletin*

by D. G. Hogarth

(from issue no. 100, 20 August 1918)

Mentor to us all was Hogarth, our father confessor and adviser, who brought us the parallels and lessons of history, and moderation, and courage. To the outsiders he was peacemaker (I was all claws and teeth, and had a devil) and made us favoured and listened to, for his weighty judgement . . . Hogarth was our referee, and our untiring historian, who gave us his great knowledge and careful wisdom even in the smallest things, because he believed in what we were making.

Seven Pillars of Wisdom, Ch. 6

Hogarth took some time to find a suitable wartime role, eventually finding it in the newly created Geographical Section of the Naval Intelligence Division (hence his naval rank), the main task of which was the compiling of geographical handbooks for intelligence purposes. By the end of 1918 more than fifty volumes had been produced, acquiring a high reputation for accuracy and impartiality. Hogarth contributed an authoritative two-volume *Handbook of Arabia* to this series. At the same time he was responsible for similar reports prepared for the Military Intelligence Department, Cairo (e.g. two reports on the Marmara region of Turkey) and for handbooks issued under the aegis of the Arab Bureau, notably a *Handbook of Hejaz* which made extensive use of material from the *Arab Bulletin* (such as Lawrence's descriptions of Feisal and his brothers in Item VI of *Secret Despatches*). In addition he was much involved in establishing the format, style and tone of the *Arab Bulletin*, and was therefore the obvious person to sum up that journal's achievements in its hundredth number.

The 'intervals of absence' mentioned in paragraph five refer to periods in 1916 when he was in London co-ordinating the work on these various publications; his appointment to a similar intelligence role in 1917 at General Allenby's headquarters

in Palestine also took him away from regular contact with the *Bulletin*, though
the initials 'DGH' continued to appear under important articles to the end of the
campaign.

The Arab Bulletin

Our hundredth number offers occasion and excuse for a retrospect of the
career of the *Arab Bulletin* since it started more than two years ago. It has
changed its character in some respects during that period, as it has changed
its name: for it began as *Arab Bureau Summaries* published under the
authority of the Foreign Office, but in connection with the General Staffs at
that time. The Arab Bureau which had barely attained to a separate existence, was dovetailed into the Military Intelligence Office, Cairo, directed by
Brig.-Gen. G. F. Clayton, and widely known by its telegraphic address,
'INTRUSIVE'. The headquarters of the General Staff, then at Ismailia, issued
an *Intelligence Bulletin*, and to this *Arab Bureau Summaries* were originally
intended to be a supplement, the first suggestion of them having been made
by Captain, now Lieut.-Colonel T. E. Lawrence.

Half-a-dozen numbers followed the General Staff model, being typewritten by the Roneo process. The idea of printing soon arose, partly owing to
imperfect execution of the reproductive process, which made the sheets difficult to read, but more from the existence of a small confidential military
staff at the Government Press, which, having at that time light work, was
able to take on the printing of the *Arab Bureau Summaries* as its chief duty.
For the first number so printed, a new name, *Arab Bulletin* was adopted, and
when the earlier typewritten issues were printed off immediately afterwards
to complete the set, the name was made retrospective.

It had been proposed at first to issue numbers, not every day like the
Intelligence Bulletin of the General Staff, but at short irregular intervals, as
necessary matter came in. Seven numbers accordingly appeared in twenty-
four days of June 1916. But the adoption of printing inevitably retarded production, though the Press gave every facility, and by October the *Bulletin* had
fallen to four numbers a month. A year later even this rate proved for a time
impossible to maintain, as the confidential work thrown by the General Staff
and the Admiralty on the Government Press increased rapidly. The difficulties became so great in the latter part of 1917, that the *Bulletin* was on
the point of either returning to Roneo or disappearing altogether.
Fortunately, however, other pressure decreased at the Press, and it became
possible again to produce a weekly issue. On the whole this rate has been
sustained up to the present, the Press doing its part regularly and promptly
if the Editor does likewise.

Since it was as easy to write it in decent English as in bad, and much more
agreeable, the *Arab Bulletin* had from the first a literary tinge not always
present in intelligence summaries. This quality turned, in one respect, to its
disadvantage. Coupled with good type and paper, it seems to have impaired

the respect paid to the confidential character of the *Bulletin* by some of its limited circle of recipients. The Arab Bureau soon learned that its publication was in gratifying, but very inconvenient, demand. It began to go the round of large departments, both military and civil; it was not always kept within official precincts; and unauthorised knowledge of its existence led to certain demands to see it regularly, which could not be resisted. Towards the end of 1917 the list of recipients was revised and restricted, and other precautions were taken to preclude the dangers of over-circulation; but some uncertainty how far it goes still remains to render the task of editing delicate and difficult.

This uncertainty, added to the comparative slowness of the production of this *Bulletin*, and the ever increasing interval which the Editor knows must elapse between the date of its production and the date of its delivery into the hands of most recipients, led to considerable modification of its original purpose. Instituted as a summary of the latest Arab intelligence, it has developed rather into a medium of considered appreciations. Its actual reason for existence, as it appears to the present writer (its first editor, who has continued to edit it ever since except during certain intervals of absence from Cairo) is threefold.

Firstly, it aims at giving reasoned, and as far as possible definitive, summaries of intelligence, primarily about the Hejaz and the area of the Arab revolt (Cairo being in closer touch with this than with other Arab areas), and secondarily about the other Arab-speaking countries – such summaries to be compiled, as far as possible, by those in possession of all news, secret or otherwise, but not necessarily to contain all that news. In practice, however, it has not been found possible for the staff to deal equally with all, or nearly all, the Arab-speaking area. Arab Africa, for instance for which it is dependent on the Force in Egypt's Intelligence and the Frontier Districts Administration, has passed more and more out [of] the *Bulletin*'s purview. That part of Syria, which is still in enemy hands, can hardly be dealt with at all to any good purpose. Mesopotamia and Iraq are left to the MEF and the Mesopotamian Political Department, except as regards affairs east of the Euphrates. On most of the Gulf regions, for which we are dependent on the government of India, information is seldom vouchsafed. In the beginning the *Arab Bulletin* had taken on too wide a field: and some distant areas outside the special competence of its members have had to be jettisoned – for example, Persia. Others, like Abyssinia and Somaliland, which were introduced later into its scope, had better be dropped out of it again, since the Arab Bureau can add little or nothing to the official reports circulated independently.

Secondly, the *Arab Bulletin* aims at giving authoritative appreciations of political situations and questions in the area with which it can deal at first hand.

Thirdly, it aims at recording, and so preserving, all fresh historical data concerning Arabs and Arab-speaking lands, and, incidentally, rescuing from oblivion any older facts which may help to explain the actual situation: likewise, any data of geographical or other scientific interest, which may be brought to light by our penetration of the Arab countries during the present war. It is part of the Editor's purpose that a complete file of the *Bulletin* since its beginning should be indispensable to anyone who hereafter may have to compile, for official use, a history of Arabs during the last three years, an intelligence handbook of any Arab district, or even a map of Arabia. As full an index as possible has been issued at the end of each year, on the presumption that departments and officials receiving the *Bulletin*, keep complete files, and have these bound for future reference. We have some reason to know that this presumption is not altogether justified.

Needless to say, this threefold aim has neither been kept always in view nor fully realised. Nor has it been possible to act up to any respectable standard of Arab scholarship – the variant orthography, which each index reveals, would refute any such claim! But the fact that the *Bulletin* has been suffered to reach its hundredth number and approach a thousand and a half pages, may be taken as consolatory evidence that it fills a felt want in the present war.

The Editorship of the Arab Bulletin

Hogarth states clearly (paragraph five above) that he was the principal editor of the *Arab Bulletin* and he is named as the 'regular editor' by A. W. Lawrence in his Foreword. However, two editions bore the name of T. E. Lawrence on the contents page and for most of the war the *Bulletin* appeared over the name of the Director of the Arab Bureau, Captain (later Major) Kinahan (later Sir Kinahan) Cornwallis. For interest, all the officers named in this way are listed below. With one exception all editions were datelined 'Arab Bureau, Savoy Hotel, Cairo'.

Edition no. 1	Captain T. E. Lawrence, for Director, Arab Bureau
2–8	Lt-Cmdr D. G. Hogarth, RNVR, Acting Director, Arab Bureau
9	Captain T. E. Lawrence, for Director, Arab Bureau
10–12	Lt-Cmdr D. G. Hogarth, RNVR, Director, Arab Bureau
13–16	Lt-Cmdr D. G. Hogarth, RNVR, Acting Director, Arab Bureau
17–24	K. Cornwallis, Captain, Director, Arab Bureau
25–111	K. Cornwallis, Major, Director, Arab Bureau
112	C. A. G. Mackintosh, Major, A/Director, Arab Bureau
113–14	H. Garland, Captain, A/Director, Arab Bureau

Appendix B

Foreword to the First Edition of *Secret Despatches*

by A. W. Lawrence

With the exception of the article 'Syrian Cross-Currents' which has not hitherto been printed, the contents of this volume were included in the confidential paper called *The Arab Bulletin* which was issued at Cairo from 6 June 1916 to 6 December 1918. According to an editorial in the hundredth number, Captain T. E. Lawrence originated the idea of the paper. To supplement an *Intelligence Bulletin* circulated by the General Staff of the Egyptian Expeditionary Force, the Arab Bureau (a branch of the Intelligence) began producing *Summaries* of political news received from the Turkish Empire, Arab and other Moslem countries, and Abyssinia. After six of these had been issued in typescript, in rapid succession, the *Bulletin* received its final title and shape as a printed magazine. Henceforth its tendency was to appear at less frequent intervals and to contain articles of more lasting value. Of the first few numbers only twenty-six copies were printed, for distribution to the British authorities – civil, military or naval – in the Near and Middle East, and to the Foreign Office, War Office and Admiralty in London; the contents were to be treated as 'strictly secret'. Later, the *Arab Bulletin* obtained a wider circulation. The names of contributors were then stated freely, whereas in the early issues articles were not signed nor even initialled; isolated instances do however occur in No. 9, and it may be significant that this (as well as No. 1) appeared under the imprint of 'T. E. Lawrence, Captain. For Director, Arab Bureau'. The regular editor was D. G. Hogarth.

In his own set of the *Bulletin* T. E. Lawrence noted the authorship of a large number of unsigned articles. He is thereby known to have been responsible for at least ten items, before he left the office to participate in the Arab revolt; and one anonymous report, upon negotiations at the fall of Kut, is also plainly his work (it has been published by David Garnett, *The Letters of T. E. Lawrence*, page 208). As these early articles do not come within the scope of the present volume, some particulars may usefully be given here.

No. 9   9 July 1916. Page 82. Article entitled 'Hejaz News'. Author's
             manuscript notes: *July* corrected to *June*, page 83, line 8; *TEL* at
             end, page 84.
             Page 85. 'Translation of Proclamation . . . by the Sherif.'
             Englished by TEL at end, page 88.

No. 18   5 September. Page 206. 'Note by Cairo' (on the handling of
             oriental labour). *TEL* at end, page 207.
             Page 210. 'Hejaz Narrative', *TEL* at end.

No. 22   19 September. Page 263. 'Further information of the Stotzingen
             Mission.' *Papers interpreted by P. Graves and TEL* at end of
             documents, page 272. 'Conclusion' *by TEL*, page 272; *TEL* at
             end, page 274.
             Page 276. 'Summary of Information Given by Turkish Prisoners
             Captured at Bir Aar.' *TEL* at end, page 278.

No. 23   26 September. Page 291. 'Notes' (on Diary of 1st Lieut. Grobba).
             TEL at end.
             Page 304. 'Note by Cairo' (on Arab and Turk Dispositions).
             TEL at end.

No. 26   16 October. Page 372. 'Note' (on Hejaz situation). *TEL* at end,
             page 373.

This edition includes all material ascribed to T. E. Lawrence, either by the text of the *Arab Bulletin* or by his own marginal notes, after the time of his first visit to the Hejaz. His manuscript notes have been reproduced in italics inside square brackets, except for some verbal corrections which have been incorporated in the new text. The only omissions are: some cross references inserted by the original editor of the *Bulletin*; a superfluous *neither* in the manuscript paragraph of 'Military Notes' (in the second sentence, which read *can neither increase neither their number*); in 'The Sherifial Northern Army', the word *Damascene* correcting the description *Bagdadi Officer* which is written in an unidentified handwriting beside the name of Rasim; do. in the same handwriting on the following line (about Abdullah). On the authority of *Seven Pillars of Wisdom* the text of 'The Raid at Haret Ammar' has been altered to read *ten box-wagons* instead of *two*, and *upended into the hole* instead of *the whole*. No doubt many other slips remain uncorrected, for as a rule the proofs cannot have been read by the writer. Comparison with his later accounts of the same incidents is not always helpful because of the extent to which they were re-written. The first of the post-war versions was impersonal and picturesque, to suit its purpose; it occupies three unsigned articles in *The Times*, of 26, 27 and 28 November 1918. Into *Seven Pillars of Wisdom* he introduced a personal element which had been excluded from the despatches, and in places the tone is completely different. An extreme instance is the treatment of the battle of Seil el-Hasa, the despatch on which had been composed as a bitter parody (according to the last sentences of Chapter 86 of the public edition); and after the award of a DSO on the strength of it, his reports on the remainder of the campaign tended to minimise his own share in events.

For the benefit of anyone who may consult the *Bulletin*, the following is a complete list of changes now made in the text on the authority of the manuscript notes. In 'Military Notes', *600* for *1,500* as the number of Arab infantry in the Turkish forces. In 'Raids on the Railway', *Mufaddhil* for *Mufaddlil*, *Tleih* for *Tleib*, *Serum* for (one occurrence only of) *Serun*, *Unseila* for *Unseih* (this correction is in an unidentified handwriting), Arabic letter *qaf* for *j*. In 'Wejh to Wadi Ais and Back', *bulging* for *bulbous, 8 a.m.* for *Sam*.

The very sincere thanks of the publishers and editor are due to Sir Stephen Gaselee, in his capacity of Librarian of the Foreign Office, for allowing the publication of official material previously held secret; and to Mr Philip P. Graves, part author of 'The Turkish Hejaz Forces and Their Reinforcement'.

Notes to the Secret Despatches

Abbreviations

AB *Arab Bulletin*

JW Jeremy Wilson, *Lawrence of Arabia: The Authorised Biography* (Heinemann, London, 1989; paperback Minerva, London, 1990)

MB Malcolm Brown (ed.), *The Letters of T. E. Lawrence* (Dent, London, 1988; paperback Oxford University Press, Oxford, 1991); published in the USA as *T. E. Lawrence: The Selected Letters* (Norton, New York, 1989; Paragon Press, New York, 1991)

SD T. E. Lawrence, *Secret Despatches from Arabia* (Golden Cockerel, London, 1939)

SP T. E. Lawrence, *Seven Pillars of Wisdom* (Jonathan Cape, London, 1935)

Secret Despatches from Arabia

I. Letter from Sherif Feisal

AB 29, 8 November 1916, I, 418

This despatch was written in accordance with the discussion mentioned in the following article, as shown by the marginal note 'Oct. 24, T.E.L. and Feisal'.

Ali was the eldest of the four sons of Sherif Hussein of Mecca, Feisal III. See 'Personal Notes on the Sherifial Family' (pp. 79–80) for Lawrence's descriptions of all four brothers.

II. Extracts from a Diary of a Journey

AB 31, 18 November 1916, I, 454–60

This and the following five reports all resulted from Lawrence's first visit to Arabia, 16 October–4 November 1916 – a remarkable outpouring of some twenty thousand words of which it could be rightly claimed that they affected the whole course of the Arabian campaign. They relate to *SP*, Book I, 'The Discovery of Feisal'.

An editorial note preceding this first report, entitled 'Arabia/Hejaz/ Summary of News', presents a more hopeful update of the situation as described in somewhat pessimistic terms by Lawrence:

> The scare which was circulated at Rabegh during the last week in October has died down, and there seems little cause for immediate anxiety . . . Reports show that the Turkish advanced headquarters are still at Bir Derwash, and that there

is a distinct shortage there of cereals, meat and forage. Feisal reports negotiations with the Billi and seems somewhat confident of winning them to the
Sherif's [i.e. Sherif Hussein's] side.

III. Extracts from a Report on Feisal's Operations

AB 31, 18 November 1916, I, 460–5
As stated in his Foreword, A. W. Lawrence restored certain manuscript notes by
TEL, printing them in italics between square brackets – though it was clearly not
his intention to make good all editorial omissions or alterations. In the case of this
report some passages which he did not restore are perhaps worth redeeming, being
part of what was clearly a first formulation of Lawrence's important affirmatory
statement in SP, Ch. 15, pp. 107–8: 'At these close quarters the bigness of the revolt
impressed me etc., etc.'

SD has an insert as follows (see p. 72): '[Looked at locally the bigness of the Revolt
impresses me] – followed by a line space, evidently indicating an intentional omission; the original text, as preserved in the copy of the report held in the Public Record
Office (FO 882/5), reads: 'A thing which has struck me rather forcibly while in the
Hejaz is the bigness of the revolt. Looked at from Egypt it loses some of its proportion, in our engrossment in the office telephones, and canal defence, and the communiqués. Yet here we have a well peopled province' (text continues as printed).

A second passage worth redeeming occurs eight lines later after the phrase 'a Holy
War against us'; here the original text continues: 'and fighting them [i.e. the Turks]
with the full and friendly consciousness that we are with them and are on their side.'

A third passage occurs as a new paragraph at the end of the next sentence, following the phrase 'behind the firing line' and before the italicised sentences in square
brackets. It reads:

> The Beduin of the Hejaz is not, outwardly, a probable vehicle for abstract or
> altruistic ideas. Yet again and again I have heard from them about acts of the
> early Arabs or things that the Sherif and his sons have said, which contain all
> that the exalted Arab patriot would wish. They intend to restore the Sheria [i.e.
> Islamic religious law], to revive the Arab language, and to rebuild the prosper-
> ity of the country.

The thought occurs that perhaps Lawrence's enthusiasm was too much even for
his sympathetic Cairo editors.

IV. Sherif Hussein's Administration

AB 32, 26 November 1916, I, 474–8
It is noteworthy that, as in the extract quoted above, Lawrence used the form 'Sherif
Hussein', not the more imposing 'Grand Sherif Hussein' frequently adopted. On this
point D. G. Hogarth's Handbook of Hejaz offers an interesting comment:

> 'Grand Sherif' is a European invention. The Arabs have always called the prince
> of Mecca 'Emir' and addressed him as Seyyidna (Our Lord). [Note: Lawrence
> uses a variant translation of this form 'Sayidna' in 'Personal Notes on the
> Sherifial Family' (pp. 79–80).] From the Turks he had the titles 'Highness' and
> 'Pasha', his sons being commonly called 'Beys' [as in 'Letter from Sherif Feisal'
> (pp. 61–2)]. These Ottoman titles, however, are no longer used in Hejaz, and,
> if any title is prefixed to the names of the royal princes, it is, in conversation,
> 'Sidi,' and, on paper, 'Emir'.

Hogarth goes on to refer to Hussein as 'The King, Sherif Husein Ibn Ali'; plainly he and Lawrence were at one in their usage in this matter.

V. Military Notes

AB 32, 26 November 1916, I, 478–80
There are various omissions in the version given in SD: perhaps the most interesting in the section summed up as '[*Argument against landing foreigners at Rabugh.*]'. Lawrence made the point that he thought encouragement to the Arabs 'would follow from the landing of instructional and technical contingents, and the exact opposite would be the effect of the landing of a combatant force'. He also stressed that there were other vital requirements quite apart from the matter of Allied troop support on the ground:

> The assistance required by the tribal army is: a) money b) rifles c) food d) Light machine-guns e) Mountain guns f) Any sort of guns g) Aeroplane reconnaissance. The value of e. f. and g. is purely moral; it will cost us a certain amount, but not more than a and c . . . and is quite as important in keeping the force in being.

VI. Personal Notes on the Sherifial Family

AB 32, 26 November 1916, I, 480–2
Note in the light of the notes on 'Sherif Hussein's Administration', above, that Lawrence calls Ali, Abdullah and Feisal by the term 'Sidi', meaning 'My Lord' while the youngest son Zeid is called 'Sherif' – in this context plainly a lesser title than that given to his brothers (see Glossary, p. 311, where Sherif is defined as an honorific title reserved for a noble relative of Mohammed).

For a similarly enthusiastic description of Feisal, see Lawrence's letter to his mother, 16 January 1917 (M. R. Lawrence, *Home Letters of T. E. Lawrence and His Brothers* (Basil Blackwell, Oxford, 1954), p. 333; also *MB*, p. 101).

VII. Nationalism among the Tribesmen

AB 32, 26 November 1916, I, 483–4
There is an important editorial comment on this report in AB 41 (II, 57):

> What was said by TEL (in our No. 32 p. 483) about the political character of the tribes is borne out sufficiently by the facts. Wherever there have been active operations the Beduins have come out when and where required and have kept out, and no tribe or clan in those areas has operated against the Sherif . . . Accordingly the Emir's pretensions to be the accepted leader of the tribal population of Hejaz may fairly be said to have been justified from the first, and to be so still.

VIII. The Turkish Hejaz Forces and Their Reinforcement

AB 32, 26 November 1916, I, 485–9
The text in AB is preceded by the note: 'Compiled from information in possession of GHQ (EEF).'

According to A. W. Lawrence's Foreword, Philip P. Graves was part-author of this report. Philip Graves was a correspondent of *The Times* and a civilian member of the intelligence circle in Cairo; before the war he had gained a reputation as a considerable expert on Balkan politics. In collaboration with Hogarth he worked on the compiling of military reports on the Marmara region of Turkey in 1915. He later edited the *Memoirs of King Abdullah of Jordan* (Cape, London, 1950), in which he vigorously defended Abdullah against Lawrence's somewhat dismissive assessments. He was the half-brother of the poet Robert Graves, with whom Lawrence forged an important friendship after the war.

The two final paragraphs were omitted in *SD*; see the supplementary despatch, 'The Turkish Hejaz Forces and Their Reinforcement' (pp. 197–8).

IX. Sherif Feisal's Army

AB 34, 11 December 1916, I, 530
Lawrence's brief report was editorially annotated, as follows (II, 531):

Note by Arab Bureau. No. 1 is the name of a tribe east of Mecca, along the Arafat road.

No. 2 evidently drawn from the Shawafi clan of the Erwa, the chief subsection of the Beni Malik Juheinah. No. 3 from another sub-section of the same section. No. 6 from the settled Juheinah.

Nos. 4 and 7 are well known Harb units.

The preponderance of Juheinah is due to the large proportion of settled cultivators in the tribe, as compared with the Harb.

X. Diary of a Second Journey

AB 36, 26 December 1916, I, 548–51
This report relates to Lawrence's second visit to Feisal in December 1916; from now onwards his work would be in Arabia, with occasional visits to Cairo, Jidda, later Beersheba, Jerusalem, etc., as required. For the early stages of what was to become virtually a two-year involvement, see *SP*, Book II, 'Opening the Arab Offensive', pp. 117ff.

XI. Genesis of the Hejaz Revolt

AB 36, 26 December 1916, I, 558

XII. The Arab Advance on Wejh

AB 41, 6 February 1917, II, 60–2
See *SP*, pp. 143–69. For Lawrence's mood at this time, see his letter to Lt-Col. S. F. Newcombe, 17 January 1917: 'This show is splendid, you cannot imagine greater fun for us, greater vexation and fury for the Turks.' (*MB*, pp. 102–3.)

XIII. The Sherifial Northern Army

AB 41, 6 February 1917, II, 63–4.

XIV. Feisal's Order of March

AB 41, 6 February 1917, II, 65–6

XV. Nejd News

AB 41, 6 February 1917, II, 69–70
Nejd is a large area of central Arabia which at this time was a source of political and religious dispute between Sherif Hussein and Ibn Saud of the Wahabi dynasty of Ryadh: as a rough rule of thumb, the Wahabi sect represented a back-to-the-Koran movement not dissimilar to today's Muslim fundamentalism.

XVI. With the Northern Army

AB 42, 15 February 1917, II, 74–80
This despatch comprises excerpts from a report made by Lawrence to Lt-Col. Wilson on 8 January 1917. In his review of *SD* in *John O' London's Weekly* (17 November 1939), John Brophy commented approvingly on its felicity of style:

> In the most objective passages the personality of the writer emerges clear and vivid. The guerrilla leader retains his aesthetic eye, and pauses in a military report to note the young grass of the desert, 'a lively mist of pale green here and there over the surfaces of the slate-blue and brown-red rock' [*sic*].

The section 'Feisul's Table Talk' contains references to three notable German activists in the Middle East. Major von Stotzingen had been instructed by the German military authorities to open up contacts between the Turkish-held territories and German East Africa. Leo Frobenius, African explorer and, after the war, an outstanding social anthropologist, had adopted Bedouin disguise while engaged in a propaganda mission to the Red Sea area; he had been found out and forced to retire with ignominy. Baron Max von Oppenheim combined the twin functions of archaeologist and Chief of the Kaiser's Intelligence Service in the Middle East; his popular name in Cairo was 'The Spy'.

XVII. Syria: The Raw Material

AB 44, 12 March 1917, II, 107–14
This despatch is preceded by the note, 'Fragmentary notes written early in 1915, but not circulated'. See also 'Syrian Cross-Currents' (pp. 162–6). A *TLS* review of 3 February 1940 singled out this report as one of the best in *SD*, describing it as 'a piece of solid good work'. Since Lawrence wrote it – as is indicated at the head of the article – in early 1915, several months before the Arab Revolt began, his reference to Damascus is particularly interesting: 'Damascus is a lode-star to which Arabs are naturally drawn, and a city that will not easily be convinced that it is subject to any alien race.'

XVIII. Geographical Notes and the Capture of Eshref

AB 44, 12 March 1917, II, 121–2
For the capture of Eshref Bey see *SP*, pp. 159–61. Lawrence described Eshref as 'a notorious adventurer in the lower levels of Turkish politics'.

XIX. Raids on the Railway

AB 50, 13 May 1917, II, 207–17
This and the following three reports relate to the important period when Lawrence left Feisal at Wejh to visit Emir Abdullah at Wadi Ais, principally to stimulate the

latter into more effective campaigning. Lawrence was ill throughout the journey and subsequently spent ten days lying in a tent suffering from boils, dysentery and malaria (see inserted note in italics in 'In Sherif Abdullah's Camp' (p. 130)). It was during this period, he later claimed, that he thought out the strategy and tactics of the Revolt. The relevant chapters in *SP* are 33 and 59.

This report relates to *SP*, Ch. 34, being a description of his first raid after his recovery. It is notable for its fine descriptive writing, including the account of the desert sandstorm.

XX. Notes on Hejaz Affairs

AB 50, 13 May 1917, II, 226–7

Dated 26 April, these notes on miscellaneous topics were collected by Lawrence during his sojourn with Abdullah in Wadi Ais.

XXI. Wejh to Wadi Ais and Back

AB 51, 23 May 1917, II, 232–40

During the journey to Wadi Ais, according to *SP*, Ch. 31, there occurred one of the most distressing events of Lawrence's war: the execution of a member of his party who had murdered another member belonging to a different tribe. It goes without saying that this episode is not referred to in his report to Cairo. For a comment on the authenticity of this event see *JW*, pp. 382–3 and 1060–1.

Under 13 March, Lawrence refers to 'Shakespear's death'. Captain W. H. I. Shakespear, a British officer who had been Political Agent in Kuwait until 1914 and had then served as an adviser to Ibn Saud, had been killed in a tribal battle in January 1915. That he is described here as 'wearing full British uniform and a sun-helmet . . . [and] was therefore easily picked out' doubtless had a bearing on Lawrence's favouring the wearing of Arab clothes. See *JW*, p. 1043, where Shakespear's death is linked to 'Twenty-Seven Articles' (pp. 142–7).

XXII. In Sherif Abdullah's Camp

AB 51, 23 May 1917, II, 240–2

For Abdullah's interest in European politics, the Somme, etc., see *SP*, Ch. 34.

There is a long gap at this point in Lawrence's appearances in *AB* due to the fact that from 9 May until 6 July he was engaged in the Akaba expedition in the company of Sherif Nasir and the Howeitat chief Auda abu Tayi; for Lawrence's account of this remarkable period in *SP* see Book IV, 'Extending to Akaba'. However, there were occasional speculative references as to his likely whereabouts and activities in *AB*: see 'Intelligence Report: The Northward Move' (p. 200) and 'Extract from an Intelligence Report under Heading "Arabia/Hejaz" ' (pp. 200–1).

XXIII. The Howeitat and Their Chiefs

AB 57, 24 July 1917, II, 309–10

This report is most noteworthy for its introduction on to the stage of Auda abu Tayi.

XXIV. The Sherif's Religious Views

AB 59, 12 August 1917, II, 333–6

Also under discussion at Lawrence's meeting with King Hussein was the Sykes–Picot agreement, the Franco-British-Russian understanding as to the carving up (not to the advantage of their Arab allies) of the Ottoman Empire after the war. Sir Mark Sykes and M. Georges Picot had just visited the Sherif and the latter had asked Lawrence to visit him in Jidda so that he could speak on this very contentious matter to a British officer whom he trusted to pass on his views to the appropriate authorities. For Lawrence's letter to Colonel C. E. Wilson, British agent at Jidda, reporting on his conversation with the Sherif see *MB*, pp. 112–13.

Sykes–Picot was plainly not a fit subject even for *AB*; hence Lawrence's report concentrates on the somewhat less controversial, though also extremely important, subject of the Sherif's religion.

XXV. The Occupation of Akaba

AB 59, 12 August 1917, II, 336–40
The text in *AB* is preceded by an editorial note: 'The following account by Captain Lawrence supplements information already given on pages 307–8 above. The irregularity of the Hejaz mail service is responsible for the delay in its publication.' The information referred to is reprinted as 'Extract from an Intelligence Report under the Heading "Arabia/Hejaz"' (pp. 200–1).

XXVI. The Sherif and His Neighbours

AB 60, 20 August 1917, II, 346–7

XXVII. Twenty-Seven Articles

AB 60, 20 August 1917, II, 347–53
This important document, first published in *SD*, has subsequently been published in David Garnett, *The Essential T. E. Lawrence*; John E. Mack, *A Prince of Our Disorder: The Life of T. E. Lawrence*; and in *JW* (Appendix IV).

Lawrence added the following note, to Major Cornwallis, when submitting the original handwritten manuscript (preserved in PRO file FO 882/7): 'Dear K.C. This isn't bad stuff – in the absence of F. please chuck it in the Bulletin, if you approve. TEL'. The spacing appears to indicate that the words 'in the absence of F.' is linked to the first phrase, not the second, which suggests that by 'F' Lawrence meant Feisal – the implication presumably being that, Feisal not being present to command his attention, Lawrence had had time for once to concentrate on the philosophy, as opposed to the strategy and logistics, of the Allied/Arab campaign.

For Lawrence's view on Arab labour, see 'Note by Cairo on Arab Labour' (pp. 194–5).

A comrade-in-arms of Lawrence and observer of his methods who has not, I believe, been sufficiently credited is Major F. G. Peake, commander of the Egyptian Camel Corps in the later stages of the campaign and later commander of the Arab Legion. In a note written in 1963 (held in the Bodleian Reserve Collection) he described Lawrence's relationship with the Arab leaders and how he influenced the course of the campaign:

His position was not comparable to that of a GOC who has his headquarters far behind the front line and issues his orders through Staff Officers. That would never have worked satisfactorily with Bedouin. He was always very conscious of the fact that he was a European and a Christian and also that the desert tribesmen were proud people, jealous of their freedom and fanatical as regards their religion. He therefore carefully avoided any overt display of authority. All his plans, so far as the Arabs were concerned, were discussed in conference with the head Sheikhs, often while sitting round the camp fire in the evening. His strong personality and knowledge of the Arabs of the desert no doubt enabled him unobtrusively to get his plans adopted, without rousing the latent antipathy to all who are not of their race and religion. For the same reason, he always wore Arab clothes, rode with the tribal Chieftains, but not ahead of them, ate their food, slept on the ground in their camps, and charged with them in battle. The only observable difference between him and his warriors were that his clothes were spotlessly clean and he wore a gold agal (head rope) which had been given to him by the Amir Faishal [*sic*], the nominal Commander in Chief, in the midst of the Arab soldiers.

In other words, Peake saw the successful carrying out of the precepts of 'Twenty-Seven Articles' in practice.

XXVIII. The Raid at Haret Ammar

AB 65, 8 October 1917, II, 401–4
The final version of this story is in *SP*, Chs 61–7, where the two gun-instructors, Yells and Brook, are renamed respectively – after their weapons – Lewis and Stokes.

Although hailed as a successful operation, this raid did not achieve its main aim, which was to deal with the Turkish railway strong-point at Mudowara; this was not finally achieved until August 1918: see note from *AB* 100 quoted below (p. 301). However, like all such forays, it undoubtedly had its positive side, since any destruction of Turkish locomotives and rolling stock (of which the Turks had a strictly limited supply) helped to tip the balance in favour of the Allied situation overall (and therefore assisted Allenby's task in Palestine). A note in AB 66, 21 October 1917, p. 415, states that the Turks admitted losing twenty-seven killed and forty-two wounded, in contrast to the figures given by Lawrence on p. 301. When forwarding Lawrence's report on the raid to his superiors at GHQ, Brigadier-General Clayton stated: 'The success of this small operation should have effects considerably beyond the importance of the action itself. It will raise the spirit of the Arabs throughout and will without doubt be reported throughout Arab districts and its magnitude will not lose as the news travels [*sic*]. It should have an excellent effect on the Arabs throughout.' Clayton also commended 'the gallantry of Major Lawrence and the successful manner in which he managed his irregular force' (document in PRO FO 882/4).

XXIX. The Raid near Bir esh-Shediyah

AB 66, 21 October 1917, II, 412–15
The report is dated 10 October. This raid is described in *SP*, Ch. 68. For Lieutenant Pisani see note to 'Report: Railway Raids Northern Section' below.

XXX. Geographical Notes

AB 66, 21 October 1917, II, 421
A note in *AB* 23 July 1918 confirms that the Hejaz Railway was subsequently found by surveyors to have been placed too far to the east on the maps, as Lawrence had maintained (p. 153).

XXXI. A Raid

AB 73, 16 December 1917, II, 502–4
This relates to *SP*, Chs 71–8.

A notable companion on the first part of this raid was Captain George Lloyd, Unionist MP (West Staffordshire), later Governor of Bombay and, as Lord Lloyd,

High Commissioner of Egypt. His not always flattering account of Lawrence's performance while they were up country together (Lawrence lost his way at one time and on another occasion managed to fall from a telegraph pole) is quoted in John Charmley, *Lord Lloyd and the Decline of the British Empire* (Weidenfeld & Nicolson, London, 1987), pp. 65–6. Lloyd and Lawrence remained lifelong friends, however, and Lloyd's 1917 report concedes that his companion was

> a very remarkable fellow – not the least fearless like some who do brave things, but as he told me last night, each time he starts out on these stunts he simply hates it for two or three days before, until movement, action and glory of scenery and nature catch hold of him and make him well again.

For a reference to the later stages of this raid see 'Report: Railway Raids Northern Section' (p. 202) and 'Notes: Northern Section and Late News' (pp. 202–3).

XXXII. Abdullah and the Akhwan

AB 74, 24 December 1917, II, 511–13
Akhwan, as in this item and the next, can be taken as being the same as Wahabite: see note to 'Nejd News' above.

XXXIII. Akhwan Converts

AB 77, 27 January 1918, III, 31

XXXIV. First Reports from Tafila

AB 78, 11 February 1918, III, 35
SD omitted several sentences from the beginning of this report, but this appears to have been an intentional deletion by A. W. Lawrence and there seems no virtue in restoring them.

XXXV. The Battle of Seil el-Hasa

AB 79, 18 February 1918, III, 41–3
This despatch is preceded by the note, 'written from Tafila under date 26 January'.
   The *SP* account of the campaign which includes Tafileh (or Seil El-Hasa) is in Book VII, 'The Dead Sea Campaign'. For a later comment on what he came to believe was an unnecessary and misjudged action, see his letter to the official military historian Major Archibald Becke dated 28 December 1929, in *MB*, pp. 433–4.
   There is a further large gap at this point in Lawrence's appearances in *AB*. He was so deeply involved in the running of the campaign that he appears virtually to have abandoned filing to the Arab Bureau. However, he is referred to twice in June 1918 in relation to the visit to the Middle East of the Zionist Commission under Dr Chaim Weizmann: see 'Extract from an Intelligence Report on Arabia' (p. 203) and 'Note: Feisal and Weizmann' (pp. 203–4).

XXXVI. Report on Khurma

AB 96, 9 July 1918, III, 245–6
Introduced in *AB*: 'Col. Lawrence, arrived from Jiddah, sends the following.'
   Wadi Khurma had become a zone of dispute between Sherif Hussein and Ibn Saud. The *TLS* review of *SD* described Lawrence's report on this complex subject as

'extremely perspicacious'. It may be said that Wadi Khurma was the spark which actually led to the explosion of hostilities between Sherif Hussein and Ibn Saud and eventually to the downfall of the former. Lawrence has sometimes been reproached with underestimating the power of Ibn Saud and exaggerating that of the Sherif, but he was under no illusion as to the latter's weakness at Khurma.

For the background to this report, see *JW*, pp. 523 and 1097. Lawrence's main purpose in going to Jidda had been to take letters to the Sherif from Sir Reginald Wingate (High Commissioner, Egypt) and General Allenby, to persuade him to agree to the moving of Arab forces north to Syria. Hussein refused, largely because of his absorption with his dispute with Ibn Saud.

XXXVII. Syrian Cross-Currents

Introductory note by A. W. Lawrence: 'Written by T. E. Lawrence in 1918, on Arab Bureau paper, but not included in the *Arab Bulletin*. From the MS in the possession of Mr A. W. Lawrence.'

Not included in *AB*, but (contrary to the introductory note) printed as *Arab Bulletin Supplementary Paper* No. 1, 1 February 1918 (in PRO FO 882/14). See *MB*, p. 137, letter to his mother, 8 January 1918: 'I have an article to write for an Intelligence Report published in Egypt . . .'

Again there is a substantial gap in Lawrence's writings or references in *AB*. However, certain entries can be related to his known activities.

1. From *AB* 100, 20 August 1918, III, 279:

> On the morning of 8 August, Mudowara station was carried by a brilliant assault, and the garrison overwhelmed. The Turks lost thirty-five killed, and six officers and one hundred and forty-six men – including twenty-six wounded – were captured . . . The attackers had one officer and six men killed, and two officers and eight were wounded. The destruction wrought in this area was most thorough. A large steam pump, a windmill-pump, a water-tower with its tanks, and two wells, seventy-five feet in depth, were ruined.

This report refers to the attack on Mudowara by troops of the Imperial Camel Corps under the command of Major R. V. Buxton (later Lawrence's friend and – in peacetime – his solicitor). Lawrence was not present at the attack but had been central to its planning and the briefing of the men.

2. From *AB* 104, 24 September 1918, III, 331:

> Brilliant success has attended the operations of the mobile column of the Emir Feisal's Northern Army . . . Since 19 September, road and rail communication between Palestine and Damascus has been denied to the Turks, and the withdrawal of their Fourth Army, now in progress, will be a task of no small difficulty.

Lawrence was deeply involved in this final stage of the campaign, as is clear from the following report – his last before the end of hostilities, and the last in *SD*.

XXXVIII. The Destruction of the Fourth Army

AB 106, 22 October 1918, III, 343–50

See SP, Book X, 'The House in Perfected'. The TLS review of SD had particular praise for this report as opposed to the account in SP: 'The narrative of the final operation leading up to the capture of Damascus is far superior from the historical point of view to the personal story, if only because it omits those schoolboyish euphemisms which delighted some of Lawrence's friends but did no good to his reputation.'

With regard to the Tafas incident described on pp. 171–2, Major Peake (see note to 'Twenty-Seven Articles' (pp. 298–9)), who arrived on the scene as the massacre was in progress, stated in a note to A. W. Lawrence in 1963: 'Immediately Lawrence saw me he ordered me to round up all prisoners as they arrived and to guard them. At nightfall I had 2000 to look after.' But a massacre had taken place and Lawrence did not attempt to disown it in his report – or, later, in SP. For his vigorous defence of the Arabs on this occasion see p. 172.

Supplementary Despatches

I. Distribution List

AB 1, 6 June 1916, I, 2

This particular list, from the first issue, is as it appears in the copy of the Arab Bulletin held in the Public Record Office (FO 882/25). The last four names have been added by hand, and the figure given for the number of copies allocated to the words 'Arab Bureau' has been altered from 1 to 2.

II. Hejaz News

AB 9, 9 July 1916, I, 82–4

This and the succeeding five items date from the period preceding Lawrence's first visit to Arabia. They are included because of their relevance to the Arab Revolt; they also show that Lawrence was already an acknowledged expert on many aspects of the revolt before he left Cairo. (Indeed, as we now understand, he bizarrely underplayed his role in SP by suggesting that he went to Arabia half casually, to use up some available leave. On the contrary: he was sent to report in detail and at length – and readably, in a form in which those in high places would take notice – on the state of the revolt in the Hejaz.)

This despatch is of especial interest in that it is a situation report on the revolt just over one month after it started in early June 1916.

III. Note by Cairo on Arab Labour

AB 18, 5 September 1916, I, 206–7

As is explained in A. W. Lawrence's Foreword, the authorship of these pieces is indicated by T. E. Lawrence's pencilled notes in his own copy; however, this text would be traceable to Lawrence even if no such proof were available. The 'British undertaking' in the vicinity of the Baghdad Railway to which he refers is clearly the archaeological dig at Carchemish in which he was involved from 1911 to 1914 (see Introduction to the Secret Despatches, p. 59), and the techniques of labour control which are advocated read almost like an early draft of sections of his classic 'Twenty-Seven Articles' (pp. 142–7).

IV. Hejaz Narrative

AB 18, 5 September 1916, I, 210

V. Note on the Garrison of Medina

AB 20, 14 September 1916, I, 243
The note is a postscript to an item entitled 'Extracts from Report by Colonel Wilson on his meeting with Sherif Feisal Bey at Yanbo, 27 and 28 August 1916' and is a correction to an estimate given by Feisal to Colonel C. E. Wilson – the British Representative in Jidda – that there were about '6,000 [Turks] in Medina and on lines of communication'. Wilson's report is also of interest in that it gives a very positive reaction to the character and calibre of Feisal: 'Feisal is about 28 years of age and struck me as being an exceedingly nice man, well educated, and altogether impressing me very favourably.' This would undoubtedly have been in Lawrence's mind when he went to meet Feisal just over a month later.

This item is not referred to in A. W. Lawrence's Foreword but is ascribed to TEL in his Bodleian Library notes.

VI. Note on the Hejaz Military Situation

AB 26, 16 October 1916, I, 304
It is noteworthy that Lawrence arrived in Jidda on his first, crucial visit to Arabia on the day on which this issue was published.

VII. The Turkish Hejaz Forces and Their Reinforcement

AB 32, 26 November 1916, I, 489
These paragraphs, by TEL and P. P. Graves, were previously omitted from 'The Turkish Hejaz Forces and Their Reinforcement' (pp. 82–6); they should follow the words 'at one stroke, all three campaigns' on p. 86.

VIII. Intelligence Report

AB 37, 4 January 1917, II, 4
This report, indicating that the Turks had offered a reward for Lawrence's capture, shows how quickly the Turks became aware of his activities, and of his importance.

IX. Hejaz: The Present Situation

AB 47, 11 April 1917, II, 161–2
The cross-reference to p. 144 is to a report by Lieutenant Colonel S. F. Newcombe, describing his first expedition against the Hejaz Railway, published in issue 46. Beidha is described as a small oasis three miles to the west of the main route taken by Newcombe and sixty-six miles from the Arabs' Red Sea coastal base at Wejh.

X. Note: Wejh Map (Provisional Sheet)

AB 52, 31 May 1917, II, 260
The route reports referred to in issues 50 and 51 are 'Raids on the Railway' (pp. 111–21) and 'Wejh to Wadi Ais and Back' (pp. 122–30).

XI. Intelligence Report: The Northward Move

AB 56, 9 July 1917, II, 300

This item appeared in the *AB* on the day on which Lawrence reached Suez following the successful conclusion of the Akaba expedition, having been written while Lawrence was engaged in the 'coloured adventures' described in 'Extract from an Intelligence Report under the Heading "Arabia/Hejaz"'.

XII. Extract from an Intelligence Report under the Heading 'Arabia/Hejaz'

AB 57, 24 July 1917, II, 307–8

XIII. News of Anazeh Tribes

AB 65, 8 October 1917, II, 407–8

The significance of this report can be gauged from an *AB* article of the previous November, 'The Anazeh Tribes and Chiefs' (*AB* 32, I, 489–90), by D. G. Hogarth, written 'in view of the part which . . . they might presently have to play in the Near Eastern situation'. The article described 'the Anazeh of the Syrian Desert' as 'numbering, at least, a quarter of a million souls and owning over half a million camels . . . They are constantly spoken of in official reports, and even by native Intelligence agents, as a *Tribe* – in the singular. It would be much less misleading to call them a *People*.'

Nuri Shaalan of the Ruwallah tribe, referred to in this despatch, was one of the most influential and formidable of the Arab tribal leaders. For his confrontation with Lawrence on the subject of British motives in the Middle East see *SP*, Ch. 48.

Some 'Rualla Anazeh' (*sic*) were involved in the Akaba expedition: see 'Extract from an Intelligence Report under the Heading "Arabia/Hejaz"' (pp. 200–1).

XIV. Report: Railway Raids Northern Section

AB 71, 27 November 1917, II, 473

This report relates to the extended incursion into Turkish-held territory described in 'A Raid' (pp. 154–6). As stated in Lawrence's account, the attack on a train took place on 11 November, not the 7th as given in this despatch; 7 November was the date of the abortive attempt on the bridge. This correction is confirmed in 'Notes: Northern Section and Late News' on p. 202. See also *SP*, Chs 75–8.

The Lieutenant Pisani referred to was a French artillery officer with whom Lawrence was able to collaborate. He had been with Lawrence on the raid near Bir esh-Shediyah (see pp. 150–2). Later he was attached, as was Lawrence, to the Arab delegation at the Paris Peace Conference.

XV. Notes: Northern Section and Late News

AB 72, 5 December 1917, II, 490

These two items conflict with the assertion by a recent biographer (Lawrence James, *The Golden Warrior*, Weidenfeld & Nicolson, London, 1990) that Lawrence had returned to Akaba by 21 November and therefore could not have been in Deraa at the date given in *SP* for his capture and humiliation by the Turks. The implication is clear from these reports that he was not effectively back at base until much later – in fact, at the time indicated in *SP*.

For a detailed – and, I believe, entirely convincing – critical analysis of James's claim see Jeremy Wilson, 'Documentary Proof or Wishful Thinking: Lawrence James on the Deraa Episode' in *The Journal of the T. E. Lawrence Society*, Vol. I, No. 1, spring 1991.

It might also be added on common-sense grounds that if Lawrence had, as James implies, invented the Deraa episode it would have been absurdly negligent to have dated it at a time when he was known to have been in Akaba. He was far from his base for substantial periods during his two years in Arabia and would have had numerous convenient dates at his disposal.

XVI. *Extract from an Intelligence Report on Arabia*

AB 91, 4 June 1918, III, 178
Dr Chaim Weizmann was a prominent Zionist and the future President of the World Zionist Organization and the Jewish Agency for Palestine; later he became the first President of Israel. Major William Ormsby-Gore (later Baron Harlech) had been a member of the Arab Bureau in 1916–17; known for his pro-Zionist views, he was at this stage British liaison officer to the Zionist Commission of which Wiezmann was head.

For the background to this and the following despatch, 'Note: Feisal and Weizmann', see Wilson, 'Documentary Proof or Wishful Thinking', pp. 512–14 and 1095. GHQ Cairo considered it important that Lawrence should be at the meeting between Weizmann and Feisal, but Lawrence had left on a mission before the notification of date reached Akaba.

XVII. *Note: Feisal and Weizmann*

AB 93, 28 June 1918, III, 208
This report shows evidence of an optimism – largely shared by Lawrence – about the future relations between the Arabs and Jews that was not to be justified by later events. Cf. Weizmann's contribution to *T. E. Lawrence by His Friends*, ed. A. W. Lawrence (Jonathan Cape, London, 1937), p. 221: '[Lawrence] did not think the aims and aspirations of the Jewish people in Palestine contrary to the interests of the Arabs.' Lawrence's post-war article 'The Changing East' (pp. 248–59) is also a relevant document in this context.

XVIII. *Notes on Camel-Journeys*

AB 111, 24 May 1919, IV, 71–3
'G. Harland' is plainly H. Garland – Bimbashi, later Captain Herbert Garland, MBE, MC, who had been commissioned in the Egyptian Army in 1916 and had initially been sent to the Hejaz to train Arabs in the use of explosives. He was the inventor of the 'Garland' grenade, of which 174,000 were supplied to the Mediterranean Expeditionary Force. Lawrence made use of such grenades during his forays against the Hejaz Railway (see p. 116). Garland was briefly Acting Director of the Arab Bureau in 1919 and was responsible for the last two issues (113 and 114) of the *AB*. It is unclear whether 'G. Harland' was a printer's error, or whether Garland chose to make his comments on Lawrence's claims under an easily penetrable pseudonym. For Lawrence's views on Garland's relative unsuitability for working with Bedouin tribesmen see *JW*, pp. 375 and 1058.

Acknowledgements

This book owes its existence to the imaginative persistence of Michael Leventhal of Greenhill Books, who came to me some years ago with the thought that among the legion of books about T. E. Lawrence space might be found for a volume specifically devoted to him as a soldier and military thinker. I replied that I had in effect produced one already, in that in 1991 – as fully explained in the Preface – I had put together a collection of his wartime and post-war writings. As time went by and the world changed, it became evident that his instinct was correct, and that the moment was ripe for a new book with a new title for a new situation. I congratulate him on his perception and thank him warmly for his sustained, and sustaining, enthusiasm and support. It was he too who suggested that the book might be the more valuable for a scholarly Foreword by an authority well versed in Middle Eastern studies, and I am delighted that Professor Michael Clarke of King's College London agreed to provide one. Since certain comments by Professor Clarke quoted in *The Times* in 2003 – and reproduced here in the General Introduction – were crucial in persuading me that the book was a viable project, there could have been no one better able to fulfil this important role and I am most grateful to him.

David Watkins of Greenhill Books has proved a rigorous, stimulating and highly professional editor; above all I owe to him the clarity with which a volume consisting of numerous disparate components has been organised into a comprehensible whole. He has been ably assisted by his copy editor, Neil Titman. I offer my thanks to him and to Mark Bolland who supplied the excellent index. My thanks also to Servis Filmsetting, who designed the pages, and the designer of the dust jacket, Chris Shamwana.

On a further personal note I must add that I have been conscious throughout the publication process of the benign support of the founder of Greenhill Books, Lionel Leventhal.

As is the case with all my publications on T. E. Lawrence, this book was undertaken with the encouragement and support of the Trustees of the Seven Pillars of Wisdom Trust; it is good to add that the earlier volume of which this is to a substantial extent a reformulation, as described above, was undertaken with the personal approval of T. E. Lawrence's brother, the late Professor A. W. Lawrence. Crown copyright material, i.e. the wartime despatches in Part One and the first item in Part Two, is reprinted courtesy of the National Archives (all items are from Foreign Office FO 882/25–7).

With regard to material from other sources: the extract from *Lawrence of Arabia: The Authorised Biography of T. E. Lawrence* by Jeremy Wilson is reproduced by permission of J. and N. Wilson; the extract from E. M. Forster's *Abinger Harvest* is reproduced by permission of the Provost and Scholars of King's College, Cambridge, and the Society of Authors as the Literary Representatives of the Estate of E. M. Forster; the extract from Wilfred Owen's poem 'The Parable of the Old Man and the Young' is included by permission of Professor Jon Stallworthy, the text being taken from his edition of *The War Poems of Wilfred Owen* (Chatto & Windus, 1994); extracts from the Introduction by Kathi Frances McGraw to *T. E. Lawrence, A 20th Century Perspective* are printed by permission of the author; and the final item in the book is reprinted with permission from *Encyclopædia Britannica*, copyright ©1929 by Encyclopædia Britannica, Inc.

Photographs are reproduced by courtesy of the sources named in the List of Illustrations: I am particularly pleased to record that the majority of them are from the unique Lawrence Collection in the Photograph Archive of the Imperial War Museum, an organisation to which I have been attached as a freelance historian since 1989.

A number of highly valued friends helped me with the making of the book, in particular with the reading of and commenting on my numerous items of introductory matter. Thus I should like to record my great gratitude to Jack Flavell, Peter Metcalfe, Jeremy Wilson and Kathi Frances McGraw, who not only encouraged me in my efforts but also saved me from numerous pitfalls. The text of the General Introduction was also read by Angela Godwin, curator of the 2005–6 Lawrence Exhibition at the Imperial War Museum, with which I have been privileged to be involved as consultant. Finally I offer my thanks to my wife Betty for her scrupulous scrutiny of my text and her invaluable help in reading and correcting the proofs.

Select Bibliography

Robert B. Asprey, *War in the Shadows: The Guerrilla in History* (Doubleday, New York, 1975; MacDonald and Jane's, London, 1976)

Ian F. W. Beckett, *Modern Insurgencies and Counter-Insurgencies: Guerrillas and Their Opponents since 1750* (Routledge, London and New York, 2002)

Ian F. W. Beckett (ed.), *The Roots of Counter-Insurgency: Armies and Guerrilla Warfare, 1900–1945* (Blandford Press, London, 1988)

John Bierman and Colin Smith, *Fire in the Night: Wingate of Burma, Ethiopia and Zion* (Random House, New York, 1999; Macmillan, London, 2000)

Malcolm Brown (ed.) *The Letters of T. E. Lawrence* (Dent, London, 1988; Oxford University Press, Oxford, 1991); published in the USA as *T. E. Lawrence, The Selected Letters* (Norton, New York, 1989; Paragon Press, New York, 1991)

Cyril Falls, *The First World War* (Longmans, London, 1960)

E. M. Forster, *Abinger Harvest* (Edward Arnold, London, 1936)

David Garnett (ed.) *The Essential T. E. Lawrence* (Jonathan Cape, London, 1951; Dutton, New York, 1952; Oxford University Press, Oxford, 1992)

David Garnett (ed.) *The Letters of T. E. Lawrence* (Jonathan Cape, London, 1938; Doubleday, Doran, New York, 1939; Spring Books, London, 1964)

T. E. Lawrence, *The Mint: A Day-Book of the RAF Depot between August and December 1922* (Jonathan Cape, London, and Doubleday, New York, 1955)

T. E. Lawrence, *Oriental Assembly* (Williams & Norgate, London, 1939; Dutton, New York, 1940; Imperial War Museum, London, 1991, 2005)

T. E. Lawrence, *Secret Despatches from Arabia* (Golden Cockerel, London, 1939)

T. E. Lawrence, *Seven Pillars of Wisdom: A Triumph* (Jonathan Cape, London, 1935; Doubleday, Doran, New York, 1936)

T. E. Lawrence, *Seven Pillars of Wisdom: A Triumph*, 1922 (Oxford) Version (Castle Hill Press, Fordingbridge, Hants., 1997)

John J. McCuen, *The Art of Counter-Revolutionary War: The Strategy of Counter-Insurgency* (Faber & Faber, London, 1966)

John E. Mack, *A Prince of Our Disorder: The Life of T. E. Lawrence* (Weidenfeld & Nicolson, London, and Little, Brown, Boston, 1976; Oxford University Press, Oxford, 1991; Harvard University Press, Cambridge, MA, 1998)

Kathi Frances McGraw and Andrew Carvely, *T. E. Lawrence, A 20th Century Retrospective* (Andrew Carvely Corporation, Summerduck, VA, 1998)

Scott R. McMichael, *Stumbling Bear: Soviet Military Performance in Afghanistan* (Brassey's, London, 1991)

John A. Nagl, *Counterinsurgency Lessons from Malaya and Vietnam: Learning to Eat Soup with a Knife* (Praeger, Westport, CT, 2002)

David E. Omissi, *Air Power and Colonial Control: The Royal Air Force, 1919–1939* (Manchester University Press, Manchester and New York, 1990)

Jon Stallworthy (ed.), *The War Poems of Wilfred Owen* (Chatto & Windus, London, 1994)

Stephen E. Tabachnick (ed.), *The T. E. Lawrence Puzzle* (The University of Georgia Press, Athens, GA, 1984)

Stephen E. Tabachnick and Christopher Matheson, *Images of Lawrence* (Jonathan Cape, London, 1988)

Stanley and Rodelle Weintraub, *Evolution of a Revolt* (The Pennsylvania State University Press, University Park, 1968)

Jeremy Wilson, *Lawrence of Arabia: The Authorised Biography* (Heinemann, London, 1989; Minerva, London, 1990; Atheneum, New York, 1990)

Trevor Wilson, *The Myriad Faces of War* (Polity Press, Cambridge, in association with Basil Blackwell, Oxford, 1986)

Glossary

Aalim   Learned man
Abu . . . Akhu . . .   Father of . . . Brother of . . .
ADC   Aide-de-camp
Ageyl   Camel-corps
Allah yinsur el Din   'God give victory to the Religion'
ASC   Army Service Corps
Ashraf   Plural of Sherif

Bab-Arab   Commissioner for Bedouin Affairs
Bedu   Bedouin
Belediyeh   Municipality
Bir   Well

Cadi   Civil judge
CGS   Chief of General Staff
CO   Commanding Officer

Dhelul   Camel
Dhurra   Indian corn
Dira   Grazing-ground

EEF   Egyptian Expeditionary Force
Emir el-Muminin   'Commander of the Faithful' (caliph's title)
Ethil and **Tarfa**   Tamarisks

Fetwa   Religious decree

Ghadir   Pool
Ghazzu   Raid
Girbi   Water-skin
GOC   General Officer Commanding
GOC.-in-C.   General Officer Commanding-in-Chief

Habub   Dust storm
Hadhar   Settled
Harrah   Lava

Idhan   Call to prayer
Imama   Turban

Imaret   Administration of Mecca

Jihad   Holy War

Khadim   'Servants'
Kilim   Thin rug
Kufar   Atheist, corrupt, infidel

L. of C.   Line of communication

Maidan   Part of Damascus
MEF   Mediterranean Expeditionary Force
MG   Machine-gun
MI   Mounted infantry
Mofraza   Mixed Detachment
Mohafiz   Military Governor
Mohafiz Alai   Regiment used for guard purposes
Muedhdhin   Caller to Prayer
Murettab   Composite, of various units

NCO   Non-commissioned officer

OC   Officer Commanding

QF   Quick-firing

Redif   Pillion-rider on a camel
RFC   Royal Flying Corps
RGS   Royal Geographical Society
Rikab   Rider directing a camel
RNVR   Royal Naval Volunteer Reserve

SAA   Small Arms Ammunition
Sayidna   'Our Lord'
Sebil   Wayside fountain
Seil   Torrent
Sharia   Islamic law
Sherif   Religious noble of the blood of Mohammed; the 'Sherif of Mecca'
   was a vassal prince of the Turkish Empire
Shiyukh el-harrat   Sheikhs of the Quarter
Sidi   'My Lord'
SNO   Senior Naval Officer

Tarika   Religious Order
Themail   Shallow water-holes

Ulema   Learned men

Wadi   Watercourse and its valley
Wasm   Crest and cattle-brand

Yeni Turan   'New Turanian' or Pan-Turkish movement

Zariba   Fortified camp
Ziaret   Shrine

Index